Figures of Autobiography

Figures of Autobiography

THE LANGUAGE OF SELF-WRITING IN VICTORIAN AND MODERN ENGLAND

AVROM FLEISHMAN

University
of California
Press

Berkeley
Los Angeles
London

University of California Press
Berkeley and Los Angeles, California

University of California Press, Ltd.
London, England

© 1983 by The Regents
of the University of California

Library of Congress Cataloging in Publication Data

Fleishman, Avrom.
    Figures of autobiography.

    Includes index.
    1. English prose literature—History and criticism.
2. Autobiography. 3. Fiction, Autobiographic. 4. Self
in literature. 5. Figures of speech. I. Title.
PR756.A9F5 1983   828'.08   81-23163
ISBN 0-520-04666-8   AACR2

Printed in the United States of America

1 2 3 4 5 6 7 8 9

for Franz and Ilya
who provided
a (rock) musical
background

A man's life of any worth is a continual
allegory—and very few eyes can see the
mystery of his life—a life like the
scriptures, figurative. . . .
                          JOHN KEATS

No Romance sold unto
Could so enthrall a Man
As the perusal of
His Individual One—
'Tis Fiction's—to dilute to Plausibility
Our Novel—When 'tis small enough
To Credit—'Tisn't true!
                          EMILY DICKINSON

Somewhere a child's voice calls, a tune ascends
Through notes as shrill and liquid as a thrush.
Half of my life begins as one half ends.

A cloud moves. A weight presses me, is gone.
What would both lift and lighten me, yet crush
My spirit like a thunderbolt from the sun?

And all I have lost is suddenly made one.
                          ANTHONY THWAITE,
                          New Confessions

Contents

ix

Contents

Contents

Acknowledgments

THIS BOOK began to take its present form after a friend noted on the margin of an earlier draft: "Yes—what implications for the relation of language and self might this have?" It took almost ten years' head-scratching to find such answers as I have, but J. Hillis Miller is nonetheless to be thanked for his subtle prodding.

A number of other former colleagues provided similar grains of sand. My debts to Ronald Paulson and the late Earl Wasserman will be evident in the pages where I enter their domains. A present colleague, Lee Patterson, helped hold Augustine down and showed me where to press him for a polite response. Other specialized help was kindly tendered by Jerrold Cooper, Catherine Macksey, and Georg Luck.

My studies of autobiography began when I was asked to give a series of lectures at California State University at Los Angeles; my thanks to David Kubal for inviting me and to Dean John Palmer for footing the bill. An intermediate stage of competence was reached while teaching a summer seminar for the National Endowment for the Humanities; the young college teachers who pursued their own interests in autobiography were of enormous stimulation to me in pursuing mine.

As this book declined and swelled over the years, I have come to think of it as *my* autobiography; perhaps the best substantiation for this illusion is the observable growth in the two individuals closely related to me who are named in the dedication.

A few further acknowledgments. Portions of the manuscript were read by scholars in a better position to judge than myself: Sacvan Bercovitch, Margery S. Durham, and Thomas Vargish. If I have insisted on maintaining certain errors, theirs is not the blame.

Some earlier drafts have appeared in journals and a book: the Dickens, Eliot, and Lawrence in *Genre*; the Mill, Butler, and Gissing in *Approaches to Victorian Autobiography*, ed. George P. Landow (Ohio University Press); the Ruskin in *Texas Studies in Literature and Language*; the Virginia Woolf in *English Literary History*. Thanks are due the editors and publishers for permission to reprint here.

Introduction

STRUCTURING
THE CRITICISM

No ONE CAN TELL what autobiography is, yet that has not dispelled a surge of recent efforts to define it. The bookstore browser who picks up *The Memoirs of Richard Nixon* will probably be confirmed in his expectation of frequent departures from the norm in a genre nominally devoted to truth telling. But the browser leafing through *Roland Barthes by Roland Barthes* will make an even more liberating discovery in the theory of genre. Not that an alphabetical arrangement of vignettes illustrating a man's characteristics is an entirely unprecedented gambit. Over four hundred years ago the Renaissance physician Girolamo Cardano wrote his autobiography as an achronological series of diagnostic essays. There can be no iconoclasm where there are no sacred icons, and the history of autobiography resembles a library of the works of man more than it does a librarian's classification code. As the chief historian of the subject sums up:

> Hardly any form is alien to it. Historical record of achievements, imaginary forensic addresses or rhetorical declamations, systematic or epigrammatic description of character, lyrical poetry, prayer, soliloquy, confessions, letters, literary portraiture, family chronicle and court memoirs, narrative whether purely factual or with a purpose, explanatory or fictional, novel

and biography in their various styles, epic and even drama—all these forms have been made use of by autobiographers; and if they were persons of originality they modified the existing types of literary composition or even invented new forms of their own.[1]

Any study of autobiography ought to be at least as open to innovation as are autobiographers themselves, for they are constantly tinkering with new forms, new modes, new media in which to make a work of art somehow commensurate with themselves. Students of the subject may do well also to emulate the autobiographers in their sense of tradition as well as in their proneness to change, for in the effort to make a new work, one is always thrown back on what has already been made. Without engaging a doctrine of influence or defining a genre by historical continuities, the student of autobiography may speculate that the books an autobiographer is most likely to be reading are other autobiographies and that these will make an appearance of some kind in the work of his hand.

Although I shall, in what follows, be arguing for intertextual relations, if not historical continuity, in autobiography—even in the case of Augustine, often called the founder of Western confessional writing—it may be well to consider an apparently absolute origin to test the limits of the argument. Perhaps the earliest exercise in autobiographical narrative, a pseudoautobiographical inscription from early first-millennium Nineveh, tells the life of the founder of the first Mesopotamian empire (mid-third millennium) in a way that differs from the usual Ozymandias-like declarations:

> Sargon, the powerful king, King of Agade, am I.
> My mother was of low degree, my father I did
>   not know.
> The brother of my father dwelt in the mountain.

1. Georg Misch, *A History of Autobiography in Antiquity*, trans. E. W. Dickes, 2 vols. (London, 1950 [1907]), I, 4.

Introduction

My city was Azurpirani, on the banks of the
                              Euphrates.
My humble mother conceived me; in secret she
                              brought me forth.
She placed me in a basket boat of rushes; with
                              pitch she closed my door.
She gave me over to the river, which did not
                              rise over me.
The river bore me along; to Akki, the irrigator,
                              it carried me.
Akki, the irrigator, in the ——— brought me
                              to land.
Akki, the irrigator, reared me as his own son.
Akki, the irrigator, appointed me his gardener.
While I was gardener, Ishtar looked on me
                              with love
——— four years I ruled the kingdom.[2]

Here is an autobiography which can owe little or nothing to
a generic tradition for its images. But to say that there is no
text to condition this as autobiography is to scout the evident
pressure of an enormous fund of mythological belief, doubtless central to the religious culture of its time and place. The
myth is, moreover, of the kind that surpasses temporal and
regional boundaries and places this text amid the myriad articulations of the "myth of the birth of the hero"—the "monomyth," as it has been called.[3] Not only does the inscription
echo the legends of the hero's obscure origins and early ex-

2. In the *University Library of Autobiography*, ed. several hands,
15 vols. (New York, 1918), I, 3. For a more scholarly translation than
that in this rare anthology, see *The Ancient Near East*, ed. J. B. Pritch-
ard, 2 vols. (Princeton, 1958), I, 85–86. My grasp of the complex cultural situation of this "pseudo-autobiography" was belatedly broad-
ened by Brian Lewis, *The Sargon Legend: A Study of the Akkadian
Text and the Tale of the Hero Who Was Exposed at Birth* (Cambridge, Mass., 1980).
3. These terms have been made common coin by such studies as
Otto Rank's *The Myth of the Birth of the Hero* (1910) and Joseph
Campbell's *The Hero with a Thousand Faces* (1949) and its successors.

posure—in common with Moses, Romulus, and other political founders—but it introduces a tutelary figure and a divine protectress to authenticate the passage from lowly to exalted status. These clearly formulaic gestures bestowing supermundane afflatus on the king cannot have been employed to inspire in the beholder anything less than conviction about an individual's distinctive career. Myth makes truth, in historical as well as in literary autobiography. The paradigm of exile and return, of alienation and repossession, is, moreover, a frequent self-conception and connects this archaic document with autobiographies written at many a later juncture in other civilizations—not least in English literature of the past two centuries.

As we approach our own time, the dazzling aura created by mixing history and mythology, the original and the received, comes to be displayed without embarrassment, even with enthusiasm, on the part of many autobiographers. One such is that lifelong practitioner of autobiographical fiction, Italo Svevo, whose *Confessions of Zeno* (1923) has most often been read in association with his friend James Joyce's more famous autobiographical experiments in *A Portrait of the Artist* and *Ulysses*. The intensity of Joyce's persistence in autobiographical writing pales beside Svevo's continuous rewriting of his life. Embarking on yet another fictional rendering of his experience, Svevo wrote:

> A new era begins for me with this date. From these days I discover in my life something important, the only important thing that ever happened to me: the description I made of a part of it. . . . How alive is that life and how definitively dead is that part which I didn't relate. . . . I also know that that part which I recounted was not the most important. It was made the most important because I fixed it in words. And now what am I? Not he who lived but he who described. Oh, the only important part of life is the regathering [*raccoglimento*]. When everyone understands this as clearly as I do, everyone will write. Life

4

will be literaturized. [*La vita sarà letteraturizzata.*] Half of humanity will be dedicated to reading and studying what the other half will have noted down. And if regathering occupies most of our time, in that way it will be subtracted from real, horrible life. And if one part of humanity rebels and refuses to read the musings of the other, so much the better. Each one will read himself. And his own life will become more clear or more obscure, but it will repeat itself, it will correct itself, it will crystallize itself.[4]

The fine fantasy of Svevo's musings should not be allowed to detract from the seriousness of his sense of life and literature. Some will find regrettably romantic his sweeping rejection of life as "real, horrible," but the utopian alternative, the spectacle of everyone's reading one another's autobiographies, has its own appeal. Indeed, some will observe that, for better or worse, such a situation will be soon upon us if the present outpouring continues.

The core of Svevo's insight is less sweeping and less a matter of taste, for it is based on a feature of every autobiography that is perhaps too obvious to be worth mentioning: that it is a book. (I moot here the question of other arts as autobiographical media[5] and trust that the material status of Sargon's inscription makes no serious exception to the rubric "book.") For the writer—and for the willing reader—the

---

4. Quoted by Susan P. Machala in her interesting study, "The Convergence of Autobiography and Fiction in the Nineteenth and Early Twentieth Centuries," Ph.D. dissertation, Johns Hopkins University, 1976, pp. 240–41; the original text is in Italo Svevo's *Opera Omnia*, 4 vols. in 5 (Milan, 1968), III, 372. The translation in my text is by Dr. Machala.

5. An accounting of nonliterary autobiographies would include much of Smetana's music, most of Fellini's films, the sequence of Rembrandt's self-portraits, and such mixed media entities as Louis Zukofsky's *Autobiography* (1970), consisting of musical scores with brief prose links. Perhaps the ultimate autobiography, where medium and subject are one, is the work by a contemporary artist who sits with a sign announcing, "I will sit under this sign for _x_ minutes."

book turns the autobiographer into a new being: not the person who lived its events but the person who wrote it. The events themselves are inevitably transformed from what they were (not necessarily important) to what has been made—into literature. Svevo claims that in their new existence these events are alive, the original events dead, and we may take this as a metaphoric distinction between kinds of writing. The autobiographer keeps his life vividly present; otherwise the events become recoverable only by the act of resuscitation known as biography. The new status of human existence under the sway of autobiography is given in the formula, "Life will be literaturized." This transformation of personal life provides also for an ongoing activity under the new conditions of existence: "Each one will read himself."

Whether so much can be claimed for every autobiographer's activity or for the achievements of autobiography collectively is more than I shall undertake to demonstrate. But some share of Svevo's enthusiasm will perhaps be communicated to those who closely inspect a substantial number of autobiographical works, seeking neither biographical information nor even personal communion with their authors but only the range of experiences expected and derived from works of art.

Amid the hum of activity in the reading and writing of autobiography, there may arise voices objecting to the brace of texts I have chosen to frame the subject. Is the pronouncement ascribed to Sargon a genuine piece of autobiography, fragmentary as it is, riddled with legend as it must be, different as its reception must have been from that of a modern Western book? And is Svevo's declaration and practice of imaginatively distorting the facts of his life a fitting model of anything but autobiographical fiction, not autobiography itself? Corresponding to the rising awareness of such questions on the part of many readers is a boom in critical writing on the subject in the past decade. While the range of recent accounts of autobiography is as wide as the spectrum of contemporary literary theory—taking in all shades of critical ideology, the major psychological schools, and a variety of philosophical positions as well—the main lines of approach may be drawn without excessive distortion along six axes.

Truth

Still undoubtedly the most widely held view may be called the literalist or purist position, which maintains that an autobiography is a self-written biography designed and required to impart verifiable information about the historical subject. The classic statement of this position is given in a dialogue from *Don Quixote*:

> "If you want to know anything about my life, know that I am Ginés de Pasamonte whose life story has been written down by these fingers that you see here. . . . What I would tell you is that it deals with facts, and facts are so interesting and amusing that no lies could equal them."
>
> "And what is the title of the book?" asked Don Quixote.
>
> "*The Life of Ginés de Pasamonte.*"
>
> "Is it finished?"
>
> "How could it be finished," said Ginés, "when my life is not finished as yet?" [6]

Cervantes's satire depends on the spectacle of a galley slave spouting an autobiographer's braggadocio, as well as on the literary competition implicit in Ginés's aspiration to outdo in his life the picaresque exploits of the fictional Lazarillo de Tormes. A more profound undercutting of the naïve claim to autobiographical truth lies in the closing joke. The claim of completely rendering the facts of an ongoing life gives every purportedly complete autobiography an element of fiction whereas *The Life of Ginés* remains incomplete as the victim of a manic fidelity to fact. Where at least one inven-

---

6. Cervantes, *Don Quixote*, in the Putnam translation (many editions), Pt. I, ch. 22.

tion is required, others are likely to follow, and the commonsense notion that autobiographies ought to be veracious is usually accompanied by a grudging recognition that self-dramatization, special pleading, or some other rhetorical motive makes them anything but strictly true. In the biographer Leslie Stephen's words, an autobiography is valuable "in proportion to the amount of misrepresentation it contains. ... it is always curious to see how a man contrives to present a false testimonial to himself."[7]

Stephen's skepticism is the sardonic side of a positive literalist position—although it also trenches on a distinct approach, which I shall consider under the rubric of "expression" theories. The strongest case for autobiography as truth telling is given in the influential formulation of Georges Gusdorf. For Gusdorf, the autobiographer tells a truth only he can know, the report of how his experience looked or felt from an inside view: "le témoignage d'un homme sur lui-même, ... la recherche de sa plus intime fidélité."[8] This valorization of subjective truth or, more properly, of a true account of subjectivity, derives in the French tradition from Montaigne, where its coupling with a disciplined philosophical skepticism suggests an underlying linkage between subjective truth and epistemological doubt. True to his heritage, Gusdorf is willing to embrace error, omission, fiction, and imposture insofar as they contribute to the revelation of the inner man.

A like tincture of dubiety touches even apparently straightforward affirmations of autobiographical truth. Both a comprehensive historian of English autobiography and a persistent contributor of theoretical essays in recent years

7. Leslie Stephen, *Hours in a Library*, 4 vols. (London, 1909 [1874]), IV, 185.

8. Georges Gusdorf, "Conditions et limites de l'autobiographie," in *Formen der Selbstdarstellung*, ed. G. Reichenkron and E. Haase (Berlin, 1956), p. 118. The essay has been translated by James Olney for his collection, *Autobiography: Essays Theoretical and Critical* (Princeton, 1980).

argue stolidly for the autobiographer's intention to set down "nothing that is not literally and factually true" and "never to falsify his facts for a fictional purpose," yet both acknowledge that the intention is perceptible only as a rhetorical claim or an audience impression. The autobiographer "wishes to be understood" as truthful and strives to "sound as truthful as possible"; his actual achievement of these laudable goals wisely remains untested as a normative standard. Similar transformations of truth criteria into authorial purport and reader expectation will be considered below under the heading of "convention" theories, but we already find here reasons for the widespread critical shift from canons of historical statement to those of self-imaging, rhetorical persuasion, and narrative technique.

The most sophisticated version of the truth-telling approach is that of Francis Hart in a healthily contentious article. Hart's loyalties remain with the historical model of autobiography, but his efforts to distinguish this model from the fictive run a tenuous course: "In understanding fiction one seeks an imaginative grasp of another's meaning; in understanding personal history one seeks an imaginative comprehension of another's historic identity. 'Meaning' and 'identity' are not the same kind of reality and do not make the same demands."[9] One might, however, reflect that these two terms are all but synonymous, according to the widespread view, as expressed by Josiah Royce, that "the Self is not a Thing, but a Meaning embodied in a conscious life."[10] Historic identity is the wake the self makes in enacting its meaning, and following that wake in autobiography is precisely to grasp a meaning.

A more persuasive interaction between the factual and the fictive elements of autobiography emerges from Hart's

9. Francis R. Hart, "Notes for an Anatomy of Modern Autobiography," in *New Directions in Literary History*, ed. Ralph Cohen (Baltimore and London, 1974), p. 224; the quotation below is from p. 228.
10. Josiah Royce, *The World and the Individual*, 2nd ser. (New York, 1959 [1901]), p. 269.

exercises in practical criticism, illustrating his polemic against new-critical norms of organic unity. Holding that this is a species of writing where authorial intention is rarely unchanging or univocal, he finds that the unfolding of shifting intentions issues in multiform and variegated works: "Every autobiography can appropriately and usefully be viewed as in some degree a drama of intention. . . . The total emergent reciprocity of situation and activity and pattern is what is formative or distinctive." This keen awareness of the complexity of even the simple autobiographical intention to tell the truth should make a salutary corrective to the purist view. But Hart may have departed the truth seekers altogether in his subsequent discussion of the personal focus of an autobiography as either an "inductive invention" or an "intentional creation"—narrowing the gap between truth and fiction to the vanishing point.

Building upon the strength of Hart's argument, we might conclude that the unstable character of autobiographical intention is one of the inveterate conditions that call on the autobiographer to fictionalize—that each shift of intention generates a new fiction in behalf of a totalized account of one's life (the ultimate fiction). Two further implications from the complexity of autobiographical intention may also be drawn: that it is the variety of intentions—both as distinguishing one writer from another and as dramatically engaged within an individual writer—that accounts for the multiplicity of genres and media that autobiographers have appropriated to their enterprise. Further, that intention itself will always remain an induction from the evidence of texts—even an explicit statement by the writer being only a part of the text that further complicates its formulation. The intention to "tell the truth about oneself," like other imaginative projects, is a fictional premise which may issue in highly rewarding constructions of the self, but it makes a poor Archimedean point on which to base an origin, practice, or test of literary performance. But this is to anticipate the "deconstruction" theories to be discussed below.

Introduction

Meaning

"Although nobody," writes André Malraux in his *Anti-Memoirs*,[11] "now believes that the object of the self-portrait, or even the portrait, from the effigies of the Egyptian sculptors to the Cubists, was simply to imitate nature, people still believe it of literary portraiture." This looks like, though it is probably not, the last word on autobiographical truth, but it opens up a world of speculation on the aesthetic burdens of self-portraiture. An outstanding book by Roy Pascal, *Design and Truth in Autobiography*,[12] moves to redefine the terms of its title by replacing the familiar correspondence norms of truth with those of coherence. The autobiographer gives an order to the facts of his history, an order not inherent in them but necessarily of his own devising and therefore a reflection of himself that is more profoundly informative than the data that he manipulates. Pascal has effectively shifted the discussion from the realm of truth to that of meaning. What is the *meaning* of an autobiography in the sense that we ask for the meaning of any other work of art?

Although not distinctively hermeneutical in their critical operations, proponents of meaningfulness in autobiography tend to adopt a view of personal identity that we have already touched on. Conceiving of the self as a process rather than a determinate structure, Pascal takes Wilhelm Dilthey's idea of *Selbstbesinnung*[13] as a "search for one's inner standing": "The life is represented in autobiography not as something established but as a process; it is not simply the narrative of the voyage, but also the voyage itself. There must be in it a sense of discovery, and where this is wanting, and the auto-

11. André Malraux, *Anti-Memoirs*, trans. Terence Kilmartin (New York, 1968 [1967]), p. 6.
12. Roy Pascal, *Design and Truth in Autobiography* (Cambridge, Mass., 1960); the quotations below are from pp. 182, 160.
13. See Wilhelm Dilthey, *Pattern and Meaning in History: Thoughts on History and Society*, trans. and ed. H. P. Rickman (New York, 1961), pp. 95–112, esp. pp. 100–01 on autobiography.

biography appears as an exposition of something understood from the outset, we feel it is a failure, a partial failure at any rate." Even more than the evident Procrusteanism of this definition, the results of its application must give one pause: "I do not think one can evade the conclusion that the supreme task of autobiography is not fulfilled in modern autobiography. It has of course rarely been fulfilled. . . ." Given such standards and the handful of successful cases, a prospective autobiographer might well turn from the task. If he should, by some misadventure, find himself understanding his life before writing it, he had better not write it at all—or he must feign a voyage to a land where he has already arrived. The latter case is doubtless the more frequent, but what does this invention of a quest myth do to Pascal's implicit ideal of sincerity?

Closely associated with the quest for meaning in autobiography is the concept of a life, the inspiration of the quest whose goal is the "meaning of [my] life." In this formulation, the object represented in an autobiography would be neither entities nor events but the life itself. What does such a conception of autobiography as life entail? The philosopher who has done most to make the term "life" a philosophic one—Dilthey—presents a number of descriptive categories to help us characterize a life, but even his follower Pascal would not seek to raise them to a universal standard for autobiography.

If we cannot say that a life story is a representation of a life, lacking a consensus on what a life is, we may still retain the term by building on its common usage. Many autobiographies employ the genitive form in their titles—*The Life of . . . by Himself*, or just *My Life*—but go on to propose the existence of another entity in their claim to tell the story of that life. There may be a redundancy here, as "life" and "story of a life" are equivalent terms in their literary reference. The existence of this ambiguity suggests that a life is not something that precedes autobiography but is identical

to it, that is, that an autobiography does not represent or repeat a life but instead constitutes it, brings it into existence.
"Life" means nothing in the individual (as distinct from the
biological) realm until it is told in life stories. Autobiography
is not, then, an imitation of something already there, found
or given, but the creation of a new being, a life—not one to
take up space and people the earth, perhaps, but one that exists as an aesthetic object.

Convention

As there grows a wider agreement on what constitutes a
literary life, even in the absence of consensus on what life is
in the busy, living world, there is likely to be sharper awareness of autobiography as a verbal artifact rather than as a
natural phenomenon. This foregrounding of the medium in
critical perspective has encouraged recent efforts to define
the genre as a cultural institution, taking account both of its
long history in the Western tradition[14] and of its characteristic rhetorical features, those which signal an author's awareness of working within a tradition and which condition an
audience's expectations in receiving a given text. Discussion
of autobiography has been enriched by this dual approach to
its generic status, which avoids the rigors of abstract definition in favor of literary-historical context and the dynamics
of convention and reception.

The first of these inquiries was fostered by Northrop
Frye's brief words on autobiography in *Anatomy of Criti-*

14. A caveat: autobiography's reputation as a peculiarly Western
phenomenon—often coupled with claims for its invention by Augustine or its efflorescence in modern times—is as susceptible to refutation
by example as are similar claims for the "rise of the novel" with the
advent of Western capitalism. The *University Library of Autobiography* includes excerpts from Avicenna's and al-Ghazali's Arabic works;
such classic Oriental novels as *The Tale of Genji* and *The Dream of
the Red Chamber* have been found to contain an autobiographical dimension. I shall return to this cultural egocentrism in a later chapter.

cism, which placed it squarely among the forms of prose fiction (while emphasizing fiction's connotations as something *made* rather than as something illusory):

> Autobiography is another form which merges with the novel by a series of insensible gradations. Most autobiographies are inspired by a creative, and therefore fictional, impulse to select only those events and experiences in the writer's life that go to build up an integrated pattern. This pattern may be something larger than himself with which he has come to identify himself, or simply the coherence of his character and attitudes. We may call this very important form of prose fiction the confession form, following St. Augustine, who appears to have invented it, and Rousseau, who established a modern type of it.[15]

It is doubtful that any reader will assent to all the propositions in this definition—particularly the primacy of the confessional mode, only one of those available to the autobiographer. Yet fictional creativity, selective construction, and the goal of an integrated image of the self have marked the activity of making autobiography from its inception (as we shall see in greater detail below).

Frye was spare and suggestive in linking autobiography and other forms of fiction in their historical development, but further studies have emphasized the interaction of this genre with others as they came to be in history. Scholes and Kellogg's *The Nature of Narrative*, in developing the richness of emergent fictional forms in the ancient world, placed autobiography squarely within this evolution:

> The prose writers of the Roman Empire developed the first-person journey narrative as an art form and also established the pattern of the inward journey, the autobiography, in its two usual forms—the apology

15. Northrop Frye, *Anatomy of Criticism: Four Essays* (New York, 1968 [1957]), p. 307.

and the confession. All these developments can be illustrated from the works of four men who came from various parts of the Empire in the period from the first to the fourth centuries A.D.: Petronius, Apuleius, Lucian, and St. Augustine.[16]

The virtue of this approach is to seek the origins of autobiography in a culture and not in an individual inventor, for the latter may be representative of the former while realizing only some of its potentialities. Going beyond Augustine, Scholes and Kellogg describe the role of picaresque pseudo-autobiography in Petronius, the mythmaking and conversion drama of Apuleius, and the self-anatomizing aspects of Lucian's first-person satirical pieces. Such an approach anticipates that later developments in narrating a life story will be similarly complicated by novelistic, eschatological, and didactic impulses, and expressed in terms closely related to the formal properties that link these generic variants from the outset.

A similar awareness of the historically fluid career of autobiography among related genres marks the work of Philippe Lejeune and Elizabeth Bruss. Lejeune, in a useful survey of French autobiography (at least, post-Rousseau), shows himself alive to the close association between the rise of eighteenth-century autobiography and the prevalence of the pseudoautobiographical novel (a subject that has been studied in fine detail by Philip Stewart):[17]

> authenticity began to be imitated in the novel before
> it was retrieved and interiorized by autobiographers:
> the autobiographer came into his own only by imitat-
> ing [novelists] as they imagined what it was to be an
> autobiographer. A singular game of mirrors, which

16. Robert Scholes and Robert Kellogg, *The Nature of Narrative* (London, Oxford, and New York, 1968 [1966]), p. 73.

17. Philip Stewart, *Imitation and Illusion in the French Memoir-Novel, 1700–1750: The Art of Make-Believe* (New Haven and London, 1969).

shows that sincerity is learned, that originality is imitated, and that it is not a question of the genius of a
few individuals, but of a general transformation in the
notion of the individual through the appearance in society of a new type of narrative.[18]

With a similar sensitivity to the shifting historical forms for
self-presentation—both within a writer's career (as borne out
by comparing his autobiography with his other writings)
and from period to period, cultural imperative to cultural
imperative—Bruss has traced the main lines of English autobiography through four centuries by seizing on four writers'
distinctive responses to "the changing situation of a literary
genre." [19]

Despite Lejeune's and Bruss's awareness of the historical
evolution of genres and of the permeable membrane of each
autobiographical mode in its literary and social relationships,
both scholars fall into a well-known trap of generic criticism:
the codification of norms, be they theoretically universal or
historically derived, be they laid up in Aristotle or demonstrated in the formal traits of specially selected texts. With
Lejeune, the set of favored conventions reaches considerable
elaboration in his later writings,[20] but all this linguistic and
historical sophistication is in the service of maintaining his
initial account of what he calls "le pacte autobiographique":

We admit only those authors who themselves ask to
be admitted. The autobiographical declaration of intention can express itself in different ways—in the title,
. . . the dedication, most often in the ritual preface, but
sometimes in a concluding note (Gide) or even in

18. Philippe Lejeune, *L'Autobiographie en France* (Paris, 1971), p.
47; my translation. The quotations that follow are from pp. 25, 28.
19. Elizabeth W. Bruss, *Autobiographical Acts: The Changing Situation of a Literary Genre* (Baltimore and London, 1976).
20. These essays are collected in Philippe Lejeune, *Le Pacte autobiographique* (Paris, 1975).

interviews granted at the time of publication (Sartre); but in any case, the statement is obligatory.

Lejeune uses the term *pacte* to denote the conventional understanding between writer and reader—the one, signing himself as committed to tell the truth (whether or not in fact he does so); the other, considering himself authorized to take the text as truth not fiction.[21] Beyond the convention-*making* sense of the term *pacte*—that is, an agreement to accept an arbitrary formula as indicating certain roles or responses—an unfortunate aura of legislative authority hangs over it (as it does over Bruss's term *act*). The authoritative tone is present even when Lejeune seeks to limit the pact to an intention and not a performance of truth telling: "What distinguishes autobiography from the novel is not an unattainable historical exactitude, but only the sincere *project* of recapturing and understanding one's own life. It is the existence of such a project that matters, and not an ultimately impossible sincerity." What is essential, then, is not the pact as a verbal marker in the text but as an antecedent "sincere project"— though this origin is never determinable or simple, as the disclaimer of "impossible sincerity" suggests. It is a "project" much like Pascal's norm of the quest for meaning and falls

21. In Bruss's formulation: "Whether or not what is reported can be discredited, . . . the autobiographer purports to believe in what he asserts" (p. 11). This transformation of the truth criterion for autobiography into a purported truthfulness criterion derives from Bruss's speech-act theory: "What is vital for creating the illocutionary force of the text is that the author purport to have met these requirements [for truth] and that the audience understand him to be responsible for meeting or failing to meet them" (p. 11). But this play of conventional roles not only removes the author's responsibility actually to tell the truth (it is enough that he purport to do so) but may also qualify the reader's "understanding" of the author's responsibilities (it is sufficient that the reader perceive the author to be so purporting and not necessary that he believe him to speak the truth). That is, if the truth claim becomes merely a speech act, all roles become conventional—a desirable condition, in which art may do its work!

into the same place with other professions of autobiographical good intentions.

Lejeune is well aware that the medium in which this project is enacted must employ the techniques of narrative that make for an audience's conviction, not necessarily for truth: "The paradox of autobiography is that the autobiographer must carry out this project of impossible sincerity using all the usual tools of fiction. He must believe that there is a fundamental difference between autobiography and fiction even if, in fact, to tell the truth about himself, he uses all the novelistic techniques of his time." In this ironic situation, all that Lejeune is able to salvage as a firm generic ground is the autobiographer's "belief" in such a distinction—which comes down to little more than a will to believe, a working premise for a fictional activity. Conventionalism extends, then, to the autobiographer's intention and shifts his qualifying performance from a pact in which he purports to be truthful to a pact in which he purports to play the role of truth teller.

When the study of genre history points to the absence of a "fundamental difference" between fiction and autobiography, it would be churlish to require of autobiographical writers a faith in that distinction which is denied the literary historian. The most stable conventions we can hope to find in autobiographies are the rhetorical traces of a literary tradition, by which writers play the role of desiring to have their work read in that generic context. Sincerity may be desirable as well but is neither reliably ascertainable nor requisite for generic affiliation. Nor is a naïve adoption of the rhetorical pact demanded of the audience; as narrative genres develop and intermingle, readers become increasingly aware of their "singular play of mirrors." Indeed, many come to welcome a text's self-referentiality, or *mise en abyme*, which invites their complicity in the author's task of artfully manipulating his medium. It is my impression that a wide audience of modern readers has reached a higher sophistication in regard to autobiography than some members of the critical fraternity, so that it welcomes displays of fictionality, artfulness, and even tailoring of the facts in behalf of skilled performance in an autobiographical role.[22] The sincere project of truth telling, like the quest for self-discovery, seems a latter-day version of Romantic norms and is being superseded as a conventional expectation in the continued evolution of the genres.

Expression

By contrast with the historical relativity of the generic model, another approach to autobiography assumes that any text—but especially an autobiography—is inevitably an emanation of its author, so that it reveals his uniqueness by a *natural* process even without his intended or executed design to do so. The motto for this approach is the naturalist Comte de Buffon's maxim "Le style est l'homme même," but its methods need be in league neither with the Enlightenment nor with the Romantic-expressive tradition. Instead, it may seize its opportunities to apply linguistic analysis to authorial idiolects, the bearers of an autobiographer's individuality. Such studies build upon older methods of philological stylistics, for example, those of Leo Spitzer, who sought the keys to an author's distinctive view of the world in his habitual deviations from normal usage, whether in grammar, diction, or other traits.

22. Bruss's final chapter, on Nabokov's self-deconstruction in *Speak, Memory*, is fully aware of the changing patterns of reception to which a number of modern autobiographers have responded and contributed: "Conscious experimentation and deliberate violation of literary codes and models have accelerated the slow and largely accidental process of literary history in this century. This paradoxical convention of the unconventional has naturally touched autobiography as well as poetry and the novel—giving us, along with free verse and the *nouveau roman, Anti-Memoirs* as well" (*Autobiographical Acts*, pp. 128–29). And further: "Identity can no longer seem impermeable to the conditions and techniques of the autobiographical act. . . . Sincerity can offer no guarantee, since it is a creation of will and appearance, and may be as easily feigned or as much a chimera as anything else." So much for the truth claim as a credible speech act.

A sketch of the expression theory, its links to the "deviation" approach to stylistics, and its assimilation of recent linguistic thinking is the much reprinted essay by Jean Starobinski, "The Style of Autobiography."[23] Starobinski uses the findings of the linguist Emile Benveniste on the tenses of historical and discursive narration to make more precise the co-presence in autobiography of a narrated past and a narrational present—the latter sometimes more highly foregrounded than the former. Similarly, the distinctions among the autobiographer's self-referential pronouns—not only in the special case of autobiography in the third person but even among the usages of a first-person narrative—are correlated with his dual role as narrator and subject matter of the work.[24]

The greatest virtue of the expression theory lies in shifting critical attention from the past represented in an autobiography to the implied or explicit present of its narrative situation. The author engaged in the exacting task of writing his life becomes the locus of the text's expressive reference: "No matter how doubtful the facts related, the text will at least present an 'authentic' image of the man who 'held the pen.' . . . Style as 'form superadded to content' will be judged above all on its inevitable infidelity to a past reality [i.e., to the man who acted]. . . . Style as [linguistic] deviation, however, seems rather to exist in a relation of fidelity to a contemporary reality" (i.e., to the man who writes). Yet the

23. Jean Starobinski, "The Style of Autobiography," in *Literary Style: A Symposium*, ed. (and trans.?) Seymour Chatman (New York and London, 1971), pp. 285–96; the quotations below are from p. 287.

24. Another linguistic potentiality engaged by Starobinski's essay (and the discussion that is printed with it) is the concept of pronouns as *shifters*, referring directly to nothing outside the text but operationally defined only by reference to other elements of the code. For a brief discussion of the autobiographical I as a shifter, see Eugene Vance, "Augustine's *Confessions* and the Grammar of Selfhood," *Genre*, 6 (1973): 2–4. Other articles in this and the following number of *Genre*, both devoted to autobiography, make telling application of linguistics to the interpretation of individual works. See also a later collection of essays on autobiography in *Genre*, 12, no. 1 (1979).

Romantic mythology that underlies this shift of attention suffuses it at the next breath: "In this case, the very notion of style really obeys a system of organic metaphors, according to which expression proceeds from experience, without any discontinuity, as the flower is pushed open by the flow of sap through the stem." It is hard to tell whether Starobinski is urging our assent to this naturalistic view of what happens in autobiography or merely rehearsing some characteristic gestures in the tradition. In either case, the organic metaphor seems dated as a poetics and unconvincing as a genetics of autobiography.

Though it generalizes about the proper use of linguistics in making discussion of autobiographical discourse more precise, Starobinski's essay moves quickly to the distinctive and complex play of tenses and pronouns in such writers as Augustine and Rousseau. In contrast to his impulse toward the individual author, other appropriations of linguistics have moved toward elaborate schemas of the universal characteristics of the genre, restricting the range of acceptable articulations and categorizing works in conformity with a preordained set of formulas.[25] In the cases where these schemas are used to categorize autobiographies as to type of discourse, the most evident effect is that of a decorating scheme with many dangling ends of fabric and wallpaper. In the more fortunate cases, the system once established is simply put away in favor of a functional account of the author's style and the experience of reading his prose.

25. E.g., Lejeune, *Le Pacte autobiographique*, in the title essay; and Bruss, *Autobiographical Acts*, ch. 1. The former devotes extended discussion to pronouns and the role of proper names; the latter treats a host of grammatical and rhetorical features in their autobiographical roles—resulting in a two-page table of "some linguistic markers sensitive to context." Both the excessive specification of Lejeune's language norms (though less marked in his discussion of pronouns) and the broad generality of Bruss's view of autobiographical language render them of scant utility in practical criticism. But Lejeune is developing more supple methods in his more recent essays, e.g., "Autobiography in the Third Person," trans. E. Tomarken and A. Tomarken, *New Literary History*, 9 (1977): 27–50.

These efforts to codify the linguistic workings of the genre suggest by their abstractness or irrelevance to most empirical cases that the proper role of language study lies in the analysis of individual texts. There is no set of stylistic or linguistic traits to identify autobiography as such: neither pronouns, tenses, grammatical structures, or other categories can be standardized or limited in application. Theoreticians of first-person autobiography, who have carefully extended their range to third-person works, must nerve themselves to consider that a canonical text, Augustine's *Confessions*, is written largely in the second person, addressed as it is to God throughout. The autobiographer's options are as wide as language and literature themselves.

Myth

Closely related to the expression theory is the view that an autobiographer does not merely press out some of his inner substance with his stylistic traits but that he automatically creates additional substance, a birth which may be considered a new self. While this intuition is never articulated in the bald terms given here, it underlies the thinking of critics influenced by Jung, who employs a version of the auto-biographical creation myth in his account of psychic life in general. For Jung, life is a process of integrating the several parts of the mind, the conscious and unconscious aspects of living; and his followers see autobiography as the creation of a "personal myth" (Jung's term in his own autobiography)[26]—a unification of the disparate elements and latent impulses of the autobiographer's life. From this standpoint, writing one's autobiography is the healthiest thing one can do for oneself.

The fullest application of Jungian psychology to auto-

26. Carl Gustave Jung, *Memories, Dreams, Reflections*, ed. Aniela Jaffé, trans. R. Winston and C. Winston (New York, 1965 [1961]), p. 3.

biography, James Olney's *Metaphors of Self*,[27] expounds the "meaning of autobiography" at length and with conviction. Although it deals with the verbal texture of a number of autobiographical works, it shows only sporadic inclinations to translate into literary terms the process by which psychic integration is brought about. To trace this sequence, I shall make use of a comparable practitioner of literary psychology, Charles Mauron, though cognizant that his Freudian orientation would make commerce between these two versions of personal myth a strain for their exponents.

After treating in detail the repetitive images and situations that mark the *oeuvre* of a number of classic French authors, in a manner resembling that of the Geneva school of phenomenological criticism, Mauron sums up his account of the process, using the example of Baudelaire's complex of images, the "carriers of the Chimera":

> This figure groups the obsessive representations and thoughts which were peculiar to Baudelaire. Another writer might equally well speak of hair, of prostitute or actor, of hindrance and fall: he would have other memories, other psychic and physical gestures. He will group other images and compose them in a new manner. Singularity and repetition thus create characteristic figures. The imagination of a given writer seems to attach itself to only a limited number of such figures. He varies them more than he exchanges them for others. . . . What results in each case is a small number of dramatic scenes, whose action is as characteristic of the writer as it is of the participants. Their constellation comprises the personal myth.[28]

Mauron swiftly covers a sequence of operations, which I shall discuss under four heads: memories and their traces in

27. James Olney, *Metaphors of Self: The Meaning of Autobiography* (Princeton, 1972).

28. Charles Mauron, *Des Métaphores obsédantes au mythe personnel: Introduction à la psychocritique* (Paris, 1963), p. 209; my translation.

23

images; repetition, or its psychological concomitant, obses-sion; composition or "groupement" (which I have translated as "constellation"); and dramatic scene and action.

To begin with the first items, one must note an implicit qualification to Mauron's account. Although many a (per-haps every) writer recycles his memories, since they emerge spontaneously throughout his work as transposed images, an autobiographer deals directly in memories and attempts to describe them vividly in verbal images. Here the author's intention may count for something determinable, for there is a difference between passively playing out one's personal myth in the obsessive images that screen one's past and set-ting out resolutely to describe those scenes and to foreground those images. What new screens may enter in the process of description are, of course, to be attended to as they emerge, but they will be second-order transformations, not the pri-mary veils of the memory work.

A further stage is reached with a writer's persistent return to selected images throughout his career; much the same re-iteration can often be observed within the confines of a single autobiographical text. Mauron's account of this apparently compelled repetition entails a psychological theory of obses-sion whereas Olney ascribes it to universal metaphysical pro-clivities hidden in the depths of Jungian archetypal theory. Both psychological critics speak of a priori mental forms as determining these predispositions;[29] the one tends to reduce them to clinical symptomatology, the other to a mystical daimon. Neither explanatory theory is, however, needed to account for an autobiographer's act of repetition, for it dif-fers in kind from obsession. An obsessive is bound to repeat, often reenacting as well as returning to the past in language and thought. An autobiographer may be an obsessive but

29. Olney follows Jung in describing the archetype as "a priori and inherent, the *donnée* of human existence" (*Metaphors of Self*, p. 131); Mauron calls the personal myth "une forme a priori de l'imagination" (*Des Métaphores*, p. 218). The quotations from Olney that follow are from *Metaphors of Self*, pp. 34, 87.

insofar as he turns to autobiographical writing, he has shifted from direct reenactment (including acts of speech) to the language of review, revision, and representation. Such repetition is never simply the same again but will inevitably generate novel features: the same anew.

This reflection brings us to the third of Mauron's stages, that of composition or grouping, where we can speak of a newly emergent pattern not given in the psychic *données*. Describing a comparable process, Olney emphasizes novelty in the writer's achievement: "The self expresses itself by the metaphors it creates and projects, and we know it by those metaphors; but it did not exist as it now does and as it now is before creating its metaphors." This new self created in autobiography is linked to the evolving pattern of images, which moves toward completing what is nascent but incomplete in life: "We see Montaigne completing himself in the completion of his portrait. Hand in hand the two move to the destined and foreseen but unknown end, the man becoming complete as the metaphor describes and defines him, the portrait being finished as the man comes to richest maturity." This sense of a progressive emergence of identity in the articulation of metaphor (despite regrettably vague notions of destiny or prophecy) is more illuminating in the study of autobiography than Mauron's reduction of the writer's creativity to the role of autoanalysis (in his chapter devoted to that subject).

Nevertheless, Olney's invocation of metaphor in his title *et passim* is not as conducive to tracing the creative process in autobiography as its prominence might suggest. Although recognizing the importance of metaphoric language in autobiographical self-creation, Olney does not valorize the compositional qualities of this verbal activity but only its existential value for psychological ends. Olney's accounts of expanding metaphors, even in what he calls "duplex" as opposed to "simplex" autobiographers, accumulate their interweavings in a "web" of evolved selfhood, but nowhere is there a recognition that language has a dynamic structure of its own, to which the evolving structure of personal identity may be set up as a parallel but to which it is not identical. For Olney's account of the fusion of text creation and self-creation has no point of interaction between literature and psychology, between language and mental life, lacking a recognition that language has an action, a life of its own.

Particularly noticeable by its absence is an awareness of the dramatic action that takes place within and among metaphors, an awareness that literary criticism has inherited from William Empson and Kenneth Burke and that is succinctly formulated by Frye: "The assumed metaphors in their turn become the units of the myth or constructive principle of the argument. While we read, we are aware of a sequence of metaphorical identifications; when we have finished, we are aware of an organizing structural pattern or conceptualized myth."[30] What Frye explains in the reading process is also true of the constructive process by which the myth or argument is set forth. It is the tale told by these metaphors—the drama of the metaphors themselves—that is the mythos of autobiography, for the *way* in which metaphors dynamically become myths is the general model for the way in which autobiographical narrative generates a self or personal myth.

This sense of process is captured in Mauron's *poetics of personal myth*. It has no necessary reference to traditional mythology except as those myths are sometimes employed to focus a writer's metaphoric dramas. (Olney, in his turn, scarcely refers to traditional myths as shaping autobiographical narratives although he mentions the Jungian conceptualization of them as archetypal structures of the mind.)[31] It is,

30. Frye, *Anatomy of Criticism*, p. 353.
31. Even Olney's careful tracing of the interwoven and modulating motifs of the *Four Quartets* treats them not as an "imitation of events" but as an "imitation of a process," i.e., of the "evolving self" (*Metaphors of Self*, p. 301). While the autobiographical status of this and other Eliot poems is open to debate, Olney seems to give away too much (temporal reference, referrable place names, biographical incidents) in an effort to focus the poems' action on inner development. The latter may well be the proper subject of narrative, but it is diffi-

Introduction

indeed, important to distinguish at least three senses of *myth*
in these formulations: the traditional body of tales that may
serve as resources of metaphoric identification, the mythos
or narrative that the autobiographer may construct of his
metaphors in sequence, and the created identity or new self
that he forms in the process of writing. Yet the convergence
of these three senses in the autobiographical situation suggests that they are not incidentally related but are closely
implicated in the creative activity to which the mythic view
of autobiography gives us access.

What emerges from these studies of the making of personal myth—despite their psychological or literary vagaries—
is the need for attention both to narrative and to metaphoric
action in autobiographical texts. Their implications go well
beyond the received idea that autobiographies are or contain
narratives—the telling of a story of change over time. One
implication is that the criticism of autobiographical narratives may take as its subject the twin proceedings in which
metaphoric sequences are shaped into literary, and obsessive
images are transformed into personal, myths. We may eventually come to agree, if not that these two enterprises are
essential to autobiography, at least that their tandem movements may lead to the creation of individually focused and
uniquely achieved works of art.

Structure

In contrast to the mythic approach to autobiography,
which sees metaphors and symbols as the stuff or substantial
element of psychic life and is therefore sanguine about the

cult to narrate except as connected with points of reference in the
external world. For a useful reminder of the story-telling inclinations
of even the most inward autobiographers, see Alfred Kazin, "Autobiography as Narrative," *Michigan Quarterly Review*, 3 (1964): 210–
16. For an exploration of the problems of narrating inner processes,
especially of the time sense, see Janet V. Gunn, "Autobiography and
the Narrative Experience of Temporality as Depth," *Soundings*, 60
(1977): 194–209.

autobiographer's ability to use this material for psychic integration, another movement in post-Freudian psychology has grave doubts about the possibilities of integration and is therefore skeptical about the direction of autobiography to that end. The Lacanian school—whether it is considered structuralist or poststructuralist in relation to other currents of Continental thought—has devised complicated models of mental structure that anticipate protracted internal tension rather than eventual integration. It holds promise, at best, for our recognition of an essential lack or *manque à être* in patients and nonpatients alike—sometimes garishly expressed in a revised formulation of the castration complex. But Jacques Lacan and his followers have a potential interest for the study of autobiography because their structural account of mental processes suggests a corresponding structural analysis of the writer's self-picturing. Indeed, their chief terminological resource is an appropriation of the structural methods of linguistics to the inner psychic drama.

In place of the Freudian and Jungian furnishings of the mind, Lacan posits that its inner workings are structured on the model of interpersonal discourse. Explaining one of his simpler symbolic pictures, he writes:

> This schema signifies that the condition of the subject [S] (neurotic or psychotic) depends on what is being unfolded in the Other [A]. What is being unfolded there is articulated like a discourse (the unconscious is the discourse of the Other)—a discourse whose syntax Freud first sought to define for those fragments of it which come to us in certain privileged moments, dreams, slips of the tongue or pen, flashes of wit.[32]

I shall not attempt an adequate explanation of the "Other" (with either a small or capital initial letter) who speaks in

32. Jacques Lacan, "Traitment possible de la psychose," in his *Ecrits* (Paris, 1966); this passage is translated and quoted in Anthony Wilden, *The Language of the Self* (Baltimore and London, 1968), p. 107. See also Jacques Lacan, *Ecrits: A Selection*, trans. Alan Sheridan (New York, 1977).

this internal discourse, when one expositor spends several pages listing the alternative denotations of the term.[33] Nor shall I offer to resolve the ambiguities of the twin aphorism that the unconscious is both "articulated like a discourse" (or, elsewhere, "structured like a language") and is the "discourse of the Other." But the implication of greatest interest for the student of autobiography is that normal self-reference is marked by anxiety, alienation, and incompletion—or by Lacan's equivalents of these widely perceived modern conditions. To quote a characteristic Lacanian quandary: "It is not a question of knowing whether I am speaking about myself in conformity with what I am, but rather that of knowing whether, when I speak of it, I am the same as that of which I speak. . . ." Beyond the usual cruxes of self-division and existential identity, this attention to the subject's language—particularly when speaking of himself, from the moment of his identifying himself as the object of his discourse—opens special problems for the writer of autobiography.

Again, in contrast with the prevailing image of the autobiographer as engaged in a refined form of narcissism—and in contrast to the tacit expectation of other critics that the autobiographer is likely to be pleased with the meaning he discovers or approving of the image he projects—the Lacanian narcissist is inclined to be rightly appalled at his view in the mirror. Going well beyond the plain man's skepticism of autobiography as a geriatric art form designed to fend off death for a time—or at least to properly compose a death mask[34]—the literary practitioners of structuralism have placed Narcissus with Oedipus as the twin demigods of self-inquiry under the fatal necessity of self-deconstruction.

33. Wilden, *Language of the Self*, pp. 262–69; the quotation from Lacan below is from Wilden, p. 183.

34. Discussions of death in (or as) autobiography from other points of view include Barrett J. Mandel, " 'Basting the Image with a Certain Liquor': Death in Autobiography," *Soundings*, 57 (1974): 175–88; and Mutlu K. Blasing, *The Art of Life: Studies in American Autobiographical Literature* (Austin, Tex., and London, 1977), preface.

In *A Structural Study of Autobiography*,[35] Jeffrey Mehlman has treated the work of four modern French writers as the creation neither of a new or symbolic or integrated or especially attractive self but as a process of deconstructing the apparently stable structure in which the self has reached written form. For this perception of the writer's apparently fated tendency toward self-deconstruction, Mehlman applies the insights of another poststructuralist thinker, Jacques Derrida, into writing in general, of which autobiographical writing is a salient instance. In *Of Grammatology*,[36] Derrida argues that writing by its very nature not only places but displaces its subject, for the marks in the text are always the signs of his absence rather than his presence. Given this distantiation, it is not only the critic who comes upon a text with a will to deconstruct it; the autobiographer's own activity is deconstruction—practiced upon the self because the subject is himself.

Taking one of the most fecund of modern autobiographers, Michel Leiris, as his paradigm, Mehlman describes his account of Leiris's *oeuvre* as the "hidden center" of his own undertaking:

> For, in his effort to posit a poetics and ethics of autobiography, Leiris has pressed the question of the genre to its extreme and produced the most far-reaching experiment in the impossibility of becoming alive *(bio)* to oneself *(auto)* in the elusive realm that the French call *écriture (graphie)*.... My effort has been, in each [autobiography], to reach that level of analysis at which a persistent textual organization is revealed, whose coherence throws into jeopardy the apparent intentions of the author and expropriates him in an intertextual circuit of relations, which this study would indeed constitute.

35. Jeffrey Mehlman, *A Structural Study of Autobiography* (Ithaca and London, 1974); the quotation below is from pp. 13–14.
36. Jacques Derrida, *Of Grammatology*, trans. G. C. Spivak (Baltimore and London, 1976 [1967]).

Mehlman extends this approach to a work that apparently moves toward self-discovery, Proust's autobiographical novel, as well as to a work by a staunchly self-affirming mind, Sartre's, which nevertheless becomes the record of how he "became a stranger to himself." Adapting Mauron's methods of attaching psychological significance to repetitive figures, myths, and images, Mehlman's *A Structural Study of Autobiography* is among the most impressive readings of personal myth available.[37]

A number of issues touched on in Mehlman's programmatic statement raise further speculations, however. The critic acknowledges that a writer may have an "apparent intention" to discover or create himself but that this project will be defeated by the conditions prevailing in the realm of *écriture*. This formulation seems to grant the possibility of a desire to work against the determinate conditions of the medium, but the word *apparent* calls even the authenticity of such an intention into doubt. By upholding the medium over the maker in the passive unfolding of an "intertextual circuit of relations" that expropriates him, Mehlman, in common with the more scientifically oriented structuralists, may be yielding to determinism. Such a withdrawal from personal freedom—from even the possibility of gaining a partial victory over one's medium—would in another period have been perceived as an instance of Sartrian "bad faith." Yet in this, as in other deconstructionist criticism, there is one will, one freedom that seems able to resist the tide of deconstruction by its own language. This aspect of the critical project emerges clearly in the final phrase quoted above. To acknowledge that the final "circuit" or structure of relations is constituted by the critical study rather than by the works "expropriated" is to claim control of the writing mechanisms by which the autobiographer is controlled. One need not

37. A number of articles demonstrating a structuralist or poststructuralist approach have been published in recent journal issues devoted to autobiography: *Genre*, 6, nos. 1–2 (1973); *New Literary History*, 9, no. 1 (1977); and *Modern Language Notes*, 93, no. 4 (1978).

solve the metaphysical puzzle as to the inherence of structure in the system or in the systematizing mind in order to perceive the will to power exercised in the critic's demonstration of the autobiographer's powerlessness.[38]

An unlooked-for consequence of this deconstruction of the writer's power over his language is a diminution of the power of writing itself. For all the focus on language in psychology and literature, the structuralists who succeeded Claude Lévi-Strauss have tended to call into doubt the capacity of any language to order decisively, to represent adequately, and to embody symbolically. When Mehlman describes autobiography as the genre that "proclaims the impossible dream of being alive to oneself in the scriptural," he joins in a broader tendency to see representation and other displacements of the subject as a kind of death. The apparent primacy given to linguistic structure as the model for other organizations confers, moreover, no privilege on language as interpreter or norm, for the isomorphism of, for example, language and self is of a negative kind. Just as language displaces any subject, when the subject is, as in the case of autobiography, the self, language becomes the model of the self's inclinations toward self-alienation—toward the evasion of identity and the responsibilities of identification with/as oneself that has been widely observed in contemporary culture.

Yet a more promising option in employing the structuralist approach opens when the tendency of the self to become other in writing is seen neutrally as a process of self-alteration. Altering, becoming other, need not be taken as making strange but may be remaking. From this position, the death of self in autobiography may be seen as a sloughing off of the dead self, as exorcism of the living yet baleful one, or as the inveterate need or habit of tinkering with oneself in language, of which the poet speaks:

---

38. For Mehlman's account of his structure and its origins in the methods of Mauron and Lacan, see his *Structural Study of Autobiography*, pp. 16–17; the quotation below is from p. 163.

> The friends that have it I do wrong
> When ever I remake a song,
> Should know what issue is at stake:
> It is myself that I remake.[39]

If there is inescapable alteration in the act of writing autobiography, it is an alchemy comparable with the Freudian injunction to displace id with ego: there where living was, let writing be.

If autobiography is not merely the drive to be other but the drive to exist in another medium, something may be done to reconcile the varied and apparently mutually exclusive drives that writers have displayed. The move to write oneself down as a text combines the impulse to confirm the self as it is (the same) and the impulse to become or to make it strange, ideal, or permanent (the other). Thus, the genre is not only inherently incomplete—lacking, at the very least, the moment of the writer's death—and metaleptic (combining past acts and present narration, history and discourse); it is transubstantiative as well. Each autobiographical utterance embalms the author in his own prose, marking his passage into a form that both surrenders him to death and yet preserves his name, acts, and words. Given this transformation of self into text, the deconstructive character of language need be construed as the autobiographer's self-destruction no more vividly than as his self-creation.

Perhaps the most satisfactory way of taking the writer's alteration is through Derrida's concept of writing as supplement—the mark of an absence, which yet supplies something of what is lacking in life or lost in writing. And here we come upon a rationale for the frequently observed repetitive image, chain of metaphor, or projected myth in so many autobiographies. Just as a metaphor may generally be read as a vehicle that makes up the lack of an adequate literal de-

39. W. B. Yeats, *The Variorum Edition of the Poems of W. B. Yeats*, ed. Peter Allt and R. K. Alspach (New York, 1968 [1957]), p. 778.

scription for its tenor, so autobiographical metaphor may be seen as a supplement that fills the space left by the self, which, in the act of writing, absents itself. The other self written in autobiography may also serve as a supplement to fill many a lack felt in a variety of ways in life—such motivation is legion. The homology of language and self is one neither of identical substance, then, nor of isomorphic pattern but of reciprocal dynamics.[40]

Such a way of relating autobiography to the action of language avoids a number of critical pitfalls. First to be eschewed is the so-called "metaphysics of presence," which cherishes a hope of recovering the true author or real self in the text; he will always be displaced in language or—in traditional terms—transformed into a work of art. Again, the symbolic status of an autobiographical text is relieved of the biological passivity with which the expression theory would endow it; the text is an icon, by virtue of its similar (perhaps identical) mode of operation, not an indexical sign resulting from the life processes of the author (to employ C. S. Peirce's terms).

Finally, the result of an autobiographical enterprise neither is guaranteed by nor inevitably fails in its high aims. The action of metaphor is to build the qualities of the associated vehicle into the concept of the tenor; similarly, autobiographical metaphors expand the self beyond its original confines (which were at most provisional). It is generally agreed that autobiographies relate the self to larger constructs in history, society, or philosophy; the self seeks not merely a context of definition but a way of appropriating its

40. I have been helped throughout this discussion by private communications and published writings of Michael Ryan: "Self-De(con)-struction" [review of Mehlman], *Diacritics*, Spring 1976, pp. 34–41; "Narcissus Autobiographer: *Marius the Epicurean*," *English Literary History*, 43 (1976): 184–208; and "A Grammatology of Assent: Cardinal Newman's *Apologia Pro Vita Sua*," in *Approaches to Victorian Autobiography*, ed. G. P. Landow (Athens, Ohio, 1979), pp. 128–57. On the present point and a number of others, my own departures from Ryan's Derridean reading should be evident.

world to itself. In the formation of personal myth out of a train of metaphors, the autobiographer enhances his condition, extends himself beyond his unwritten self. At the same time, he opens himself to a play of language that takes him beyond his original intentions, he becomes part of the realm of interpretation, and he condemns himself never to be known as a simple essence. To this new person sent into the world by autobiography, one may give the name *supernumerary*, combining qualities of the Yeatsian mask, the structuralist Other, and perhaps the Jungian archetype. He is an extra, a "substitute in case of necessity"; in theatrical terms, "one not belonging to the regular company, who appears on the stage but has no lines to speak." Quite naturally, for his role is to bear the script, in which the play of self is written out.[41]

One result of this survey of current opinion is to make it clear that there are no agreed norms for a genre of autobiography. The canons of a standard of truth (or even of purported truth), of a quest for meaning (whether as goal

41. I am conscious that this account fails to specify a concrete relation between the mythos of metaphors constructed in the text and the personal myth constituted as a self. I shall try to be more precise about the displacement of life by language and the reciprocal destruction and creation of self in what follows. But, in common with all authorities I have encountered or read, I don't know the self well enough to do more than entertain it as a premise. Yet I am not prepared to surrender one term of the relation between language and self entirely, as some have done, dropping the unknowable self as a fiction and collapsing it in the linguistic vortex of the text. The self may not be something preexistent that generates autobiography, but it is not identical to the resulting autobiography itself. Fluctuating and imperceptible, as philosophers from David Hume to Abraham Caplan have never tired of showing, it is nevertheless "'somewhere in the room"—as Dickens's Mrs. Gradgrind insists, even though she cannot say who bears her pain. I pursue the problem obliquely in an Envoi and have developed my position on the referentiality of literature in *Fiction and the Ways of Knowing: Essays on British Novels* (Austin, Tex., and London, 1978).

or process), of a set of conventional markers or consistent rhetorical gestures, of an inevitable self-expression or personal myth or dialectic of desire—all are broadly enlightening but are useful only operationally in exhibiting the behavior of one or another self-writing. Autobiography is not generically distinguished by formal constituents, linguistic register, or audience effects, yet it is not quite whatever a person makes of it. In writing, he joins with a long succession of other writers bent on the same folly, devoted to the same calling. This is not a company set apart from other mortals, for autobiographers are only so part time (there may be a few modern exceptions, to be discussed below). As writers or actors in their own times, they will stamp their autobiographies with the marks of the literary and other cultural movements in which they are engaged. Autobiography therefore has no history as a genre but it is steeped in history; its continuities are intertwined with the historical processes of culture at large.

Despite an author's being locked into a productive system of figurative language, beyond his necessary generation of a supernumerary text, the autobiographer can add his own voice to the putatively self-regulating linguistic enterprise. He can always comment on his own text, on the recalcitrance of language, and on the choices of the working craftsman in the throes of his self-imposed task. By adding his voice to the text that is to produce his image, the writer may not be able fully to control the mechanisms by which he works, but he can at least assert his struggle with them—even though he does so in language. Naming the shadow that falls between will and craft, intention and expression, does not resolve the discrepancy by fiat, nor is an assertion of resistance to the medium a performative declaration of independence from it. But in the course of his authorial self-references, the autobiographer emerges most clearly: not as one who lived but as one writing for his life.

What, then, makes an autobiography better or worse, successful or unsuccessful—or is it possible to fail entirely in self-writing? No prescriptions for procedure or estimation will be forthcoming here. If there are to be axiological distinctions between *classes* of autobiography, we may ascribe higher value to those works where *mise en abyme* occurs, for its absence in another breed of writings designed to obscure their own artificiality has led to their relegation to the class of memoirs. The self-conscious autobiographer may ask himself: What am I doing in the act of writing this? His book becomes an answer to this question, as it comes to dramatize the challenge and response of writing autobiography itself. Nor is this a totally hermetic or centripetal movement; the answer to such queries is sometimes framed—by those writers with a lively sense of their predecessors—in terms of that question posed and answers given by previous writers. From such gestures emerges a historical tradition, not as a generic code but as an ongoing and ever-changing stream of influence and originality.

I must conclude this review of six approaches to autobiography on a note resembling the research report of a negative outcome of an experimental design. Certain studies look for the defining characteristics of a theoretical genre, with an essence or eternal nature; others propose historical generalizations of certain shared features—in a manner approximating the family resemblance definitions of Wittgenstein. Both these enterprises fail to take hold of autobiography's protean forms: the one because autobiography cannot be derived from an abstract theory of genres; the other because a variety of pragmatic criteria are always introduced to delimit the range of works considered—otherwise all writings that make some arguable reference to the author might be welcome.[42] It is not necessary to take the extreme

42. This review of the current approaches to autobiography lends support to the sweeping contention of Paul de Man that the subject is ill served by current efforts to treat it as one genre among others: *Modern Language Notes*, 94 (1979): 919–30. De Man enforces his view not simply by noting the poverty of efforts to preserve narrow normative distinctions and to maintain autobiography's purity as his-

position of some genre critics that only historical conventions determine a genre—and that since modified audience expectations and authorial manipulations of tradition constantly occur, a genre may last only as long as the individual work or, as a sensible compromise, some few decades.[43] We may instead take the consensus of recent revisions of genre theory to apply with special force to autobiography. It is not only volatile in its changes but so profuse in its variety of forms as to make no urgent claim for a place among the genres.

Yet this negative conclusion need not relegate autobiography to the margins of literature, among the parasitical or scrappy works that surround the canonical texts. Instead of

---

torical reference, despite its manifest symbiotic relationships with poetry and fiction. He makes his point by drawing attention to the metaphoric character of autobiographies—which is only a special case of the inveterately figurative dimension of language in general. More questionable is his merging of autobiography with literature at large: "Autobiography, then, is not a genre or a mode, but a figure of reading or of understanding that occurs, to some degree, in all texts" (p. 921). On this assumption, de Man feels empowered to treat not merely *The Prelude* but Wordsworth's *Essays upon Epitaphs* as metaphoric enactments of autobiographical prosopopoeia, the calling into play of a fictive addressee, speculatively endowing it with a voice and a face. A curious contradiction besets this project of submersion, however, for it mingles all texts in a common pool yet selects certain ones called autobiographies as especially suitable for illustrating the nature of texts in general ("The interest of autobiography, then, is not that it reveals reliable self-knowledge—it does not—but that it demonstrates in a striking way the impossibility of closure and of totalization [that is the impossibility of coming into being] of all textual systems made up of tropological substitutions" [p. 922]). If autobiography can serve as this striking illustration, it must have, if not the defining characteristics of a genre, at least such distinctive marks as those that lead most readers to take *The Prelude* as autobiographical and not *Essays upon Epitaphs*.

43. See Gustavo Pérez Firmat, "The Novel as Genres," *Genre*, 12 (1979): 269–92, for some strict discipline on the standards for generic definition and for the temporal limits of audience consensus. On the historical career of genres, see Firmat's notes for references to Todorov, Jauss, and Guillén.

asking what is autobiography and arriving at such disheartening results, we may ask how the age-old activity of writing life stories has organized itself at various periods of literary history. This emphasis on the activity rather than on the corpus of works corresponds to a sense of the subject latent in its name. *Autobiography* seems to refer from the outset to the writing process rather than to its results. Self-life-writing becomes, from this standpoint, less a compound of substantives than an account of an ongoing action. (I shall abbreviate to *self-writing* in what follows.)

This activity has a history since it is a series of human events, but that history is so intercalated with other acts and occurs over such long stretches of time that it can hardly be written in a totalizing fashion but only with local continuities. (The experience of Georg Misch in his lifelong dedication to the task should be regarded neither as a sad nor a noble example but as testing of the limits of the possible.) It is desirable that a literary-historical study of autobiography be historically specific, limiting not only its period of analysis but also the lines of force that it seeks to draw to other cultural phenomena. It is the purpose of the opening chapter to describe a set of such phenomena as they converge in a great book, Augustine's *Confessions*, showing how it draws on the resources of Christian and pagan culture and sketching their transmission to later autobiographers, among the wider body of Augustine's recipients. This selective account makes no pretense to be even the partial history of a genre but claims only to set out the most telling evidence for the study of some important autobiographies in nineteenth- and twentieth-century England. To what extent these works are worth examining in their own right and to what extent they are illuminated by shared religious concerns, figurative language, and narrative imperatives will be for the reader to judge.

PART I

Traditional
Figures

—

To TELL THE STORY of his life may seem as unmediated an action as a writer can perform, given his expertise in the subject and the singular authority he can exert over it. Yet after brief reflection, the lessons we have learned about cultural codes, symbolic forms, and cognitive archeology will be found to bear with special weight on autobiography, making it one of the most sensitive registers of the idea of human existence and the pattern of individual life in a given society. At the simplest level, it is the necessities of narrative that assert themselves. The need to shape a story will lead the writer to the story types that prevail in his culture; similarly, the desire to conceive a protagonist will be abetted by the character types that have predominated in those stories. As an influential statement of the imperatives of narrative puts the matter: "All knowing and all telling are subject to the conventions of art. Because we apprehend reality through culturally determined types, we can report the most particular event only in the form of a representational fiction. . . ."[1]

How do these narrative fictions come into play in autobiography? Although the details of any particular event may be told in an unmotivated chronological sequence—a *story*, to use E. M. Forster's well-known distinction—the longer

1. Robert Scholes and Robert Kellogg, *The Nature of Narrative* (London, Oxford, and New York, 1968 [1966]), p. 151.

influences and intentional relations of events require an activity of the kind known to literature as *plotting*.[2] Since original plots are notoriously few and since the autobiographer may share most fictional masters' difficulty in inventing them, these plots are likely to be variants of the accumulated cultural stores. It would be easy but pointless to construct an ideal developmental structure or narratological lexicon of the plots employable in telling a life story; they are elaborated in forms as various as the society's complexity of experience permits. We learn little about the manifestations of the Oedipus complex by referring them back to the structure of the Oedipus myth.

There are a few intrinsic limitations on autobiographical plots, derived from the peculiar situation of the autobiographer: for example, his inability to end his story with his own death—although certain writers have chipped away at this constraint by writing from a point of view *d'outre-tombe* (as in Chateaubriand's *Mémoires d'outre-tombe*: 1848). These general conditions limit the story but not the plot of autobiography, for even an incomplete chronological sequence can be told in a way designed to inspire a sense of finality, if not of resolution. Similarly, an effort to conform the autobiographer's life story with the archetypal critics' universal plot—from birth to death, including exemplary actions comparable with the rituals of initiation, wedding, trials and tests, scapegoating of the protagonist and/or defeat of his antagonist, ascendancy and at least proleptic funeral[3]— would come under the suspicion of obliterating his choice of a finite and particular image of himself. Autobiographers have sometimes availed themselves of the archetypal forms

2. To avoid overcomplication of the narrational machinery—given the thickets of semantic terminology to follow—I omit references to the formidable body of structuralist theory that has grown around this distinction.

3. I follow a typical listing of archetypal patterns in Northrop Frye, *Anatomy of Criticism: Four Essays* (New York, 1968 [1957]), p. 105.

of ancient drama and tribal ritual (for example, John Cooper Powys's *Autobiography*: 1934), but most have shown commendable pertinacity in resisting universal schemas, preferring to pick and tinker among varied resources like Claude Lévi-Strauss's image of the culture-making *bricoleur*.

The relation posited here between individual life stories and the plots profferred by the institutions of culture presupposes more general dealings between autobiography and history. Everyone recognizes that the form and content of autobiographies change with times and places, but the point of impact of these changes on the shape of narrative has remained obscure perhaps because overburdened by weighty historicist conceptions. Georg Misch, whose lifelong studies of autobiography make the strongest claim yet to constitute a generic history, ascribes to the subject several kinds of historicity:

> Though essentially representations of individual personalities, autobiographies are bound always to be representative of their period, within a range that will vary with the intensity of the authors' participation in contemporary life and with the sphere in which they moved. . . .
> Thus the characteristic self-revelations provide us with an objective, indeed, a demonstrable image of the structure of individuality, varying from epoch to epoch. Accordingly a history of autobiography offers an alluring prospect: as men's accounts of their concrete existence follow one another, whether they are merely stereotyped or show a personality in its individual manifestation, there pass vividly before us in a continuous series of self-portrayals the permanence and changefulness of the values of life. In this way autobiographical works, while to all appearance emerging by chance, and associated only through relations of literary form, make up an intrinsically connected series, which enables autobiography to be comprehended as a kind of organic whole that has

developed constantly with the general civilization of
the various ages and peoples, down to our own day.[4]

Three distinct historicist generalizations are to be found in
this program, and they will probably be received in our day
with descending degrees of confidence.

Few will dissent from the opening proposition that an
autobiography, like other works of art or historiography, is
"representative" of the period or culture in which it was
produced. This idea verges on tautology since scholarly
periodization frequently relies heavily on the images of personality exhibited in autobiographies. Cellini has been employed to help define the Renaissance, Rousseau the early
Romantic era, and Malraux and Nabokov have been pressed
into similar service for the present age. About Misch's claims
of a coherent development in the "values of life" from age
to age, which is paralleled in a "continuous series" of self-
portrayals somewhat like a portrait gallery, there will be
greater skepticism. Not only are current readers less imbued
with late-Hegelian assumptions about world-historical progress, but even those with convictions about the cohesive
nature of autobiography will be wary of granting its history
the integrity of an "organic whole," with a determinate intrinsic development. It is with Misch's middle propositions
that there will be partial agreement but also keen desire for
elaboration. What is the precise point of differentiation between autobiographies that are "merely stereotyped" and
those that exhibit "individual manifestation" since neither
one nor the other kind can be purely stereotyped or purely
individual? And how do these works draw on the life and
thought of their periods, so as—both of them!—to be representative?

One would like to be able to observe, if not to codify,
the process by which the choice and tinkering among available plot forms is made. How does an individual autobiogra-

4. Georg Misch, *A History of Autobiography in Antiquity*, trans.
E. W. Dickes, 2 vols. (London, 1950 [1907]), I, 12–13.

pher build up a repertory of plots and select from them elements that are right for himself? A recent historian of autobiography has provided some useful terms for tracing this process:

> Cultures compress [their] essential values and convictions in human models. In our Western tradition there were such ideal models as the Homeric Hero, the Hero of the Germanic peoples, the ideal of the Roman *pater familias*, the Stoic Wise Man, Aristotle's *aner megalopsychos* (the great-minded man), the ideal of the truly committed Monk and Saint, the true Knight, the Good Burgher, the true Scholar. The most startling ideal of all, the model most forcefully reminding us of the force of models, was the ideal expressed in the *Imitatio Christi*. . . .
>
> When men, with their eyes fascinated by the attractive power of their models, write their autobiographic accounts, they will have scripts for the basic outlines of their lives. The story of their selves can be fitted into basic literary forms.[5]

5. Karl J. Weintraub, "Autobiography and Historical Consciousness," *Critical Inquiry*, 1 (1975): 837–38. Weintraub's main thesis is that modern autobiography celebrates individuality and eschews conventional norms of personality: "The most dominant personality conception of modern Western man does not fit the model type; it is even antithetical to the very thought of a model" (p. 838). The culture-bound cultural historian, valuing the historicist paradigm of the growth of self-consciousness, fails to recognize that modern individuality may be merely another normative ideal of the same artificiality and temporal limitation as the formally specific models of earlier periods. The argument is carried out at length in Weintraub's *The Value of the Individual: Self and Circumstance in Autobiography* (Chicago and London, 1978), which selects for discussion premodern works that ostensibly illustrate historical models but are actually denigrated for failing to conform to the norms of modern individualism, by which autobiography is here generically defined: none of the ancients "opened up their souls in the inwardness of genuine autobiography" (p. 1). Thus, an example of medieval autobiography is severely judged whereas Renaissance examples are cherished for anticipating modern self-consciousness: "Such dependence on role models

The generative process that is merely hinted at in the second paragraph is perhaps a more important phase than the enumeration and selection of models. Given the initial image of an ideal figure, a plot comes into play: the tale of how that figure came to be. It is a projection of the ideal into time, a narrativizing of personal qualities. In order to tell one's personal story, the standard scenes, images, and formulas of the pattern narrative will be appropriated. Since more than one of these ideals may be held by the same individual—for example, *Imitatio Christi* and the good burgher or true knight —the narrative will have to be dovetailed to obviate the more apparent discrepancies between them as well as the more painful indications of the man's falling short of the ideal.

Such ideal cultural figures have served to inspire men not only in their self-conceptions and modes of behavior but in their narrativizations. Yet cultural historians like Karl Weintraub are reluctant to trace the working out of these narrative images, perhaps because their marked conventionality seems unliterary to an older notion of original literary production. When Weintraub makes his own selection of works for close study, they rarely illustrate images and actions but instead exemplify philosophical ideas. Moreover, this historian is apt to take greater interest in the extraordinary than in the stereotyped works—an odd choice for one seeking to establish representative texts for various periods. The autobiographies most worth discussing hold, to be sure, something more than the stereotypes provided by the dominant culture. The outstanding minds in any age no doubt write autobiography to establish their distinctiveness along with their adherence to cultural norms. But the most curious aspect of the urge to establish a unique identity, evident in modern times as in every period, is its persistent need to draw on the images, actions, and patterns of other stories in

is not found in the autobiographies of authors who seek to understand themselves as an individuality. The more a human being possesses a sense of ineffable individuality, . . . the less will he find comfort in models" (p. 89).

order to tell one's own. The "basic literary forms," which Weintraub mentions only in passing, are the instruments with which autobiographers make themselves unique, by creative reenactment, revision, and reversal.

The case for a continuous history of the genre has yet to be demonstrated, then, but there are continuities to be traced in the language of autobiography. By this overused word I mean neither formal characteristics nor a specific terminology (although these may come into play), but a larger set of verbal operations that makes the writing of a life story possible. In order to set down either the image of a self or the working of a plot, most writers have recourse to the fund of traditional notions and conventional rubrics that make up the lingua franca of literary discourse. These verbal formulas, iconographic images, and intellectual commonplaces have been variously denominated, whether as motifs, topoi, or conventions, but I shall use the term *figure* as most supple in its applications.[6] It is my contention that a number of figures show a high incidence in autobiographical writing down through Western history and that a motivated reference to the past may be detected in their usage at certain key periods. Since a total demonstration would rival Misch's in length and learning, I shall trace only a few lines of continuity between the ancient world and the modern and devote sustained attention to a group of related figures in nineteenth- and twentieth-century English autobiographies. The test case offered by this procedure may serve as an indication

6. The classic study of the term as a symbolic mode is Erich Auerbach, "Figura," in *Scenes from the Drama of European Literature* (New York, 1959), which distinguishes the historical lines of its application to "plastic form," to rhetorical tropes, and to Christian types. The ambiguities of "figures of word and figures of substance," and of figural vs. (or =) historical or literal, are traced here and welcomed in my discussion below. For the literary-historical implications of the alternative terms, see E. R. Curtius, *European Literature and the Latin Middle Ages*, trans. W. R. Trask (New York and Evanston, Ill., 1963 [1948]), esp. pp. 70ff. For more tendentious distinctions between them, especially in defining "theme" and "motif," see Scholes and Kellogg, *Nature of Narrative*, pp. 27–28.

of the wider applicability of the figurative approach to the autobiographies of other periods.

A further refinement of the term *figure* is called for, given its pleasant ambiguity in referring to individuals as well as to verbal expressions. The word derives from the Latin for *form* or *shape* (including the shade of the departed). When we say that an autobiography presents the *figure* of a man, we dwell on a mental image of him along with the linguistic strategies by which that image has been conveyed. There is something *personal*, not only verbal, in an autobiographical figure, and to grasp the dual burden of word and self in the most favored figures, we must have recourse to the father of autobiographical figuration, Augustine. For it is his autobiography, which has been made paradigmatic in so many accounts of later self-writings, that best exhibits forms of language perhaps more important for self-portrayal than any others.

The *Confessions* became a model for Western autobiography because Augustine knew how to model his life on the lives of Adam, Moses, Jesus, and Paul (as a number of authorities have shown, whom I shall cite below). The similarities, along with the differences, among these figures are not, of course, utterly startling since some of them are emphatically modeled on the others, according to the system of narrative imitation in Judeo-Christian culture that is called *typology*. It is widely assumed that typology refers to a Christian mode of interpreting and conforming the Old Testament to the New, and indeed in that form it became the hallmark of medieval and later narratives not only in the religious but in the literary sphere. But as there is nothing entirely new under the sun, even the Christian mode of renewing old stories had its precedents in the Old Testament itself. A leading exegete describes *typology* in the prophets as follows:

> The past is only recalled as a foundation for future hope. As God had set man in Paradise so must Israel wait to be brought into a New Paradise. This is pre-

cisely the essence of typology, which is to show how past events are a figure of events to come. These events, recounted in themselves, are not particularly important. There is no striving to bring back again these past events. . . . the question is not of return (*Wiederkehr*) but of a new creation. . . .[7]

This formulation invites a number of distinctions from other modes of thought that might be confused with typology. For modern readers, perhaps the readiest association is with archetypalism, a theory of the perennial recurrence of certain characters or situations; the denial of a wish to return to an earlier state should help to distinguish the typological hope for a new and better time from the archetypal idea of cyclical replication. Further, the use of the term *figure* by Jean Danielou points to the guardedly symbolic character of typology. Its practitioners' effort is to focus on the literal level of texts and to seize upon historical facts, in opposition to allegorical interpretation, which they often disdain as merely speculative by comparison with the literal and its historical promise. Yet the method is required to take events and persons as *signs*, thereby referring them one to another, if not to an anterior realm of ideas. The type or original figure *means* its antitype or fulfilled promise, which is in turn a figure. Both are personal; both are symbolic.

The traditional use of typology as a way of reading the Old Testament tended to restrict its application to pre-Christian history, but, as might be anticipated, so pregnant a mode of explanation came ready to the hand of later religious interpreters of contemporary historical experience, both collective and individual. Although the formula "Prophecy implies future fulfillment; typology asserts that the consummation has occurred"[8] may seem to rule out lat-

7. Jean Danielou, *From Shadows to Reality: Studies in the Biblical Typology of the Fathers*, trans. Wulstan Hibberd (London, 1960 [1950]), p. 12.

8. Thomas M. Davis, "The Traditions of Puritan Typology," in Sacvan Bercovitch, ed., *Typology and Early American Literature*

ter-day applications, it was clear that Christ's role in history is not yet finished and that the hopes raised by his advent will not be fulfilled until his second coming. Not only is there ample scope for future-oriented applications of typology, but present events stand to be clarified under its aegis. As another commentator puts it, playing on several implications of the word *reform*: "The prophets not only foretold the coming of Christ, but they are also the great exemplars of all authentic reformers within the Church. . . . Furthermore, all through Christian history, typology, the *sacramentum futuri*, the mystery of expectation and anticipation of Christ and the Church in the Old Testament, acted as a stimulus for further reform in the spirit of the Gospel. . . ." Each of the two senses of reform that emerge here is promising for the spiritual autobiographer, as well as for the Christian historian. He may identify himself with the train of sacred figures in Scripture and their later avatars in church history so that his own experience of personal reform becomes inscribed in a line of reformers of heroic or even divine stature. But this procedure has its obvious hybristic risks. As a more humble alternative, the self-writer may set going echoes of his heroes so as to show his personal life as guided by their example, his turnings and waverings as having their precedents even in the stories of the saints, his wayward course made clear as working toward the same end of embodying Christ in the world.

Augustine was not a premier exponent of the typological method of interpretation among the Church Fathers, but he made a striking use of its symbolic properties when setting out his own life. In this as in other modes of figuration, the *Confessions* may be studied as a rhetoric of the possibilities of self-writing.

(n.p. [Amherst, Mass.], 1972), p. 43; the quotation following is from p. 42, where Davis cites Gerhard B. Ladner.

1

Augustinian Figures

—

THE VIEW that Augustine is the inventor of autobiography
is so squarely placed among our cultural presuppositions that
it would take a Nietzsche to dispel it entirely. The very title
of his work hints at a reason for this firm belief. It is from
savoring the *Confessions* of a saint that we derive our comfortable notion of autobiography as, from the first, guilt-
ridden self-exposure. From another starting point, a reader
of the panegyrical self-trumpetings of antiquity might surmise that true autobiography is a lost art in our time. Georg
Misch has explained this skewed sense of Augustine's priority
in some detail. An ignorance of ancient autobiography, combined with a teleological impulse to show development toward modern European forms, leads a number of historians
to a distorted view:

> Augustine's work gained such immense repute that
> many other autobiographers emulated it, and their
> achievement makes a whole class of spiritual auto-
> biography. . . . The secular autobiography that has
> competed with religious autobiography since the Ren-
> aissance is thus understood as a secularization of a
> Christian possession.
>   . . . In reality the channel for all the essential ten-
> dencies of autobiography was cut in the ancient

53

world, and Augustine's work is not a beginning but a completion.[1]

It is with the shadowy hinterland of Augustine's predecessors and contemporaries that Misch's early volumes are concerned, but no amount of background matter will suffice to overcome the fixed idea of his status *sui generis*. An acceptance of Augustine's governance by the laws of literary tradition and influence may be gained, however, by reconsidering one of the canonical passages of autobiography, his conversion in a garden at Milan.

The great Augustinian scholar Pierre Courcelle has isolated four distinct elements of the scene in ancient tradition: the sudden apparition (in this case a voice), as found in African "vision" literature; the admonition by a children's game, as in a host of classical didactic works; the *sortes*, or opening at random, practiced on a variety of privileged texts in both Jewish and pagan as well as Christian culture; and the formula "Take and read," widely used to encourage scholars in both Christian and pagan writings.[2] To discover a network of philosophical and literary convention is not, of course, to discount the historicity of the event narrated— no more than it calls in question the originality of any writer who makes creative use of tradition. But it is clear to all that Augustine was filled with the working materials of classical rhetoric from his profession as a teacher of the subject. His experience at the turning point of his life was *from the moment itself* an act of literary interpretation, for he chose to take the formulaic phrase, surrounded by a context of infantine innocence, as a divine command and followed out that interpretation by the further literary act of opening a book. It is not alone Augustine's writing of his life that may

1. Georg Misch, *A History of Autobiography in Antiquity*, trans. E. W. Dickes, 2 vols. (London, 1950 [1907]), I, 17.
2. Pierre Courcelle, *Les Confessions de Saint Augustin dans la tradition littéraire: Antécédents et postérité* (Paris, 1963), pp. 127–63; see also Courcelle's *Recherches sur les Confessions de Saint-Augustin* (Paris, 1950), pp. 188ff. ("Le 'Tolle, lege'; fiction littéraire et réalité").

be construed as a literary activity but his continuous readings in the enactment of it.

To this dense interplay of traditional motifs we may add a host of others found in this scene and elsewhere in the *Confessions*. The garden setting which forms a biblical context for the conversion scene, especially in its complementary relation to the earlier pear tree theft, which reenacts the fall; the pilgrimage and quest overtones, which so closely resemble the travels of other philosophical seekers in the late Roman world (both these motifs are discussed by Courcelle); the language of dramatic crisis, which Augustine self-consciously introduces in a metaphor drawn from medical terminology (Bk. vi, ch. 1) and which becomes a consistent figure for the central phase of the conversion process—these are well-known instances of literary convention become indistinguishable from personal experience.[3] We may hypothesize that Augustine stands at a watershed in Western autobiography because he begins the active employment of the full range of Christian life models and classical literary devices. He is not the inventor of autobiography but the master of autobiographical figuration, and his authority lies less in determining the choice of figures than in demonstrating the art of figurative self-writing.

As we review Augustine's self-writing as a place of mediation between classical and Christian literature, we come upon a more restricted type of autobiography on which he exerts direct influence. The *Confessions* are said to begin the con-

3. This discussion by no means exhausts the full range of topoi in this scene, nor any of the theological and linguistic issues raised by the text. But an additional suggestion may be ventured for the relevance of the final three books, a crux in Augustinian scholarship. In shifting from the interpretation of his own life to the interpretation of the first book of the Bible, Augustine may be seen not merely as substituting one genesis story for another but as foregrounding the problem of interpreting *any* text, including his own narrative. His conclusion, appropriately enough, emphasizes the polysemy of authoritative texts (*Confessions*, Bk. xii, ch. 31), among which his own work must be included.

fessional mode, to invent the formulas and mark the number of phases into which subsequent works in this subspecies will fall. When we inquire what it is that Augustine may be said to normalize—since his work as a whole is so strikingly different from every other text, even those written directly in imitation of it—there are only a few standard contents of the spiritual autobiography tradition that leap to mind. Crisis and conversion there must certainly be, given the exemplary role such texts are required to play, yet to isolate these does as little justice to Augustine's larger narrative view of his life as it does to the manifold power of his bequest.

It has been observed that the story of the *Confessions* is told as a series of movements—in geographical space as well as in intellectual and spiritual position—and that this dual journey has its analogues in self-writings from Socrates's *Apology* (in Plato's transcription) to Newman's *Apologia* and beyond. Additionally, it has been noted that the last book of the narrative section of the *Confessions* (Bk. IX) reaches a second climax with the meditation on last things by Augustine and his mother as they linger at Ostia on the final leg of their earthly journey back to North Africa. Scholars have placed this journey in relationship with his earlier moves to Carthage, Rome, and Milan and have recalled the epic echoes of Aeneas's similar movements, as reflected in numerous allusions to (and sneers at) the *Aeneid* throughout the *Confessions*.[4] Finally, there are innumerable biblical references and verbal plays on the language of expulsion, exodus, prodigal wanderings and other journeys of life, which thoroughly orchestrate Augustine's peregrinations.[5]

4. For an incisive comment on the relationship, see Eugene Vance, "Augustine's *Confessions* and the Grammar of Selfhood," *Genre*, 6 (1973): pp. 14–15; Vance cites fuller exposition in Harold Hagendahl, *Augustine and the Latin Classics* (Göteborg and Uppsala, 1967). The relation is summarized in John O'Meara, "Augustine the Artist and the *Aeneid*," in *Mélanges offerts à Christine Mohrmann* (Utrecht, 1963), pp. 252–61.

5. For a study of Augustine's method in biblical allusion, see Georg

Augustinian Figures

To say that Augustine invents the genre of autobiography or the special mode of spiritual autobiography is not, then, to say that he establishes a set of contents but that he demonstrates the power of figurative narration to order the chronicle of this-worldly events by a set of traditional figures, the chain of metaphors assuming the shape of myth. We are not surprised to find that it is primarily biblical figures that are called on to relate the individual life to a conception of human destiny at large. To discover that decisive events in this life story have ample parallels in the religions of the ancient world[6] is not to rob it of its Christian saliency but is to acknowledge the wider religious grounding of the journey in quest, the conversion process, and the pattern of exile and return in the Judeo-Christian tradition.[7] Within this cultural penumbra, the specific plots and metaphoric terms of much of Western autobiography can be shown to have derived from the figurative language of the Bible, as first appropriated for self-writing by Augustine.

He is the first to see his life as a synthetic enactment of the heroic lives honored by his religion, and insofar as he writes of his own repetition of historic acts, he writes typologically. As this reenactment is an individual instance of universal patterns—for the careers of certain of these heroes are

---

N. Knauer, *Psalmenzitate in Augustins Konfessionen* (Göttingen, 1955).

6. Edgar Wind, *Pagan Mysteries in the Renaissance* (New York, 1968 [1958]), p. 37 *et passim*, on *conversio*, *remeatio*, and their artistic figures; on the concept in antiquity, see Arthur D. Nock, *Conversion* (Oxford, 1933).

7. As Northrop Frye succinctly gives the biblical schema:
There are thus two concentric quest-myths in the Bible, a Genesis-apocalypse myth and an Exodus-millennium myth. In the former Adam is cast out of Eden, loses the river of life and the tree of life, and wanders in the labyrinth of human history until he is restored to his original state by the Messiah. In the latter Israel is cast out of his inheritance and wanders in the labyrinths of Egyptian and Babylonian captivity until he is restored to his original state in the Promised Land. (*Anatomy of Criticism: Four Essays* [New York, 1968 (1957)], p. 191)

readily associated with the "monomyth" of problematic origins, quest, ritual death and resurrection—his autobiography achieves universality, that is, significance for any reader irrespective of religious affiliation or even of cultural context. This is only to say that the life story is truly mythic, that is, a structured system that orders disparate materials into significant form. It is also to say that autobiographies in which such myths function may be works of art, transcending the particularity of historical narrative (individual, nonrepeatable events) to achieve the wider referentiality of aesthetic objects.

It is in behalf of grasping the myth of the *Confessions*—and the aesthetic activity that transforms the personal into the universal—that I offer the following rubrics. Derived from the language of that text, they no more exhaust the work than they prescribe a paradigm for autobiography; their analytic utility will be tested in the chapters that follow. But although later writers will focus on one or more of these phases, it is Augustine who most comprehensively assembles them.

A. *Natural Childhood.* Augustine's account of his own and of human childhood in Book I is so widely cited an exercise in Augustinianism that it is difficult to imagine the impression it would make on a hypothetically naïve reader. Written in the midst of his protracted argument with Pelagius—for whose heretical status Augustine is largely responsible—the account is at pains to deny infantile innocence, to expose the child's perverted will, and to excoriate the sins of boyhood. Its closing paean of praise for God's gifts of existence, life, and feeling—and of a "trace of your own most mysterious unity from which I took my being" (Bk. I, ch. 20, p. 63)[8]—has been taken as a referral to divine grace even

8. *The Confessions of St. Augustine*, trans. John J. Ryan (Garden City, N.Y., 1960)—valuable not only as a translation but for its references to biblical quotations and allusions; citations are from this text.

of the few innate capacities that contribute to salvation. But it is also part of a sustained effort to strike a balance, best represented in a single passage by the following:

> Therefore, O Lord my God, you have given to the infant life and a body, which, as we see, you have thus furnished with senses, equipped with limbs, beautified with a shapely form, and for its complete good and protection, have endowed with all the powers of a living being. For all such things you command me to praise you and to confess you, and to "sing to your name, O Most High." . . . But "if I was conceived in iniquity," and if my mother nourished me within her womb in sins, where, I beseech you, O Lord my God, where or when was your servant innocent?
>
> (Bk. 1, ch. 7, p. 50)

The two quotations from Psalms signal not only the terms of Augustine's argument but also the opposed views of human nature in the biblical tradition, which he adopts with perhaps greater enthusiasm for the negative pole than a perfectly balanced mind might desire.

No one who has read the glowing account in the *City of God* of the human condition before the Fall will be inclined to think the *Confessions'* version of childhood an Edenic state. The paradisal images of country or garden scenes that appear in a tributary stream of later autobiographies are absent from Augustine's self-writing. We need not speculate on his psychic motivations regarding his parents—his absent or wayward father, his authoritative mother—to explain his ascetic scorn of the child's life of the senses; doctrinal reasons would be sufficient. Yet we may take note of one element with evident psychological components: hatred of his early education. Augustine's account prepares the way for Dickens

---

The definitive Latin edition is that of Martin Skutella, reprinted with additional apparatus in the *Bibliothèque Augustinienne* (Bruges, 1962), vol. 13.

and other rebels against tutorial cruelty.[9] Even in this circumstantial account he couches mundane indignities in figures of an overarching myth: "Yet if I was slow at learning, I was beaten. . . . Thus were both toil and sorrow multiplied for the sons of Adam" (Bk. 1, ch. 9, p. 51). He does not, to be sure, oppose this system to another, more liberal, one, and his main charges lie against the hedonistic content of pagan studies and the worldly aims of rhetorical training. Yet there is room for idyllic scenes of learning that would warm the heart of later educators: "I learned [Latin] without any fear and torture, even in the midst of my nurses' caresses, the little stories of those smiling around me, and the happy games with playmates. I learned those Latin words without any load of punishment from others urging me on, for my own heart urged me on to bring forth its thoughts" (Bk. 1, ch. 14, p. 57).

9. Cf. Robert Pattison, *The Child Figure in English Literature* (Athens, Ga., 1978). Pattison's linkage of the child figure to the history of autobiography is founded on a sharp disjunction between the Augustinian and the Pelagian views of the child; it leads him to a striking formulation: "Autobiography and Original Sin enter the world together, and the author of them both was St. Augustine" (p. 18). Unfortunately, this neat correlation will no more stand up to historical tests than do other generic claims. The inadequacy of Pattison's initial disjunction as a norm derives from an oversimplification of the original controversy: the debate was not over the child's innocence vs. his sinfulness but over man's capacity to return to the high estate he had lost. The exacting Pelagian challenge to man to fulfill his responsibility for self-improvement stands behind the Romantic flowering of autobiographical *Bildung* works—so that reprobation, guilt, and confession cannot be the original sources for all later self-writing. The linking of autobiography to an Augustinian view of the child and of human depravity is shown here to be based on an old-fashioned (but still widespread) view of the genre as inclining to a definite moral position: "The autobiographical impulse from its appearance in Augustine to the present seems necessarily to contain the idea of confession and hence of guilt" (p. 109). This content-weighted generic view leads Pattison to misread many of the autobiographical texts among his collection of child figures: even Dickens's little boys lost are found to be monstrous by dint of their inherent sinfulness—a view that the critic ascribes to the novelist!

B. *Fall and Exile.* Augustine's second book is given to his sixteenth year, a somber time of sexuality in which an illegitimate son was conceived (although he leaves that fact to be deduced from later evidence). His sensual descent, below the condition of original sin, has consequences much like those of the latter: "My comeliness wasted away" (Bk. II, ch. 1, p. 65; citing Daniel 10:8). The author artfully arranges his narrative to make his personal fall a reenactment: "In a garden nearby to our vineyard there was a pear tree, loaded with fruit that was desirable neither in appearance nor in taste" (Bk. II, ch. 4, p. 70). The temptations of his fall are not Adam's, of course, whose fruit was appealing and who may have been drawn or pushed to take it, but his motivations are those which Augustine ascribes both to original and subsequent sin: perverted will—"We did this to do what pleased us for the reason that it was forbidden." The consequences are as fatal as those of the prototype: "I loved to go down to death." And the pleasures of self-destruction are shared and mutually fostered, though not between the sexes: "But my pleasure lay not in the pears: it lay in the evil deed itself, which a group of us joined in sin to do" (Bk. II, ch. 8, pp. 74–75).

Augustine's repetition of the Fall in individual experience, as well as his repetition of the language of Genesis and of later commentaries, is vigorous and explicit. More subtle is the book's closing medley of figures—the Fall, the expulsion into a desert, and the wayward prodigal son—artfully achieved in one sentence: "I fell away from you, my God, and I went astray, too far astray from you, the support of my youth, and I became to myself a land of want" (Bk. II, ch. 10, p. 76). The gloss is Luke 15, in which the prodigal's wanderings take him to such a land; Augustine metonymically transfers the dearth of the land to the condition of the youth and then applies that personal attribute to himself. We find here *in nuce* all the elements of the wilderness condition of the fallen but also the premise of their redemption upon return to God the father, "the support of my youth."

Both the bitterness of expulsion after the Fall and the hope of salvation consequent upon a return are conflated here.

c. *Wandering-Journey-Pilgrimage*. The three figures are not identical, and care must be given to sorting them out to follow the writer's variable emphases. Augustine's main emphasis seems to be on the journey in quest—although his name is often associated with the *peregrinatio* theme.[10] From the beginning of Book III, his movement is purposively intellectual and professional, though wrongly directed; it is even geographically consistent, moving northward from Thagaste to Carthage, then on to Rome, Milan, and Cassiciacum, at the foot of the Alps, before turning around to return home. The worldly movement and its otherworldly concomitant motion are from the first explicit: "I began to rise up, so that I might return to you" (Bk. III, ch. 4, p. 81; citing Luke 15 again: "I will arise and go to my father . . .").

Augustine is quite explicit on both the literal and symbolic levels of the journey figure: "Why I went from the one place and went to the other you knew, O God, but you did not reveal it to me or to my mother, who bitterly bewailed my journey and followed me down to the seashore. . . . you preserved me, all full of execrable filth, from waters of the sea and kept me safe for the waters of your grace" (Bk. V, ch. 8, p. 123). As he moves on in Roman cities and society, he generalizes his apparent and his real progress in the language of the life journey, capturing the sensations of physical movement through the world:

> O tortuous ways! Woe to my proud soul, which hoped that if it fell away from you, it would have something better! It turned and turned again upon its

10. See Robert J. O'Connell, *St. Augustine's Confessions: The Odyssey of Soul* (Cambridge, Mass., 1969), *passim*, for the neoplatonic roots of the *peregrinatio animae*, in which the soul falls away from the One, endures a period of wandering, suffers an illness and conversion, and returns to its source. See also pp. 188–90 on Augustine's self-figuration as Adam, in line with his conformation of his autobiography with his anthropology.

back and sides and belly, but all places were hard to it, for you alone are rest. Behold, you are present, and you deliver us from all wretched errors, and you put us on your way, and you console us, and you say to us, "Run forward! I will bear you up, and I will bring you to the end, and there also will I bear you up!" (Bk. vi, ch. 16, p. 155; citing Psalm 31 [32] and Isaiah 46)

At one point, however, Augustine changes the accent of his figure to stress the trial and testing of the wilderness, the purification of pilgrimage, the promise if not the fulfillment of return: "It is one thing to behold from a wooded mountain peak the land of peace, but to find no way to it, and to strive in vain towards it by unpassable ways, ambushed and beset by fugitives and deserters, under their leader, the lion and the dragon. It is a different thing to keep to the way that leads to that land, guarded by the protection of the heavenly commander . . ." (Bk. vii, ch. 21, p. 180; citing Deuteronomy 32 and Psalm 90 [91]). A Pisgah sight of the promised land is all Augustine has during his outbound journey; these are also moments of implicit identification with Moses as spiritual pathfinder. The journey at such points is a combat against allegorical beasts and martial adversaries; much of the wilderness figuration of the spiritual autobiography tradition begins here.

D. *The Crisis.* Augustine calls his liminal stage by this name, fully aware of it as a figure—although not a biblical one. He describes his mother's watching over him in "the wavering, doubtful state in which I then was. She felt sure that through this state I was to pass from sickness to health, with a more acute danger intervening, through that paroxysm, as it were, which doctors call the crisis" (Bk. vi, ch. 1, p. 134). The adoption of medical imagery is only an apparent departure from the language of eschatology, however, for the dominant metaphor is of salvation, transferred from a bodily to a spiritual condition (*salus*—"health" or "salvation"). Augustine goes on to say that his state is a sickness only a step away from "acute . . . paroxysm," a medical analogy for which it is more difficult to locate a spiritual tenor. The sense of reaching an overflow point brings to mind Aristotle's similar appropriation of medical terms in defining the effect of tragedy. Although he does not say so, Augustine may have been thinking of his life as a drama, as well as an illness, and recognizes that it must reach a purgative climax before its resolution.

The content of the crisis is, of course, not only spiritual but intellectual; Augustine gives us a detailed commentary on the stages of his dispute with pagan thought and an unexampled insight into the divided will of the imminent convert. He also gives us enough information about his personal affairs for us to recognize that his troubles were also passional and moral—what, in another context, we would have no trouble in recognizing as a tragic love affair. Having lived for fifteen years with an African woman, the mother of his son Adeodatus, he is faced with his mother's very worldly concern that he be properly married and to a more respectable wife. He is led to dismiss the woman and contract an engagement, and though he thinks his worst sin is taking on another mistress to tide him over, Rebecca West may well have noted the deeper guilt: his crude terminating of the deeper liaison.[11] Some anxiety that this may indeed be the case comes through in his account of the affair:

> In the meantime my sins were multiplied. The woman with whom I was wont to share my bed was torn from my side as an impediment to my marriage. My heart still clung to her: it was pierced and wounded within me, and the wound drew blood from it. She returned to Africa, vowing that she would never know another man. . . . I procured another woman, but not, of course, as a wife. By her my soul's disease

11. Rebecca West, *St. Augustine* (1933), in *Rebecca West: A Celebration* (Harmondsworth, 1978 [1977]), pp. 189–90; for West's larger thesis on the origins of Western neurosis in Augustine's theological sublimation of his Oedipal relation to a domineering mother, see pp. 168ff.

would be fostered and brought safe, as it were, either unchanged or in a more intense form, under the convoy of continued use into the kingdom of marriage. Not yet healed within me was that wound which had been made by the cutting away of my former companion. After intense fever and pain, it festered, and it still caused me pain, although in a more chilling and desperate way.

(Bk. vi, ch. 15, pp. 153–54)

The underlying figure is the same medical terminology that had colored the account of spiritual crisis, and the two kinds of illness metaphor may be taken as referring to twin aspects of the man's condition—religious and interpersonal, intellectual and emotional. The double work of the metaphor is furthered by the considerable physical specificity given to its picture of human love. Heart, pierced, wound, blood, cutting away, fever, pain, festering, and chilling: in this semantic chain we have most of the materials for an ideology like courtly love, vivid in its bodily immediacy yet open to translation as a spiritual system. Augustine's crisis is, then, the paradigm of such metaphoric usages in spiritual autobiography, but only in the *Confessions* does it become a total figure for the man—with the result that the saint's iconographic symbol has come down to us a heart pierced by an arrow.

E. *Epiphany and Conversion.* I intend the term *epiphany* in both its Christian and its modern critical senses, for in such works as Augustine's one senses a personal appropriation of the biblical epiphanies in which Christ appears, transfigured. The showing forth of the divine—the equivalent not merely of the *anagnorisis* of tragedy but of the *epopteia* of ritual—is as necessary to an autobiographical climax as the conversion or *peripeteia*. (Neither one is strictly necessary; they come to be expected in the wake of Augustine.)

The climactic "Tolle, lege" episode in Book VIII is focused on a manifestation of the divine, if not to the eye then to the ear. All conspires to establish the garden scene as the "point of epiphany" (in Frye's term) at which the divine enters into or touches the human and terrestrial. The setting also, of course, annuls the prior garden of the Fall and the orchard of Augustine's personal repetition. The voice is vouchsafed in answer to a direct appeal: " 'And you, O Lord, how long? How long, O Lord, will you be angry forever? Remember not our past iniquities. . . . Why not now? Why not in this very hour an end to my uncleanness?' " (Bk. viii, ch. 12, p. 202; citing Psalms 6 and 78 [79]). The response is immediate; out of the freeplay of the world's sounds, Augustine construes semantic significance: "And lo, I heard from a nearby house, a voice like that of a boy or a girl, I know not which. . . ." The doubt appears to be of the singer's sex, but the simile suggests that it is only apparently a child's voice, more certainly a heavenly call. A second intervention of the supernatural follows: the *sortes biblicae*. Again, Augustine is aware of the dangers of subjective arrangement of the random and unmotivated; he treats the *sortes Virgilianae* with great skepticism on another occasion (Bk. iv, ch. 3, p. 96). But here the entire text is divine and guidance to the appropriate communication is made by personalizing the communicator: "Not in rioting and drunkenness, . . ." announces Paul (Romans 13)—another weak vessel converted and eventually beatified. Now Augustine can identify himself with another recalcitrant receiver of the Word even while receiving it from God. Finally, he sums up by using an appropriate figure for the narrative event: "For you had converted me to yourself . . ." (Bk. viii, ch. 12, p. 203)—playing on the word's root meaning of turning around to indicate the shift from the worldly to the divine.

F. *Renewal and Return.* Following the garden epiphany, Augustine and his friends withdraw to a country villa at Cassiciacum—"far from the madding world we found . . . delights in your paradise that are eternally fresh . . . in that mountain flowing with milk, your mountain, that richest mountain" (Bk. ix, ch. 3, p. 208; citing Psalm 67 [68]). The estate was probably in the approaches to the Alps, to be sure, yet this is no earthly mountain but a forest of eschatological figures. Augustine does not use the language of archetypal rebirth but the more specifically Judeo-Christian terms of the renovation following apocalypse: "How you levelled me down by making low the mountains and the hills of my thoughts, how you made straight my crooked paths and smoothed the rough . . ." (Bk. IX, ch. 4, p. 209; citing Isaiah 40 and Luke 3, which directly quotes the "voice in the wilderness"). Although the mountain withdrawal seems a move upward, out of the mundane world, the tropes of leveling suggest that the convert's ascendance is to be in spiritual rather than stratospheric space.

The party of acolytes (at least Augustine and Monica, but probably other African friends) turns about and tends toward their earthly starting point, but halfway home they pause at Ostia, and the true space of their movement is revealed: "We proceeded step by step through all bodily things up to that heaven whence shine the sun and the moon and the stars down upon the earth. We ascended higher yet by means of inward thought and discourse and admiration of your works, and we came up to our own minds. We transcended them, so that we attained to the region of abundance that never fails, in which you feed Israel forever upon the food of truth . . ." (Bk. IX, ch. 10, p. 221; citing Ezekiel 34 and Psalm 77 [78]). This *askesis* draws on biblical figures, to be sure, but its neoplatonic parallels have been much commented; thus, the language of pagan conversion (*epistrophe*) and reunion with the divine (*remeatio*) is drawn into the narrative and thence into autobiographical tradition.

In the course of giving form and meaning to the final stages of life to be recounted in his autobiography, Augustine gives specifically Christian turns to the figures and myths of classical literature, like rebirth and return. He also creates figured formulations of elements of a life story to which he might be thought indifferent, like the role of parents in his formation. Much has been made of how little Augustine makes of his father and how much he makes of his mother, but even the most psychologistic of interpreters would be aware that he regards them in metaphoric terms that are far from those of our Freudian times.

In particular, these terms are Christian figures. At the outset, Monica is "the mother of my flesh," as distinct from the Church, which is named "the mother of us all" (Bk. I, ch. 11, p. 53).[12] At the moment of Augustine's *askesis*, however, at what may be termed his rebirth into a supernatural sphere, it is Monica who enacts even more vividly the same transformation. It is as though the son's rebirth enabled the immaculate reconception of the one who bore him: " 'Son, for my own part, I now find no delight in anything in this life. What I can still do here, and why I am here, I do not know, now that all my hopes in this world have been accomplished. . . . I see you his servant, with even earthly happiness held in contempt. What am I doing here?' " (Bk. IX, ch. 10, pp. 222–23). It is not only the *contemptus mundi* theme that Augustine wishes to emphasize here but also the providentialism of his mother's role. Having fulfilled it, she is ready to depart, but in the process she is assimilated to the Church to which she had been antithetical. No longer the fleshly mother, "she took care as though she had been mother to us all, and she served us as though she had been a daughter to all of us" (Bk. IX, ch. 9, pp. 220–21).

There are perhaps not so many literal returns to the earthly place of origin in most lives, but there is always the possibility of bringing the origin into literary play in a self-writing that concludes with renewal. Augustine does not take up this option even though he returned to Africa; the narrative of the *Confessions* ceases at this point. The ultimate return is to the divine source after death and in perpetuity, but Augustine signifies this step only by testaments of faith, not visionary enactments. Yet traces can be found of figurative dealings

12. See, on this image as on many another, Peter Brown, *Augustine of Hippo: A Biography* (Berkeley and Los Angeles, 1967), p. 212.

with the divine origin itself, bringing into the text an evocation of the beginning.

After a meditation on memory—a *locus classicus* for the subject—the final three books are devoted to a philosophical and allegorical exegesis of the first book of the Bible. The fitness of this apparent appendage to an autobiography has been much debated, and a consensus has formed around the ideas that Augustine continues his confession as a confession of his beliefs and continues his record of vocation by exemplifying his priestly function as expositor of the faith. To these motivations another may be adduced. The text's turn to Genesis is the figurative equivalent of the return to origins acted out in the work at large. The identification of the individual with the race, which has been everywhere at work in the *Confessions*, enables the inquiry into personal origins to be sublimated as an inquiry into the earth's and mankind's creation. Thus, in its mode of writing as well as in the subject matter described, the *Confessions* institutes a characteristic change at the end of many autobiographies. This change has been well described by M. H. Abrams—in recounting the return to origins in *The Prelude* and other nineteenth-century works—as a version of the Hegelian *Aufhebung*, in which the same comes 'round anew, the circle is closed, the life completed, but all at a higher level of value or being.[13] In the *Confessions*, not only does the hero of the tale achieve this uplifting or sublimation, but the rhetorical register of the text is raised from the personal to the generic, from the historical to the philosophic, from the experiential to the metaphysical.

13. M. H. Abrams, *Natural Supernaturalism: Tradition and Revolution in Romantic Literature* (New York, 1971), *passim*.

2

Spiritual
Figures

——

WITHOUT ATTEMPTING to follow such scholars as Misch and
Courcelle through the vast libraries that surround Augustine—stretching back to the ancients and beyond the Middle
Ages into modern times—one may cite a few cardinal works
that illustrate the continuity of certain autobiographical figures. A relatively simple case of direct imitation of the *Confessions* is Gilbert of Nogent's story of his life (*De vita sua*:
ca. 1115). As Courcelle sums up his borrowings, it becomes
apparent that Gilbert not only tailors his own experience to
conform to the saint's and indulges in formal imitation—for
example, of the second-person grammatical form and the
lyrical invocations that begin each book—but also that he
adopts a number of the figures singled out above. The salvific,
church-related mother figure, the biblical *sortes*, the tissue
of scriptural citations, all conspire to make the work a reenactment not only of a life but of a text.[1] While this may
relegate Gilbert's autobiography to the arid places of medieval conventionalism or literary pastiche, it may also be seen

1. I follow Pierre Courcelle's summary of these features, *Les Confessions de Saint Augustin dans la tradition littéraire: Antécédents et
postérité* (Paris, 1963), pp. 272–76. For the conventionalism of the
medieval language of self-reference (which suggests a negative answer
to the problem raised in the title), see Paul Zumthor, "Autobiography
in the Middle Ages?" *Genre*, 6 (1973): 29–48.

as an extreme and highly visible instance of a process that attends all autobiographical writing in some degree and with varying richness of illumination.

A more engaging example of the continuity of figures may be selected from a period in which cultural development, personal style, and literary procedure show the marks of growing individualism. In the later Middle Ages, as singularity and invention become more highly prized and exhibit themselves in a number of autobiographies, the selective use of tradition emerges most clearly in the figures of which autobiographers avail themselves. In *The Book of Margery Kempe* (ca. 1438), the vehement individuality of a high-strung (if not hysteric) visionary is mediated by conventional language (perhaps supplied by her clerical scribe) so as to express a unique personality in the formulas of typical experience.[2]

At a crucial juncture in the history of selfhood—if it can be said to have a history—Petrarch ascended Mount Ventoux (1336), reaching a high point of individual assertion. An equal high in self-awareness is attained when the proto-Renaissance man turns from the landscape of southern France to look into the spiritual dimension of his enterprise. He does so by means of a *sortes*, employing neither Virgil nor the Bible but a book that "I always have about me," the *Confessions*.[3] He reads: "And men go about to wonder at the heights of the mountains . . . but themselves they consider not." This is, of course, an unwarranted rebuke for one of the most introspective men of all time, but Petrarch takes it as encouragement to continue in his traditional tendency to interpret the journey, the mountain, the ascent, etc., in an

2. E.g.: "This creature was inspired with the Holy Ghost [who] bade her that she should . . . make a book of her feelings and revelations." For Kempe's transcribers, see R. W. Chambers's introduction to *The Book of Margery Kempe* in W. Butler-Bowdon's edition (London and Toronto, 1954 [1936]); the above quote is from p. 3.

3. *Petrarch, The First Modern Scholar: A Selection from His Correspondence*, ed. J. H. Robinson (New York and London, 1914), pp. 316–17.

Augustinian fashion. Although Petrarch's account is given in a letter—composed to the moment at an inn after the descent—and thus makes no attempt at autobiographical dimensions, in his *Secretum*, constructed as a dialogue between "Augustine" and "Francesco," a broader self-evaluation is conducted by mingling the monitory image of Augustine with motifs drawn from ancient dialogues and from monastic initiation procedures.

We may conclude that the *Confessions* not only provides incidents and formulas to which even a ground-breaking autobiographer has recourse in telling the story of his career but that Augustine himself becomes a figure—a symbolic exponent of the enterprise of autobiographical writing itself. In this complex figure are marshaled not only the example of the sinner become a saint (for which Petrarch had perhaps a too-ready inclination) but also a discipline of self-scrutiny, which both encourages close interpretation and draws back from self-indulgent introspection. In mingling these aspects of Augustine, Petrarch anticipates the exemplary Renaissance autobiographies that engage Christian paradigms for highly individual portraiture.[4] We may venture, then, the generalization that Augustine becomes the enduring figure of autobiography, and his/its presence will be discovered in a number of nineteenth- and twentieth-century works—some as inevitable as Newman's apology, others as unexpected as Gosse's family romance.

Autobiography in the Renaissance continues to be highly figurative, as in the Middle Ages; it adapts, of course, traditional resources for new situations[5] and widens the oppor-

4. See Jonathan Goldberg, "Cellini's *Vita* and the Conventions of Early Autobiography," *Modern Language Notes*, 89 (1974): 71–83.

5. See Leslie P. Fairfield, *John Bale: Mythmaker for the English Reformation* (West Lafayette, Ind., 1976), pp. 136ff., for the hagiographic conventions employed to characterize a Protestant bishop's persecution by the Church—a nice instance of stealing the opposition's thunder. Bale's brief narrative (1553) is sometimes taken as the first English autobiography (as distinguished from Kempe's edited testimony).

tunities for choosing figures appropriate to an individual view of oneself. It is in its range of options rather than in degree of conventionalism that Renaissance autobiography "makes it new." The strong conventionality of one of the favored forms of autobiographical writing in the period, the sonnet sequence, is a case in point.[6] In prose, the emergence on the Continent of several highly individualized self-studies by no means argues against the tendency of the age toward employing traditional figures in behalf of claims for representative, though colorfully personalized, standing. In the most articulate of these works, the classically furnished Montaigne continually presents himself as a nonesuch but enlists the models of Socrates, Cato, and Cicero in his self-imaging. As an authority on the art of the age sums up the dual mode of individual distinctiveness and traditional expressions of typicality:

> Renaissance autobiography was not distinguished by any new sincerity, intimacy or vivacity. . . . Rather than personal confession, humanists preferred to use the *impresa*, an emblem, either modest or proud, which gave a sort of public definition of its bearer. The Renaissance clearly excelled in such symbolic projections: hence the ultimate expression of personality reflected in their tombs.[7]

The motifs making up these composite constructions, whether in plastic or verbal art, were drawn from codes as diversified as the culture itself: by Girolamo Cardano, from the formulas of astrology and medicine; by Sir Kenelm Digby, from the conventions of arcadian romance; by Herbert

6. See Rudolf Gottfried, "Autobiography and Art: An Elizabethan Borderland," in *Literary Criticism and Historical Understanding*, ed. Phillip Damon (New York, 1967), pp. 109–34.

7. André Chastel, *The Age of Humanism: Europe 1480–1530*, trans. K. M. Delavenay and E. M. Gwyer (New York, London, and Toronto, 1963), p. 205. Stephen Greenblatt's *Renaissance Self-Fashioning: From More to Shakespeare* (Chicago and London, 1981) appeared, alas, too late to help in these formulations.

of Cherbury, from "the chivalric ideals of the twelfth century."[8] There was in these choices little reference to the figures of autobiography that had grown in the ancient and medieval worlds, but even among secular authors Augustine was occasionally invoked. Yet the general impression given by this busy time of recycling and origination is of a casting about among the received materials for a configuration of images and linguistic procedures that could command general assent for a man's self-portraiture.

At the juncture of the seventeenth century, a number of forces moving in European civilization at large came to play a shaping role in the writing of autobiography. It is not my intention to rehearse the influence of the Reformation, the civil wars, and a host of political and social factors in effecting this change; I shall, hopefully without distortion, limit myself to the subject of Augustinian language as it exerted itself in autobiography. One caveat seems called for with respect to certain cultural presuppositions about Puritanism that color a number of accounts of autobiography. There exists a diffused assumption that Puritanism and related Protestant movements encouraged ethical and eschatological self-examination to a degree that revived (or brought into existence) an impulse toward self-consciousness obscured in the long night of conventionalism—hidden, it would seem, since Augustine himself. This habit of inward searching brought into being not only the large number of subliterary confessional works of the seventeenth and eighteenth centuries, among them the first examples of English autobiography, but furthered the tendencies toward subjectivity and particularity of description that mark the modern consciousness and the subsequent development of autobiography.

There is no refuting this congeries of propositions in detail, but a number of points ask to be recalled. Whatever gain

8. Paul Delany, *British Autobiography in the Seventeenth Century* (London, 1969), p. 21; see pp. 45, 58, 67 for examples of Augustinian imitation and p. 31 for his sweeping rejection of such influence (quoted below).

in inwardness was made in the development of spiritual autobiography, it was made in a set of received rhetorical, narrative, and figurative terms, which in turn became conventionalized in their new formulations. It is a question neither
of new wine in old bottles nor old wine in new but of corporate industriousness in fermenting and decanting the vin-
tage. Further, these spiritual figures were not the only comprehensive and powerful semantic systems for conveying
inwardness, as witness the contemporary library of non-
Puritan writings in which accounts of the self, its history
and destiny, are foregrounded. We may recall not only the
elaborate formal patterns of meditational and devotional
poetry and prose, which recent scholarship has closely described, but also the broad division introduced by Joan
Webber between the "conservative Anglican" and "radical
Puritan" styles of self-expression.[9]

The "Anglican" writers are among the jewels of the age
and Donne's *Devotions*, Herbert's *Temple*, Browne's *Re-
ligio Medici*, and even Burton's *Anatomy of Melancholy*
have always been felt to give access to their authors' minds
and lives. We have, nevertheless, some difficulty in recognizing them as autobiographical writings since their "metaphysics" are so special to the age that they must be
expounded by our learned exegetes. The spiritual autobiography tradition is, on the contrary, very much with us, having
become a staple not only of later English literature but of
American culture since its founding by the Puritans.[10] We
have no doubts about the writings of Bunyan, Fox, and their
lesser comrades as "truly autobiographical" since they anticipate some of our own habits of mind, but our very familiari-

9. Joan Webber, *The Eloquent "I": Style and Self in Seventeenth-
Century Prose* (Madison, Wis., 1968), pp. 3ff. See also Margaret Bot-
trall, *Every Man a Phoenix: Studies in Seventeenth-Century Autobiography* (London, 1958).

10. Daniel B. Shea, Jr., *Spiritual Autobiography in Early America*
(Princeton, 1968). See also Mason I. Lowance, Jr., *The Language of
Canaan: Metaphor and Symbol in New England from the Puritans to
the Transcendentalists* (Cambridge, Mass., 1980).

ty with their forms of expression hinders our seeing them as conventional in their turn—in figurative language as well as in standardized narrative.

This would seem a familiar syndrome of cultural myopia, given our inability to *think the code* because we employ it in ongoing life. Yet spiritual autobiography and its later avatars are all the more to be appreciated as literary treatments of life when they are recognized as networks of figurative characterization, standard incidents, and—a recrudescence in self-writing—biblical typology. For this purpose, too, a body of historical criticism has been growing that facilitates the reading of seventeenth-century spiritual autobiography and subsequent appropriations of its content and procedures. The alternatives are not, then, to be drawn up as between secular artifice and spiritual inwardness but between two broad tendencies of self-figuration—the one experimental and far-reaching in its search for adequate tropes of self-formulation, the other more consistent in approaching certain canonical texts for organizing schemas and metaphorical expressions. That the second mode became the more hackneyed model for imitation may have been inevitable, but it also widened the lexicon of figurative terms for later writers trying to set down their moral identity and its struggles.

The cultural basis for the emergence of a popular set of autobiographical conventions was the struggle for and limited success in establishing an experientially tested religion. When so much of this conflict was fought over right language, it is no wonder that the Reformation itself was not only a conceptual but a verbal shift. Perry Miller sums up Augustine's contribution to the Puritan frame of mind:

> The same subjective insight, the same turning of consciousness back upon itself, the same obsession with individuality, the same test of conclusions not so much by evidence or utility as by the soul's immediate approbation or revulsion—these qualities which appear in Augustine almost for the first time in Western thought and give him his amazing "modernity,"

reappear in force among the early Puritans. . . . New England diarists had not the literary genius of the author of the *Confessions* and the *Soliloquies*, nor could the divines put autobiographies into their sermons; still at their more pedestrian pace they followed his example in relying for the demonstration of original sin and innate depravity upon an analysis of the soul.[11]

This highly interiorized vision of religious experience was at the same time a recasting of the individual believer's life into a dramatic narrative. The drama, with its burden of ritual conflict, irony, and high expectation, allowed each participant to see his private life as significant in the theologically interdefined and value-weighted language of his religion. To supply its personal models, this bibliophile community was provided with authoritative heroes and narrative situations that could without excessive stretching be applied to the legal, military, and other conflicts in which the sectarians engaged, as well as to the grand enterprise of founding a new community along divinely sanctioned lines.

The most obvious model was, of course, the central figure in the religious drama, but the evident impediments in making Him the pattern of a finite life were mediated by adducing other heroes, whose careers were structured to follow much the same pattern as the deity's. Reading backward and forward in the sacred texts, a number of elevated, persecuted, questing, and redemptive figures were to be found. In at least one case, David, the form of his utterance had much in common with the example of his life so that imitators paid heed not only to the life but to its rhythms of expression: "The alternate despair and exaltation of the Psalmist, and the intensity of his conversations with the Lord, create a dramatic confrontation between man and God which spiritual autobiographers from Augustine onward strove to emu-

11. Perry Miller, *The New England Mind: The Seventeenth Century* (Cambridge, Mass., 1954 [1939]), pp. 22–23; the quotations below are from p. 5. Miller's opening chapter is also the *locus classicus* on the tenets of essential Puritanism and its key linguistic items.

late." Reading forward from the central event, Jesus's immediate followers were to be found undertaking the pattern of
His experience and narrating passages from their lives in an
exemplary way. Paul's influence on Protestant self-writing
flowed as much from the account in the *Acts* and elsewhere
of his conversion as from the cast he gave to Christian doctrine.

Augustine's version of the Christian patterning of a life
was continually available for writing personal experience,
but its continuing influence has been debated, for example,
by Paul Delany: "The line of descent from Paul to Augustine
is clear enough; but it did not continue uninterrupted down
to the British spiritual autobiographers of [the seventeenth
century]. Instead, they returned to the fountainhead of the
Pauline epistles and, with a few exceptions, were remarkably
little influenced by the *Confessions*." Yet the direct imitation
of his autobiography may have been only a small portion of
Augustine's endowment for Puritanism generally and for
spiritual autobiography in particular. As Perry Miller sums
up the issue: "There survive hundreds of Puritan diaries and
thousands of Puritan sermons, but we can read the inward
meaning of them all in the *Confessions*." It was Augustine
who made David's and Paul's experience available for autobiographical writing. Along with the pervasive appearance
of Augustine's self-reflexive habits of mind go the questioning mode of introspection, a rhetoric of subjective testimony,
and—as we shall see—certain figures of typological characterization. Neither in doctrinal nor in methodological inheritance does the Augustinian current flow as strongly as in the
figures of his self-writing—the exile, the journey, the epiphanic moment, etc.—which become shaping powers in a
number of seventeenth-century autobiographies.

Recent studies of spiritual autobiography and its fictional
successors have taken up their linguistic endowment from
other forms of Puritan writing. Perhaps the best known of
these studies, by George Starr, derives certain organizing
schemas used by these autobiographers from the ongoing

needs of evaluating experience in daily devotions: "Since every man is responsible for the well-being of his own soul, he must mark with care each event or stage in its development."[12] Among the schemas employed by the autobiographers that Starr assesses are those of the spiritual physician ("Self-searching is an heart-anatomy"); of mercantile accounting ("he is the best Christian that every day in the Evening taketh an account of his spiritual losses and gains"); and of voyage logs recording signposts and milestones through "the land of our peregrination, and [aspiration] after a better country." Starr's salient point, though he does not make it an extended issue, is that these Christian figures were modulated through contemporary experience, particularly the Puritans' engagement in bourgeois activities: "Just as seafaring tended to supplant overland pilgrimages in the imagery of peregrination, trade gradually overshadowed husbandry in the imagery of labor."

In addition to the metaphoric schemes derived from worldly experience—and, in the cases of commerce and maritime voyaging, closely linked to the rise of capitalism with which Protestantism has been associated—there was also an autobiographical appropriation of the sermons and chapbooks in which "Scripture Similitudes" were employed to give significance to life. There were a number of handbooks for the interpreting and usage of such figures, including Keach and Delaune's *Tropologia: A Key to Open Scripture-Metaphors* (1682) which declared in its title the age's self-consciousness of figurative language and its practical uses.

But the main supply of figurative terms was directly from the Bible, especially where these were cognate with experience in social, as in personal life. Owen Watkins has shown that certain figures popular among the spiritual autobiographers were based on more collective applications of biblical interpretation in the allegorical or moral mode: "To all Puri-

12. George A. Starr, *Defoe and Spiritual Autobiography* (Princeton, 1965), p. 5; the quotations following are from pp. 6n., 11, 25.

tans the calling of the Israelites out of Egypt was a prefiguring of the release of man from bondage to sin."[13] These interpretations were often handled in the local and emphatic
way that Starr describes as "allusive shorthand," leading to
no consistent pattern of identification between the autobiographer and a biblical personage: "Because the Bible showed
all types of men meeting God, anyone could find some parallel to his own experience in what had happened to patriarchs,
kings, prophets, or humbler people. Arise Evans [a typical
Puritan] was anointed like David, called like Abraham, and
eventually driven to justify himself like Paul." Beyond this
habit of casual identification, however, there were traditional
currents at work making for greater formal consistency and
disciplined interpretation in the writing of a life.

One such current was the example of Augustine, to whom
Watkins assigns a signal role in the shaping of seventeenth-
century autobiography: "It is perhaps not surprising to find
Augustine's experiences referred to more often than those
of any other man except the apostle Paul." He is able to locate this influence in the language and structure of accounts
of childhood which base themselves on the narrative of the
Confessions but find support in Augustine's other writings
on, e.g., the growing effects of original sin. Such self-writings
as Robert Blair's *Autobiography* and Richard Norwood's
Confessions are shown to be creatively Augustinian in their
language and form.

To distinguish among the varied sources and expressions
of figurative language in spiritual autobiography, we may
benefit from another study, which, like Starr's, follows the
tradition to its later transformations in such forms as Defoe's
"pseudoautobiographical" novels. J. Paul Hunter makes us
aware of the larger tendency of that language to constitute
a "Puritan myth," assimilating both biblical narratives and
contemporary experience:

13. Owen C. Watkins, *The Puritan Experience: Studies in Spiritual
Autobiography* (New York, 1972), p. 210; the quotations following
are from pp. 211, 59, 56.

They leaned most heavily, however, upon three metaphors. The metaphor of spiritual warfare suggested the conflict between good and evil that continually raged, both in the hearts of men and in the events in which men participated. The metaphor of the journey expressed the transitory nature of man's position in this world and suggested the progress necessary to deliver him to his heavenly goal. The metaphor of the wilderness combined the implications of the first two, suggesting the conflicts and temptations of the human soul journeying toward its promised land, as well as the barren condition of an unregenerated soul fallen from its original garden state.[14]

14. J. Paul Hunter, *The Reluctant Pilgrim: Defoe's Emblematic Method* (Baltimore, 1966), p. 103; see also pp. 113-14 for the transition from figurative treatment of personal experience to the codification of "pilgrim allegory." An alternative sequence in seventeenth-century self-writings has been perceived by L. D. Lerner, "Puritanism and the Spiritual Autobiography," *Hibbert Journal*, 55 (1957): 373-86: "There is a fixed pattern of development which can be related to a theological scheme. This pattern has five main stages: serious childhood, sinful youth, legal righteousness preceded by a struggle, and final illumination" (p. 374). The phrasing, as well as the brevity of the analysis, creates problems in evaluating this schema; "preceded by" may be a slip for *preceding* since Lerner goes on to give "legal righteousness" as the third stage and "spiritual struggles" as the fourth (p. 375). Moreover, the fifth stage tends to evaporate in the narratives, as Lerner explains:

> Indeed, this last stage, like the second, involves a contradiction: there is no mistaking the ecstasy of the illumination that follows spiritual crisis, and it is clearly a sign of real regeneration; but there is no stage in Christian morals of winning through, no final period in which one is no longer subject to temptation. Attempts to show this last stage are always liable to betray self-righteousness (carnal security), and the wisest autobiographer is perhaps he who stops immediately after his illumination, or who (like Bunyan) makes no claim that his struggles have ended. (p. 376)

A schema subject to these limiting conditions—and one of whose canonical texts best illustrates a standard departure from the pattern—is perhaps better suited to the conventionally formal works of ordinary sectarians than to the more complexly inspired and distinctive texts of the greater Puritan and Quaker writers.

Hunter traces these commanding metaphors through their fine elaboration in terms of armor and tactics, sea conditions and compass readings, exodus events and spiritual drought. Although he does not follow these figures in the autobiographies of the period, Hunter emphasizes their use in the biographies of exemplary men of the time.

Hunter goes on to trace the development of such metaphors to the later stage of allegorization, when specific biographical applications are replaced by "epitomical" situations or personified abstractions, and finally to the stage of fictionalization, when the narrative of a hero's career is further freed from historical or theological constraints. Two stages in this development, which Hunter scrutinizes in Defoe, are highly charged for autobiography as it comes to mingle in mode and language with the emergent novel form. Metaphors may be employed in fiction, as in autobiography, either for heightened local implication or as a controlling narrative pattern; the two activities may be exemplified by the casual allusiveness of *Moll Flanders* and the systematic applications of *Robinson Crusoe*. Two outstanding works of spiritual autobiography show the working of each mode as distinctively as do the somewhat later developments in fiction.

In a famous passage of *Grace Abounding to the Chief of Sinners*, John Bunyan describes his decision to continue to bear witness to his faith despite the repression of the Restoration regime, which has threatened him with further imprisonment. He thinks, of course, of the consequences for his wife and children, and especially for the blind daughter "who lay nearer my heart than all I had besides":

> Poor Child! thought I, what sorrow art thou like to have for thy portion in this world? Thou must be beaten, must beg, suffer hunger, cold, nakedness, and a thousand calamities, though I cannot now endure the wind should blow upon thee: but yet recalling my self, thought I, I must venture you all with God, though it goeth to the quick to leave you: O I saw in this condition I was as a man who was pulling down

> his house upon the head of his Wife and Children; yet
> thought I, I must do it, I must do it: and now I thought
> of those *two milch Kine that were to carry the Ark of*
> *God into another Country, and to leave their Calves*
> *behind them*, I Sam. 6. 10, 11, 12.[15]

The passage, for all its emotive force and directness of expression, is a tissue of tropes, from the hyperbolic simile of
the man pulling his house down to the submerged metaphor
of the wager with God. Yet it is the concluding biblical citation that carries greatest imaginative sweep, if worked out
in its metaphoric implications. For the two milch kine on the
errand of the Lord are not merely driven by men, though
deprived of their sucklings, but are moved by a more powerful force: "And the kine took the straight way to the way of
Beth-shemesh, and went along the highway, lowing as they
went, and turned not aside to the right hand or to the left
. . ." (I Samuel 6:12). Though they feel the pangs of natural
instinct, they are subject to the control of a supernatural di-
rective—just so Bunyan in his choice of twelve more years of
martyrdom.

In contrast to the precise parallelism and revelatory power of Bunyan's biblical figure, George Fox's usual style for
his *Journal* disdains the arts of rhetoric in its Quaker mini-
malism. Yet when describing a choice similar to Bunyan's
in its life-shaping consequences, Fox employs a welter of
biblical terms that leaves the plain style far behind:

> On a certain time, as I was walking in the fields, the
> Lord said unto me, "Thy name is written in the
> Lamb's book of life which was before the foundation
> of the world"; and, as the Lord spake it, I believed,
> and saw it in the new birth. Then, some time after, the
> Lord commanded me to go abroad into the world,
> which was like a briery, thorny wilderness; and when

15. John Bunyan, *Grace Abounding to the Chief of Sinners and The*
Pilgrim's Progress, ed. Roger Sharrock (London, New York, and
Toronto, 1966), p. 100.

> I came, in the Lord's mighty power, with the word of
> life into the world, the world swelled, and made a
> noise like the great raging waves of the sea. Priests
> and professors, magistrates and people, were all like a
> sea when I came to proclaim the day of the Lord
> amongst them, and to preach repentance to them.[16]

Given the richness of traditional and original tropes, from
the theological terminology of the "new birth" to the expanded metaphor of the troubled sea, it might be overlooked
that the disturbing role which the Lord's prophet is asked
to play is compared with the entry of the word of life into
the world. The terms bring us back to the first chapter of
John, who, while carrying the Greek metaphysics of the
logos into the Gospels, parallels the other evangelists by recounting the Baptist's heralding of the Lamb of God. This
chapter is, then, the place where not only the word (verse
1), life (verse 4), and light (verse 9) come into the world
but that in which the Baptist himself describes his emulation
of Jesus's vocation, baptizing with water like "he which
baptizeth with the Holy Ghost" (verse 33).

To return to Fox. Far be it from his humility to make a
direct comparison of himself with John, but the train of
semantic borrowings strongly suggests that he envisions his
ministry as a typological repetition of the Baptist's. His further references to his entry into his world, bringing distur-
bance but also the light and life of the word, bear out his
governance by that same Holy Spirit to whom John ascribes
his baptismal function: "I was sent to turn people from darkness to the light. . . . I was to direct people to the Spirit that
gave forth the Scriptures . . . for I was in that Spirit by which
they were given forth . . . when the Lord God and His Son
Jesus Christ sent me forth into the world. . . ." We find here

16. *The Journal of George Fox*, Everyman edition (London and
New York, 1949), p. 20; I cite this widely available abridgement of the
definitive edition, ed. Norman Penney (Cambridge and Philadelphia,
1911).

a typological figure shaping an autobiographer's account of his entire career; Fox takes up the language of the Johannine Gospel in order to affirm his life as a reenactment of the herald's mission, troubling his world with potent words but bringing them the Word itself.

Despite the considerable attention accorded *Grace Abounding* on the strength of its close connections with *The Pilgrim's Progress*—whose allegories slip into subsequent English autobiographies at all periods with astonishing ease— it is nevertheless not Bunyan's autobiography that most tellingly employs typological figures. Bunyan's metaphoric prose does most of the work of evoking significance; his biblical citations are interlinear, so to speak, rather than structural, and his identification with biblical personages is locally illuminating rather than typologically identifying him in a universal role or shaping the stages of his life. The power of this writing cannot be gainsaid, to be sure, and the metaphoric mode represents a viable option throughout the history of self-writing.

With Fox's *Journal*, however, we are never in doubt as to the transcendent significance of any given act. No committed typologist, Fox is only occasionally explicit in his associations with the biblical antitype. When he and James Nayler are beset by the inhabitants of Walney Island (at a town called Cockan!), the precedents are clear: "They fell upon [Nayler], and all their cry was, 'Kill him, kill him' " (ch. 3, p. 75; a similar, though lesser martyrdom is meted out to Fox himself). At his trial before Judge Fell, a typological reference is invoked in action: "I told him, when Paul was brought before the rulers, and the Jews and priests came down to accuse him, and laid many false things to his charge, Paul stood still all that while" (ch. 4, p. 77). No slave to other men's types or stages, Fox is likely to fall in with the broad lines of Christian figuration at times and places of his own choosing, but fall in with them he does. His crisis—"a strong temptation to despair"—comes on him as early as the third page of his text; his conversion and, even more clearly,

his Edenic return occur in the first chapter: "I knew nothing
but pureness, and innocency, and righteousness, being renewed up into the image of God by Christ Jesus, to the state
of Adam, which he was in before he fell" (ch. 1, p. 17); and
his epiphany occurs only a few pages after, as we have seen
in the passage examined above (ch. 1, p. 20).

Though the natural childhood and fall are only schemati-
cally noted—"When I came to eleven years of age, I knew
pureness and righteousness" (ch. 1, p. 1)—Fox's book is filled
with the journeying in quest and in ministry, the primary
matter of other Augustinian autobiographies. It would nevertheless be foolhardy to choose between Fox and Bunyan in
determining the fountainhead of the English autobiographical tradition, for the resonance of their metaphors rever-
berates throughout the nineteenth century and continues to
echo in autobiographies as secular as Siegfried Sassoon's (see
Chapter 14 below) or e. e. cummings's (*The Enormous
Room*: 1922), and in autobiographical novels as experimental
as Dorothy Richardson's (see Chapter 19 below).

Yet for a time there was a pause. We have come to think
of the eighteenth century as the period in which, for all their
persistence in displaced forms, the symbolic codes of the
medieval-Renaissance world picture lost their controlling
force in literary expression. These diminished "cosmic syn-
taxes," as Earl Wasserman termed them,[17] included—along
with the great chain of being, the analogous planes of Creation, the microcosm-macrocosm homology of man and the
universe, etc.—the Christian design of history and the individual's place within it. In particular, the active model of
Christ and other biblical heroes is notably absent from most
eighteenth-century autobiographies that have come down
to us. Nevertheless, certain figures of the typological tradi-

17. Earl R. Wasserman, *The Subtler Language: Critical Readings of
Neoclassic and Romantic Poems* (Baltimore, 1959), p. 11.

tion persisted in the popular imagination and found their way into the fiction and art of the age.

Amid the gradual but cumulatively sweeping change in religious thinking in the eighteenth century, the language of self-representation registered many of the barometric signs marking the period's cultural atmosphere. One sign of the times was observable in the fortunes of typology itself. A study that declares, with only mild qualification, that "modern theology began in England at the turn from the seventeenth to the eighteenth century" goes on to identify the shifting currents in the typological reading of the Bible as indicators of this modernity. Citing Protestant theologians who used typology "to locate the events of their day vis-à-vis the narrative framework of biblical story and history," Hans Frei concludes: "This kind of prophecy, rather than an anachronism, was the sign of a new cultural development, for its emphasis was on [present] events, on their likely course and on the hidden signs and references to this 'real' world of past and future history, spread through the Bible." [18] The success of biblical references in rendering contemporary life patterned and meaningful was also the seed of typology's degeneration—or, alternatively expressed, of a perspectival shift away from the dead past and toward the present living world.

This shift was marked by a special form of figuration, *abstracted typology*, which, despite its name, emphasizes the concrete and here-and-now. Such figures are "drawn away from the theological field of action, although there may be religious significance in the way each is introduced." [19] Paul

18. Hans W. Frei, *The Eclipse of Biblical Narrative: A Study in 18th and 19th Century Hermeneutics* (New Haven and London, 1974), p. 4; see also pp. 142–43 for a striking comparison of developments in Germany and England, differentiated by the relative importance of the realistic novel.

19. Paul J. Korshin, "The Development of Abstracted Typology in England, 1650–1820," in Earl Miner, ed., *Literary Uses of Typology from the Late Middle Ages to the Present* (Princeton, 1977), p. 148; the subsequent discussion summarizes pp. 148–65 *et seq.*

Korshin gives four general reasons for the rise of abstracted typology in the eighteenth century: the "politicizing of theological contexts" in the civil wars and their aftermath; the concomitant confusion in terminology, not only of various kinds of symbolism but also of sacred and secular ranges of reference; the enlargement of the number of genres using typology—from the narrow group including homily, divine poetry and apologetics, with only a limited extension into epic and pastoral, to the post-Restoration expansion into satire, character writing, prose and verse fable, and, most significantly for autobiography, prose narrative; and finally, early eighteenth-century theological controversies about the meaning of Old Testament prophecies. (An "enlightened" age found it increasingly difficult to believe that they were meant to be taken as literal predictions, with the result that moral or other "rational" implications were even more strongly preferred.) A number of analogous developments may be noted in English literature of the period as they bear directly on the writing of autobiography.

The eighteenth-century modification in typological habits of mind could not by itself cause a marked change in the writing of autobiography. The increase in sheer numbers and varied conditions of men would by itself account for the proliferation of self-writings; add to that the widespread journal-keeping habits of a Samuel Pepys or a James Boswell and one would anticipate large stocks of recorded experience, if not the summative views taken by autobiographies written with temporal perspective. Spiritual autobiographies continued, of course, to proceed regularly from the continued revivals of religious enthusiasm, like Methodism or the Great Awakening in America. What was missing was the fusion of the two currents, of religious patterns of thought about the shape of a life and the sensitive recording of daily experience. The great "dissociation of sensibility" that has been held to shape or misshape the post-Renaissance mind is nowhere more sharply focused than in the disjunction of the so-called "normal vision" of the eighteenth-century secular self-writings from the formulaic responses of the numerous spiritual autobiographies of the period.[20]

What fusion occurred may be looked for in the realm of form not content; as Patricia Meyer Spacks has shown, some of the emergent techniques in fictional narration were concurrently being practiced in the self-writings of the time, often by the same authors, working first in one then the other medium. Yet there remains reason to doubt Spacks's comfortable conclusion that artistic means yielded a coherence like that of religious self-writing: "The spiritual autobiography of the period explicitly declares that lives have plots arranged by God. But every memoir reiterates the first part of that statement: autobiographies affirm the art of life . . . as stoutly as they affirm human identity."[21] The plots that secular authors devise for their lives must, if they lack a pattern book like the Bible, come from somewhere else. In the absence of an alternative, the threat of randomness or dispersion hovers not only over the subject of experience for David Hume or

20. On the "normal vision," see John N. Morris, *Versions of the Self: Studies in English Autobiography from John Bunyan to John Stuart Mill* (New York and London, 1966), in a chapter on Edward Gibbon and Roger North. For a critique of Morris's apparent slighting of the richness of spiritual and other modes of self-writing, see Donald Greene, "The Uses of Autobiography in the Eighteenth Century," in *Essays in Eighteenth-Century Biography*, ed. P. B. Daghlian (Bloomington, Ind., and London, 1968), pp. 64–65. Morris might more easily be faulted for the modernist norms by which he judges approvingly anticipations of soul searching and religious angst in writers before and after the eighteenth century—while singling out Boswell and Cowper as "agents of the new."

21. Patricia Meyer Spacks, *Imagining a Self: Autobiography and Novel in Eighteenth-Century England* (Cambridge, Mass., and London, 1976), p. 302. For all Spacks's emphasis on narrational techniques shared by the two kinds of narrative, it is hard to detect what precisely these are—apart from a few standard items like "unreliable narrators." Spacks has also written extensively on other aspects of autobiography, particularly on women's lives and the vocational model.

Boswell but over their narratives (or, in Hume's case, lack of narrative) as well.[22]

A development tending to make up for the lack of divine plotting in ordinary experience has been noted by Ronald Paulson in a study of the furnishing of eighteenth-century fiction with the character types provided by popular culture. Although Paulson casually varies his terminology for these cultural images (models, types, paradigms, etc.), he notes genuine cases of typological reference in Defoe, Fielding, and, in art, Hogarth. These readable icons, spatially or temporally juxtaposed with the main action of novel or engraving, are to be distinguished from the previous century's active modeling of lives on biblical precedents. The eighteenth-century writer's use of biblical types as foils for present-day characters was most often by way of contrast, usually in behalf of satiric reduction of the contemporary. A case in point is the well-established relation: Joseph Andrews/Joseph and Parson Abraham Adams/Abraham. Paulson corrects the received view that biblical associations create a dignified elevation of the characters by remarking on "the loose fit that results when [they are] placed on a human being."[23] Contradictions, if not travesties, of biblical parallelism are readily discoverable in the novelist's and artist's use of the figures of the prodigal son, good Samaritan, and other biblical persons. The emphasis shifts to the sad disparity or comic bathos of contemporary men surrounded by echoes of the heroic past. With all its inheritance of traditional topoi, the age cannot fully believe in their modern applicability—thus the hollow ring that follows from invoking the authority of the past:

22. See Robert H. Bell, "David Hume's Fables of Identity," *Philological Quarterly*, 54 (1975): 471–83; and his "Boswell's Notes Toward a Supreme Fiction: From *London Journal* to *Life of Johnson*," *Modern Language Quarterly*, 38 (1977): 132–48, for the anxieties of finding a form for telling the pattern of a life, given the " 'Humean' notion of personal identity" (p. 140), which Boswell embodies.

23. Ronald Paulson, *Popular and Polite Art in the Age of Hogarth and Fielding* (Notre Dame, Ind., and London, 1979), pp. 153ff.

Spiritual Figures

"*Any* structure that is identifiable and redolent of the past is going to be inappropriate to a situation here and now."

In full accordance with the secular shift of emphasis from the antitype at the center of history to what I call the *after-type* at the forefront of consciousness, and in line with the desire to discriminate the sharply felt (and often lamentable) present from the now receded past, autobiographical writers in the eighteenth century employ typology alongside increasingly particular details of immediate situations—that is, in the mode that has come to be called realism. In a series of studies of eighteenth-century autobiographies, Robert Bell notes a number of features in the new technique of rendering. These are already present in Bunyan's well-known account of his crisis during a game of "cat," a potential conversion situation for which Augustine's *Confessions* provides the model:

> The event is keenly particularized. . . . Bunyan renders, with much more attention than Augustine, his perspective at the time. . . . The third, and most telling, departure from Augustinian narrative is that Bunyan is much less confident of his present authority. . . . Bunyan is in the process of becoming a spiritual *exemplum*, but the process is never fully realized. It remains symbolic, and must be constantly verified.[24]

Bell traces the intensification of realism—and the problematizing of the autobiographer's relation to the models for his experience—in a succession of autobiographies from Hume and Boswell to Rousseau and Franklin. Concomitant with the increased particularity with which the present or after-type is treated is the increased imaginativeness with which the biblical type is rendered. What was previously interpreted historically and literally now becomes, Bell says, symbolic whereas the prosaic present becomes an endless field

24. Robert H. Bell, "Metamorphoses of Spiritual Autobiography," *English Literary History*, 44 (1977): 108–26; see also Bell's "Moll's Grace Abounding," *Genre*, 8 (1975): 267–82.

91

LIBRARY ST. MARY'S COLLEGE

for metonymic extension and digression. Boswell, the prodigal son diverted by a thousand sights, even on his way home; Franklin, the good husbandman of industrious and social projects but unable to balance his carefully reckoned books of moral credit and debit;[25] the repeated appeals to the Bible, including a self-application of the parable of the barren fig tree, in William Cowper's *Memoir*[26]—a pathetic reiteration, even when the text closes with a turn to better courses; all are intent on recalling yet denying the power of authoritative figures fully to account for their lives.

25. For a fine treatment of the scene, see Robert F. Sayre, *The Examined Self: Benjamin Franklin, Henry Adams, Henry James* (Princeton, 1964), pp. 28ff.

26. "Memoir of the Early Life of William Cowper, Esq.," ed. Maurice J. Quinlan, *Proceedings of the American Philosophical Society*, 97 (1953 [1816]): 366–82.

3

Romantic
Figures

——

Prominent among the myriad forces acting to modify the
forms of European culture, a number of revivals of Christian
piety were under way in the eighteenth century. (This rationalistic period witnessed, after all, the creation of some of
the greatest monuments of Christian art since the northern
French cathedrals: the church music of Bach and the biblical
music dramas of Handel.) This later phase of the Reformation—felt particularly in Germany and England but not confined to those Protestant lands—may be called, after the model
of recent political movements, international pietism ("l'inter-
nationale piétiste").[1] Lutheran (or Hussite) versions of self-
searching like that of the Moravian sect; evangelical tendencies charged with emotional fervor, like Methodism within
the English church; Catholic counterparts like the quietism
of Madame Guyon and Archbishop Fénelon; philosophical
equivalents like the emotive and individual emphases of the
German Counter-Enlightenment—these varieties of religious

1. Georges Gusdorf, "De l'autobiographie initiatique à l'autobiographie genre littéraire," *Revue d'histoire littéraire de la France*, 75
(1975): 957–94. Further underscoring of the importance of biblical
models for Continental self-writing emerges in Derek Bowman, "The
Path of Life: Attitudes to the Bible in Some Autobiographies of the
Seventeenth and Eighteenth Centuries," in *Essays in German and
Dutch Literature*, ed. W. D. Robson-Scott (London, 1973), pp. 65–88.

experientialism can be detected throughout the century and feed the later developments that we have come to call Romanticism. Their influence on literature is well attested by their secular sublimation—evident from Shaftesbury's seminal role—in the sentimental fiction and landscape poetry that marked the so-called Age of Sensibility. It is in this larger stream that the flowering of Romantic autobiography is to be studied and not by some sudden revelation of a historicist mentality or a sharp shift of the scales toward the value of the individual.

If we consider narrative language alone, compared to the writings of the movement's participants, it would be difficult to demonstrate the role of religious pietism in the making of literary autobiography. Gusdorf's instancing of the pietist model of the "Schöne Seele" for Goethe is more clearly operative in the novel *Wilhelm Meister* than in the autobiography *Poetry and Truth*. Yet the shaping power of religious sensibility in self-writing is subtle and pervasive. It works its way by encouraging the popular practice of reflective diary keeping (the well-documented rise of the *journal intime*),[2] by the higher valuation placed on feeling, memory, and introspection in literature at large, and by what may be called the rediscovery of the Bible by those who turned away from rationalism toward myth and away from plain prose toward symbolic language. To the question that has been asked about nineteenth-century autobiography—where was Jean-Jacques?[3]—we may reply that he was already at work in the eighteenth, moving men in the direction of a literature of self-examination, self-accusation, and self-mythologizing.

2. For the relation of genres, see Jacques Voisine, "De la confession religieuse à l'autobiographie et au journal intime, entre 1760 et 1820," *Neohelicon*, 2 (1974): 337–57. See also Alain Girard, *Le Journal intime* (Paris, 1963).

3. Ample discussion of Rousseau's *Confessions* in relation to—and in departure from—his life will be found in the magisterial work of Jean Guéhenno, *Jean-Jacques Rousseau*, trans. J. Weightman and D. Weightman, 2 vols. (London and New York, 1966 [1962]).

Enlightenment, revolution, and romanticism have become the historiographical names for aspects of a new spirit abroad in late eighteenth-century Europe, one of whose manifestations was the articulation of individualism that issues in the modern ego and its varied forms of expression, better and worse. On the positive side of the account, presumably, is the proliferation of nonreligious autobiographies, among them the celebrated three by which the leading figures of French, German, and English letters made their life stories into test cases for new concepts of personal life. Yet even a cursory overview of Rousseau's *Confessions*, Goethe's *Poetry and Truth*, and Wordsworth's *Prelude* shows in high relief the traditional resources of autobiography to which even innovators turn in the plotting of their highly individual lives. The *Confessions* may be seen as a succession of Edenesque landscapes in each of which primal innocence and happiness are partially achieved, invariably to be followed by a fall—merited or unmerited—and expulsion. Similarly, Goethe enjoys a garden of innocent sexuality, the so-called Sesenheim idyll, artfully conveyed in literary terms derived from Oliver Goldsmith—an idyll which degenerates in the common light of the social world.[4] Although the Edenic state and its aftermath are more distinctly recalled in the former work, the journey in quest of vocation—which evokes resonant Old and New Testament figures—is stronger in Goethe's autobiography. Rousseau's call to his life's work on the road to Vincennes is not as saliently positioned as the moment for decision between Italy and Weimar with which Goethe concludes his narrative. (Further fragments of his great confession, the *Italian Journey* and *Conversations with Eckermann*, were later to pick up the story.) The figures of autobiographical tradition will be found to appear as powerfully in these ground-breaking works as they had in conven-

4. A penetrating literary study—not limited to the points at issue here—is Marjorie Perloff, "The Autobiographical Mode of Goethe: 'Dichtung und Wahrheit' and the Lyric Poems," *Comparative Literature Studies*, 7 (1970): 265–96.

tional spiritual autobiographies; what is new is the aesthetic freedom with which they are employed, fulfilling the tendencies toward present orientation, circumstantial realism, and localized typological reference that we have seen growing in the eighteenth century.

When we come to Wordsworth, it is no longer possible—at least not since the appearance of M. H. Abrams's *Natural Supernaturalism*—to regard his autobiographical poem as an expression *sui generis* of a unique life design. By calling attention to the figures that it shares with spiritual autobiographies from Augustine down (although it is still not clear how much Wordsworth was directly affected either by Augustine or by seventeenth-century writers),[5] Abrams has established *The Prelude* as a Romantic version of themes and forms that have haunted autobiography since its earliest exemplars. To cite Abrams's summary formulations:

> the Wordsworthian theodicy of the private life (if we want to coin a term, we can call it a "biodicy"), belongs to the distinctive Romantic genre of the *Bildungsgeschichte*, which translates the painful process of Christian conversion and redemption into a painful process of self-formation, crisis, and self-recognition, which culminates in a stage of self-coherence, self-awareness, and assured power that is its own reward.
>
> . . . In *The Prelude*, then, the justification of seeming evil turns on a crisis and inner transformation, parallel to Augustine's agony and conversion in the garden at Milan. [Augustine's conversion is "instant and absolute" whereas] . . . In Wordsworth's secular account of the "growth" of his mind, the process is

5. On the role of eighteenth-century spiritual autobiography in shaping Romantic self-writing, see Richard E. Brantley, *Wordsworth's "Natural Methodism"* (New Haven and London, 1975); and Frank D. McConnell, *The Confessional Imagination: A Reading of Wordsworth's Prelude* (Baltimore and London, 1974), pp. 28ff.; see esp. McConnell's comparison of Fox's and Wordsworth's mountain visions, pp. 83ff.

one of gradual recovery which takes three books to
tell in full; and for the Christian paradigm of right-
angled change into something radically new he sub-
stitutes a pattern . . . in which development consists of
a gradual curve back to an earlier stage, but on a higher level incorporating that which has intervened.[6]

Abrams goes on to show how other typological motifs, especially those of the pilgrim and the prodigal, mark the narratives of quest and self-discovery with which Romantic poetry is filled.

While displaced versions of the Christian *peregrinatio*

6. M. H. Abrams, *Natural Supernaturalism: Tradition and Revolution in Romantic Literature* (New York, 1971), pp. 96, 113–14. Another approach to the biological aspect of the Romantic and post-
Romantic garden or place of origin is Martha R. Lifson, "The Myth
of the Fall: A Description of Autobiography," *Genre*, 12 (1979): 45–67.
Lifson's examples include Boswell, Rousseau, Wordsworth, De Quincey, Thoreau, Adams, James, Lillian Hellman, Anaïs Nin, James Bald-
win, Nabokov, Muir, Leonard Woolf, Genet, and others. Her speculations on the motives for persistent focusing on childhood garden
scenes and their loss are listed in the second part of her article: the confessional urge to deal with one's earliest sins, the desire to recall and
recapture creative potentialities, a tendency to return to origins in
order to review one's career from the beginning, an effort to recapture
the timeless feeling of childhood (as an anticipation of, or prevention
of the movement toward, death), a literary appropriation of the topoi
of pastoral in the desire to envisage an ideal realm or state of mind,
and a recapitulation of the eternal act of creation by the Word in the
autobiographer's verbal creation: "The autobiographical narrator bears
witness to himself and by means of words brings an image of the
'garden'—order, light, coherence, stability, timelessness, fame, imagination—into being as he shapes himself and sets himself in a scene" (p.
67). Some of these impulses may be endemic in autobiographical
writing generally; others—the confessional urge, in particular—certainly are not. All these motives lack specific grounding in the cultural history of the nineteenth and twentieth centuries, as well as
reference to the literary traditions which both shape and serve autobiographical expression (with the exception of the appropriation of
pastoral). Most strikingly absent from Lifson's study of the myth of
the Fall is any sustained reference to the Bible; her illustrations show
no sign of having been formed in a Christian culture.

are widespread in a number of Romantic genres—witness "The Rime of the Ancient Mariner," *Prometheus Unbound* (which has been called Asia's "spiritual journey"), and *Melmoth the Wanderer*—they are equally evident in the autobiographical narratives of the major poets. It is a mistake to isolate *The Prelude* in the English Romantic period, for this is not the sole—nor even the first—long poem to tell the growth of a poet's mind. By 1804, Blake had composed *Milton*[7] while the first version of *The Prelude* was in progress; and in 1809, as he was producing the first copies of this prophetic book, Byron began *Childe Harold's Pilgrimage*, at which he worked intermittently until 1818.[8] In all three poems, we find enormous boldness matched by considerable diffidence—as is reflected in protracted composition and delayed publication—but in all three there shows itself as well an urgency to tell a tale of personal exploration and "mental fight" as the worthy subject of a poem on an epic scale. It is notable, moreover, that the figures of these poetic autobiographies—in addition to the obligatory modifications of epic conventions—are drawn from the stores of autobiographical tradition. Selected to cover individual situations and deployed according to the needs of extended narrative, the stages of spiritual autobiography are placed in the foreground of these poems of intellectual prodigals on pilgrimage for self-discovery and poetic power.

Blake and Byron are well practiced in a limited number of the stages through which autobiographies have long moved—the one in Edenic innocence and epiphanic vision,

7. See the commentary in William Blake, *Milton*, ed. K. P. Easson and R. R. Easson (Boulder, Colo., and New York, 1978), pp. 135ff.; see also its bibliography for three recent, full-length studies of the poem.

8. Robert F. Gleckner, *Byron and the Ruins of Paradise* (Baltimore, 1967), pp. 43ff., 295–96; for the questing motif throughout the nineteenth century, see Georg Roppen and Richard Sommer, *Strangers and Pilgrims: An Essay on the Metaphor of the Journey* (New York, 1964).

the other in roving journeys in quest of self and in moments of crisis racked by guilt. It is Wordsworth who traverses each of the six points we have plotted in the fullest autobiography, Augustine's, and its comparable fullness helps make *The Prelude* the greatest English autobiographical work in any form. To demonstrate Wordsworth's mastery of the figurative possibilities of self-writing, it would be easy to show that in this, as in other respects, *The Prelude* moves over ground that was prepared before. It is also important to recognize the poem's clear signs of its conception, if not under the sway of Augustine, at least with a scope commensurate to that of the *Confessions*. I apologize for citing passages already well known in the histories of Romanticism and modern consciousness and shall try to single out phrases that attest to the awareness of origins, which gives Wordsworth a watershed place in the autobiographical tradition.

The early books of *The Prelude* recount a childhood in an Edenesque landscape not so much innocent as sheltered and governed by powers of some capacity to overawe:

> Fair seed-time had my soul, and I grew up
> Fostered alike by beauty and by fear:
> Much favoured in my birth-place, and no less
> In that beloved Vale to which erelong
> We were transplanted. . . .
>   (Bk. 1, lines 301–05)[9]

The almost immediate sequel to initial garden possession is sin and a fall into the moral realm. After recounting the ten-year-old's bird-stealing forays (robbing not only ravens' nests but snares set by other trappers), the decisive sin of

9. The reference is to the vale at Hawkeshead, the first in a series of vales—of which Grasmere is the final place of return. I cite the Norton edition of *The Prelude*, ed. J. Wordsworth, M. H. Abrams, and S. Gill (New York and London, 1979); although this text makes a parallel arrangement of the 1805 and 1850 versions of the poem, I quote only from the latter.

theft is told. "It was an act of stealth / And troubled pleasure," Wordsworth says of his boat stealing and elaborates
the guilt-ridden consciousness of his transgression in the
aspects of the landscape:

> . . . a huge peak, black and huge,
> As if with voluntary power instinct
> Upreared its head. I struck [the oars] and
> struck again,
> And growing still in stature the grim shape
> Towered up between me and the stars . . .
>
> . . . after I had seen
> That spectacle, for many days, my brain
> Worked with a dim and undetermined sense
> Of unknown modes of being; o'er my thoughts
> There hung a darkness, call it solitude
> Or blank desertion.
>
> (Bk. i, lines 378–95)

The autobiographer is clearly working in the Old Testament figures of an angry mountain god, inducing internal-
ized guilt in the primitive in order to lead him to a higher
culture, as Freud has shown for Moses. If Wordsworth's language of "unknown modes of being" expresses an untradi-
tional religious sense, his "solitude / Or blank desertion" is
specifically resonant of Adam at the Fall.

The continuation of this early-begun process is traced in
the books that record Wordsworth's schooltime and Cambridge years, his anxiety-ridden pursuits among books, and
his further epiphanic visions, for example, on crossing (or,
more precisely, on descending from) the Alps (Bk. vi, lines
619–40). But the process of education is not perceived as
equally an alienation until the young man passes to a brief
residence in London and protracted wanderings in France—
carrying the standard equipment of pilgrims both mundane
and spiritual, the "scrip and staff" (Bk. ix, line 36). London
is a place of exile, colored by hellish sensations epitomized
in Bartholomew Fair: "what anarchy and din, / Barbarian

and infernal—a phantasma, / Monstrous in colour, motion, shape, sight, sound" (Bk. vii, lines 686–88). A later stopping place, Paris at the time of the September massacres, is disclosed as a Dantean dark wood: "The place, all hushed and silent as it was, / Appeared unfit for the repose of night, / Defenceless as a wood where tigers roam" (Bk. x, lines 91–93).

From here it is a short narrative step—although over three years in biographical time—to the "crisis of that strong disease" (Bk. xi, line 306), which Wordsworth experienced in 1796:

> . . . now believing,
> Now disbelieving; endlessly perplexed
> With impulse, motive, right and wrong, the ground
> Of obligation, what the rule and whence
> The sanction; till, demanding formal *proof*,
> And seeking it in every thing, I lost
> All feeling of conviction, and, in fine,
> Sick, wearied out with contrarieties,
> Yielded up moral questions in despair.
> (Bk. xi, lines 297–305)

Almost immediately, grace descends ("Thanks to the bounteous Giver of all good!") in the form of a ministering sister who "Maintained for me a saving intercourse / With my true self" (Bk. xi, lines 334, 341–42). Epiphany does not follow—how should it, when the poem has recorded revelatory experiences at almost every age?—but instead we get a general theory of epiphany, the famous definition of the "spots of time" (Bk. xii, lines 208–25).

The general must be enforced by the particular, however, and at the beginning of his concluding book Wordsworth devises one of his most striking *anachronies* (to use Gérard Genette's term), reverting to an experience of 1791, the ascent of Mount Snowdon, for his climactic mountain epiphany. The passage is too well known to be dwelled on here, but one might call attention to the influx of typological language at precisely this point in the poem. The vision of mist and sea from the mountain peak is interpreted as "the type / Of a majestic intellect," "the emblem of a mind / That feeds upon infinity" (Bk. xiv, lines 66–71). Beyond the ample scope the passage gives for commentary on Wordsworth's dealings with "transcendent power" and "that glorious faculty" of Imagination (Bk. xiv, lines 75, 89), the language marks a fulfillment of the typological mode first seen on the descent from the Alps, when landscape features were read as "Characters of the great Apocalypse, / The types and symbols of Eternity" (Bk. vi, lines 638–39).

Another form of return is suggested by the closing books of *The Prelude*, the return to childhood scenes, natural sources, and, more specifically, the Lake District. But this return in space to an earlier time is not narrated in these books; there is even an acknowledgment of weakening memory—something that worried Wordsworth enough to become the provocation for another great poem, the Intimations Ode. Despite a gathering of early images and the beneficial effects ascribed to them, there is some skepticism of any return:

> . . . The days gone by
> Return upon me almost from the dawn
> Of life: the hiding places of man's power
> Open; I would approach them, but they close.
> I see by glimpses now; when age comes on,
> May scarcely see at all; and I would give,
> While yet we may, as far as words can give,
> Substance and life to what I feel, enshrining,
> Such is my hope, the spirit of the Past
> For future restoration.
> (Bk. xii, lines 277–86)

The hint is dropped here that it is not in geographical space nor even in mental recovery of time past that the return is to be enacted but in the writing of autobiography.

In this sense, the completing stage of Wordsworth's life

as conceived in *The Prelude* is the writing of the poem itself.
But this universally acknowledged truth is difficult to locate
in the formal design of the poem, ending as it does only with
declarations of an autobiographical project but no narrative
of its execution—only the evident existence of the text itself.
M. H. Abrams has taught us to discover a *mise en abyme*,
the presence of the poem as a fulfilling object within its own
fabric, in its opening pages.[10] Turning back to its beginning,
the text achieves the recurvate form better known in such
works as *Finnegans Wake* and other narratives of return and
renewal. The opening "Glad Preamble," which Wordsworth probably composed on a walking tour in the Lake
District with Coleridge in November 1799, is all at once a
declaration of mental independence, a resolution to move to
Dove Cottage, Grasmere, and an announcement of inspiration by a "sweet breath of heaven" that wakens a "corre-
spondent breeze" within the poet and "is *now* [my emphasis]
become / A tempest, a redundant energy, / Vexing its own
creation" (Bk. 1, lines 33–38). Despite the continuing difficulties of maintaining and expressing such an infusion
(which Geoffrey Hartman has keenly observed),[11] Wordsworth declares to Coleridge that the resulting words are
prophecy:

10. Abrams, *Natural Supernaturalism*, pp. 287ff.; note also the articulation of an idea all readers have sensed but none has expressed so
clearly:
 Only now does [Wordsworth] identify the aspect of the vale
 which had all along made it the goal of his tortuous literal, spiritual
 and poetic journey. That goal, as in all the ancient genre of the
 circuitous pilgrimage, is home—*Home at Grasmere* [which
 Abrams proceeds to link to *The Prelude* at this juncture]. . . .
 The place in which, "on Nature's invitation" (line 71), Wordsworth's literal and metaphoric wanderings have terminated is
 identified, after the venerable formula [of the Christian quest], as
 a home which is also a recovered paradise.
11. Geoffrey Hartman, "A Poet's Progress: Wordsworth and the
Via Naturaliter Negativa," *Modern Philology*, 59 (1962): 214–24. See
also David P. Haney, "The Emergence of the Autobiographical Figure
in *The Prelude, Book 1*," *Studies in Romanticism*, 20 (1981): 33–63.

> ... to the open fields I told
> A prophecy: poetic numbers came
> Spontaneously to clothe in priestly robe
> A renovated spirit singled out,
> Such hope was mine, for holy services.
> (Bk. i, lines 50–54)

There follows the text proper of *The Prelude*.

———

The Romantic conversion of the Christian *peregrinatio* into displaced forms of exile or alienation, spiritual and geographic wandering, and return to the self in lieu of a literal return home has been described by Harold Bloom as the "internalization of quest-romance."[12] It is striking that the prose self-writings of the period—including such outstanding works as *Confessions of an English Opium-Eater*, Leigh Hunt's *Autobiography*, and the *Biographia Literaria*—show few signs of traditional figuration in their themes and diction, although De Quincey is a partial exception. It was left to the verse autobiographies to unfold the process of self-discovery as a narrative journey over time and space.

Yet the emphasis placed here on the Romantics' recycling of older autobiographical materials should not obscure the decisive modulations that their imaginations played on those resources. It is not necessary to fall in with received views of the Romantic rebellion against inherited orthodoxies—not even in the Bloomian version in which the poets both are influenced by and swerve from their predecessors—to gain a grasp of their originality in reclaiming biblical and other figures for their self-writings. Blake, Byron, and Shelley create syncretic myths out of biblical and pagan iconography, revivifying the Fall and exile, Satan and his Promethean version, and various prophetic wisdom figures who guide the pilgrim-prodigal-wanderer on his way to a paradise

---

12. See his essay with that title in *Romanticism and Consciousness: Essays in Criticism*, ed. Harold Bloom (New York, 1970), pp. 3–24.

within the imagination. But the valences of these forces have been altered, if not reversed, from their initial polarities. As Sacvan Bercovitch puts the case, applying the language of Augustinian theology to the poets' plotting of their lives:

> Theological displacement is defined by Augustine, in a famous passage [of *De Trinitate*], as the *"experimentum medietatis,"* a "trial of the center" in which the ego overcomes the soul. The Puritans applied this concept to the unsuccessful auto-machia, the false pilgrim's regress from Christ to the self; following Augustine, they found their main examples in Lucifer and Prometheus. The Romantics, we might say, redefined the *experimentum medietatis* as a victory of the soul. Having claimed the self as its own absolute—in Coleridge's words, a "manifestation of the Eternal and Universal One"—they outlined a Promethean auto-machia which ascended *through* the Center of Indifference to an affirmation of the self as divinity incarnate.[13]

As he goes on to explain, the Romantic displacement of traditional Christian figures followed directly from this transvaluation of values, moving from a desired suppression of the ego to an assertion of the soul or self and an all-but-identification of deity with it.

Bercovitch also draws some of the implications of this displacement of theological language for autobiography—at least for American self-writers, though a number of English authors come equally to mind. Although Wordsworth is careful—increasingly during the long years of revising *The Prelude*—to qualify the claims of the imagination and the self-determining power of the individual mind, Emerson (for reasons we cannot review here) "can omit such considerations"; "he recasts Romantic autobiography into auto-

13. Sacvan Bercovitch, *The Puritan Origins of the American Self* (New Haven and London, 1975), pp. 163–64; for Bercovitch's remarks on Wordsworth, Emerson, and Carlyle, see pp. 170–75.

American-biography" and can take the Romantic equation of history and biography a step further by positing that "all biography is autobiography." Such opportunities and temptations may help to explain why the Romantic prose autobiographies fall short of the mythic scope of the major poems. Whether in De Quincey's anguish of drug-induced imaginings[14] or in the growth of mind that reaches definition in Coleridge's primary and secondary imagination, even selectively circumstantial narrators of personal fall and exile, crisis and epiphany cannot baldly assert the self as alpha and omega—they have suffered and depicted too many of its lapses and weaknesses along the way. The poets are better placed to figure the struggles and triumph of the self on a level of generality that avoids the most painful self-recriminations, although one of the foremost of them, Byron, cannot refrain from perpetuating his "trial of the center."

For these reasons, we must put in doubt the easy assumption that places the flowering of modern autobiography in the Romantic period. There has always seemed to lurk a contradiction in the view that autobiography begins with Augustine and comes into its own among the Romantics, for the Augustinian confession aimed at self-transcendence whereas the poets, in one form or another, affirm the transcendent self. It would be an anomaly in the history of ideas if a great outburst of the individual imagination were to find its appropriate form in the sacred book of self-suppression and chastizement of the ego, the will and the body—with grave doubts even of the memory. Even among the Romantics there were those who were wary of the imagination's grand

14. See Karen M. Lever, "De Quincey as Gothic Hero: A Perspective on *Confessions of an English Opium-Eater* and *Suspiria de Profundis*," *Texas Studies in Literature and Language*, 21 (1979): 332–46. See also Elizabeth W. Bruss, *Autobiographical Acts: The Changing Situation of a Literary Genre* (Baltimore and London, 1976), for the readjustments between De Quincey's self-writings. I am not aware that these two well-known sides of Coleridge have been studied in the context of the *Biographia Literaria*.

claims to sovereignty, happiness, or godhead; two men born in the heyday of Romantic selfhood (Keats and Carlyle, both in 1795) were rightly alarmed at some of the possibilities and pitfalls now opened to them. But only the latter was to outlive the period, continuing to grapple with the grandeur and misery of self in his self-writings.

It is almost inevitable that we find Thomas Carlyle at the juncture between the spiritual autobiography tradition and modern self-writing, given his deep roots in Calvinist theology and its broad Augustinian heritage and his excruciated struggle to resist orthodoxy without falling into impiety. *Sartor Resartus* has always been known to mark this struggle, but it now becomes possible to see an array of cultural forces converging at the precise point on which the action of *Sartor* and the conversion process turn: the place called "Center of Indifference." This central chapter has been accurately observed to rest upon the "trial of the center" in Augustinian thought,[15] but although all acknowledge it as the turning point of the protagonist's conversion, its transmutative power remains to be specified. In this symbolic reenactment of his personal drama, Carlyle gives a further turn to the Romantic displacement of the *experimentum medietatis*, reconverting it from a victory of the self to a subtle adjudication of ego and world, mind and its objects, personal and divine will. To inquire into Carlyle's thought and language in striking these balances is to begin the study of traditional figures in Victorian autobiography.

The process by which this multiple conversion is effected must be given its own space in the next chapter, but we may already be in a position to anticipate some of the directions in which the following studies of Victorian and modern autobiographers will move. It has often been observed that the Victorian poets inherit the Romantics as a dangerous cargo,

15. G. B. Tennyson, *"Sartor" Called "Resartus": The Genesis, Structure, and Style of Thomas Carlyle's First Major Work* (Princeton, 1965), pp. 310-15.

which it is their lifelong business to demystify and desexualize. Some such hypothesis may be advanced for the Victorian autobiographers; inheriting the resources of writing life stories from a tradition at once confessional and affirmative, they also inherit the diffidence already observable in some of the Romantics, not merely about the "unmanly" or "ungentlemanly" attention which self-publication draws but about the self-exaltation which a Victorian "prophet" must draw back from. The extreme caution exercised by most of the Victorians about the assembling of materials for their biographies is even more painfully evident in their autobiographies—the symbolic disguises of Carlyle, the lifelong suppression of his text (and of rage in the text) by Mill, the tormented apologies for publication by Newman. Yet one and all make the effort to universalize the self in figural terms, aware of the necessary failure of the disguise yet resigned to bear the consequences—fully realized in the debunking biographies by modern critics.

These writers and the novelists who gain courage to narrate—though only in the more fully fictionalized form of autobiographical novels—their falls, exiles, and renewals confront the problems of self-writing at their most attenuated point, given the conflicting yet strangely consorted demands of Christian tradition and Romantic precedent. How they severally made a virtue of such necessities, the varied ways in which individual works dramatically enact their conflicting imperatives, must be left to the detailed analyses that follow. But we may already hazard the claim that the Victorian age was the great age of English autobiography, before a number of modern authors, following closely in its figurative patterns, went on to expand its lexicon of selfhood in the languages of our own time.

PART II

The Figures of the Prophets

——

IT WOULD NOT BE ENOUGH to say that in the Victorian age self-writing becomes widespread; it becomes specialized as well. This is the period in which we discover gypsy autobiographies—or at least would-be gypsies like George Borrow; erotic autobiographies, of which at least one authentic example, *My Secret Life*, has come down to us; and even, if only as a fictional construct, an equine item: *Black Beauty: The Autobiography of a Horse*. With the tendency to play up one or another aspect of the self, there develops a wider range of metaphorical resources and an extension of the name and notion of autobiography to works of poetry and fiction. (*Aurora Leigh* and *Jane Eyre*, while not their authors' autobiography, are cast in that mold, and the latter is subtitled with that term.) At the start of any investigation of the undisputed masterpieces of Victorian self-writing, one notes their placement before a broad hinterland of pseudo-, quasi-, and neoautobiographies.

The Victorian period is still widely regarded as an age of egoistic authoritativeness, even though the studies initiated by Walter Houghton have opened up its underside of doubt, anxiety, and shunning of the self. The leading intellectual currents all stress selfhood in one or another way: Elie Halévy's famous thesis establishes a parallel between such unlikely bedfellows as laissez faire individualism and Evangelical religious activism; the philosophical hedonism at the base of Utilitarian ethics encouraged self-scrutinizing even as the doctrine widened to calculate the common good beyond personal satisfactions; and the applications of Darwinism in social thought compensated for the individual's insignificance, by comparison with the species's fortunes, with manly encouragement to struggle and endure. In this cultural climate, the leading proponents of one ideology or another become heroes—and are required to be models—of individualism. One result of this veneration of the heroic image is the sorry history of burnt letters, official biographies, and—a Victorian invention?—a self-created biography (or autobiography posing as biography), *The Life of Thomas Hardy*.

Thus, it comes about that we think of the great Victorians as creatures of biography—either as subjects for hagiography, as in the vest-pocket religions of the Browning societies and their like or as objects of ridicule, in the wake of Lytton Strachey. We might do better to think of them as creators of commanding self-images, in many cases surviving into our own age of skepticism and research. It is a short step from this awareness to the perception, now on the verge of general acknowledgment, that the Victorian age was one of great autobiographical activity, in which a number of masterpieces were created and in which the variety and importance of this aesthetic enterprise were thoroughly explored. Prefiguring the trend in contemporary English letters, in which every important writer and many a literary hanger-on must write his autobiography well before resigning himself to creative silence, the Victorians exhibit self-writings in prose and poetry, fiction and nonfiction, by almost all the leading figures of the age. In *In Memoriam*, "Switzerland," *Modern Love*, and Hopkins's "terrible sonnets," the poets devised new versions of or alternatives to the sonnet sequence—the series of distinct lyrics linked by a narrative line—to make a way for their impulse toward self-writing. And each of the major novelists is represented by at least one autobiographical novel—although in Trollope's case, he is better represented by an autobiography.

How did such an outpouring come about, given the firm

restraints on public posturing and the apparent inappropri-
ateness of seventeenth- and eighteenth-century and even
Romantic models of self-writing? A man does not sit down
to write his autobiography in cold blood, without a language
somewhere at hand for the enterprise. I return to autobiographical figures, as they figure (for) the Victorians.

Perhaps the most examined passage of Romantic poetry,
at least in quarters where literary terminology comes under
discussion, is Wordsworth's paean to natural objects at the
Simplon Pass in Book VI of *The Prelude*:

> Characters of the great Apocalypse,
> The types and symbols of Eternity,
> Of first, and last, and midst, and without end.
> (lines 638–40)

The very magniloquence of the rhetoric may tend to dampen
the vibrations of religious language in which this and much
of *The Prelude* is couched. This use of the word "types"
has, however, drawn attention in the recent revival of interest in typology, and Wordsworth's apocalyptic note has
been connected to its primary source in biblical prophecy.
We do not know precisely what Wordsworth understood
by *type*, but it is likely to have come to his pen as readily as
the phrase "types and emblems" did to his contemporary
Francis Jeffrey,[1] editor of the *Edinburgh Review* and least
likely of typologists. As the observer of a parallel phenomenon in American letters has observed: "Throughout the
nineteenth century, the terms 'symbol,' 'emblem,' 'type,' 'allegory,' and 'figure' were, through carelessness, often inter-
changeable and therefore largely negligible. The variety of

1. Quoted in E. R. Wasserman, *The Subtler Language: Critical
Readings of Neoclassic and Romantic Poems* (Baltimore, 1959), p. 182:
"that subtle and mysterious analogy which exists between the physical
and the moral world—which makes outward things and qualities the
natural types and emblems of inward gifts and emotions. . . ."

concepts about metaphor does not correspond to the variety of terms."[2] Perhaps a low but liberating note was sounded when Blake punned on the term in referring simultaneously to his substitute for printing type and to his use of biblical figures in *Jerusalem*—"Therefore I print; nor vain my types shall be" ("To the Public").

The operative word in the Simplon Pass epiphany is, in any case, "symbols." For all Jeffrey's use of "types and emblems" to refer to the signifying action of natural objects—and despite contemporary attempts to construct a poetics of natural typology, in which such objects are seen substituting in the traditional role of biblical elements—the poetics of symbolism were already in place for Wordsworth and were being codified by Coleridge for the nineteenth century. In this poetics, typology had, indeed, a role to play, and it was Coleridge who made the most vigorous call for the revival of the Bible and its language as a primer for poets as well as statesmen.[3] For all their "modernity," the Romantics were instrumental in reviving biblical reference so as to foster its interplay with other symbolic resources. What was lost, and no small loss, was the historical sense of reenactment that orthodox typologists could enjoy, the viability of a social enactment by the after-type of the ideals manifested by types and the possibility of seeing the entire shape of a man's life under the sign of biblical heroism.

It is this provision and dearth bequeathed by their Romantic ancestors that made the grandeur and misery of Vic-

2. Karl Keller, "Alephs, Zahirs, and the Triumph of Ambiguity: Typology in Nineteenth-Century American Literature," in *Literary Uses of Typology: From the Late Middle Ages to the Present*, ed. Earl Miner (Princeton, 1977), p. 282; see also in this volume the judgment of Theodore Ziolkowski that "we can no longer speak with any real precision of religious figuralism in the conventional sense when we are dealing with writers of the twentieth century" ("Some Features of Religious Figuralism in Twentieth-Century Literature," p. 354).

3. Samuel Taylor Coleridge, *The Statesman's Manual: or, The Bible the Best Guide to Political Skill and Foresight* (1816).

torian autobiography. In the absence of a stable symbolic mode for self-writing, the Victorians were led to invent new techniques of composition, developing a palette of the myths, symbols, and other debris of classical and Christian culture. Recent commentators on nineteenth-century art have made us aware of the vivid and self-conscious way in which a number of Victorians employed typology, but their greatest contribution to our grasp of the poetics of the age lies in highlighting the expedients to which those authors were put. Thus, George Landow has not only shown the systematic use of typology in the art of William Holman Hunt but has also indicated the severe displacement which types must undergo in the hands of a lapsed Christian poet like Dante Gabriel Rossetti.[4] Similarly, Linda Peterson has traced a series of types in Browning's self-conception at various stages of his career;[5] the broad implication of these varied figures is that the poet could rest content with none of them but availed himself of one after another to express the special pangs of his vocation at crucial junctures. It is the absence of an overarching form for his life that one misses in the local applications of typology by Browning and other poets (Browning's own term for such references is *symbol*, in a passage quoted but misread by Peterson). If we are to find types functioning as structural principles that order the shape of a career, it is to the autobiographies of the period that we must look. But structural figures need not be exclusive and totalizing in a given life; it is the extended juxtaposition and dramatic in-

4. See George Landow, *William Holman Hunt and Typological Symbolism* (New Haven and London, 1978); and his " 'Life touching lips with immortality': Rossetti's Typological Structures," *Studies in Romanticism*, 17 (1978): 247–65. Landow has recently published a survey of the subject, of which I have not been able to take account: *Victorian Types, Victorian Shadows: Biblical Typology in Victorian Literature, Art, and Thought* (London and Boston, 1980).

5. Linda Peterson, "Biblical Typology and the Self-Portrait of the Poet in Robert Browning," in *Approaches to Victorian Autobiography*, ed. G. P. Landow (Athens, Ohio, 1979), pp. 235–68; see p. 250 for Browning's use of the term *symbol*, discussed below.

terplay of competing self-images that is the life of autobiographical language. Such a dynamic of self-imaging may also
be found in a number of autobiographical novels of the period, which splendidly exhibit this symbolic action.

The power generated by symbolic interactions in structuring a life precludes the possibility of establishing a single
set of figures as the dominant one in Victorian self-writing.
Some scholars have elected the Exodus pattern of wandering
and return to a promised land as the Victorians' most potent
inheritance from the spiritual autobiography tradition,[6] but
the proliferation of these motifs throughout post-Renaissance
literature diminishes the particularity of their appeal in the
nineteenth century. But the Victorians were endowed with
widespread sources of imagery, in which the Christian
peregrinatio (filtered through the Romantic poets) was only
one strand. In the exfoliation of these patterns in Western
art and literature, traditional typology is not left behind, but
a new symbolic action is generated: the enriching of a biblical heritage with the whole history of its aesthetic versions,
where what counts is not the specific content of the original
figure but its malleability for life fashioning. The type becomes a palimpsest, and the developing schemas of using
such overdetermined or polysemous figures make up a grammar of self-writing.

If one were to elect a single figure as the central one for
the nineteenth century, however, it might well be the large
possibilities offered by the myth of the Fall. A useful article
by Martha Lifson has collected the evidence of a widespread
appearance of the Fall pattern throughout Western autobiography, and in this larger fund the Victorians have an
important share.[7] But here the universality of the figure leads

6. E.g., ibid., pp. 238–39. For a more supple application of biblical
patterns to the figurative stances of nineteenth-century writers in
America, see G. Thomas Couser, *American Autobiography: The
Prophetic Mode* (Amherst, Mass., 1979).

7. Martha R. Lifson, "The Myth of the Fall: A Description of Autobiography," *Genre*, 12 (1979): 45–67.

one to doubt its distinctive presence in Victorian or modern culture; Lifson tends to employ archetypal terminology and to invoke universal human experience in order to explain the ubiquity and abundance of the figure. Nevertheless, one may observe a host of Victorian writers appealing to their Adamic qualities, setting their childhood in an Edenic garden or leafy landscape, and bewailing the loss of their original endowment and their difficulties in resuming a state of innocence to take relief from the busy, vicious world. In this complex of attitudes and the biblical imagery attached to it, however, a number of associated trains of imagery may be traced to other sources. The garden scenes are often couched in the language of the classical *locus amoenus*, reminding us that the educational texts of these writers were as often pagan as Christian. Similarly, the figure of the child who stands in these gardens is laden with secular attributes, which the Romantic poets had added to the store of virtues that the Gospels had allegorized with it.[8]

The Victorians, to adapt Dylan Thomas's phrase, "dreamed [their] genesis" but showed no inclination to leave their exodus and return out of account. Neither one phase nor another of the biblical process was to be preferred in imaging a life, if only because the experience of alienation and recovery was as widespread as the memory of initial bountifulness. Just as the myth of the Fall is spelled out in a complex of figures—Adamic innocence, paradisal fruitfulness, diabolic temptation, etc.—so the sequence of figurative stages following upon that original state could be variously worked out in narratives of individual life.

Yet the potentialities of the biblical sequence for providing figures in which to register the successive stages of a life do not ensure that every—or that any—autobiographer will systematically take them up. Not only the special features of each man's experience but the selective leaning of every

8. See Peter Coveney, *The Image of Childhood* (Harmondsworth, 1967 [1959]); and Robert Pattison, *The Child Figure in English Literature* (Athens, Ga., 1978).

imagination toward one or another evocative symbol ensures that the autobiographical monomyth will remain an ideal reconstruction rather than an operative design. Several Victorian and modern autobiographers specialize, as it were, in one or more figural stages: Carlyle and Muir, the phases of exile and return; Dickens and Sassoon, those of childhood and Fall; Newman and Joyce, crisis and epiphany; etc. Curiously, we shall find that certain turn-of-the-century authors like Gissing and Gosse are among the most comprehensive employers of such figures, leading to speculation that their more or less self-conscious role was to recirculate the working symbolism of their predecessors and to give it a critical new turn before it passed into the hands of modern writers. When we come to Lawrence, Yeats, Richardson, and Woolf, some of these figures achieve a powerful reassertion on the same grand scale on which the Victorians employed them.

The experience of exile from an initial state of security is often expressed in figures that have as their burden the problem of self-consciousness as the Victorians inherited it from the Romantics. In place of the traditional gentlemanly apology for excessive self-regard in writing one's autobiography, the Romantics substituted *anxiety*—anxiety that their inwardness was either unmanly (Keats), or poetically unproductive (Byron), or unfathomable (Coleridge). These anxieties did not have to await the Victorians for full expression, but they emerge dramatically among them. In response to similar misgivings, Carlyle adapted from the Germans his "anti-self-consciousness theory," in Mill's phrase; describing his own adoption of it, Mill affirms the value of "the internal culture of the individual" but adopts the Carlylian strategy for maintaining it: "Those only are happy (I thought) who have their minds fixed on some object other than their own happiness.... Aiming thus at something else, they find happiness by the way."[9] This strategy of indirect progress through

9. *Autobiography of John Stuart Mill* (New York, 1924 [1873]), p. 100; for fuller textual discussion, see ch. 5, n. 3 below. Taking up the question of self-consciousness, a challenging generalization about

oblique self-promulgation is merely a special application of the broad awareness fostered by the Romantics that though self-consciousness—indeed, consciousness itself—is at the root of our problems, having brought alienation into the world, it is nevertheless only through self-consciousness that this separation is to be transcended:

> The modern age, unhappily, has moved to the very extremity of dividedness, for "never since the beginning of Time was there . . . so intensely self-conscious

---

Victorian autobiography has recently been put forward by Elizabeth K. Helsinger ("Ulysses to Penelope: Victorian Experiments in Autobiography," in *Approaches to Victorian Autobiography*). Helsinger makes a series of distinctions among the Victorians—including a number of poets whose lyric explorations of self accompany, if they do not join, the corpus of extended autobiographies:

> The prose autobiographies of the high Victorian period, with the exception of Ruskin's *Praeterita*, show few radical departures from a tradition which reaches from Wordsworth back to St. Augustine. The major Victorian poets, however, expressed in the 1850s their discontent with Wordsworth's sublime egotism, and experimented with poetic structures which would allow them to explore a different concept of selfhood. These poetic alternatives to spiritual or crisis autobiography prepare the way for Pater's Penelope [artistic exploration that takes the form of "that strange, perpetual weaving and unweaving of ourselves," described in *The Renaissance*]. (p. 4)

Helsinger goes on to trace the poets' preference for a transcendent, "eternal landscape of the past" to the traditional conception of life as a temporal quest; e.g., Arnold's impatience with excessive self-consciousness is figured in his frustration with the image of the "river of our life" and its "purposive movement in a single direction." Eventually, Pater discovers that the "deliberate pursuit of patterns of consciousness" is "morbid, self-involved, and probably fruitless as romantic questing. But those patterns can be suggested indirectly, by using literary forms and structures new to autobiographical writing. Tennyson and Browning are the great Victorian pioneers, using fictional more often than actual autobiography for their experiments" (p. 24).

A number of literary-historical adjustments need to be made before this thesis can become workable. First, there is some doubt that the implied centrality of *The Prelude*, not as a model but as a molted skin, can be maintained. Helsinger's starting point in Wordsworth's

a Society." . . . Carlyle echoes Schiller's assertion that the culture which had inflicted this wound must heal it, and like his predecessor, he suggests that the fall of man was a happy division that will lead to a greater good. Is not "the symptom of universal disease, yet also the symptom and sole means of restoration and cure?"[10]

It is this willingness to undertake the fallen condition of self-consciousness and to express it in the fallen language of symbolism that enables Carlyle to write the seminal Victorian autobiography.

---

notion of "life as a movement in a single direction" is undermined by the evidence of circular form, substitutive places, and opening rather than closure at the point of return. Next, the rubric of Victorian prose autobiography as "a program of internal questing, identified with romanticism"—avoided by the poets through "deliberate turning outward of the self"—sounds like an account of these autobiographies' problem *and* resolution—as worked out in *Sartor*, Mill's *Autobiography*, and the *Apologia* (in theological terms). Ruskin's *Praeterita* will not be found the only "puzzling anomaly" in an otherwise homogeneous tradition of prose autobiographies.

For the final thrust of Helsinger's argument, however, a logical and affective, rather than literary-historical, adjustment is required. The reason that the Victorian poets turned from Wordsworth's "sublime egotism" is, in her view, their discomfort in the act of intense self-consciousness—a moral feeling with which Helsinger happens to agree: "In fact, Victorian critics and poets were right when they said that the quest for identity was usually painful and fruitless; their conviction that it was ethically wrong insured that they would find such selfhood a burden, and turn aside from internal quests" (p. 6). There is a curious *non sequitur* in this argument. It may well be, as the first clause of this sentence has it, that the "quest for identity was usually painful and fruitless," but it does not follow that "painful and fruitless" behavior is "ethically wrong." Certain critics may have thought so; perhaps the only poet who ever did was Hopkins.

10. M. H. Abrams, *Natural Supernaturalism: Tradition and Revolution in Romantic Literature* (New York, 1971), p. 308.

4

Carlyle's
Sartor

THE
OPEN SECRET

Carlyle was the transmitter, from the Romantics to the Victorians, not only of philosophical organicism but of its associated theory of symbolism. The new note he added to the accepted wisdom about the organic symbol was a volitional and creative one, to complement, if not fully to replace, its attributes of quasi-biological passivity and quasi-mystical unconsciousness. To invigorate a poetic symbolism that was said to come as naturally as leaves to the tree or not at all, Carlyle envisaged a universal human activity of symbol making in which not only pragmatic worldly skills but spiritual aspiration and imaginative conception were made concrete life in the form of symbols.

The strength of the transcendental imagination in Carlylian symbolism has long been acknowledged but at the expense of the Puritan element in his culture, to which it has often been juxtaposed.[1] Although the immediate influence of Scottish Calvinism may well have been as stultifying in its literalism and antipathy to fiction as some have proposed, the

---

1. E.g., A. Abbott Ikeler, *Puritan Temper and Transcendental Faith: Carlyle's Literary Vision* (n.p. [Athens, Ohio], 1972).

larger Protestant tradition that Carlyle inherited was laden with representational systems of which he could readily avail himself. Allegory, typology, and the broader mythic resonance attached to the first books of the Old Testament were part of the grain and tissue of his mind, and we have only to consult a recent summative article on the biblical references in *Sartor Resartus* to sense how close the language of Scripture was to the nub of his pen.[2]

The figures of this language were not so much normative for Carlyle as generative. They are the materials out of which he fashions a rhetoric for his thought and a poetics for his self-promulgation. After collecting the several biblical figures in which one of the Carlylian personae in *Sartor* is portrayed—Diogenes Teufelsdröckh as Old Testament prophet, Christ figure, exiled Israel, fire-baptised martyr, all-but-returned Moses, and microcosm of the macrocosmic Adam Kadmon—one is assured only of the synthetic tendency of the book's figurative mode. Neither typology, allegory, nor even a worldwide mythic lexicon will do justice to Carlyle's symbolic imagination, for it is larger and more interesting than the sum of its parts. It may well be true, as one student of nineteenth-century symbolism has claimed, that Carlyle creates a personal version of typological thinking and that his category of "intrinsic symbols," as opposed to the received and arbitrary extrinsic ones, is really a formula for traditional typology.[3] But the symbolism of *Sartor* and other high-Carlylian writings operates by superimposing varied biblical references over figures derived from classical and

2. Joseph Sigman, "Adam-Kadmon, Nifl, Muspel, and the Biblical Symbolism of *Sartor Resartus*," *English Literary History*, 41 (1974): 233–56. The fullest account of *Sartor*'s tropes is G. B. Tennyson, *"Sartor" Called "Resartus": The Genesis, Structure, and Style of Thomas Carlyle's First Major Work* (Princeton, 1965).

3. Herbert L. Sussman, *Fact into Figure: Typology in Carlyle, Ruskin, and the Pre-Raphaelite Brotherhood* (Columbus, Ohio, 1979), p. 9. Sussman's study of the roots of Victorian typology in Carlyle complements George P. Landow's claims for Ruskin's similar influence in *The Aesthetic and Critical Theories of John Ruskin* (Princeton, 1971).

other cultures, by deliberately blurring the liaisons between symbols and the systems from which they are derived, and by building up larger structures for its figural personae—of which Teufelsdröckh is only one. This synthetic mode of symbolism is engineered not only to prophetically exhibit a heroic, transcendentalist view of modern life but also to promulgate the figure of the prophet himself—which is the autobiographical burden of this nongeneric work.

The origins of *Sartor Resartus* have been so often rehearsed that they can be seen to anticipate almost any of the faces this multifaceted book ultimately reveals. It is well known, for example, that Carlyle in 1827 was writing an autobiographical novel, *Wotton Reinfred*, that deals with an unhappy love affair and conflates his experience with at least three women. To express the personal, Carlyle seized so firmly on the popular fiction conventions of the day—the plot which turns on a revelatory locket, the appearance of a mysterious stranger, a setting in wild, vaguely Gothic scenery—that writing this sublimated version became unsatisfactory, and a new set of conventions became desirable. Similarly, the germ of *Sartor*'s symbol and subject has been located in Carlyle's 1830 journal entry: "I am going to write—Nonsense. It is on 'Clothes.'" [4] But an equally decisive turning may have been made when the first version of the theme, the two articles he wrote for *Fraser's Magazine*, were rejected in 1831, and he recognized another desideratum: "I can devise some more biography for *Teufelsdreck* . . ." (p. xxv). Looking at the origins of the book prospectively rather than from our critical distance, the problem for the still struggling and no longer young author who had confined himself mainly to translation and literary hack work was to

4. Quoted in *Sartor Resartus: The Life and Opinions of Herr Teufelsdröckh*, ed. Charles F. Harrold (New York, 1937 [1834]), p. xxv. Here as elsewhere, this invaluable edition will be employed as a gathering place of Carlyle's *oeuvre* and accumulated scholarship; full references to the sources will be found in Harrold's critical apparatus. This edition will be cited parenthetically in my text.

find a language, a set of figures that could sustain the speculative thought, the personal experience, and the peculiar personality of one of the most distinctive men of any age, who nevertheless insists on establishing himself as the spokesman and prophet for his age.

Writing and publishing, then, become acts of promulgating oneself before the world, but the ironies that attend every such interaction of the public and the private self become particularly attenuated in Carlyle. Not only in his personality but in his social vision and eventually in his metaphysics as well, the distance between the individually held core of truth and the dissipation of that thought in its various forms of manifestation—in language, in journalistic or other media, in the marketplace of ideas—becomes a fall from original purity. More concretely, the would-be social reformer must communicate his radical, if not revolutionary, critique to the very society he finds blind and corrupt; the pharmacist-physician of social disease must adjust his prescriptions to the claptrap of political shibboleths—the reformer must claim to be more profoundly conservative than the Tories. It is the traditional problem of the prophetic voice crying in the wilderness, not mitigated even when the outlander (a Scotsman in this case) arrives at the babel of voices in the metropolis.

To mediate that discordance, to place himself both within and without the community of discourse, Carlyle falls back on a narrative option that later became a hallmark of modern fiction, the device of multiple narrators or personae. For his radical and alien side, he erects the outlandish image of Diogenes Teufelsdröckh to convey the mystical, intellectual, Germanic, Promethean, heroic, and faintly absurd side of himself and his message—burdens emblematized in the six bags of autobiographical fragments and the Germanic text, which he opens to the British public. To receive this burden and to convey it to his compatriots, there is raised the equivalent of Scott's dry-as-dust editor, in this case a comically befuddled, skeptical, and resistant but earnest inquirer into the vagaries of the documents set before him. It should be evident that this artful multiplication of entities for conveying the message is no arbitrary convenience or mere means, for it corresponds to the twin elements in Carlyle's personality, vision and doctrine.

Although the initial splitting of the narrative focus between Teufelsdröckh and the editor represents a structural division within Carlyle's internal dynamic and stance in the world, the proliferation of figures that goes into the making of the former persona alone reflects the infinite nuances of that face of the self. From Diogenes's initial associations with the devil and his modern avatar, the Sansculottist (Bk. 1, ch. 3, p. 16), the Wandering Jew (Bk. 1, ch. 3, p. 17), a comic version of the Faustian polymath (Professor of Things in General at the New University of Don't-know-where), the Menippean satirist at his lofty elevation above the earth (although his "watch-tower" has also been taken as a biblical prophetic one),[5] we become aware of a tropology of vast and devious knowledge, as much a condition of alienation, perhaps of original sin, as of authority and wisdom.

To this synthetic wisdom figure, severely marked by the taint of forbidden and self-destructive knowledge, another equivocal figure is added in Part II, as the biographical fragments are sifted to compose a narrative of the hero's origins. Adamic motifs have been employed earlier, but we now find a full passage of preference for the Edenic imagination of innocent youth: "a certain prospective Paradise" from which even the Tree of Knowledge is not excluded (Bk. 11, ch. 5, pp. 132–33). The tale of Teufelsdröckh's delivery to his foster parents by a mysterious stranger is, of course, straight out of the storehouse of *Märchen* conventions,[6] and he is further specified as a Fortunatus when making his *Wanderjahre* wanderings (Bk. 11, ch. 6, p. 153). Even his "unchristian" Christian name is given point when its reference to divine

5. Sigman, "Adam-Kadmon," pp. 234–35.
6. See Tennyson, *"Sartor" Called "Resartus,"* pp. 190–93 *et passim* for the *Märchen* materials.

origins rather than to fallen wisdom (re: the Cynic philosopher) is foregrounded (Bk. ii, ch. 1, p. 86). To the equivocal figure of the prophet of Part I there succeeds an equally equivocal figure of everyman, born in unknowable circumstances and pursuing an iron but imponderable fate.

The common function of these explanatory metaphors and mythological associations is to obscure as well as to reveal the hero. As Carlyle, or his editor-persona, puts it: "From this point, the Professor is more of an enigma than ever. In figurative language, we might say he becomes, not indeed a spirit, yet spiritualised, vaporised. Fact unparalleled in Biography . . ." (Bk. ii, ch. 6, p. 153). It is not only the present sentence that resorts to figurative language but, as we have seen, the entire characterization of the protagonist and the associated self-imaging by his creator. So extended and self-conscious an enterprise cannot have been made *in spite of* its evident shortcomings as a clarification. There is here at work a systematic program to obscure as well as to reveal the hero and the author behind him. Nor is this a mere sportive coyness or early-Victorian diffidence on Carlyle's part; it is well known how much trouble his *Reminiscences*, written late in life, caused him,[7] but the present mode of concealment shows less a bashful anxiety than a disciplined and controlled ambiguity. It is not to Carlyle's guilty egotism that we must account his powerfully presented and as powerfully withdrawn self-image but to his larger vision of things—to the philosophy of clothes, language, and symbol-

7. In Carlyle's closest approximation of conventional autobiography, the *Reminiscences* (1881), there are touches of the old master of Rembrandtesque portraiture but little of the volcanic energy that marked his career for better or worse. The *Reminiscences* are, indeed, organized as biography rather than autobiography, a series of portraits of some significant others in Carlyle's early life; the second longest, on his wife, gives only hints of what later biographers were to reveal about their extraordinary relationship. Even with these distancing maneuvers, Carlyle was extremely uncomfortable in the autobiographer's role and repeatedly questioned the soundness of his enterprise, even proposing that the manuscript be destroyed after his death.

ism that is the subject of *Sartor*. The thought and the thinker, form and content of the work, are inextricably entwined,
and the "open secret" is written into the portraiture—the
autobiography given/denied in the work—just as it is in the
universe it envisages.

———

Carlyle's symbolic theory has been so heavily commented
upon that a further review must aim to touch only on its
characteristic turns of mind. The consequence of the view
that "all visible things are emblems" (Bk. I, ch. 11, p. 72),
beyond its transcendentalist reformulation of a Platonic-
Christian idea, is the dual attitude that such a view entails
toward the realm of matter in particular and toward sym-
bolization in general. " 'Whatsoever sensibly exists,' " writes
Teufelsdröckh in his oracular style, " 'whatsoever represents
Spirit to Spirit, is properly a Clothing, a suit of Raiment, put
on for a season, and to be laid off' " (Bk. I, ch. 11, p. 74).
This ascetic ambivalence toward the body is extended then
toward the realm of culture, to which the clothes philosophy
metaphorically extends. Human nature is seen under the
same rubrics: " 'Nay, if you consider it, what is Man himself, and his whole terrestrial Life, but an Emblem; a Clothing or visible Garment for that divine ME of his, cast hither,
like a light-particle, down from Heaven?' " (Bk. I, ch. 11,
p. 73). The condition of human life thus presupposes a fall
of spirit into the realm of matter, but it carries the irradiat-
ing force of light, which can transfer significance from
spirit to spirit. In this double role, all cultural forms are implicated in communication and imposture: " 'Clothes gave us
individuality, distinctions, social polity; Clothes have made
Men of us; they are threatening to make Clothes-screens of
us' " (Bk. I, ch. 5, p. 41). And it is especially language that
bears the double marks of its more general origins: " 'Examine Language; what, if you except some few primitive
elements (of natural sound), what is it all but Metaphors,

recognised as such, or no longer recognised; still fluid and florid, or now solid-grown and colourless?'" (Bk. i, ch. 11, p. 73). Metaphoric language has two states, both native to it: fluid and solid, energetic and material, communicative and stultifying, alive and dead (as the passage goes on to say).

Carlyle anticipates, it would appear, not only the post-Kantian philosophy of cultural forms in Ernst Cassirer's symbolic theory but also the more ironic view of culture—indeed, of reality—in the poststructuralist theory of *differance*. Where Carlyle's idealism would part company from Jacques Derrida's antimetaphysics is in holding fast to an ultimate reality that is not deferred, that does not come into play in the course of a differential system of symbolic relations; what they share is the same lively sense of imposture in the process, the same readiness to pinprick the naïve assumptions of truth and value traditionally ascribed to mere signs. Given this corrosive insight into the mere formality of what passes as stable and natural, there should be no surprise in discovering that autobiography is a prime target for Carlylian deconstruction.

The text of *Die Kleider* in hand, the sanguine editor wants to take the style-is-the-man theory a step toward its revelatory potential: "His Life, Fortunes, and Bodily Presence, are as yet hidden from us, or matter only of faint conjecture. But, on the other hand, does not his Soul lie enclosed in this remarkable Volume . . . ?" (Bk. i, ch. 3, p. 27). The autobiographical text is, then, a place for hiding a "Bodily Presence" as well as revealing a soul, and even the latter is "enclosed." Thus, the committing of life to language entails the same dual movement and effect as symbolism in general: Speak, and thou shalt hide.

To the editor, historical specialist in biographical documentation and representative of Carlyle's professional self, there is, of course, a norm of truth for autobiography and biography. Their usual guarantees as historical disciplines are, however, broadly undercut by the satire of the editor and his opening procedures. The appeal to historical data is lampooned in the image of the six bags' full of fragments, arranged and perhaps arrangeable only by zodiacal signs. The historian's commitment to truth telling is burlesqued as a form of gossipiness when the bags' supplier, Hofrath Heuschrecke, is allowed to dilate on the popular rage for exact information about celebrities: " 'Biography is by nature the most universally profitable, universally pleasant of all things: especially Biography of distinguished individuals' " (Bk. 1, ch. 11, p. 76). And the final grace of the historian's craft, his urge toward chronological ordering and causal intelligibility, is annulled by the character of the materials that go to make up a man's totality, his theoretical work and indeed the *mental* character of his life: "Then again, amidst what seems to be a Metaphysico-theological Disquisition, 'Detached Thoughts on the Steam-engine,' or 'The continued Possibility of Prophecy,' we shall meet with some quite private, not unimportant Biographical fact" (Bk. 1, ch. 11, p. 78). The editor is wise enough to conclude his own project: "Biography or Autobiography of Teufelsdröckh there is, clearly enough, none to be gleaned here: at most some sketchy, shadowy fugitive likeness of him may, by unheard-of efforts, partly of intellect, partly of imagination, on the side of Editor and of Reader, rise up between them" (Bk. 1, ch. 11, p. 79). These words apply, *pari passu*, to *Sartor Resartus* as an autobiography of Carlyle.

The dual energy of *Sartor* in concealing as well as in revealing its author is at work in the two primary materials of Carlyle's being, which correspond to the divisions of *Die Kleider*, the "Historical-Descriptive" and the "Philosophical-Speculative" (Bk. 1, ch. 4, p. 34). That is, Carlyle needs to imbed his thought in the living tissue of his personality and in at least selected aspects of his career, in order that it be understood as the sincere expression of a committed thinker. But the synecdochic relation of thought and life may readily be reversed, as in the above quotation in which the biographical facts are found imbedded among the larger texts of Teufelsdröckh's thought. The quandary of the hermeneutic circle applies to the creator of autobiography as much as it does to its interpreter. He cannot tell his life without images, yet these images obscure as much as they convey his pure self-conception. The constriction of this circle is felt with particular acuteness when these images are the traditional figures of autobiography.

The notion that to tell the story of a life, there may be recourse to a myth or other pattern of life as found in history or legend is open to the same duality of perception and attitude as that appropriate to all symbolism. The voice of the editor merges with Teufelsdröckh's story of his life in Book II, producing a series of allusions by which the early life of the hero is both magnified and mocked. This merger of mythologizing and skepticism is performed by the editor in quoting Teufelsdröckh's Romantic version of biblical figures, yet he is willing to believe in its efficacy: "This Genesis of his can properly be nothing but an Exodus (or transit out of Invisibility into Visibility" (Bk. ii, ch. 1, p. 81); " 'The Andreas and Gretchen, or the Adam and Eve, who led thee into life . . . were, like mine, but thy nursing-father and nursing-mother: thy true Beginning and Father is in Heaven . . .' " (Bk. ii, ch. 1, p. 86); " 'the fair Life-garden rustles infinite around, and everywhere is dewy fragrance, and the budding of Hope' " (Bk. ii, ch. 2, p. 91); " 'Those hues of gold and azure, that hush of the World's expectation as Day died, were still a Hebrew Speech for me; nevertheless I was looking at the fair illuminated Letters, and had an eye for their gilding' " (Bk. ii, ch. 2, p. 93); " 'The past, then, was all a haggard dream; he had been in the Garden of Eden, then, and could not discern it!' " (Bk. ii, ch. 5, p. 143); "He quietly lifts his *Pilgerstab* (Pilgrim-staff), 'old business being soon wound-up'; and begins a perambulation and circumambulation of the terraqueous Globe!" (Bk. ii, ch. 6, p. 147); " 'A hundred and a hundred savage peaks, . . . there in their silence, in their solitude, even as on the night when Noah's Deluge first dried! Beautiful, nay solemn, was the sudden aspect to our Wanderer' " (Bk. ii, ch. 6, pp. 150–51); "Poor

Teufelsdröckh! . . . Thus must he, in the temper of ancient Cain, or of the modern Wandering Jew, . . . wend to and fro with aimless speed" (Bk. ii, ch. 6, p. 156); etc.

Eventually, biblical allusion falls away from even this qualified centrality, and the distinction between Old Testament types and modern after-types is made explicit: "It is all a grim Desert, this once-fair world of his; wherein is heard only the howling of wild-beasts, or the shrieks of despairing, hate-filled men; and no Pillar of Cloud by day, and no Pillar of Fire by night, any longer guides the Pilgrim" (Bk. ii, ch. 7, p. 161). In place of strict typological reference to Genesis and Exodus as a coherent image of the self, Carlyle yields to the syncretic tendency of his mythmaking throughout. In the three famous chapters of his crisis and conversion, he performs a significant adaptation and reformulation of the pattern of Christian heroism that Augustine bequeathed to the spiritual autobiography tradition. Side by side with the models of *askesis*, Carlyle sets the figures of Romantic self-hood that descend from classical myth. On one and the same page we find: "Did not Paul of Tarsus, whom admiring men have since named Saint, feel that *he* was 'the chief of sinners' . . . ?" and: "To the unregenerate Prometheus Vinctus of a man, it is ever the bitterest aggravation of his wretchedness that he is conscious of Virtue, that he feels himself the victim not of suffering only, but of injustice" (Bk. ii, ch. 7, p. 160). Attempting to avoid the opprobrium of autobiographical self-revelation, Carlyle has his editor dismiss these figures as "symbolical myth all" (Bk. ii, ch. 7, p. 166n.), yet with the network of scholarly annotation that establishes the literalness of many of his statements about Teufelsdröckh-Carlyle's mental crisis and suicidal despair the disclaimer becomes truer than perhaps the author intended.

Into the crisis and conversion formula, Carlyle pours layers of reference to a wide variety of symbol systems. For "The Everlasting No," there are literary models ready to hand in the Romantic context: Schiller's *Die Räuber* provides a fitting model of a tormented hero declaring the ultimacy of his will to affirm himself despite his self-lacerating impulses (Bk. II, ch. 7, p. 167n.).[8] For religious models of (potential) prophets going through their spiritual testing by worldly fires, there is a string of biblical references that needs no amplification here.[9] To these primarily Old Testament sources, Carlyle adds the Christian lore of baptism, fused with the imagery of fire that attends the Pentecost and its issuance in inspired speech. And to round off the syncretic movement of his prose, he adds a grace note allusion to Baphomet, a figure which is itself a compound of mishandled Moslem, deviant Christian (Templar), and contemporary literary texture (Bk. II, ch. 7, p. 168n.)—a sort of symbol of synthetic symbolism itself.

The most striking image—an auditory more than a visual one—that emerges from the crescendo of "The Everlasting No" is that of the Protestant mind and its chief spokesman, Luther:

> "Thus had the EVERLASTING No (*das ewige Nein*) pealed authoritatively through all the recesses of my Being, of my ME; and then was it that my whole ME stood up, in native God-created majesty, and with emphasis recorded its Protest. Such a Protest, the most important transaction in Life, may that same Indignation and Defiance, in a psychological point of view, be fitly called."   (Bk. II, ch. 7, p. 167)

Unwilling to take on himself the Romantic figure of Promethean self-assertion and rebelliousness, Carlyle finds a way to endow his individualism with a religious aura and his ego with a positive, liberating function. Having traced the Augustinian "trial of the center" (self versus soul) toward the self and alarmed by the danger of making it a self-

8. The underlying model for the chapter's title and for the figure of its implied antagonist is another Romantic mythic creation, Goethe's Mephistopheles.

9. See Sigman, "Adam-Kadmon," pp. 238–39.

worshipping deity, he avoids the Satanic implications of world defiance by casting them onto the Mephistofelian figure that underlies the chapter from the outset. In its place, he rears a figure that can say no to the no—empty of content as yet but as sure of its ground as was Christ against his adversary: " 'The Everlasting No had said: "Behold, thou art fatherless, outcast, and the Universe is mine (the Devil's"; to which my whole Me now made answer: "*I* am not thine, but Free, and forever hate thee!" ' " (Bk. II, ch. 7, pp. 167–68).

———

The succeeding stages of the conversion process have been traced by Charles Harrold and other commentators,[10] moving from the initial, blatant, but empty affirming of the self through the intermediate stage of acknowledging the indifference of the not-self. "The Center of Indifference" chapter is an assemblage of scenes of meaningless worldly existence, whether in history (the battlefield of Wagram) or nature (the "infinite Brine" seen from the North Cape). But Carlyle's articulation of the dialectical process at work suggests that his advance from the positive but merely formal self, through the merely negative rejection of not-self, will arrive at some higher positive plane ("from the Negative Pole to the Positive"—Bk. II, ch. 8, p. 182). The emergence into "The Everlasting Yea" is by way of a return to origins, a renewal of exilic and Promethean figuration, and a divestment of the figures of redemption which have been acquired in the exultation of previous struggles. "Temptations in the Wilderness!" the chapter begins and declares several times over that the temptations are at an end, the wilderness traversed, the pilgrim staff laid aside, and the possession of a promised land assured. The hero even specifies a New Testament antitype for his collection of prefigurative trials and

10. The fullest comparison of Teufelsdröckh's and Carlyle's own conversion is Carlisle Moore, "*Sartor Resartus* and the Problem of Carlyle's 'Conversion,' " *PMLA*, 70 (1955): 662–81.

purgations: " 'Here, then, as I lay in that CENTER OF INDIF-FERENCE; cast, doubtless by benignant upper Influence, into a healing sleep, the heavy dreams rolled gradually away, and I awoke to a new Heaven and a new Earth. The first pre-liminary moral Act, Annihilation of Self (*Selbst-tödtung*), had been happily accomplished; and my mind's eyes were now unsealed, and its hands ungyved' " (Bk. II, ch. 9, p. 186).

But the figure of an entry into an apocalyptically re-deemed world is surely hyperbolic—not an assertion of the antitype but a metaphorical exultation—for the hero and his author have not won through to a transcendental realm or beatific state. Indeed, the third phase of the conversion pro-cess is not transcendence but a return to the desert of this world; its vigorous cry of affirmation is not directed to a redeemer but to the conditions of life in this world. " 'Not so easily can the old Adam, lodged in us by birth, be dis-possessed. Our Life is compassed round with Necessity; yet is the meaning of Life itself no other than Freedom, than Voluntary Force: thus have we a warfare; in the beginning, especially, a hard-fought battle' " (Bk. II, ch. 9, p. 183). And afterwards? Work, the fate of the old Adam. Self-annihila-tion, the return to the desert, the acknowledgment of fallen nature, the ethic of renunciation (*Entsagen*), which Carlyle imports from Goethe, the "Worship of Sorrow," which he resurrects from medieval and latter-day pietists—these ele-ments of asceticism are carefully picked over among the debris of Christian culture to make a "new Mythus" (Bk. II, ch. 9, p. 194). It is no accident that precisely at the juncture between his conversion and his going forth to prophecy, Carlyle places the figure of George Fox, the man who made himself a suit of leather—and an autobiography to boot.

It is true that Carlyle translates Fox's gospel message in his own terms: "A man God-possessed, witnessing for spiri-tual freedom and manhood" (Bk. III, ch. 1, p. 207). But this set of values is the moral equivalent of the burden of the spiritual autobiography of the seventeenth century, one of the foremost carriers of the strain of Augustinian piety into the modern world. *Sartor Resartus* may be seen, then, as traditional not only in its figures but in its purport; what is new is its symbolic method and its grasp of that two-edged sword. Although its pattern of conversion departs in many respects from the formulas of Puritanism, its outcome is a modern renewal of the Protestant work ethic: " 'Produce! Produce! . . . Work while it is called Today; for the Night cometh, wherein no man can work' " (Bk. II, ch. 9, p. 197).

It was this image of the self—of himself—that Carlyle established for Victorian autobiographers in whatever forms they chose. Coming as it does (in book form) within a year of the start of Victoria's reign, *Sartor* becomes the paradigmatic text for a line of autobiographical novels of crisis and conversion while the most significant autobiographies of the time (Mill's, Ruskin's, and even Newman's) are written, as it were, in its margins. Carlyle's position as the "major prophet" of the age has, of course, been widely attested, and the role of his protective self-images in enforcing his claims to authority has been ably described.[11] Equally, the peculiarities of *Sartor Resartus* as a prose work have been observed since Wilhelm Dilthey's ground-breaking review of J. A. Froude's biography of Carlyle, which located the homology of form, content, and personal presence in the peculiarities of the style: "All these eccentricities do not hide the ingenious and appropriate structure of the work from a careful reader, for it makes transcendental idealism incarnate in a man, a life, and a symbolic expression of its doctrine."[12] Yet it needs to be specified that this homology is not accidentally related to the autobiographical character of the work but is of its essence.

---

11. E.g., in Albert LaValley, *Carlyle and the Idea of the Modern: Studies in Carlyle's Prophetic Literature and Its Relation to Blake, Nietzsche, Marx, and Others* (New Haven, 1968).

12. Wilhelm Dilthey, "*Sartor Resartus*: Philosophical Conflict, Positive and Negative Eras, and Personal Resolution," trans. Murray Baumgarten and Evelyn Kanes, *Clio*, 1, no. 3 (1972): 49–50.

The conversion that takes up the center of *Sartor*'s narrative is, after all, only the middle phase of its autobiographicality. The dual personae of outcast hero and mediating editor may stand as a composite self-image for the author on beginning his autobiography. But how can we redeem the third and final book for autobiographical activity? A hint comes from a probing extension of the idea of conversion in an article by Walter Reed:[13] It is not simply the hero who is converted in the crisis narrative, but the materials of the philosophy and of the life are converted from dead to living matter by the power of metaphorical transformation. The personae act upon one another in the internal dynamics of the prose so that the editor is gradually converted from a skeptical and apologetic presenter to a lively advocate of Teufelsdröckh and his ideas; and the reader is handsomely invited to join in a social conversion that is already at hand in society: "Have many British Readers actually arrived with us at the new promised country?" (Bk. III, ch. 9, p. 267). That "actually" means *now*, as the seed working toward its flowering is now in place: "Our own private conjecture, now amounting almost to certainty, is that, safe-moored in some stillest obscurity, not to lie always still, Teufelsdröckh is actually in London!" (Bk. III, ch. 12, p. 297).

The several conversions which take place in Book III of *Sartor*—from a personal to a social range of reference, from a complex view of the power of symbolism to a simpler stripping away of the detritus of outworn symbols, from a metaphorical to a sententious style heavily committed to formulation in maxims—all these are aspects of the major conversion of the self that is dramatically enacted in the prose.[14] For the ultimate aesthetic triumph of *Sartor* as au-

13. Walter Reed, "The Pattern of Conversion in *Sartor Resartus*," *English Literary History*, 38 (1971): 411–31, for the transformative power of metaphor, which Reed finds in the work's autobiographical and social-theoretical levels of reference.

14. For Carlyle's effective conversion of himself into the figure of the prophet and the succession of hero-prophets throughout his career,

tobiography lies in its enactment of the dual function of all symbolism, according to Carlyle's precocious insight—that it simultaneously hides as it reveals, absents as it presents, defers as it manifests. So with the autobiographical symbol by which this autobiography operates. Its final movement is to take away all that has been given and leave only the space of Carlyle without his substance. Like the seed of regeneration waiting to sprout, like Teufelsdröckh lying latent in London, Carlyle makes himself available for the Victorian age, but only as a potency. It is for the age to make his prophecy come true, to heed if not fully to grasp his message, to make the words take on flesh. Yet like all prophets, Carlyle can never be fully known by the populace. There must always stand between them the symbols in which they meet but which persist in their oddity and distraction. Thus, *Sartor Resartus* is the book in which Carlyle reveals and hides himself, like the absconding god whom he witnesses.

---

see David DeLaura, "Ishmael as Prophet: Heroes and Hero-Worship and the Self-Expressive Basis of Carlyle's Art," *Texas Studies in Literature and Language*, 11 (1969–1970): 718-19; see also the classic chapter devoted to Carlyle's prose in John Holloway, *The Victorian Sage: Studies in Argument* (New York, 1965).

5

Mill's
Autobiography

TWO DEITIES

———

THE LIST OF ATTRIBUTES missing from John Stuart Mill's
Autobiography is as impressive as the gathering of prose
qualities that recommend other great books. A general history of English autobiography sums up its aporias: no sensory description, no dramatic plot, no dialogue, that is, no
narrative but explanation and argument.[1] So systematic a
negation would appear to derive from an insistence on recording only certain kinds of phenomena—those that can be
labeled causes and effects—rather than from a fit of inad-
vertence. This economic principle may be derived from
Mill's philosophy both in logic and psychology as well as
from his notorious insistence on literal truthfulness. Yet the
effect of such a stylistic choice—in this case, firmly controlled
by the author's impersonal personality—may be as powerfully metaphoric as the vigorous expressions of a Wordsworth or a Carlyle. Like *Sartor Resartus*, Mill's *Autobiography* deploys figures to conceal as well as to reveal its subject,
but these are not the received tropes of Christian typology.
Rather, Mill sensitively registers the overtones and ambigui-

---

1. Wayne Shumaker, *English Autobiography: Its Emergence, Materials, and Form* (Berkeley and Los Angeles, 1954), pp. 142ff.

ties in his significant others, patiently building a super-individual resonance in one case and sweepingly inflating another to superhuman standing. The result is to mytho-poetically expand these characterizations to the status of mythic figures and to relate them to one of the fundamental myths of its century, the myth of progress. In the course of fitting out this underlying plot, the *Autobiography* renews and revises some of the fundamental concepts of the individual long held in the Western tradition.

The image that arises from the *Autobiography* is that of a thoroughly transparent being, who is nonetheless opaque to himself. There is no room in Mill's intellectual system for inexpressible mysteries or obscure revelations, and there is little wavering in his objective estimation of himself. Bitter-ness appears and passion rises sometimes to a lyrical pitch, but Mill does not inquire more deeply into himself than he can know. It is all too easy for psychoanalysts to probe a man who tells us that the turning point in his mental crisis was the relief of tears when reading about a boy who vowed to take the place of his dead father for his family—and who tells us this without giving any sign of recognizing the Oedipal feelings about his own father which the scene brings to the surface.[2] Mill's disturbed feelings may come into play, but they hardly come to consciousness, and it is not sur-prising to find that this work—made famous by its exposé of an educational system that forced a boy to perform intel-lectual wonders at the expense of normal physical and social development—was written partly as a defense, though a criti-cal one, of that very system.

Mill's rationalism has some room for myth, however, and

2. For a specialist diagnosis, see A. W. Levi, "The Mental Crisis of John Stuart Mill," *Psychoanalytic Review*, 32 (1945). The linguistic ambiguities of the text are even more compelling evidence of psychic ambivalence toward the father and the education; see James Mc-Donnell, "Success and Failure: A Rhetorical Study of the First Two Chapters of Mill's *Autobiography*," *University of Toronto Quarterly*, 45 (1976): 109–22.

the one he grasps to give shape to his own career is a synec-
doche of the myth prevailing in his society. The myth holds
that life *is* progress, in accordance with his liberal faith in
human progress through educational enlightenment and utilitarian reform. He announces this part-whole relation of self
and social progress in his statement of aims for the autobiography: "It has also seemed to me that in an age of transition
in opinions, there may be somewhat both of interest and of
benefit in noting the successive phases of any mind which
was always pressing forward, equally ready to learn and to
unlearn either from its own thoughts or from those of others."[3] There are few men who can claim so much for their
own development and not meet with derision, but Mill is
one of those men who so impress us with their honesty that
we are willing to suspend our skepticism.

The same transparency, which both lucidly manifests and
suggestively mythologizes the subject's mind, also acts in a
dual way on its objects—in particular, on the chief objective
presence in the *Autobiography*, James Mill. In spite of the
diminished instruction in religion of which he speaks ("I
grew up in a negative state with regard to it"—ch. 2, p. 30),
the younger Mill was able to perceive the strong elements
of Christian culture that persisted in the elder, despite his
avowed agnosticism and antipathy to Christian beliefs. The
first fact set down in the chapter devoted to James Mill's
"character and opinions" is his education "in the creed of
Scotch presbyterianism" (ch. 2, p. 27), and although this is
soon buried under James's movement through deist thought
to a testy agnosticism, it remains a nodal point for the intellectual traits that are later adduced. Filling in for the stern

3. *Autobiography of John Stuart Mill, Published from the Original
Manuscript* (New York, 1960 [1873, but written mainly 1854-]), p. 1.
This long standing edition—which I have checked against the defini-
tive text in the Toronto edition of Mill's *Collected Works*, vol. 1, ed.
J. Stillinger and W. Robson (Toronto, 1980)—will be cited in my
text.

father-god engaged in perpetual warfare against the diabolic enemy, James Mill deploys an equivalent root concept, one of great antiquity even within Christian history: "The Sabaean, or Manichaean theory of a Good and Evil Principle, struggling against each other for the government of the universe, he would not have equally condemned; and I have heard him express surprise, that no one revived it in our time. He would have regarded it as a mere hypothesis; but he would have ascribed to it no depraving influence" (ch. 2, p. 28). Although the father changes the valences in the correlation of these principles with the Christian god—"Think (he used to say) of a being who would make a Hell . . ." (ch. 2, p. 29)—the essential polarization and contentiousness of his Calvinist world picture remains intact.

A second feature, by no means limited to but proverbially associated with the Calvinism in which James Mill was raised, is its indifference or antipathy to pleasure—not merely of the sensual kind but with a more sweeping distrust. In both Mills' utilitarianism, pleasure as well as pain must have its reckoning in the rational calculation that attends ethical decision making, yet there is a deficiency of commitment to that side of the ledger that makes its accounting bloodlessly abstract. John Stuart expresses his awareness of this weakness of the system when whittling his father's beliefs down from an epicurean pleasure-pain calculus, through a stoical resignation to the painful side of the account, to a cynical indifference to the pleasure balance:

> But he had (and this was the Cynic element) scarcely any belief in pleasure; at least in his later years, of which alone, on this point, I can speak confidently. He was not insensible to pleasures; but he deemed very few of them worth the price which, at least in the present state of society, must be paid for them. . . . He thought human life a poor thing at best, after the freshness of youth and of unsatisfied curiosity had gone by. . . . For passionate emotions of all sorts, and

for everything which has been said or written in exaltation of them, he professed the greatest contempt.
He regarded them as a form of madness.

(ch. 2, p. 34)

Elie Halévy has established the thesis which connects the
Puritan individualism of the Evangelical movement with the
origins of philosophic radicalism[4] so that the analogy between these contemporary opponents and their apparently
opposite minds gives no cause for surprise. What is striking
is to find one of the participants in the fray show all but explicit awareness of the underlying similarity and its cultural
origins. Thus, Protestantism becomes mythologized and converted to a libertarian set of values: "He taught me to take
the strongest interest in the Reformation, as the great and
decisive contest against priestly tyranny for liberty of
thought" (ch. 2, p. 30).

A third relationship between the rationalistic father and
the deep-laid cultural assumptions which he unwittingly enacted in raising his son derives from the theology of grace,
with its strong predestinarian conviction and its underlying
assumption of all but universal depravity. Checking a youthful sign of self-satisfaction in acquired knowledge, James
Mill has recourse to the rhetoric of this theology: "He
wound up by saying, that whatever I knew more than others,
could not be ascribed to any merit in me, but to the very
unusual advantage which had fallen to my lot, of having a
father who was able to teach me, and willing to give the
necessary trouble and time; that it was no matter of praise to
me, if I knew more than those who had not had a similar advantage, but the deepest disgrace to me if I did not" (ch. 1,
p. 24). A number of points call for attention: the underlying
fatalism of predestinarianism ("fallen to my lot"); the quick
chastisement of pride in personal attainments ("could not be
ascribed to any merit in me"); the double bind with regard

4. Elie Halévy, *The Growth of Philosophic Radicalism*, trans. M.
Morris (London, 1929).

to the employment of innate resources ("no matter of praise
. . . the deepest disgrace"); the self-satisfaction exhibited by
the conveyer of these good tidings ("the very unusual advantage of . . . having a father who was able to teach me");
and the ascription of free will only to the human substitute
for god, not to filial humanity ("a father . . . willing to give
the necessary time and trouble"). This cast of mind goes beyond Oedipal rivalry and the aggression against the potentially competitive son, which might be called a Laius complex. It draws on the root assumptions of the Puritan mind,
so strongly enunciated in the Pauline epistles: "For by grace
are ye saved . . . : Not of works, lest any man should boast"
(Ephesians 2).

A final trait may be ascribed to James Mill's origins in
the Judeo-Christian tradition, but it is harder to pinpoint the
tropes by which the writer of the *Autobiography* makes his
awareness of its provenance felt. Yet since this is the most
dramatically important of the father's stock Puritanical aspects, it needs to be made explicit that this paternal rationalist is a highly unreasonable man,[5] that his distaste for pleasure and passion is accompanied by a potent sexual appetite,
and that his carefully planned educational scheme is well
calculated (not necessarily mathematically) to produce the
deleterious consequences in the autobiographer's personality,
which the text then proceeds to expose. The character study
of the father begins with a certain awe of his departures from
strict conformity with rational principles:

> In this period of my father's life there are two things
> which it is impossible not to be struck with: one of
> them unfortunately a very common circumstance,
> the other a most uncommon one. The first is, that in
> his position, with no resource but the precarious one
> of writing in periodicals, he married and had a large
> family; conduct than which nothing could be more

5. In the sense in which Gradgrind eventually declares Bounderby
to be "unreasonable"—*Hard Times*, Bk. III, ch. 3.

opposed, both as a matter of good sense and of duty, to the opinions which, at least at a later period of life, he strenuously upheld. The other circumstance, is the extraordinary energy which was required to lead the life he led, with the disadvantages under which he laboured from the first, and with those which he brought upon himself by his marriage.

(ch. 1, p. 2)

We need not rehearse the stages of the educational project and may assent to all the defenses Mill erects against his own and others' censure—nor need we discount the impressive achievements that came of it, in childhood and in the subsequent career. Yet we can perceive the dual image of child and man with some astonishment and regret: "I was constantly meriting reproof by inattention, inobservance, and general slackness of mind in matters of daily life. My father was the extreme opposite in these particulars: his senses and mental faculties were always on the alert; he carried decision and energy of character in his whole manner, and into every action of life . . ." (ch. 1, p. 25). The final judgment of this first sketch—to be complemented by the even more deeply divided encomium in the chapter that records the father's death—is particularly telling as delivered by one rationalist about another: "He had not, I think, bestowed the same amount of thought and attention on this [the practical side of life], as on most other branches of education; and here, as well as in some other points of my tuition, he seems to have expected effects without causes" (ch. 1, p. 26).

Given this image of the repressive father couched in the attributes of the Puritan deity, we are not surprised that the son's inevitable mental troubles are described in the language of spiritual autobiography. Somewhat self-consciously—for theological conceptions are not easily handled by such a thinker as Mill—he makes resort to one of the formulas of the spiritual autobiography paradigm: "I was in a dull state of nerves, such as everybody is occasionally liable to; unsusceptible to enjoyment or pleasurable excitement; one of those moods when what is pleasure at other times, becomes insipid or indifferent; the state, I should think, in which converts to Methodism usually are, when smitten by their first 'conviction of sin' " (ch. 5, p. 94). Most of this analysis of his mental condition employs the categories in which he was trained, for example, pleasure and its absence, conformable to universal mental states ("such as everybody is occasionally liable to"). But "conviction of sin," even employed as a metaphor, suggests not merely guilty feelings but a more specific violation. The question must be left for the experts whether this corrosive guilt is traceable to the son's hostility toward James Mill's tutelage and personality, for the autobiographer does not have the psychiatric terminology to tell us. But he is much more explicit on the further stages of the crisis as an experienced sequence of feelings and as an illuminating alteration of his self-conception.

The famous nervous breakdown that forms the dramatic center of the *Autobiography* is precisely a crisis in the myth of progress as well as in the young Mill's development. It is in terms of his attitudes toward social progress that Mill describes the event:

> From the winter of 1821, when I first read Bentham, . . . I had what might truly be called an object in life; to be a reformer of the world. My conception of my own happiness was entirely identified with this object. . . . I was accustomed to felicitate myself on the certainty of a happy life which I enjoyed, through placing my happiness in something durable and distant, in which some progress might be always making, while it could never be exhausted by complete attainment. . . . It was in the autumn of 1826. I was in a dull state of nerves. . . . In this frame of mind it occurred to me to put the question directly to myself, "Suppose that all your objects in life were realized; that all the changes in institutions and opinions which

you are looking forward to, could be completely effected at this very instant: would this be a great joy
and happiness to you?" And an irrepressible self-
consciousness distinctly answered, "No!" At this my
heart sank within me: the whole foundation on which
my life was constructed fell down. All my happiness
was to have been found in the continual pursuit of
this end. The end had ceased to charm, and how could
there ever again be any interest in the means? I seemed
to have nothing left to live for.

(ch. 5, pp. 93–94)

Lest there be any temptation to see these words as a political recantation, it should be clear that Mill is not saying
that he renounced the goals of progress, nor even that he
could not see others living happily in a perfected world. He
conceives of happiness as movement (or as being *in* a movement), and progress is for him distinctly a felt state of
change; any arrest of this motion, even by completion of the
task, would be to arrest the excitement of transition, which
is, for him, the ambience of happiness. In a truly utilitarian
way, Mill had strategically mapped out for himself a life of
continual happiness by setting up a goal beyond his grasp;
the sudden threat of realizing it and having "nothing left to
live for" seemed to him not fulfillment but death.

What may be gained from such a negative discovery is a
positive image of the self as process. The individual does not
possess a given nature but is always moving beyond himself;
the self is a progressive (but also quite possibly regressive)
activity, always in course of formation. Such a view of
the self as composed of interactions with others—as a continual shifting of roles or masks in response to life's situations—was later to be developed by the sociologist George
Herbert Mead. In Mead's pragmatist theory of social dynamics, which has gained wide favor in our time, the self is
not what it is but what it does. Mill, however, did not generalize from his own experience to state a process view of
the self perhaps because he recognized its dangerous impli-

cation (which Sartre was to face) that if the individual is always in the making, he is never fully formed—that the self is *nothing in itself*.

The literary and other materials that Mill poured into this apparent vacancy are too well known for detailed enumeration. The emotional utility of Wordsworth, the sentimental catharsis produced by reading an autobiography—despite an astonishing obliviousness to the parallels between himself and the young Marmontel who wishes to "supply the place of all that they had lost" (ch. 5, p. 99, that is, of the father)[6]—and a fresh recognition of "the internal culture of the individual" all serve to connect Mill with the contemporary Romantic culture which his father's eighteenth-century-type education had caused him to overleap. By the early 1830s he has almost caught up with the times, though his first reading of *Sartor Resartus* in manuscript means little to him, and it is two years until he can receive it "with enthusiastic admiration and the keenest delight" (ch. 5, p. 123). By means of these texts, a displaced equivalent of the conversion process is enacted: not by the palmary words of Scripture and associated gnomes but by the language of the poets, the seeker in crisis receives a vision of "the perennial sources of happiness, when all the greater evils of life shall have been removed" (ch. 5, p. 104). It is a secular utopia, to be sure, but, nonetheless, an epiphanic moment and a beatific state.

A key place in this conversion must be accorded to the changed standing of the previous authority figure in the newly emergent consciousness. With the challenge of Thomas Babington Macaulay's critique of his father's political doctrine laid down, John Stuart discovers the truth of some of his strictures, the inadequacy of his father's response to them (ch. 5, p. 111) and the need to synthesize strict rationalism

6. See *Memoirs of Marmontel*, trans. Brigit Patmore (New York, 1930), pp. 36–37, for the scene in all its lachrymose but palpably Oedipal trappings.

in political thought with wider experience of the living condition of men and women: "If I am asked what system of political philosophy I substituted for that which, as a philosophy, I had abandoned, I answer, no system: only a conviction, that the true system was something much more complex and many sided than I had previously had any idea of ..." (ch. 5, p. 113, that is, from his father).

Mill's conversion toward Romantic ideology in politics and psychology, under the "influences of European, that is to say, Continental, thought, and especially those of the reaction of the nineteenth century against the eighteenth" (ch. 5, p. 113), inspired his vocation to devise a logic that can embrace love and other transindividual sensations. It is a conversion expressed in the language and with the enthusiasm of converts to other creeds: "Much of this, it is true, consisted in rediscovering things known to all the world, which I had previously disbelieved, or disregarded. But the rediscovery was to me a discovery, giving me plenary possession of the truths, not as traditional platitudes, but fresh from their source: and it seldom failed to place them in some new light ..." (ch. 5, p. 118). Mill goes on in the same sentence to record his continued adherence to certain previously acquired truths, which he now saw new virtue in; but the very length of the sentence is the sign of his straining to keep everything under control even while acknowledging the illumination of the "new light." The same strain is manifest in the filial duties completed in the next chapter, in which he has not only to record the "Commencement of the Most Valuable Friendship of My Life" but also to pay obsequies to the memory of his father, who died in the same decade. The heroic portrait painted in this leave-taking is a substantially reduced one; it is largely taken up with such qualifications as James Mill's moderate position beside Bentham's in the history of their movement and with attempts to explain his already marked loss in reputation. Consigning his father to the shades in the same gesture by which he takes on the new ethos of his own century, Mill's epitaph runs: "As Brutus was called the last of the Romans, so was he the last of the eighteenth century: he continued its tone of thought and sentiment into the nineteenth (though not unmodified nor unimproved), partaking neither in the good nor in the bad influences of the reaction against the eighteenth century, which was the great characteristic of the first half of the nineteenth" (ch. 6, p. 143).

The major progress in Mill's life may be described as a shift from one authority figure to another, from a demanding and angry father-god to a goddess of loving kindness and emotional enrichment. An ideal figure of life and fruitfulness replaces a patriarchal authority of law and order. For if James Mill began as an insistent force for John Stuart's mental progress, he emerges as a conservative stumbling block in the latter's efforts to make Benthamism more humane and subtle in its progressive program. The transition in the *Autobiography* from James Mill's to Harriet Taylor's predominance represents the turning point in John Stuart Mill's formulation as a self.

The shift also marks a change of stylistic mode in the *Autobiography* and simultaneously a change in Mill's representation of himself. All these differences come down to the emergence of a more or less conscious mythology:

> she became to me a living type of the most admirable kind of human being. I had always wished for a friend whom I could admire wholly, without reservation & restriction, & I had now found one. To render this possible, it was necessary that the object of my admiration should be of a type very different from my own; should be a character preeminently of feeling, combined however as I had not in any other instance known it to be, with a vigorous & bold speculative intellect. Hers was not only all this but the perfection of a poetic & artistic nature . . . in any true classification of human beings such as I are only fit to be the

subjects & ministers of such as her; & . . . the best thing
I, in particular, could do for the world, would be to
serve as a sort of prose interpreter of her poetry. . . .[7]

The language of this mythology, even in its curtailed
version in the final text of the *Autobiography*, conveys not
only the force of religious enthusiasm, nor only the moral-
aesthetic values of the Romantic culture which Mill had begun to acquire. Its terms are themselves drawn from Romantic mythology and carry something of its underlying
world view. As Mill develops her, Harriet Taylor becomes
a literary construct whose closest analogues are not other
historical or fictional personages but the symbolic deities of
Romantic poetry—Asia, Moneta, Astarte. These tutelary
mother goddesses command the same powers to complete
the deficient male protagonist, as Taylor does for Mill. One
might generalize from their effects to the promises laid out
in Jung's doctrine of the womanly anima, but Mill's specific
model for the feminine being who could complete him lay
closer to hand in Shelley's "Epipsychidion." Not only the
magna mater and her combinatory functions but also the
figure of the poet himself, given enormous afflatus in Romantic aesthetics, comes out in the portrait, both in its vatic
and its questing aspects. In comparing Taylor with Shelley,
in a much derided passage, both the intense seeking and the
high achievement of the ideal poet are captured. This is
idealism, to be sure, not of the philosophic kind but of the
poetically mythological: Mill did not convert to metaphysical idealism but made ideals an active force in his conception
of things, particularly of those closest to him.

Such frank personification of his highest humanistic ideals
has been almost universally scorned, and Mill was conscious

7. *The Early Draft of John Stuart Mill's Autobiography*, ed. Jack
Stillinger (Urbana, Ill., 1961), p. 179; I cite this early formulation for
its tropological fullness, somewhat muted in the final text as edited
by Helen Taylor.

enough of the predictable reaction to suppress such passages as the above and yet deliver almost equally high encomiums.[8] For Mill really *believed in* Harriet Taylor, and when we put the case so, we raise the question, what sort of belief is that? It is not, clearly, belief of the same kind as Mill obtains from his inductive-deductive method or any other technique in his *System of Logic*. Nor would it be fair to say that he was simply operating according to blind faith in his personal life while eschewing all irrational forms of intellectual conviction. When he uses the term "living type," we can find in the phrase the broad supernaturalism of Wordsworth's "types and symbols of eternity" combined with a notion borrowed from Comte's "religion of humanity" that a figure like Christ is a symbol representing the highest ideals of mankind. Taylor is such a symbol, not merely of Mill's own "best self" but of human perfectibility. Her perfection as a wife or thinker is less important to Mill—as it should be to us—than her power as an inspirational mythos.

The mythology at which Mill hints is not quite as bizarre as its formulation, in his intellectual context and with his hyperbolic enthusiasm, may suggest. We get a hint of its symbolic force in his claims for Taylor's potentialities as a political leader: "Her profound knowledge of human nature and discernment and sagacity in practical life, would in the times when such a *carrière* was open to women, have made her eminent among the rulers of mankind (ch. 6, p. 131). If we speculate about the social period Mill has in mind, it seems that only the purported prehistorical matriarchy—already being touted by such anthropologists as J. J. Bachofen

8. See Michael St. John Packe, *The Life of John Stuart Mill* (New York, 1954), for a summary of the vigorous positions taken in this extended pseudocritical controversy; Packe's reasonable conclusions make the Mills's excesses appear more plausible than they do in isolated quotations. The fullest treatment of the relationship is F. A. Hayek, *J. S. Mill and Harriet Taylor: Their Friendship and Subsequent Marriage* (London, 1951)—a curious production by a great economist.

(*Das Mutterrecht*: 1861)—could serve as an illustration. Mill seems in danger of making his religious elevation of Taylor's values into a literal cult, but he manages to keep to the metaphoric plane when recalling his personal experience with her:

> To be admitted into any degree of mental intercourse with a being of these qualities, could not but have a most beneficial influence on my development.... The benefit I received was far greater than any which I could hope to give; ... the rapidity of her intellectual growth, her mental activity, which converted everything into knowledge, doubtless drew from me, as it did from other sources, many of its materials. What I owe, even intellectually, to her, is, in its detail, almost infinite. ...   (ch. 6, p. 132)

Given her powers of "beneficial influence" (to which one is admitted by degrees), of transmuting the material into the ideational ("converted everything into knowledge" including his "materials"), and of "almost infinite" obligation for salvific benefits, we may say that the conversion traced in the *Autobiography* is to the ideal of human potentiality to which his previous authority figure, with its concomitant sense of the autonomous self, was incapable of binding him.

Harriet Taylor can symbolize Mill's higher self or ego ideal because she is herself a process. She is not a moral absolute like the father but a child like John Stuart, and in describing her life, Mill has scope to enlarge upon his enthusiasm for personal progress. Taylor becomes the deity not of achieved selfhood but of the power of the human spirit to develop its potentialities. She is the model of perfectibility, if not of perfection:

> It is not to be supposed that she was, or that any one, at the age at which I first saw her, could be, all that she afterwards became. Least of all could this be true of her, with whom self-improvement, progress in the

highest and in all senses, was a law of her nature. . . .
In general spiritual characteristics, as well as in temperament and organisation, I have often compared
her, as she was at this time, to Shelley: but in thought
and intellect, Shelley, so far as his powers were developed in his short life, was but a child compared
with what she ultimately became. (ch. 6, pp. 129–31)

These claims are excessive, of course, but are saved from the
ludicrous by Mill's awe at the capacity of man (and woman) to change and grow. We need not wonder, then, that
Mill concludes: "Her memory is to me a religion, and her
approbation the standard by which, summing up as it does all
worthiness, I endeavour to regulate my life" (ch. 7, p. 170).

The *Autobiography* becomes an embodiment of Mill's
self not by forming a unity corresponding to the sum of his
parts nor by generating symbols of the completed form of
his identity but in being consistently animated by the principle of change, transition, anticipation—by the informing
principle, that is, of Mill's active life and philosophical
thought. That the cost of maintaining this sense of self was
payable in social insecurity, emotional instability, and physical awkwardness was only to be expected. Mill acknowledged this price—the price of trial and error in liberal individualism—in his ethical and social philosophy and seems
gradually to have accepted it for his own life. The political
and cultural individuality celebrated in his classic essay "On
Liberty" is accompanied by a tolerance of errors and ineffi-
ciencies in the individual's actions. On the one hand, Mill's
systematic mind continued to map out and control larger
and larger areas of difficulty in politics, economics, and logic
whereas, on the other, he was aware that the special mark of
his thought was his "willingness and ability to learn from
everybody . . . in the conviction that even if [opinions] were
errors there might be a substratum of truth underneath them
. . ." (ch. 7, p. 172). This refusal of the finished and syste-

matic in favor of the variable and modulated came about not only through the shake-up of Mill's mental crisis and recovery through poetry and love but also with the help of his writing the *Autobiography* itself. In this sense his book is not only the visible image of his created self but the process through which he came to conceive and accept himself as a process.

6

Newman's
Apologia

ALONE
WITH GOD

—

U<small>NLIKE THE PROPHET</small> who hides and reveals himself in the figures that convey his doctrines—unlike the prophet who remains unaware of his self-imaging as he creates images of his dual deities—John Henry Newman is certain that he must make himself plain: "I must, I said, give the true key to my whole life; I must show what I am, that it may be seen what I am not, and that the phantom may be extinguished which gibbers instead of me. I wish to be known as a living man. . . . I will vanquish, not my Accuser, but my judges" (p. 12).[1] Even knowing the provocation of Charles Kingsley's attack on Newman, we would be at a loss to understand this urgency of self-revelation were it not for the extreme valuation on privacy that Newman sounds from the outset: "The words, 'Secretum meum mihi,' keep ringing in my ears . . ." (ch. 1, p. 15). Indeed, this profound privacy is the most remarkable aspect of this very public man, amid all his Protes-

1. John Henry Newman, *Apologia Pro Vita Sua: Being a History of His Religious Opinions*, ed. Martin J. Svaglic (Oxford, 1967 [1864]); subsequent citations are from this text. For a commentary on the biblical values of the personified "Accuser," see the article cited in n. 4 below.

tant-style manifestoes and Catholic establishment positions. It is not simply that Newman is more remote or guarded than others; he insists not only on the privacy but on the primacy of his individual soul, and perhaps it is this superb egocentrism that gives him reason for his apprehensions. Fortunately for him, his reputation as a pillar of the Church and as a Victorian sage has blunted the imputations of egotism, and Newman's self-manifestation in the *Apologia* has hardly been felt as its most striking revelation.

Beyond the monumental character of the ego it sets out, the *Apologia* is rhetoric not merely in behalf of but in demonstration of the coherence of a life. Although checking Kingsley's charges against his gentlemanly veracity and, by implication, his sexual probity (not in performance but in restraint), the apology is delivered to a wider audience that questions the integrity of the convert, that is, the wholeness of a man who converts, changes his affiliation and his mind. How can such a man be one, be himself, be what he seems? Perhaps he is only what he seems, not plain John Henry Newman but Father Newman, eventually Cardinal Newman, a thing of forms and titles. To convert is, at root, to transform substance, perhaps identity, so that an apology for conversion must establish that the convert has not essentially changed but made the potential actual. Such a demonstration requires not logical consistency alone; according to Newman's existential grasp of the reasoning process—eventually to be codified as a counterlogic in the *Grammar of Assent*— it must manifestly involve the whole man ("It is the concrete being that reasons; . . . the whole man moves"—ch. 4, p. 155). Thus, the bold act of autobiography: an act of daring not in its personal revelations but in making available to a multitude that which is by nature alone. "My secret is my own," the Latin tag intones, affirming what must be preserved even under public scrutiny: the ultimate privacy and isolation of the self (my own).

With customary bravado, Newman undertakes to defend not one conversion but two, and it must remain an open question which of these is the more fundamental a rededication. In structuring his narrative around these conversions, in sketching a dramatic series of inner and outer contentions between them, Newman makes the *Apologia* as sustained an exercise in the forms of spiritual autobiography as can be found since the seventeenth century. The mid-Victorian literature of religious crisis and conversion is, of course, copious in fiction and nonfiction, but it is rare to find an entire life conceived as such a drama, the more single-minded converts usually applying themselves to their decisive period of recommitment. Newman conceives his life as constantly changing but always one, on the model of metaphysical absolutes and sacred beings who descend into the realm of time and change. Such self-confidence extends to the autobiography as well: "I cannot help thinking that, viewed as a whole, it will effect what I propose to myself in giving it to the public" (ch. 1, p. 15). Such a sacrifice is made only by beneficent beings whose giving of themselves "to the public" often serves to establish them as enduring images of potent individuality.

The first conversion is a Protestant one, under the aegis of the Evangelical movement of religious enthusiasm that swept the Anglican church early in the nineteenth century. This childhood phase in the initial chapter of Newman's autobiography has never been made a focus of the same kind as the climactic turning in the fourth act of his five-chapter drama. Yet this quiet prologue, the equivalent of childhood reveries in other self-writings, may be the more decisive of the two passages. Long before the working out of his highly sophisticated religion, there are the elementary forms of the religious life: "I used to wish the Arabian Tales were true; my imagination ran on unknown influences, on magical powers, and talismans. . . . I thought life might be a dream, or I an Angel, and all this world a deception, my fellow-angels by a playful device concealing themselves from me, and deceiving me with the semblance of a material world" (ch. 1, pp. 15–16). Newman has been called many things but never a gnostic, to my knowledge, yet here is an unmistakable deposit of gnostic disdain for the material world and a concomitant suspicion of the spiritual powers that would descend to deal with such a realm—either in the role of creating it or in the more "playful" role of promulgating the illusion of its existence. Even more poignant, in view of what follows, is the alienation of the self from its "fellow-angels," who not only deceive it with the illusion of "this world" but conceal themselves and leave the self alone in dreamlike isolation.

Into this splendid and yet vulnerable isolation, the thought of another comes, under the influence of the Reverend Walter Mayers bearing volumes "all of the school of Calvin" (ch. 1, p. 17). The "great change of thought" that took place in the boy seems at a distance difficult to specify, but Newman can still recall one doctrine in detail, though he makes clear that he is doubtful of its "divine source," that is, according to Catholic orthodoxy. It is the doctrine of final perseverance, the Calvinist assurance to the elect that their election was absolute, that God would never allow them to fall away from him:

> I received it at once, and believed that the inward conversion of which I was conscious (and of which I still am more certain than that I have hands and feet) would last into the next life, and that I was elected to eternal glory. . . . I believe that it had some influence on my opinions, in the direction of those childish imaginations which I have already mentioned, viz. in isolating me from the objects which surrounded me, in confirming me in my mistrust of the reality of material phenomena, and making me rest in the thought of two and two only absolute and luminously self-evident beings, myself and my Creator;—for while I considered myself predestined to salvation, my mind did not dwell upon others, as fancying them simply passed over, not predestined to eternal death. I only thought of the mercy to myself.
>
> (ch. 1, pp. 17–18)

Although another passage records the fading away of the doctrine in his maturity (along with an assurance that he was never tempted by its obvious openings to antinomianism), Newman retains the consciousness of his "inward conversion" as vividly as his self-consciousness at the moment of writing.

If we ask for the content of that conversion, it can only be the self's turning to the thought of another being in the world: the essential content of all conversion, the full affirmation of a god's existence. The doctrine serves, then, to modify what Newman already believed—those "childish imaginations" of his own unique existence, "isolating me from the objects which surrounded me"—and to add a new conviction: "the thought of two and two only absolute and luminously self-evident beings." It is the necessary effect of the self-affirming doctrine of election to entail an elector, a Creator, a bestower of "mercy to myself."

A further tenet of this faith must be underscored in the account of his conversion, and although Newman makes it seem a stray thought, one can deduce it rigorously from the first two premises of his conviction, himself and his Creator:

> I am obliged to mention, though I do it with great reluctance, another deep imagination, which at this time, the autumn of 1816, took possession of me,— there can be no mistake about the fact; viz. that it would be the will of God that I should lead a single life. This anticipation . . . was more or less connected in my mind with the notion, that my calling in life would require such a sacrifice as celibacy involved; as, for instance, missionary work among the heathen, to which I had a great drawing for some years. It also strengthened my feeling of separation from the visible world, of which I have spoken above.
>
> (ch. 1, p. 20)

No St. John Rivers, Newman's first thought is that Protestant missionaries must go off to the tropics alone; no wonder Kingsley was dissatisfied by the implication of what is required of a true pastor, both in Newman's example and in his apology for it. But the more profound implications of this "deep imagination" were to be spelled out on a larger canvas, in Newman's self-conception.

Celibacy for such a man would be more than a sexual choice; it represents an affirmation of the self's isolation from other men and women. We need not open again the lid of speculation about Newman and other "Oxford apostles," for the covert or unconscious homosexuality that has been ascribed to them makes Newman appear much more gregarious than his writing allows us to believe him. His "problem" was not men or women but *others*. Choosing celibacy was to choose "two and two only," the self and God. This sense of personal sacrifice and social separation was accompanied by an equally strong sense of identity—or, more accurately, of duality.

The *Apologia* opens a space where the self enacts its aloneness, and this negation of interpersonal narrative generates the peculiar curtailments of the first chapter, which many readers have found mysterious. The most remarkable evidence of Newman's strange complication of selfhood, manhood, and Godhead lies in another memoir, carefully preserved among Newman's papers—"My Illness in Sicily," published in a collection of his lifelong efforts in autobiography.[2] (Of these the most remarkable is a series of inscriptions in a schoolbook to which he continued to add until his nomination as cardinal.) The account of this brief episode in a long and busy career seems only another indication of the care Newman maintained for his own story and its preservation. Yet I think it possible to isolate this text as a

2. John Henry Newman, *Autobiographical Writings*, ed. Henry Tristram (New York, 1957), pp. 111–38. This volume also documents the extreme care which Newman took with his autobiographical documents throughout his life, explaining how he was able to write the *Apologia* so quickly; even the omitted material on the Sicily episode was treated to persistent revision, and steps were taken to put it in the hands of the editor of his correspondence. The quotes below are from pp. 138 and 124–25.

symbolic crux revealing his sense of the origins of his identity. Like almost every other phase of his career, this one was treated to a number of descriptions in Newman's letters and journals; the bare details include his taking ill while on a classical pilgrimage by mule in the interior of Sicily, his dire condition at Castro Giovanni ("the ancient Enna," as he points out), and his nursing by the guide Gennaro: "He was humanly speaking the preserver of my life, I think. . . . He nursed me as a child. An English servant never could do what he did. He had once been deranged; and was easily overset by liquor."

In this exotic situation (in a landscape which Newman has no reserve in comparing to the Garden of Eden—p. 123), a flow of partly conscious ideas and images occurred, and some are strikingly recaptured in his memoir:

> As I lay in bed the first day many thoughts came over me. I felt God was fighting agst me—& felt at last I knew *why*—it was for self will. I felt I had been very self willed—that the Froudes had been agst my coming [to Sicily]. . . . Yet I felt & kept saying to myself "I have not sinned against light." And at one time I had a most consoling overpowering thought of God's electing love, & seemed to feel I was His. . . . Next day the self reproaching feelings increased. I seemed to see more & more my utter hollowness. I began to think of all my professed principles, & felt they were mere intellectual deductions from one or two admitted truths. . . . I know I had *very* clear thoughts about this then; &, I believe in the main true ones. Indeed this is how I look on myself; very much (as the illustration goes) as a pane of glass, which transmit[s] heat being cold itself. . . . for I believe myself at heart to be nearly hollow—i.e. with little love, little self denial. I believe I have some faith—that is all. . . .

Lest there be an inclination to dismiss these lines as the ramblings of a body and mind in extremity, it should be recalled that Newman wrote them well after the event, in the seven years after the crisis of May 1833; he soberly affirms his delirious thoughts as "in the main true ones."

I shall not offer a running commentary on the nuances of his language (having of necessity omitted a number of intervening lines). What leaps to the eye is the sustained imagery of light used in expressing not only the mysterious formula of self-exculpation ("I have not sinned against light") but also in defining the self and its God: Newman is "hollow" (an empty space) but contains "clear thoughts" (an expression that is already a buried metaphor of a mental fact in optical terms). He is himself clear, "a pane of glass," and though he chooses to vary the metaphor by advertising glass's power to "transmit heat being cold itself," this makes sense only insofar as glass transmits light, a form of energy which converts into heat upon absorption in a nontranspar-ent object. Newman is thus involved in a profound dialectic with the deity. He is its way of passage into the world, a medium and transmitter; yet he fears to interrupt it by some materiality or heat of his own (for which the generic ethical term is employed: self-will).

What shall we say of this intervention, the sin against light that Newman congratulates himself for escaping at two other points in the memoir and twice again in the *Apologia*? With disarming disingenuousness, the autobiographer speci-fies that "I never have been able quite to make out what I meant" (ch. 1, p. 43), but he is at the same time aware of the easy transition from this imagery to the composition of his most popular writing, the poem "Lead, kindly light." The other repeated phrase that runs through Newman's con-sciousness at the time and through his memory afterward is the slogan "I have a work to do in England" and thus turns the historical drift of the mental-physical crisis toward the next stage in his career: "I have ever considered and kept the day [the Sunday following his return from Sicily] as the start of the religious movement of 1833," that is, of the Ox-ford Movement. But that initiating action belongs to Keble, who preached the famous Assize sermon, quite independently of Newman's return. What is there, then, in Newman's avoidance of the sin against light, which marks this as an enabling event in his role as religious leader?[3] We may take the term as symbolic shorthand for his faith that the determination "that I should lead a single life" has been the law of his conduct and a guarantee of his existence as himself. It is a preservation of his status as the pure medium to convey God's light, these the "two only absolute and *luminously* self-evident beings" in Newman's world picture (my italics).

———

After this crisis involving his bodily health, his vocation, and his commitment to celibacy, Newman enacts not the fallen condition of exile from meridional Eden but the active stance of the church militant. His continued anxieties, particularly those involving the social forces of the material world which tend to intervene between himself and God, lead eventually to his later and more famous crisis. I shall not retrace the Tract 90 controversy, well covered by intellectual history studies of the *Apologia*, but give attention to the private imaginings in which Newman's public behavior and religious affiliations are shaped. The decisive

3. Newman closes his Sicily narrative (*Autobiographical Writings*, p. 137) with a reference to celibacy that may be relevant to his sense of purity after the trip:
> The thought keeps pressing on me, while I write this, what am I writing it for? For myself, I may look at it once or twice in my whole life [*sic*], and what sympathy is there in *my* looking at it? . . . This is the sort of interest which a wife takes and none but she—it is a woman's interest—and that interest, so be it, shall never be taken in me. Never, so be it, will I be other than God has found me. All my habits for years, my tendencies, are towards celibacy. I could not take that interest in this world which marriage requires. I am too disgusted with this world—And, above all, call it what one will, I have a repugnance to a clergyman's marrying. I do not say it is not lawful—I cannot deny the right—but, whether a prejudice or not, it shocks me.

It would seem that Kingsley was not entirely wide of the mark in thinking his charge against Newman a countercharge.

scene of this conversion process, when he purportedly discovers himself to be (like) a Monophysite, is essentially an event of the imagination rather than of intellection or inspiration. The event hinges on the framing of a metaphor and the discovery of identity in that metaphor. Further, the narrative of the event is dramatically prepared with all the arts of narrational technique, reaching a climax by declaring its formal parallelism with the canonical model of all similar narratives, Augustine's *Confessions*.

"The Long Vacation of 1839 began early" (ch. 3, p. 108), he begins ominously. After the elaborate prolepsis of Chapter 2, in which Newman leaps ahead to the doctrinal controversy of 1841 which initiated his leaving the Anglican church, he returns in Chapter 3 to the origins of his intellectual change. Acknowledging that in his spiritual and social position in the Church he was "truly at home" (ch. 2, p. 76), he has applied the biblical parable of the seven years' "time of plenty" to anticipate a fated shift to another phase: "I tried to lay up as much as I could for the dearth which was to follow it" (ch. 2, p. 77). He now (1839) proceeds with his research on the history of the Church as a guarantee of his faith:

> My stronghold was Antiquity; now here, in the middle of the fifth century, I found, as it seemed to me, Christendom of the sixteenth and the nineteenth centuries reflected. I saw my face in that mirror, and I was a Monophysite. The Church of the *Via Media* [the Anglican church] was in the position of the Oriental communion [invaded by the Monophysite heresy], Rome was, where she now is; and the Protestants were the Eutychians [a more extreme heresy].
>
> (ch. 3, p. 108)

Two metaphoric chains emerge in this summative passage: the specular one, in which mirror imagery is used to open a view not only on intellectual positions ("Christendom reflected") but on individual visages ("my face in that mirror"); the other, a logical or geometrical figure, in which

three parties are placed in relation to one another on the
model of a like configuration. Newman proceeds to work
out the second of these analogies, with some astonishment at
the power of metaphor to reveal what he takes to be blind-
ingly literal truth: "I found it so,—almost fearfully; there was
an awful similitude, more awful, because so silent and un-
impassioned, between the dead records of the past and the
feverish chronicle of the present" (ch. 3, p. 109). He moves
on to other metaphors—"shadow of the fifth century," "spirit
rising from the troubled waters"—only to return to the main
figures: "the shape and lineaments of the new." The latter
apparition is used to designate an abstract tenor, the modern
world, but it catches up the sense of shocked discovery of
oneself and one's familiar but unrecognized face, from the
presiding sentence quoted above.

The discovery of one's face in a mirror is well established
as an origin both of identity and of alienation, and I believe
that the record of it in the *Apologia* is not metaphoric invention to describe an abstract discovery but the report of
a metaphoric illumination, perhaps even of an ocular experience. Newman goes on to worry this metaphor in the summative passage of his concluding chapter, in which he sets
out his articles of faith, speculating on a world without God
as a mirror in which he (Newman) failed to see himself reflected. He later raised the power of the metaphor by developing the notion of a double mirror in the *Grammar of
Assent*: "The mind is like a double mirror, in which reflex-
ions of self within self multiply themselves till they are un-
distinguishable, and first reflexion contains all the rest."[4] We

4. This figure has been studied with great penetration in Michael
Ryan, "A Grammatology of Assent: Cardinal Newman's *Apologia
Pro Vita Sua*," in *Approaches to Victorian Autobiography*, ed. G. P.
Landow (Athens, Ohio, 1979), pp. 149ff., where the rhetorical tactic
of arguing the case by an impossibility (*apocarteresis*) is extended to
other implications of Newman's mirror imagery. For Ryan, the figure
of the empty mirror becomes the figure of autobiography, not only in
Newman's conception of his writing as figuring himself but in a general Derridean deconstruction of the possibility of self-reference, self-

cannot follow this metaphoric chain through all its variations, but it should be clear that the climactic passage of this
autobiography is one in which the power of metaphor to
reveal the self—both in lived experience and in subsequent
exposition—is dramatized with stunning force.

Armed with the power of metaphor, Newman proceeds
to tell how it enabled him to find his true parallel, a literary
model crucial to his life decisions and palpable in his self-
writing. He reads an article by Cardinal Wiseman employing
the method of analogy he had himself begun to use but finds
that the Donatist controversy "was not parallel to that of
the Anglican Church" (ch. 3, p. 110). Yet the article's quotation of Augustine's words against the Donatists allows him
a mediated approach to his own condition: "Securus judicat
orbis terrarum . . ." (The world judges with assurance that
they are not good men who separate themselves from the
rest of the world). The logic of the relation comes home to
Newman since he has equated himself with the Monophysites
and must take the imputation of Augustine's judgment of
separatists upon himself. But the power of the words is not
confined to their logic: "For a mere sentence, the words of
St. Augustine, struck me with a power which I never had
felt from any words before. To take a familiar instance, they
were like the 'Turn again Whittington' of the chime; or, to
take a more serious one, they were like the 'Tolle, lege,—
Tolle, lege,' of the child, which converted St. Augustine
himself" (ch. 3, p. 110). The power of the words is itself
represented by two figures: one the chiming sounds that determined a man's life course (less serious because they had
become part of English folklore, but still serious in their
echo of children's voices); the other, the archetype of con-

---

presence, and good writing. The dialectical difficulty which this essay
discloses in Newman's (and any autobiographer's) project, nevertheless, makes his practical success in the *Apologia* seem all the more
heroic, for despite or because of his metaphors of absence the man is
there in his on-again, off-again figures. For a general review of the
work's style, see Walter E. Houghton, *The Art of Newman's Apologia*
(New Haven, 1945).

version effected through the influence of formulaic language. The latter establishes the strength of literary models in authenticating the autobiographer's experience, as well as guiding his writing of it: " 'Securus judicat orbis terrarum!' By those great words of the ancient Father, interpreting and summing up the long and varied course of ecclesiastical history, the theory of the *Via Media* was absolutely pulverized" (ch. 3, pp. 110–11). Augustine's *securus judicat* as applied to all forms of Christianity outside Rome becomes Newman's "tolle, lege," admonishing him in his climactic conversion.

There are still rough places to be gotten through before Newman can come into his own. There is the flare-up of the Tract 90 controversy (already told but again reported in this chapter); his further studies, confirming initial intuitions by the same process of analogy and metaphor, this time using the Arians ("The ghost had come a second time" —ch. 3, p. 130); and the personal loyalties that were sorely tried, both his own with respect to Oxford and those of his young Anglican followers with respect to their families (ch. 4, pp. 161–62). For these transitional movements and their difficulties, Newman has recourse to the time-honored language of exile, journey, and return. He had been "truly at home" in his time of plenty during the Oxford Movement but now must "leave my own home, to which I was bound by so many strong and tender ties" (ch. 3, p. 90). The movement from home to a true refuge in Mother Church, a figure rife throughout the *Apologia*, has been developed as an archetypal journey in a keen study of the *Apologia*'s language by Margery Durham.[5] Durham notes the biblical type

5. Margery S. Durham, "The Spiritual Family in Newman's *Apologia*," *Thought*, 56 (1981): 417–32. Durham's analysis of the work's figures includes an assembly of references to Mother Church in Newman's other writings, tracing this trope back to his early quotation of St. Cyril and forward to *The Development of Christian Doctrine*. But Newman might also have taken the phrase, "the mother of us all," from the *Confessions*, where Augustine relates it to the spiritual activities of his own mother (Bk. 1, sec. 11); see my discussion above, p. 68.

of such self-exile and new foundations in Newman's prefatory citation of Abraham's journey, among those of other wanderers. Another layer of reference is to the persistent sense of unease and movement, which he records: "For years I must have had something of an habitual notion, though it was latent, and had never led me to distrust my own convictions, that my mind had not found its ultimate rest, and that in some sense or other I was on journey" (ch. 3, p. 112). For a time, Newman is satisfied to take on the stance of an exile and wanderer: "And I am content to be with Moses in the desert, or with Elijah excommunicated from the Temple" (ch. 4, p. 145).

Newman's course is a flight from collegiate home and the security of fellows to the spiritual home and maternal embrace of the Church, but it is only the former that heavily evokes feeling and its embodying language. Indeed the true home is out of space and time and is best represented by a mathematical point: "Certitude of course is a point, but doubt is a progress; I was not near certitude yet. . . . Of that I believe I was not possessed, till close upon my reception into the Catholic Church" (ch. 4, p. 195). Yet this possession remains abstract, by comparison with the loss of the earlier, naïvely innocent home, in which he had lived among flowering emblems of sin and death:

> There used to be much snap-dragon growing on the walls opposite my freshman's rooms there [at Trinity College], and I had for years taken it as the emblem of my own perpetual residence even unto death in my University.
> On the morning of the 23rd [Feb. 1846] I left. . . . I have never seen Oxford since, excepting its spires, as they are seen from the railway.
> (ch. 4, p. 183)

Thus, the first paradise is remembered from the standpoint of a paradise within or beyond, happier far—yet it is still the one that produces evocations of celestial spires.

One of the root difficulties in Newman's taking on a new church, especially one structured hierarchically and laden with material accoutrements of faith, is the anxiety it raises about the possibility of a third entity in his dualistic world picture. When he deals with his acquirements and difficulties in Catholic theology, it is precisely in these terms that he thinks; for example, the Catholic devotion to the Virgin Mary was a sticking point with him because

> from a boy I had been led to consider that my Maker and I, His creature, were the two beings, luminously such, *in rerum naturâ*. . . . Only this I know full well now, and did not know then, that the Catholic Church allows no image of any sort, material or immaterial, no dogmatic symbol, no rite, no sacrament, no Saint, not even the Blessed Virgin herself, to come between the soul and its Creator. It is face to face, 'solus cum solo,' in all matters between man and his God.　　　　　　　　　　　　　　　(ch. 4, p. 177)

I am not concerned here to examine the degree to which this is a deviant interpretation of Catholic doctrine but only to point out that these are the considerations that Newman repeatedly makes throughout the *Apologia* in tracing his way to Rome. Only because the Church could admit him *with* his vigorous and traditionally Protestant individualism could Newman adopt it as his religious community.

Without malice be it said, there arises some doubt from the *Apologia* about the priority as between the two "luminously self-evident beings" of Newman's world. In the final chapter, in which his world view is set out with great power, Newman aims to derive his idea of the self from the idea of God but ends with something different:

> Starting then with the being of a God, (which, as I have said, is as certain to me as the certainty of my own existence . . .), I look out of myself into the world of men, and there I see a sight which fills me with unspeakable distress. The world seems simply to

give the lie to that great truth, of which my whole
being is so full; and the effect upon me is, in consequence, as a matter of necessity, as confusing as if it
denied that I am in existence myself. If I looked into
a mirror, and did not see my face, I should have the
sort of feeling which actually comes upon me, when
I look into this living busy world, and see no reflexion
of its Creator.   (ch. 5, p. 216)

Here the idea of the self seems to be prior; although he starts
with the being of God, that being is found by Newman "as
certain to me as the certainty of my own existence," of
which he is already well assured. On the negative side, the
self is again the reference point; the idea of God's nonexis-
tence is as "confusing as if it denied that I am in existence
myself." The feared absence of one's face when looking in
a mirror suggests some anxiety about his own existence but
turns out to be only a metaphor for an experience Newman
"actually" has had "when I look into this living busy world,
and see no reflexion of its Creator." It is God's being that
comes into question, never his own. There is thus warrant
for taking the self which narcissistically sees itself reflected
in a mirror as the model for God's reflection in the "living
busy world." It is the god of the egoists who scoff at denials
of their own existence.

In another passage, Newman seems even more firmly to
make the self's reality the most immediate and undeniable
fact and to derive the being of God from it: "If I am asked
why I believe in God, I answer that it is because I believe in
myself, for I feel it impossible to believe in my own existence (and of that fact I am quite sure) without believing
also in the existence of Him, who lives as a Personal, All-
seeing, All-judging Being in my conscience" (ch. 4, p. 180).
There is some reciprocity of the two beings here, to be sure,
but the main emphasis falls on belief in oneself—"of that fact
I am quite sure." With that to go on, Newman finds it impossible to believe in his existence alone and takes on the ex-

istence of another, who lives in Newman's mind or "conscience."[6]

If the suggestions I have assembled have cumulative force, they lead to a revised estimate of the meaning and form of the *Apologia Pro Vita Sua*. Although it begins in a rhetorical situation, in which Newman seeks to answer "not my Accuser, but my judges," the English Protestant public, it quickly becomes a self-manifestation in face of the great denier. The paradigm is that of scenes in which the reality of the hero or god is bodied forth: "I must show what I am, that it may be seen what I am not . . ." (ch. 1, p. 12). The apology is not so much a defense of the acts of his life as an affirmation of the life itself: I am that I am. If there is a hint of self-glorification, even self-deification, in this book, that is to be expected given the duo of beings in which Newman believed—himself and his Creator. The *Apologia*, which has been shown to draw its images and impulses from models as widely spaced as the confessional and the chivalric romance, may have its closest analogue in sacred books that reveal that the subject of their story lives.

I am not inclined to accuse Newman of excessive egoism

6. For a cogent account of the philosophical underpinnings of this predisposition, see Thomas Vargish, *Newman: The Contemplation of Mind* (Oxford, 1970), pp. 182ff. Vargish comes much closer than orthodox critics who have studied this strain in Newman—e.g., A. J. Boekraad and Henry Tristram, *The Argument from Conscience to the Existence of God According to J. H. Newman* (Louvain, 1961)—to acknowledging its vulnerability to skepticism, solipsism, and subjectivism. But Vargish is not—nor is the present argument—led to conclude Newman's displacement of God nor even his assertion of primacy; as Vargish finely puts their relation: "God and the self are still together, self-evident, in glorious league against the indifference, the ultimate irrelevance of the world" (p. 185). See also the entire concluding chapter, in which the conversion process in the *Apologia* is compared with those in Newman's novels and in which the sacramental or symbolic character of the process is related to Newman's egoism: "His development represents in his own eyes a kind of proof of the existence of God and the truth of Catholicism" (p. 186).

in making self-manifestation his chief aim. The marks of egoism are only too evident throughout his career and may be accepted as in the character of the man. It has long been recognized (by commentators from F. L. Cross to Geoffrey Faber) that what brought on Newman's flight from Anglicanism after the hostile reception of Tract 90 among the Oxford establishment was that after he had erected his bishop as an incontrovertable authority (in place of the pope as supreme bishop), the bishop had gone on to criticize him: "I published that Letter [of partial retraction] to him, (how unwillingly you know,) on the understanding that *I* was to deliver his judgment on [Tract] 90 *instead* of him" (ch. 4, p. 199). From making his bishop his pope, Newman goes on to make himself his bishop—with lasting effects. His ultimate fortunes in the Catholic hierarchy are racked by constant conflict with the English cardinals on just such issues.

Egoism is more, however, than personal pique; it is a social attitude as well, one that excludes others from one's conception of reality. There is very little acknowledgment of the reality of the world of men in the *Apologia* although there are tender portraits of Keble, Froude, and other leaders (followers) of the Oxford Movement. Newman's relation to society is largely a strategic one, as much engaged in maintaining the self as it is in changing other men's minds. It comes as a relief, then, that the closing pages of this autobiography glow with a warmth toward others that begins to grant them independent existence. The other men here are the brothers of the Birmingham Oratory, which Newman founded and in which he spent much of his life as a Catholic. He acknowledges these brothers (sons) on the penultimate page and devotes an entire paragraph to one of them:

> And to you especially, dear AMBROSE ST. JOHN; whom God gave me, when He took every one else away; who are the link between my old life and my new; who have now for twenty-one years been so devoted to me, so patient, so zealous, so tender; who have let

me lean so hard upon you; who have watched me so
narrowly; who have never thought of yourself, if I
was in question. (ch. 5, p. 252)

It is welcome, though so late in the book, to find that Newman can, after all, love another human being—albeit one who
has thoroughly denied himself in order to devote himself to
Newman. The self that reveals and affirms itself in the *Apologia* comes in the end obliquely to acknowledge the ideal
from which it all the time falls short: the selflessness of the
humble servant of others and of God.

7

Ruskin's
Praeterita

THE
ENCLOSED
GARDEN

FAVORED IN SO MANY WAYS in his material and cultural endowment in life, Ruskin has been equally fortunate in his popular and critical following. None of the other Victorian "prophets" may claim to communicate with a variety of readers in our day as Ruskin can—a predilection that, though I share it, I am unable fully to justify by the importance of his ideas. The present reputation of Ruskin's autobiography, *Praeterita*, is a case in point. It has been the focus of a recent book-length study,[1] as well as of a number of articles that capture the brilliance of its best pages. It has even been favored by attention to its biblical figures, especially the paradise motif in one chapter, and by a study of its imagery, which traces its ordering not in a linear, pathlike sequence but in an expansive, fieldlike dimension.[2] Each of these ap-

1. Jay Fellows, *The Failing Distance: The Autobiographical Impulse in John Ruskin* (Baltimore and London, 1975).
2. Pierre Fontaney, "Ruskin and Paradise Regained," *Victorian Studies*, 12 (1969): 347–56; and Elizabeth K. Helsinger, "The Structure of Ruskin's *Praeterita*," in *Approaches to Victorian Autobiography*, ed. G. P. Landow (Athens, Ohio, 1979), pp. 99ff.

proaches is convincing at the level of inquiry selected, whether it be a characteristic subject matter (Fellows), the metaphoric focus of one part of a work (Fontaney), or the narrative's connective forms (Helsinger). I shall attempt to combine the insights of these critics in a reading that finds their common ground in *Praeterita*'s domination by the figures of the garden and the Fall. What appears to be a variety of local motifs and metaphors achieves a wider resonance when related to the fund of biblical language and iconography, which writers of Ruskin's culture assimilated early and harbored long.

Ruskin sees the writing of his autobiography as a choice of passages through a series of flowered landscapes. In a preface he writes: "What would otherwise in the following pages have been little more than an old man's recreation in gathering visionary flowers in fields of youth, has taken, as I wrote, the nobler aspect of a dutiful offering at the grave of parents who trained my childhood to all the good it could attain. . . ."[3] Both images of memory—flowery field and parental grave—take their special force from the setting he establishes in the first volume of *Praeterita*, the garden or orchard behind his childhood home at Herne Hill in south London. This garden is a place of bounty and safe enclosure, though constrained by paternal prohibitions: "The differences of primal importance which I observed between the nature of this garden, and that of Eden, as I had imagined it, were, that, in this one, *all* the fruit was forbidden; and there were no companionable beasts: in other respects the little domain answered every purpose of Paradise to me; and the climate, in that cycle of our years, allowed me to pass most of my life in it" (Vol. I, ch. 2, pp. 26–27). In this Eden, Ruskin is isolated, but from his childish ego's standpoint he

3. John Ruskin, *Praeterita: Outlines of Scenes and Thoughts Perhaps Worthy of Memory in My Past Life* (London, 1949 [1885–1889]); I have checked this edition (now in an Oxford paperback) against the Cook and Wedderburn edition of Ruskin's *Works*, vol. 35. Citations are from the 1949 edition.

is central to an imagined universe; he "began to lead a very small, perky, contented, conceited, Cock-Robinson-Crusoe sort of life, in the central point which it appeared to me . . . that I occupied in the universe" (Vol. I, ch. 2, p. 27). Given these resources and restraints, two faculties were to become highly developed, visual observation and romantic imagination: "Under these circumstances, what powers of imagination I possessed, either fastened themselves on inanimate things—the sky, the leaves, and pebbles, observable within the walls of Eden,—or caught at any opportunity of flight into regions of romance . . ." (Vol. I, ch. 2, p. 28). And from these innocent faculties, cultivated in his "Eden," developed the sensibility of the artistic dictator and radical prophet of England for half a century or more.

Ruskin was aware of the strengths to be gained by joining exposure to nature and enclosure within stern parental limits: "But one farther good there was in it, hitherto unspoken; that great part of my acute perception and deep feeling of the beauty of architecture and scenery abroad, was owing to the well-formed habit of narrowing myself to happiness within the four brick walls of our fifty by one hundred yards of garden; and accepting with resignation the aesthetic external surroundings of a London suburb, and, yet more, of a London chapel" (Vol. I, ch. 7, p. 121). Yet "narrowing" is felt as deprivation as well as focus, and Ruskin's eventual revolt against the aesthetic poverty of English culture and against his Evangelical heritage were anticipated in his recognition of his parents' lofty dominion and of their narrow religious values:

> My parents were—in a sort—visible powers of nature to me, no more loved than the sun and the moon: only I should have been annoyed and puzzled if either of them had gone out; (how much, now, when both are darkened!)—still less did I love God; not that I had any quarrel with Him, or fear of Him; but simply found what people told me was His service, disagree-

able; and what people told me was His book, not
entertaining.   (Vol. I, ch. 2, p. 35)

Nevertheless, he conceives of his development as that of a
plant in a garden—"the course of my education was thus
daily gathering the growth of me into a stubborn little standard bush" (Vol. I, ch. 4, p. 75)—until it can expand in a
larger landscape.

When the Ruskins undertake a program of cultivating
their son into the foremost tourist of Europe after Byron,
his first sight of the Alps is regarded as a translation from
Eden to a yet grander realm: "Infinitely beyond all that we
had ever thought or dreamed,—the seen walls of lost Eden
could not have been more beautiful to us; not more awful,
round heaven, the walls of sacred Death. It is not possible to
imagine, in any time of the world, a more blessed entrance
into life, for a child of such a temperament as mine" (Vol.
I, ch. 6, p. 103). But even this accession from an earthly
garden to a heavenly landscape carries with it a sense of enclosure; just as the lost Eden is remembered as walled, the
higher realm is seen as bounded by a mountain wall—one
that connotes both life and death.

The movement from a cloistered virtue in the state of
nature to a paradise within or above, happier far, would be
especially familiar to a writer like Ruskin, bred on a funda-
mentalist Bible and later deeply imbibing Milton—one, we
might say, weaned on the notion of the exile from the garden as a lamentable yet foreordained displacement. The peculiar structure of Ruskin's garden calls, however, for further
specification. An abundance of trees, birds, flowers, and
breeze, together with nearby meadows and waters—even in
south London—marks this as a late appearance of the *locus
amoenus*, the pleasance of classical poetry, which is associated not only with amatory activities but also with the topoi
of the earthly paradise, golden age, and other utopian ideals.[4]

4. The *locus classicus* for the *locus amoenus* is E. R. Curtius, *Euro-*

But the special feature of Ruskin's garden is its wall, and this places it in the more distinctive tradition of the *hortus conclusus* or enclosed garden.[5] The topos descends from Canticles 4:

> A garden inclosed *is* my sister, *my* spouse; a spring shut up, a fountain sealed. Thy plants *are* an orchard of pomegranates, with pleasant fruits. . . . A fountain of gardens, a well of living waters, and streams from Lebanon.

Traditional interpretations revolve around the Virgin Mary, sealed yet fertile, but the notion of a beloved who closes herself yet still luxuriates in her loveliness is one that is available to much wider varieties of imagination.

Ruskin was so much taken with the theme that he used it as the title of a book, a collection of letters to two spinster ladies who were neighbors of his in later life (*Hortus Inclusus*: 1887). As his preface states, the Misses Beever were identified in his mind with a virginal and Edenesque vision: "In themselves, they were types of perfect womanhood in its constant happiness, queens alike of their own hearts and a Paradise in which they knew the names and sympathised with the spirits of every living creature that God made to play therein, or to blossom in its sunshine or shade."[6] These are the queens, mothers, or goddesses who rule the ideal garden in Ruskin's mind and who preside over his mythological speculations throughout his career (for example, *Sesame and Lilies, The Queen of the Air, Proserpina*).

---

pean Literature and the Latin Middle Ages, trans. W. R. Trask (New York and Evanston, Ill., 1963 [1948]), pp. 183–202.

5. For the *hortus conclusus*, see Stanley Stewart, *The Enclosed Garden: The Tradition and the Image in Seventeenth-Century Poetry* (Madison, Wis., 1966).

6. *The Works of John Ruskin*, ed. E. T. Cook and Alexander Wedderburn, 39 vols. (London, 1903–1912), XXXVII, 79. See Charles T. Dougherty, "Of Ruskin's Gardens," in *Myth and Symbol: Critical Approaches and Applications*, ed. Bernice Slote (Lincoln, Nebr., 1963), pp. 141–51, for an examination of similar texts.

The identification of his own past with a realm of feminine grace, natural fruitfulness, and solitary innocence accompanies Ruskin all his life. It contributes to his later turning toward a utopian vision of the Middle Ages, which inspired generations of English guild socialists like William Morris in a similar regressive tendency toward an age of presumed innocence. It is also marked by a sense of deprivation and impotence, which acts to fuel his ambivalent feelings toward his parents and condemns him to a love life whose scandals are made touching by his sexual naïveté. Ruskin well knows his shortcomings in personal relations and derives his preference for privacy from the vision of his garden:

> *My* times of happiness had always been when *nobody* was thinking of me; and the main discomfort and drawback of all proceedings and designs, the attention and interference of the public—represented by my mother and the gardener. . . . My entire delight was in observing without being myself noticed. . . . If only [the garden animals] would stay still and let me look at them, and not get into their holes and up their heights! (Vol. I, ch. 9, pp. 155–56)

Ruskin's delight and skill in observation—which are indeed the major factors in his contributions to art and architectural criticism and to landscape study—depend on the object of observation to stand still. Human beings are even more restless than marmots and chamois, however, and only Alps and frescoes can be called resolute under scrutiny. It was inevitable, then, that Ruskin would suffer repeated loss and frustration throughout his career, and with these the middle volume of *Praeterita* is filled.

The pressure on the wall of Ruskin's garden, which marks the point of fissure in his protected childhood, derives from his systematic travels on the Continent. It is one thing to collect the riches of the Occident at home in one's den and another to go forth to explore them, and Ruskin's enterprise inevitably led him into the "world" in its manifold senses. In a climactic chapter of *Praeterita*, "The Col de la Faucille," he describes the sixteen-year-old's trip to Switzerland and Italy and the approach to the break in the Jura from which the Alps are first seen from the west (his initial view had been from the north, at Schaffhausen):

> the chain opens suddenly, and a sweep of the road, traversed in five minutes at a trot, opens the whole Lake of Geneva, and the chain of the Alps along a hundred miles of horizon.
> . . . the Col de la Faucille, on that day of 1835, opened to me in distinct vision the Holy Land of my future work and true home in this world. My eyes had been opened, and my heart with them, to see and to possess royally such a kingdom!
> (Vol. I, ch. 9, p. 157)

Where the previous view of the Alps had been emblematized as yet another wall—with associations of "lost Eden" and the "walls of sacred Death"—the sense of discovering them anew is here expressed by variations on the word "opening." *Traductio* is twice employed to render the opening not only of the mountains but of the view, not only the future career but the sense of revelation. Biblical figures and religious terminology are rife: "vision of the Holy Land" (pilgrimage), "future work and true home" (vocation), and royal possession of "such a kingdom" (restoration or redemption). Rather than a "blessed entrance into life, for a child of such a temperament," as in the previous Alpine encounter, Ruskin here anticipates the onset of maturity and his formation as a seeker, worker, and heroic inheritor.

Events of the next years present a number of occasions for growth, and *Praeterita* dutifully lists them but with the memory of much trepidation. Sex becomes a challenge when the four daughters of the elder Ruskin's partner, the vintner Pedro Domecq, are put before him: "How my parents could allow their young novice to be cast into the fiery furnace of the outer world in this helpless manner the reader may wonder, and only the Fates know; but there was this excuse for them, that they had never seen me the least interested or anxious about girls . . ." (Vol. I, ch. 10, p. 169). After his attraction to and put-down by Adèle Domecq, the Ruskins parade other well-bred and sensitive girls before their son with alarming consequences. After he shows these girls scant attention, they are led into pragmatic marriages or remain unloved; in either case, they shrivel up and die:

> I cannot be sure of the date of either Miss Withers'
> or Miss Wardell's death; that of Sybilla Dowie (told
> in Fors [*Clavigera*]), more sad than either, was much
> later. . . . I had never myself seen Death, nor had any
> part in the grief or anxiety of a sick chamber. . . . But
> I had been made to think of it; and in the deaths of
> the creatures whom I had seen joyful, the sense of
> deep pity, not sorrow for myself, but for them, began
> to mingle with all the thoughts, which, founded on
> the Homeric, Æschylean, and Shakespearian tragedy,
> had now begun to modify the untried faith of child-
> hood.   (Vol. I, ch. 12, p. 218)

Ruskin's experience is still more literary than personal, but it is rendered more serious by the knowledge of other beings within his garden.

When Ruskin's own health is threatened, another trip to Italy is prescribed, but his deeper penetration of that peninsula encourages neither a *dolce far niente* nor a sure sense of possession. His first exposures to Florence, Rome, and Naples are uniformly distasteful, and his farthest progress south, to Mount Vesuvius, is a descent into hell: "In the same literal way in which the snows and Alpine roses of Lauterbrunnen were visible Paradise, here, in the valley of ashes and throat of lava, were visible Hell. If thus in the natural, how else should it be in the spiritual world?" (Vol. II, ch. 3, pp. 261–62). On the return trip, he again coughs up dark blood and his "father's face was very grave," but death withdraws its personal attentions, and return to the Alps brings renewal of his sense of election: "I had found my life again;—all the best of it. What good of religion, love, admiration or hope, had ever been taught me, or felt by my best nature, rekindled at once; and my line of work, both by my own will and the aid granted to it by fate in the future, determined for me. I went down thankfully to my father and mother, and told them I was sure I should get well" (Vol. II, ch. 3, p. 269).

This feeling of divine ordination marks Ruskin's choice of a career as moralist and aesthetician. He receives several abrupt and decisive revelations that set his course in drawing, painting, and architecture. Back in England, he learns to draw not something "composed" but "what was really there!" and marks the moment with an organic metaphor: "I was neither so crushed nor so elated by the discovery as I ought to have been, but it ended the chrysalid days" (Vol. II, ch. 4, p. 281). To make up for his inadequate response to Venice and Venetian painting, an artist friend points out to him the technique that makes Veronese "greater in manner" than his favorites: "From that moment, I saw what was meant by Venetian colour . . ." (Vol. II, ch. 5, p. 307). And on his next trip to Italy he makes a new response to architectural form (as has been explained by the architectural historian Stefan Muthesius)[7]—"and thereon literally *began* the study of architecture" (Vol. II, ch. 6, p. 319).

Toward these initiations, the autobiographer—writing with a knowledge of their consequences—maintains a consistent ambivalence. His discoveries started him on his lifework, he began to perceive truly or to confirm the truth of his perceptions, he was providentially reserved for his prophetic role, yet he lost a garden and its happy childhood. The topos that hovers on the verge of articulation in these ambivalent retrospects is that of bitter knowledge, the acces-

7. Stefan Muthesius, *The High Victorian Movement in Architecture: 1850–1870* (London and Boston, 1972), pp. 26–38.

sion to the truth by loss of innocence—"and O yet happiest if ye seek / No happier state, and know to know no more" (*Paradise Lost*, Bk. IV, lines 774–75). On learning the limitations of his early favorites Samuel Prout and Copley Fielding, seeing the paintings Turner exhibited in 1836 in his "later manner," and reading the derogatory article in *Blackwood's* (which moved him to begin *Modern Painters*), he can write: "The review raised me to the height of 'black anger' in which I have remained pretty nearly ever since . . ." (Vol. I, ch. 12, p. 203). And so it is with other maturations: "On the journey of 1837, when I was eighteen, I felt, for the last time, the pure childish love of nature which Wordsworth so idly takes for an intimation of immortality. . . . It is a feeling only possible to youth, for all care, regret, or knowledge of evil destroys it . . ." (Vol. I, ch. 12, p. 204).

Concerning religious knowledge, Ruskin shows the same mixed feelings: "The full happiness of that time to me cannot be explained. . . . For the world appeared to me now exactly right. . . . And I expected to bring everybody to be of my opinion, as soon as I could get out my second volume [of *Modern Painters*]; and drove down to Pisa in much hope and pride, though grave in both. . . . Yet at this moment I pause to think what it was that I found" (Vol. II, ch. 6, p. 319). "What it was" was the essentials of Christianity as portrayed on the walls of another enclosed garden, the Campo Santo cemetery—although neither Christian doctrine nor the "triumph of Death" (as some of these frescoes are called) was a "new thought to me." It is the knowledge of sin and men's guilty consciousness of it that comes as a surprise: "There is one fact, and no question at all, concerning the Judgment, which was only at this time beginning to dawn on me, that men had been curiously judging *themselves* by always calling the day they expected, 'Dies Irae,' instead of 'Dies Amoris' " (Vol. II, ch. 6, p. 322). He takes to reading Shakespeare with the same regret at the disclosure of moral complexity: "As I try to follow the clue of Shakespearian power over me since, I cannot feel that it has been anywise wholesome for me to have the world represented as a place where, for that best sort of people, everything always goes wrong; or to have my conceptions of that best sort of people so much confused by images of the worst" (Vol. II, ch. 7, pp. 337–38).

Even the discovery of Tintoretto at Venice—a watershed for his lifelong critique of the Renaissance—is seen as a deviation from an original and rightful endowment:

> But Tintoret swept me away at once into the "mare maggiore" of the schools of painting which crowned the power and perished in the fall of Venice; so forcing me into the study of the history of Venice herself; and through that into what else I have traced or told of the laws of national strength and virtue. I am happy in having done this so that the truth of it must stand; but it was not my own proper work; and even the sea-born strength of Venetian painting was beyond my granted fields of fruitful exertion.
> (Vol. II, ch. 7, pp. 340–41)

In summing up this period of awakening and setting forth, Ruskin sees it as loss and damnation: "That happy sense of direct relation with Heaven. . . . Whether I was capable of holding it or not, I cannot tell; but little by little, and for little, yet it seemed invincible, causes, it passed away from me. I had scarcely reached home in safety before I had sunk back into the faintness and darkness of the Under-World" (Vol. II, ch. 7, p. 346).

———

As if to confirm his sense of exile from an original home, it was no longer the garden of Herne Hill to which he returned. With proper bourgeois expansiveness, the Ruskins had moved to a bigger house and, of course, a bigger garden: "The Herne Hill days, and many joys with them, were now ended. Perhaps my mother had sometimes—at Hampton

Court, or Chatsworth, or Isola-Bella—admitted into her quiet
soul the idea that it might be nice to have a larger garden"
(Vol. II, ch. 4, p. 286). So the house is bought, the grounds
beautified and even turned into a genteel farm, the earth
newly possessed and progressively worked: "But, for all
these things, we never were so happy again. Never any more
'at home'" (Vol. II, ch. 4, p. 287). The new house is called
Denmark Hill, and with broad irony Ruskin marks his next
phase with the chapter title "The State of Denmark" (Vol.
II, ch. 8).

In tracing this passage from innocence to experience,
Ruskin has recourse to a metaphor closely associated with
the figures of Eden and the Fall: that of religious seclusion
as in "a fugitive and cloistered virtue." His account of the
first prospects of sexual maturity leads him to compare his
protected state with that of the Domecq girls: he was "vir-
tually convent-bred more closely than the maids themselves"
(Vol. I, ch. 10, p. 169). Initiation to the truths that Italy had
to teach does not immediately expel him from such isolation; at Pisa, despite the lessons of sin and death, he takes the
Campo Santo as another happy enclosure, adding to it "another lovely cloister . . . the cloister of San Francesco: in
these, and in the meadow round the baptistery, the routine
of my Italian university life was now fixed . . ." (Vol. II, ch.
6, p. 324). The "university" metaphor adds point to the detailed account of his "monkish discipline" that follows: his
college is a cloister all to himself. Again, when taking a rustic
cottage near Monte Rosa, where he stations himself to add
the Italian Alps to his collection (and where he suffers the
knowledge of Shakespearean tragedy), he is so snugly provided with interior comforts and external views that he can
describe it as "my mossy cell of Macugnaga" (Vol. II, ch. 7,
p. 337).[8]

8. Another Ruskin description of this retreat shows him fully conscious of his passage from innocence to experience; see *Ruskin in Italy:
Letters to his Parents, 1845*, ed. H. I. Shapiro (Oxford, 1972), pp. 161–

Yet on a later journey to the Alps, arriving at the most famous of upland monasteries, "a word was said, of significance enough to alter the courses of religious thought in me, afterwards for ever" (Vol. III, ch. 1, pp. 441ff.). Patronizing the Carthusian monk who shows him round the bare and unaesthetic Grand Chartreuse, Ruskin comments on the "effect of the scene outside upon religious minds. Whereupon, with a curl of his lip, 'We do not come here,' said the monk, 'to look at the mountains.' Under which rebuke I bent my head silently, thinking however all the same, 'What then, by all that's stupid, do you come here for at all?' " This insight into the severe limitations of the cloistered point of view begins a train of speculation not only about the religious mind but about the monks and nuns he has known, leading to the discovery that he is not cut out for monkish seclusion. Recalling a sister at the "summit of the isolated peak of lava at Le Puy," with her radiant certainty of salvation, he concludes: "It has always seemed to me that there was no entering into that rest of hers but by living on the top of some St. Michael's rock too, which it did not seem to me I was meant to do, by any means." This trail of associations leads him to recount his variety of religious experiences in "Liberal" (F. D. Maurice's Broad Church) and "Puritan" (Evangelical) congregations—in one of which his probing question is received as if he were "the serpent having, somehow, got over the wall into their Garden of Eden" (Vol. III, ch. 1, p. 454). It is clear from the famous finale of his "un-conversion" at the gloomy chapel of a small Italian Protestant sect that Ruskin fell out of communion not with Christianity but with a Christian community marked, like the Carthusian monk, by incomprehension of all outside the walls:

---

63. In its recapitulation of the themes of childhood felicity, hermitage, enclosed garden or happy valley, darkening and disappointment, recalled early associations ("home feeling"), and generalized preference for youthful insouciance over adult responsibility, this letter may stand as a synecdochic equivalent of the larger process traced in *Praeterita*.

I walked back into the condemned city [Turin], and up into the gallery where Paul Veronese's Solomon and the Queen of Sheba glowed in full afternoon light. . . . And as the perfect colour and sound [of a military band] gradually asserted their power on me, they seemed finally to fasten me in the old article of Jewish faith, that things done delightfully and rightly were always done by the help and in the Spirit of God. (Vol. III, ch. 1, pp. 460–61)

Ruskin emerges from his cloistered innocence with a rejection of asceticism and an equal affirmation of the craftsman ethic; he is well on his way to the socioaesthetic doctrines of *The Stones of Venice* and, ultimately, the socialistic economics of *Unto This Last.* But the personal consequence of losing his evangelical beliefs and the other securities of his childhood is a long tale of unsettling encounters with sexuality, religious melancholy, and manic-depressive illness. *Praeterita* stops its more or less chronological account at this point, and the remaining three chapters are filled with random memories, mainly of friends and books. Yet their very disorder is the significant mark of disturbed life and eventually disordered mind. The subsequent religious fluctuations that left him bereft of his habitual enthusiasm, his absurdly immature and shamefully broken marriage (although this does not enter into *Praeterita*), his love for a child named Rose La Touche and its disastrous effects on her mental balance—such experiences might well have given Ruskin the fixed impression that the loss of Eden was no myth but stark reality. Yet except for his depressive anxiety about the gradual darkening of the sun and increase of storm clouds in the nineteenth century, Ruskin does not maintain his vision of the Fall either in his own life or in that of mankind. Instead, in the closing chapter of his autobiography (the last that madness would allow him to write), he pays homage to the cousin who nursed him through his episodes and through her (and Rose La Touche) returns imaginatively to the garden of his childhood:

> I draw back to my own home [Brantwood], . . . permitted to thank Heaven once more for the peace, and hope, and loveliness of it, and the Elysian walks with Joanie, and Paradisiacal with Rosie, under the peach-blossom branches by the little glittering stream which I had paved with crystal for them. . . . "Eden-land" Rosie calls it sometimes in her letters.
>
> (Vol. III, ch. 4, pp. 525–26)

At this instancing of an architecturally designed recovery of the garden of his past, Ruskin stops writing, though he lived on for another eleven years. It may well be, as John Rosenberg has observed,[9] that as it approached the present, *Praeterita* became more difficult to write so that Ruskin changed direction and began to write backward toward his childhood. But this familiar geriatric turning or second childhood is distinctively expressed in Ruskin's case as a return to home, Eden, and a garden compounded of nature and art. In this return to origins and withdrawal into a carefully crafted space of memory, Ruskin identifies himself with his enclosed garden; and he creates, by writing *Praeterita*, an enclosure for his autobiographical imagination.

9. John Rosenberg, *The Darkening Glass: A Portrait of Ruskin's Genius* (New York, 1961), pp. 7ff.; see also Claudette K. Columbus, "Ruskin's *Praeterita* as Thanatography," in *Approaches to Victorian Autobiography*, p. 127n., for a Lacanian explanation using the language of Genesis.

PART III

The
Fictions of
Autobiographical
Fiction

——

ONE OF THE MOST OBVIOUS OBJECTIONS to the autobiographical novel is that it is too easy. Every writer has an overriding interest in his own development, and ever since Rousseau and Wordsworth many have conceived the story of their lives as an epic struggle against inner and outer forces. By casting these heroics in the form of fiction, the stage is set in favor of the autobiographer, who acts as both narrator and protagonist, unique source of information, and manipulator of point of view. The poet Stephen Spender decided to write autobiography and not fiction, he tells us, for just these reasons, refusing to hide behind a created hero who would represent—and cover up for—himself. He also refused the sympathy of readers who tend to identify themselves with a fictional hero; unlike a novel, "the autobiography would not allow [Spender] to escape from the harsh reality of himself, and would not invite the reader to forget his real existence. . . ."[1]

With these strategic advantages of the autobiographical novelist in mind, we can, however, take another view of his enterprise. Success in such fiction may be measured precisely by the degree to which the writer resists his temptations to self-magnification. To do this, he will create a fiction that is not simply a stylized version of the messiness of life

1. Stephen Spender, *World Within World: The Autobiography of Stephen Spender* (London, 1951), p. 310; see also Roy Pascal, *Design and Truth in Autobiography* (Cambridge, Mass., 1960), p. 163.

and a hero who is not simply an idealization of self. There may be even greater difficulty in resisting the temptation to extravagant self-denigration, as in certain contemporary examples of the form, like Philip Roth's Portnoy or Saul Bellow's Herzog. The reader of autobiographical novels must keep a wary eye on their figuration to see that it is not a case of the tailor becomingly retailored, but a freshly conceived man, or figure of the man.

If this construction of a self is to avoid self-indulgent distortion, a number of centers of interest must be established along with the central figure. Characters, locales, situations all serve to modulate an overcharged preoccupation with the individual's internal life. It is also possible to see an inherent structural relationship in autobiographical fiction, which acts to place the hero in a dimension larger than his sole self. This structure arises from the peculiarities of point of view in the narration of autobiographical novels and may best be approached by comparison with other narrative forms. A simple distinction between autobiographies and memoirs might be based on the double focus of the former; although both kinds of writing (between which no absolute discrimination can be made) narrate the past acts of a first-person figure from the point of view of a presently writing "I," in memoirs the focus of attention is almost always on the I-past whereas autobiography derives much of its interest from the complications generated by the interplay of I-past and I-present. Exceptions will come to mind, but the perspectival structure of a present writer commenting on his past self calls for our undivided attention to the dual focus of autobiography.[2]

2. The subject has been treated with enormous refinement, but without ultimate clarification, in the title essay of Philippe Lejeune's *Le Pacte autobiographique* (Paris, 1975); and in his "Autobiography in the Third Person," *New Literary History*, 9 (1977): 27–50, Lejeune stretches his strict demarcations of autobiography and fiction by developing a list of stylistic and grammatical "figures" (and of what he calls "fictive fictions"), which introduce multiple points of view into autobiographical discourse.

In autobiographical novels, one comes upon a phenomenon that has been widely perceived in fiction generally: the "implied author," whom Wayne Booth describes as the imagined figure generated by the novel as a whole.[3] This is neither the protagonist nor the narrative persona of the work, no more than it is its historical author, who lurks somewhere in another mode of being than that of his creation. Although fictions are busily employed in the course of every autobiography—being perhaps in the nature of writing and certainly in that of self-writing—in autobiographical novels this fictional construct becomes foregrounded. The dual autobiographical foci, I-past and I-present, and the distinction between subject and object, narrator and protagonist, are complicated by this third focus of a novel's activity. In both autobiographies and autobiographical novels, a presently writing persona narrates the acts and thoughts of a past personage—the same person in autobiography and often so in autobiographical novels, unless an omniscient narrator or "reflector" is employed. In every case, perspectival interest derives from the interpretations, figurations, and even distortions of the narrative voice, but only in fiction does a third personage arise from the entire narrative situation, taking in the narrator, the protagonist, and all the other figures of the work. Whereas in autobiography a writer makes a figurative representation of himself as he was (sometimes also as he is), in an autobiographical novel a writer creates a figurative version of himself as the sum of narrator, protagonist, and other fictional artifacts.[4] In self-writings where the narrator as well

3. Wayne Booth, *The Rhetoric of Fiction* (Chicago, 1961), pp. 71–75 *et passim*.

4. William C. Spengemann, *The Forms of Autobiography: Episodes in the History of a Literary Genre* (New Haven and London, 1980), pp. 119ff., reaches similar views of the wide resources of autobiographical novels (*David Copperfield*, *The Scarlet Letter*[!]), scarcely distinguishing them from the "allegorical" language and "fictive metaphors" operating in autobiographies (Carlyle, De Quincey). Spengemann's historical thesis on these nineteenth-century works sees them

as the protagonist is elaborately figured (*Sartor*, Gissing's *Ryecroft*), this distinction will tend to break down, and there will be difficulty in deciding whether to place the work among autobiographies or on the fiction shelf.

In neither mode should the creation of a figure of the self be thought of as a literal representation of the true identity of the author.[5] A verbal artifact *is and is not* commensurate with its author; as a symbol it is both a dynamic equivalent of the self and a shabby substitute for the richness of the experiencing life. A number of Continental thinkers, including the philosopher Wilhelm Dilthey, the psychoanalyst Ludwig Binswanger, and the Marxist (at least the early-Marxist) Georg Lukàcs have entertained the notion that an author is changed and "interpreted by" his own work, that he relinquishes his endowed self in order to grow and find his "genuine" self, and that this expansion occurs in and by means of the work. Paul de Man has carried us a step further in appreciating this process by pointing out the problems it involves for the author. The creation of a self is no sanguine success story but a fearful projection of oneself into inauthenticity, into role playing, and into dilution of one's subjectivity in an artificial object: "The distinction between the personal self of the author and the self that

---

as regrettably fallen from his canonical models of autobiography, which search for "true being," but this distinction is vitiated by the discovery of imaginative fictions—at the service of the "ultimate purposes of autobiography," to be sure—in Augustine, Dante, and Bunyan. Despite Spengemann's keen insight into autobiography's fictional means of allegorizing the self, his genre definitions are grounded largely in ontological categories (e.g., "absolute self"). A more interesting distinction for this historical thesis is the shift in relations between narrator and protagonist described on p. 115.

5. For a similar view of autobiography and autobiographical fiction as symbolic constructions, see Susanne Langer, *Feeling and Form: A Theory of Art* (New York, 1953) pp. 296–97—yet Langer finds that all but a few such novels fail to symbolically transform their biographical "raw materials."

achieves a measure of totality in the work becomes concretely manifest in these divergent destinies. . . . Art originates in and by means of this divergence."[6] Here the tension between the times of action and of writing, between the languages of history and of personal discourse, between the processes of self-creation and of memoir recording is stretched by an even more sweeping dichotomy that transcends autobiographical fiction and finds its way into all art: "The work must become a project aimed towards an unreachable goal and its partial success takes on the form of 'a renunciation at the very moment when it comes into being' " —as de Man concludes, following Lukàcs. That a number of novelists have made this effort and experienced the renunciation it entails is testimony not to the excessive easiness but to the surpassing difficulty and worth of the autobiographical enterprise.

Whether it is a sign of surpassing difficulty or excessive ease, the fact remains that almost all the great Victorian novelists attempted the autobiographical novel. The details of personal history in these works are usually held to a minimum, often amounting only to the *donnée* of a vocational situation (Trollope's post office experience in *The Three Clerks*),[7] an emotional entanglement (Thackeray's intensely

6. Paul de Man, *Blindness and Insight: Essays in the Rhetoric of Contemporary Criticism* (New York, 1971), p. 41; the quotation that follows is from p. 43.

7. Trollope's main act of self-writing, *An Autobiography* (1873), has had a rocky row to hoe and is not much helped by current interests in it. The chorus of objections to its frank shop talk of the professional writer would constitute material for a documentary history of the romantic idea of the artist. Such recent work as Walter M. Kendrick, *The Novel-Machine: The Theory and Fiction of Anthony Trollope* (Baltimore and London, 1980), attempts to transcend older attitudes by landing on new ones in which the author disappears in his text—the autobiography serving as a theoretical work on the practice of realism, with little attention even to the figure of the author raised by Kendrick's title. Meanwhile the book goes unacknowledged as one of the most poignant evocations of the Victorian theme of the little

ambivalent feelings about maternal and other forms of love in *Pendennis*), or a family background (Meredith's equally ambivalent feelings about his origins in middle-class tailordom in *Evan Harrington*). Although later phases of the hero's career may pick up further details of the writer's life (Thackeray's journalism career, Meredith's courtship of a wealthy young lady), many of these novels move with no certain strides toward totalization of the autobiographical figure. Indeed, greater personal investment is often to be found in other works not at all autobiographical in plot (*Henry Esmond*, *The Adventures of Harry Richmond*). Yet even when we exclude the arguable cases, like Hardy's *Jude the Obscure* and Meredith's *Ordeal of Richard Feverel*, there remains an impressive body of fully wrought autobiographical novels lying close to the major strain of Victorian fiction. To explore *David Copperfield*, *Villette*, *The Mill on the Floss*, and *The Way of All Flesh* in some detail is at once to exhibit the figurative workings of autobiographic art and to underscore the central place of such novels in the great tradition of Western fiction.

Despite appearances, the Victorian autobiographical novel was not native to the period or to the minds that produced it but, like all cultural institutions, had to be learned. The evident place to locate its school is the same as that for other developments in fiction, the eighteenth-century novel. When we read the full title of Dickens's periodical publication, *The Personal History, Adventures, Experience, & Observation of David Copperfield the Younger of Blunderstone Rookery. (Which He never meant to have Published on any Account.)*,[8] we may readily distinguish the conventional,

---

boy lost and as an outstanding act of self-penetration into the persistence of childhood anxieties in strategies for gaining security through writing.

8. Compare *The History of Pendennis: His Fortunes and Misfortunes, His Friends and His Greatest Enemy*, where the categories are strictly of the eighteenth century and preclude the self-inspection and character change of Copperfield's "Experience & Observation."

the modulated and the countergeneric elements of the work, its debts to its predecessors, and its transcendence of them.

While there were few autobiographical novels in the preceding century, there was an intensive production of works that look much like them, which have been called pseudoautobiographical novels. Although the term is open to cavils, it is useful in describing, for example, the peculiarly dissociated and determinedly superficial self-presentation of Moll Flanders, whose text has been called an imitation of a "naïve incoherent autobiography, a story really told by a real person like Moll."[9] The effort in such works is to create credibility by their likeness to authentic works of personal report and historical documentation, an effect gained not only by the verifiability of their content but by the rhetorical power of their tropes. The refinement of such illusion making, which gains its effect from its resemblance to the diction and tactics of ordinary people reporting their experience, has been held to lie at the origins of the realist tradition. Yet the sophistication of these techniques far exceeded the requirements of an illusionist surface texture and readily lent itself to the growth of Victorian and modern fiction by its probing of states of mind or internal action.

The close relationship between fiction, realism, and autobiographical art has usually been traced to the activity of eighteenth-century imitators of history and personal narrative, but another view of the relation suggests the reciprocity of all these enterprises:

> modern autobiography was not born in a break with traditional biography . . . but simply in the wake of the appearance of a new biographical form, the autobiographical novel. . . . In the case of fictional discourse, in particular, the use [of biographical formulas] is extremely seminal, because the novel of

9. Ralph Rader, "Defoe, Richardson, Joyce, and the Concept of Form in the Novel," in *Autobiography, Biography, and the Novel,* ed. Ralph Rader and William Matthews (Los Angeles, 1973), p. 41.

experience imitated a situation of interiority on the fictional level—actually the same situation as the autobiographer's. . . . here, too, authenticity began to be imitated in the novel before it was retrieved and interiorized by autobiographers: the autobiographer came into his own only by imitating [novelists] as they imagined what it was to be an autobiographer.[10]

If this account be taken to apply to English as to French developments, there emerges an even pattern of mutual influence (though undoubtedly more complex in reality). The earlier biographical narratives of popular heroes and rogues inspire imitation by publishing hacks and by picaresque novelists; these latter sometimes come to write novels in which inner experience is recounted in the same fine and convincing detail as was lavished on material things and external action; these "novels of experience" become models for the new burst of autobiography in the late eighteenth and early nineteenth centuries; and these autobiographies in their turn become exemplary for the rash of autobiographical novels of the Victorian age.

Although the term *pseudoautobiography* may sound demeaning, the autobiographical novels that take up its imitative gambits rank among the outstanding achievements of the form. *David Copperfield, Villette*, and (a pseudobiography) *The Way of All Flesh* inherit from the earlier modes not only the possibility of imitating colorfully adventurous lives but the problems of narrating any life. Although this might seem to place Victorian autobiographical novels at a third remove from reality—imitating novels that imitate nar-

10. Philippe Lejeune, *L'Autobiographie en France* (Paris, 1971), pp. 46–47; my translation. For a full discussion of the reciprocal mimesis of fiction and autobiography, see Philip Stewart, *Imitation and Illusion in the French Memoir-Novel, 1700–1750: The Art of Make-Believe* (New Haven and London, 1969); it was not novels in general but specifically pseudoautobiographies that autobiographers like Rousseau and Restif de la Bretonne imitated—in the latter case, his own pseudoautobiographies.

ratives of real life—a greater authenticity is made possible by this devious generic encounter. For the pseudoautobiography opens up the opportunity to dramatize not simply the author's life but his activity as autobiographer, that is, to figure forth not only the protagonist but the narrator of life stories. In pursuing this enterprise, the autobiographical novelist will recruit the figures of other genres in order to make a narrative of writing as well as of living. He may draw upon the rhetoric of difficulty in expression (spoken or written), the tropes of publicly presenting customarily covert activity (whether the lives of thieves or governesses), and the hero types of pagan and Christian tradition who have been used to give afflatus to the protagonists of fiction. Not all Victorian pseudoautobiographies may claim to be ultimately constitutive of their authors' lives—*Jane Eyre: An Autobiography* and *The History of Henry Esmond* can be found to refer to Brontë and Thackeray only with strenuous argumentation. But those which do figure their authors are among the most psychologically complex and aesthetically satisfying works of autobiographical literature.

8

David Copperfield

EXPERIMENTS
IN
AUTOBIOGRAPHY

▬

IT IS ONE OF THE CONFIRMATIONS of a work's greatness that it can sustain an audience of general and even young readers while scholars with a thesis to establish continue to gather about it like flies around honey. *David Copperfield*'s potential for generalizations about Victorian childhood still has its takers,[1] and its abundant matter for psychological interpretation attracts ever closer readings.[2] Although rarely placed where Dickens placed it, at the peak of his achieve-

1. E.g., Barbara Charlesworth Gelpi, "The Innocent I: Dickens' Influence on Victorian Autobiography," in *The Worlds of Victorian Fiction*, ed. J. H. Buckley (Cambridge, Mass., and London, 1975), pp. 57–71; and LuAnn Walther, "The Invention of Childhood in Victorian Autobiography," in *Approaches to Victorian Autobiography*, ed. G. P. Landow (Athens, Ohio, 1979), pp. 64–83.

2. Albert Hutter has published a series of Freudian studies of this and other Dickens novels, but the most illuminating analysis is Lawrence Frank, "Charles Dickens and the Problematic Self," unpublished ms. For a developmental view of the novel and a full bibliography (in the notes), see Robert L. Patten, "Autobiography into Autobiography: The Evolution of David Copperfield," in *Approaches to Victorian Autobiography*, pp. 269–91.

ment as a "favorite child," it has been taken as an important turning in his development. Yet there has not been as much interest in its special status as fiction nor in its claims to stand as the paradigmatic autobiographical novel of the Victorian, perhaps of any, age.

With all its power of drawing attention, *David Copperfield* (1849–1850) has tempted the more avid devotees to the literary sin of dismemberment. It is a multiplotted and sequential novel, even by Dickens's standards, all agree, and some critics have preferred either David's childhood or his adult phase—one suggesting that the first fourteen chapters alone constitute the autobiographical text whereas others have shifted the focus to the moral chastisements that the older David's "undisciplined heart" receives.[3] Lost in this fragmentation of thematic and narrative design is an awareness that the narrative voice frequently and abruptly changes, running through a number of the possible modes of narrating action and evaluating personal experience. Yet the fact that we are repeatedly asked to recall is that *all* of the text is given as from the pen of David Copperfield, that it is an autobiographical writing "never meant to be published on any account," which has somehow fallen into our hands, and that its inconsistencies are immediately referrable neither to its varied materials nor to its historical author but to its protagonist-narrator.

These varieties of narrative technique begin with a nostalgic and appropriately heightened report of earliest events in a romance or fairy tale mode.[4] The aim here is to preserve

3. For the early curtailment, see William C. Spengemann, *The Forms of Autobiography* (New Haven and London, 1980), pp. 122–23; the classic statement of the late resolution is Gwendolyn B. Needham, "The Undisciplined Heart of David Copperfield," *Nineteenth-Century Fiction*, 9 (1954): 81–107.

4. The fairy tale elements in the novel have been often rehearsed, perhaps best in Christopher Mulvey, "*David Copperfield*: The Folk-Story Structure," *Dickens Studies Annual*, 5 (1976): 74–94. See also Harry Stone, *Charles Dickens and the Invisible World: Fairy-Tales, Fantasy, and Novel-Making* (Bloomington, Ind., and London, 1979),

the special quality of childhood experience from loss and death, as the narrator specifies at the openings of Chapters 18 ("A Retrospect") and 53 ("Another Retrospect"). A narrative mode more akin to the conventions of realism is already implied in an aside in one of the above passages—"the unseen, unfelt progress of my life"[5]—but is developed only in later pronouncements on the shape of the adult career, as at the beginnings of Chapters 42 and 48. Although both of these are David's disclaimers of any intention to go into detail about his vocational development—the first, with respect to his shorthand legal reporting, the second, his productions as a novelist—they both strike the brisk note of a man determined to cover "part of my progress" (ch. 48, p. 758) and not linger over his past. These twin impulses pervade David the protagonist as well as the narrator: on revisiting "the old familiar scenes of my childhood, . . . I haunted them, as my memory had often done, and lingered among them as my younger thoughts had lingered when I was far away" (ch. 22, p. 378). Yet the same passage continues: "My reflections at these times were always associated with the figure I was to make in life, and the distinguished things I was to do." One of the first synthetic images of the ultimate autobiographer, Dickens, is the composite formed by his narrator's self-indulgent sense of his past and interwoven awareness of himself as an accomplished author who has outstripped his dreary origins.

A third mode of narration is less extensively employed and less distinctly foregrounded by the narrator himself, yet in the nature of the case it is more curious and even mystical in its notions of the self and how it came to be. The first trace of David's shadowy conception of this narrative role comes with his report of the occasion on which Micawber

which studies from this point of view aspects of the novel not usually so regarded—including the visionary Agnes scenes (pp. 274-75).

5. I quote from the Penguin edition, ed. Trevor Blount (Harmondsworth, 1966), ch. 17, p. 322, but I have checked it against the Clarendon edition, ed. Nina Burgis (London, 1980).

hints at his secret devotion to Agnes: "We have all some experience of a feeling, that comes over us occasionally, of what we are saying and doing having been said and done before, in a remote time—of our having been surrounded, dim ages ago, by the same faces, objects, and circumstances—of our knowing perfectly what will be said next, as if we suddenly remembered it! I never had this mysterious impression more strongly in my life, than before he uttered those words" (ch. 39, p. 630). Although the feeling is ascribed to the past, it is compared with a habitual "impression" that colors the present writing of the narrative at other points. When finally he discloses to himself and Agnes that he has loved her all his life, the narrator adopts this style of preternatural fulfillment: "Long miles of road then opened out before my mind; and, toiling on, I saw a ragged wayworn boy, forsaken and neglected, who should come to call even the heart now beating against mine, his own" (ch. 42, p. 937).

This third conception of a life story is one that takes over the final third of the novel as surely as the fabular and folkloric mode employed for childhood gives way to moral motifs and educative situations after David begins life anew. We may venture the hypothesis that the protagonist's life is not the only aspect of the novel that is sequential but its narrative mode as well and that this switching from one to another style and self-conception is part of a systematic (not necessarily conscious) process. The varieties of narration mark an effort to discover not merely an appropriate form but an interpretive principle by which experience can be recounted and grasped. It is an effort to discover not bare meaning but an adequate language, and in following his protagonist as he conducts this research, Dickens raises the pseudoautobiography to dramatic enactment of a personal quest. We may anticipate the conclusion that it is not in his protagonist's only but in his narrator's activity as well that Dickens establishes his self-image as man and writer.

No matter how we approach *David Copperfield*, we come face to face with the glaring presence in the novel of several paragraphs paraphrased from an autobiographical fragment, published in John Forster's *Life of Dickens* and described as a trial run for the fiction: "It was not until several months later, when the fancy of *David Copperfield*, itself suggested by what he had so written of his early troubles, began to take shape in his mind, that he abandoned his first intention of writing his own life."[6] And there they stand— the first and fifth paragraphs of Chapter 11—as an outcry of the little boy lost, set to work in the London slums and exiled from parental and all other security: "It is matter of some surprise to me, even now, that I can have been so easily thrown away at such an age. A child of excellent abilities, and with strong powers of observation, quick, eager, delicate, and soon hurt bodily or mentally, it seems wonderful to me that nobody should have made any sign in my behalf. But none was made; and I became, at ten years old, a little laboring hind in the service of Murdstone and Grinby."

The story of Dickens's degradation in a blacking (or shoe polish) factory is too well known for long recital, but I wish to focus on a phrase of his autobiographical fragment that Dickens leaves out of the novel and that seems to me a clue to the way he regarded himself: "My whole nature was so penetrated with the grief and humiliation of such considerations, that even now, famous and caressed and happy, I often forget in my dreams that I have a dear wife and children; even that I am a man; and wander desolately back to that time of my life." It is no surprise that Dickens returned to childhood memories in his dreams and in his fictions; it is a truism that he is above all the author of childhood—and of

6. I quote from the Everyman edition of John Forster's *Life of Charles Dickens*, ed. A. J. Hoppé (London, 1966 [1872–1874]), p. 20; passages parallel to those to be quoted from the novel are found on pp. 21–26; the quotation from the autobiographical fragment in my next paragraph is from p. 23.

childhood terrorized and outcast. There have been a number of probing studies of the seminal role of his childhood traumas in the formation of Dickens's works, but there is an even more intimate relation between this author's past and his present than that expressed in the formula "the child is father of the man." There is a sense in which Dickens the child *is* Dickens the man; as he says, he often forgets in his dreams "even that I am a man" and walks again as a child cast out upon the world. Dickens drew on past experience in varied ways for much of his fiction, but it was his present sense of himself as a child that he established when creating his autobiographical novel.

At the outset, Dickens expresses a conception of his books as his children, with *David Copperfield* a favorite among them: "It will be easily believed that I am a fond parent to every child of my fancy, and that no one can ever love that family as dearly as I love them. But, like many fond parents, I have in my heart of hearts a favourite child. And his name is DAVID COPPERFIELD" ("Preface to the Charles Dickens Edition," p. 47). There is nothing particularly odd in the venerable metaphor of the author as parent of his creations; what is more peculiar is Dickens's use of a personal pronoun for an inanimate object, the book ("his name is DAVID COPPERFIELD"). That a book about a child should be described in a childlike way is perhaps not so strange as it may at first seem, but there are even more curious evidences of Dickens's sense of the work as a child—and a child who is none other than himself.

To begin with, *Copperfield* presents a world inhabited by a disproportionately large number of children among its adult population. Other Dickens novels have, perhaps, more children among their characters, but none presents more childlike grownups: the Peggottys, with their innocent seafaring ways, the genial Mr. Dick in his pleasantly deranged way, Miss Mowcher in her midget stature, the castle-building Mr. Micawber—the list could be extended according to the suppleness of one's definition of infantile behavior. But the chief examples of childishness are David's mother and his first wife, and we need go no further afield than these to sense the centrality of childhood to the work.

Mother is quite simply called "Baby" (by that childless mother-aunt, Betsey Trotwood, to be sure). Babyhood is the most charitable construction we can put upon her behavior to David, in allowing him to be tormented and exiled by her second husband, Murdstone, and his partner in sadism, his sister. If we pursue the biographical implications of the novel, we may find this Dickens's way of charitably explaining his own mother's abandonment of him to the blacking factory. ("I never afterwards forgot," Dickens wrote in his autobiographical fragment, "I never shall forget, I never can forget, that my mother was warm for my being sent back" [to the warehouse].)[7] The best excuse we can make for maternal inadequacy, then, is to identify the mother with the child, as being equally impotent to deal with the demonic stepfather. The mother becomes just such another as the child himself, and the scene that lives in David's imagination is the confused one in which the child-mother exhibits her second child to David as he is sent away from home: "So I lost her. So I saw her afterwards, in my sleep at school—a silent presence near my bed—looking at me with the same intent face—holding up her baby in her arms" (ch. 8, p. 175). And at her death: "The mother who lay in the grave, was the mother of my infancy; the little creature in her arms, was myself, as I had once been, hushed for ever on her bosom" (ch. 9, p. 187). These dreamlike images are obviously open to varying interpretation, but I see them as an elaboration of David's own self-image, that is, he imagines himself as a baby, raised by a mother just as much a baby as himself. They are now dead, both of them, whereas the consciousness that was born to suffer and remember still lives.

It is quite understandable, from our sophisticated mod-

7. Quoted in Forster, *Life of Charles Dickens*, p. 32.

ern perspective, that David marries a girl just like his mother, one who is equally inadequate to the role of wife and mother in a world of cash and debt. The designation of this sweet young thing as a baby is repeatedly made; she comes to be thought of by David as his "childwife." The attractions of such a bride—and its value for one's self-image—come out clearly in David's own summary of his married life: "The more I pitied myself, or pitied others, the more I sought for consolation in the image of Dora. The greater the accumulation of deceit and trouble in the world, the brighter and the purer shone the star of Dora high above the world" (ch. 33, p. 534). But the obvious limitations of this ideal innocence as a refuge from reality come through to David in the end: "I did feel, sometimes, for a little while, that I could have wished my wife had been my counsellor; had had more character and purpose, to sustain me and improve me by; had been endowed with power to fill up the void which somewhere seemed to be about me . . ." (ch. 44, p. 713).

The relevance of these lines to Dickens's dissatisfaction with his marriage and to his nagging feeling that he had missed something in life is amply recorded in his letters of this period. What is more difficult to demonstrate but is, it seems to me, equally inescapable, is that these dissatisfactions are themselves signs of a subtle movement in Dickens's conception of himself. No longer can he conceive of himself as an expanded version of the innocent child figure who dominates his early novels with an aura of lamblike superiority to the world. In *David Copperfield*, Dickens begins to see childishness in adults as a defect—if not, as in the case of Micawber, an amiable vice—and to regard his own youthful self as a chastisable young puppy, like David. Writing the novel may be seen as the author's way of outgrowing his child self-image and acquiring an adult identity, recognizing himself as a mature man who has grown beyond the children (of all ages) among whom he has lived.

There is an even more explicit and effective controlling

symbol in *Copperfield* than the child figure. It is a complex of terms associated with the notion of birth. From the opening chapter, titled "I am Born," with its solemn announcements that "I was born with a caul" and "I was a posthumous child," we are made aware that not simply maturation but gestation is in train. The dramatic enactment of this process occurs when Aunt Betsey's rescue of David from his degradation is seen as a rebirth: "Thus I began my new life, in a new name, and with everything new about me" (ch. 14, pp. 271–72). Thus, David is recast in the child's role and made to be born again, but with far greater resources to survive.

In this phase of David's narration, Dickens sees his hero's —and, by implication, his own—identity as that of a child passing through life: not by sloughing off his baby and child selves and emerging full grown but by continually repeating his moments of birth and renewal so as to come to maturity wizened and fulfilled. This child image has been identified by Jung as a persistent figure in the human imagination, a personified ideal of redemption and creative vitality.[8] From this vantage point, it may be found that Dickens's version of the "divine child" archetype is one of his notions of his essential self. By positing his autobiographical novel as the child of his imagination, by opening it with a series of innocence and rebirth figures, Dickens begins to establish *David Copperfield* as the fictional embodiment of himself, in origin and growth.

After his return to a more or less recognizable contemporary world from the phantasmagoria of experience at the Murdstones', Creakle's school, and Murdstone and Grinby, the narrative mode changes from mythic-folkloric romance to something more closely akin to Victorian norms of realism. Although elements of his childhood world persist and

8. C. G. Jung and C. Kerényi, *Essays on a Science of Mythology: The Myth of the Divine Child and the Mysteries of Eleusis*, trans. R. F. C. Hull (Princeton, 1969 [1941]), pp. 70–100.

can raise the register of the prose when they reappear, the prevailing tone is caught when the narrator reports that he "felt, upon the whole, relieved that [the Micawbers] were gone; though I still liked them very much, nevertheless" (ch. 17, p. 322). The Micawbers will return, but in addition to echoing his standard set of verbal gestures, Mr. Micawber will be drawn into a realistic plot involving finance, crime, and psychological conflict, in which he acquits himself like a competent worldling rather than a comic gargoyle. Other fairy tale figures lose something of their fantasy and acquire psychological complexity and moral depth. Miss Mowcher, for one, reveals herself as having complex human feelings under her grotesque veneer: "If there are people so unreflecting or so cruel, as to make a jest of me, what is left for me to do but to make a jest of myself, them, and everything?" (ch. 32, p. 523). This shift of mode allows her to unmask the infantile projections of David, in his substitutive behavior with Emily and Steerforth, and to call him still "Child, child!" She even rises to a new prose style and a new moral tone in summing up her wisdom: " 'You are a young man,' she said, nodding. 'Take a word of advice, even from three foot nothing. Try not to associate bodily defects with mental, my good friend, except for a solid reason' " (ch. 32, p. 526). It is the language of realism she speaks, not the accents and the assumptions of the mythic world in which such parallels hold true.

David's business in this phase of his life is to learn as much and as fast as he can from the formerly fantastic figures who peopled his childhood. Thus, Mrs. Gummidge is converted from a stock type filling in the Yarmouth toy boat milieu to a creature of dedication and passion. "What a change in Mrs. Gummidge in a little time!" the narrator disarmingly remarks. "She was another woman. . . . I could not meditate enough upon the lesson that I read in Mrs. Gummidge, and the new experience she unfolded to me" (ch. 32, p. 520). The formula of "new experience" points unmistakably toward the special subgenre of realism that is brought into play by observed and internal transformations. We have here to do with the *Bildungsroman*, and the middle of *David Copperfield* neatly conforms with its modes of operation. David receives extensive exposure to varied social classes, becomes an observer of a number of morally attenuated domestic situations, and moves through a series of vocational options that allow him to penetrate the great world of men and affairs. He learns to see through the cozy legal system, despite Mr. Spenlow's defense of it (ch. 33), to grasp the egoism and sexual repression in the Steerforth house (ch. 32), and to weigh the complexities of marital imbalance and temptation in the Strongs' ménage, even drawing out its lessons for himself (ch. 45). Throughout, the tone is of busy experience and rapid knowledge of the world, though not where it might count most, with regard to his childish infatuation with Dora. In this, David remains a child and must live through the experience of marital frustration, sickness, and death. As the scene darkens, the narrative mode shifts these child-wife scenes from the tonality of Dora's conversations with her dog, Jip, to the darker tones of suffering humanity that can be discovered even in her childish tongue.

David's manner of handling this experience is conditioned, of course, by his continued childlike features, and the narrator's prose registers the limitations of his *Bildung* so long as he is what Aunt Betsey calls him, "Blind! Blind! Blind!" Echoing his former state of mind in the present writing, the narrator reports: "What I had to do, was, to turn the painful discipline of my younger days to account, by going to work with a resolute and steady heart. What I had to do, was, to take my woodman's axe in my hand, and clear my own way through the forest of difficulty, by cutting down the trees until I came to Dora. And I went on at a mighty rate, as if it could be done by walking" (ch. 36, p. 582). The language expresses not only the younger man's naïveté but also the industrious metaphors of Carlyle and other Victorian exponents of the work ethic. The chapter title "Enthusiasm" sufficiently declares the underlying target of its irony. But Carlylian values and the narrative terms of the *Bildungsroman* tradition are not merely objects of satire but are revealed in their profounder form when David becomes capable of taking on their directives for personal growth. As students of the subgenre have observed, its sources in the German idealist tradition—and its deeper affinities to the pietist imperative of remaking oneself in the image of God—make the content of *Bildung* not merely a cultivation of the faculties but an opening up of one's potential nature, an overcoming of alienation in the world, and a return to one's originative self.[9]

The measure of the distance David has traveled in the course of his education through error and suffering comes in the mandatory scene of distraught wandering following the Fall, in which David repeats Teufelsdröckh's (and anticipates Richard Feverel's) thrashing about in subalpine forests:

> If those awful solitudes had spoken to my heart, I did not know it. I had found sublimity and wonder in the dread heights and precipices, in the roaring torrents, and the wastes of ice and snow; but as yet, they had taught me nothing else.
> . . . In the quiet air, there was a sound of distant singing—shepherd voices; but, as one bright evening cloud floated midway along the mountain's-side, I could almost have believed it came from there, and was not earthly music. All at once, in this serenity, great Nature spoke to me; and soothed me to lay down my weary head upon the grass, and weep as I had not wept yet, since Dora died!   (ch. 58, p. 887)

This employment of the language of *Bildungsroman*, with its Goethian and Carlylian burden of spiritual fulfillment by

9. Two extended English-language treatments of the tradition are Susan Howe Nobbe, *Wilhelm Meister and His English Kinsmen* (New York, 1930); and Jerome H. Buckley, *Season of Youth* (Cambridge, Mass., 1974); also see Hans-Georg Gadamer, *Truth and Method*, trans. William Glen-Doepel (London, 1979 [1960]), pp. 10-18, for the philosophical presuppositions of the concept of *Bildung*.

communion with "great Nature," marks the transition to a third and conclusive mode for the narrator of *David Copperfield*.

In David's developmental phase, there had been indications that the experience of real things and of moral and social facts was only a preliminary education whereas some other layer of experience was required to realize a further aspect of the self. This awareness was known only as a lack of being, an aporia in his life that David projected onto the world around him or located in the negative character of his wife: "The old unhappy loss or want of something. . . . I could have wished my wife had been my counsellor; had had more character and purpose, to sustain me and improve me by; had been endowed with power to fill up the void which somewhere seemed to be about me; but I felt as if this were an unearthly consummation of my happiness, that never had been meant to be, and never could have been" (ch. 44, p. 713). In the shepherds' singing, the displacement of their voice to the clouds, and the prosopopoeic ascription of their speech to a source in "great Nature,"[10] David discovers a language in which such a spiritual void may be filled, in which "unearthly consummation" can take place. He also discovers what he takes to be the design of his life, which has been directing him in his successive stages and which he has rejected as "never . . . meant to be."

This third mode of narration is heavily weighted with the figures and thematics of the spiritual autobiography tradition. Almost at once, the void is filled not with projected voices but by a letter from Agnes. This remarkable document is not quoted but given in the rarely employed but highly expressive technique that has recently been studied as free indirect style:[11]

10. Cf. the similar scene, also in a middle-European setting, in which "nature speaks" to the hero of *The Ordeal of Richard Feverel*, in the chapter of that title (46).

11. See Dorrit Cohn, *Transparent Minds: Narrative Modes for Presenting Consciousness in Fiction* (Princeton, 1978); and Roy Pas-

She knew (she said) how such a nature as mine would turn affliction to good. She knew how trial and emotion would exalt and strengthen it. She was sure that in my every purpose I should gain a firmer and a higher tendency, through the grief I had undergone. She, who so gloried in my fame, and so looked forward to its augmentation, well knew that I would labour on. She knew that in me, sorrow could not be weakness, but must be strength. As the endurance of my childish days had done its part to make me what I was, so greater calamities would nerve me on, to be yet better than I was; and so, as they had taught me, would I teach others. She commended me to God, who had taken my innocent darling to His rest; and in her sisterly affection cherished me always, and was always at my side go where I would; proud of what I had done, but infinitely prouder yet of what I was reserved to do. (ch. 58, p. 888)

Most striking in the theological language that Agnes readily employs is the selection of spiritual formulas for the shape of an individual life: turning "affliction to good," "trial . . . would exalt and strengthen," "a firmer and a higher tendency" (though this latter term has overtones of *Bildung*), "what I was reserved to do." Agnes's prose becomes the conduit by which Dickens brings the spiritual autobiography tradition to bear on his personal situation. That it is his own situation as well as David's is borne out by their common phrase about their childhood: "done its part to make me what I was" (cf. the autobiographical fragment: "I know these things have made me what I am").[12] Dickens, like David, is most concerned to connect past and present, to bring his fabulous childhood into the same plane of reality as his industrious worldly activity, and to relate these in turn to his larger spiritual cravings (undoubtedly connected with

cal, *The Dual Voice: Free Indirect Speech and Its Functioning in the Nineteenth-Century European Novel* (Manchester, 1977).
12. Quoted in Forster, *Life of Charles Dickens*, p. 32.

his sense of the inadequacy of his marriage and of misdirection in his career during the period in which the novel was written). To have his narrator-protagonist discover a connective tissue that will make these life stages an organic whole, he has recourse to the kind of figuration at work in typology, although avoiding any specific type in the tradition, in favor of one of his own making.

The well-known image of Agnes "pointing upward" is worth reviewing in some detail, for its typological action to come clear. In the third paragraph in which Agnes is described, she is associated with a yet earlier memory formation: "I cannot call to mind where or when, in my childhood, I had seen a stained glass window in a church. Nor do I recollect its subject. But I know that when I saw her turn round, in the grave light of the old staircase, and wait for us, above, I thought of that window; and that I associated something of its tranquil brightness with Agnes Wickfield ever afterwards" (ch. 15, p. 280). This dim, religious light is augmented by the looming presence of Canterbury Cathedral, which is mentioned on the next pages and often again in the context of the Wickfield-Strong-Heep plot. This, too, becomes part of the memory construct that David makes of his second phase of childhood: "The earthy smell, the sunless air, the sensation of the world being shut out, the resounding of the organ through the black and white arched galleries and aisles, are wings that take me back, and hold me hovering above those days, in a half-sleeping and half-waking dream" (ch. 18, p. 322).

A further stage of symbolic association occurs when David turns into formulaic repetitions the language of passion and sexual sin picked up in his observation of Mrs. Strong's moral struggles. Among the phrases—of which the "undisciplined heart" has received most attention—is the climactic line, " 'Oh, take me to your heart, my husband, for my love was founded on a rock, and it endures!' " (ch. 45, p. 732). David readily applies the first "heart" phrase—as well as the associated line, "no disparity in marriage like unsuitability of mind and purpose" (ch. 45, p. 729)—to his own case (ch. 48, p. 766), but he reserves the "rock" formula for a better occasion. Yet already the implications of this version of the biblical text are laid up: "Therefore whosoever heareth these sayings of mine, and doeth them, I will liken him unto a wise man, which built his house upon a rock: And the rain descended, and the floods came, and the winds blew, and beat upon that house; and it fell not: for it was founded upon a rock" (Matthew 7; cf. Luke 6 and Matthew 16 for the better-known application to the founding of the Church upon Peter).

The shift from the child-wife, who corresponds with and is a survival of the childhood mode, to the spiritualized love who presides over David's third stage of life, occurs at the moment of death. Agnes is not merely presented in her iconlike stance, but her significance for a new conception of one's life is made explicit: "And now, indeed, I began to think that in my old association of her with the stained-glass window in the church, a prophetic foreshadowing of what she would be to me, in the calamity that was to happen in the fullness of time, had found a way into my mind" (ch. 54, p. 839). The phrases "prophetic foreshadowing" and "the fullness of time" insist that the narrator is deliberately adopting a typological mode of interpreting his experience, one that goes beyond the psychological processes of "old association." From this point on, theological language is rife in the narration; "sacred presence," "compassionate tears," "purer region nearer Heaven" are only the first in a series of divine attributes given to Agnes so that we begin to suspect that even her name carries paronomasia. If not the Lamb of God, she bears strong iconographic affinities with a succession of salvific females in the Christian tradition, and it is these—rather than the universal archetype of the anima evoked by the divine child figure of the first part—that dominate the final course of the narrative.

That the protagonist as well as the narrator are united in this view of Agnes's significance is revealed by the dialogue that is quoted—accurately, one assumes—at their moments of union. The first of these establishes the connective powers of the typological figure:

> "What I am, you have made me, Agnes. You should know best."
> "*I* made you, Trotwood?"
>
> . . .
>
> "As you were then [at Dora's death], my sister, I have often thought since, you have ever been to me. Ever pointing upward, Agnes; ever leading me to something better; ever directing me to higher things!"
>
> (ch. 60, p. 916)

He does not on this occasion quite convince Agnes of her symbolic power, as her surprised emphasis ("*I* made you, Trotwood?") shows. David goes on to connect his iconic construct with his first observations of her in childhood, and when she tries to reduce their mutual feeling to the sentiments of fellow orphans, he insists that his intuition of her was prophetic and *narrative*, "almost as if I had known this story."

Their second and decisive moment of union draws two conclusive gestures from David's declaration that he has loved her all his life. The more strikingly espoused of these is in the language of typology, which we have reviewed: "I held the source of every worthy aspiration I had ever had; the centre of myself, the circle of my life, my own, my wife; my love of whom was founded on a rock!" (ch. 62, p. 938).[13] But the other is even more powerful for being given in the language of a narrative. The narrator formulates the moment as one of fated self-consciousness, in which the protagonist connects his past and present selves: "Long miles of road then opened out before my mind; and, toiling on, I

13. This figure of center and circumference has been associated with medieval definitions of God's existence in J. Hillis Miller, *Charles Dickens: The World of His Novels* (Cambridge, Mass., 1958), pp. 157–58.

saw a ragged way-worn boy, forsaken and neglected, who should come to call even the heart now beating against mine, his own" (ch. 62, p. 937). The protagonist's "then" is not the narrator's "now," to be sure, but in fashioning this complex figure from the materials of the first narrative mode (the image of the way-worn child), the narrator completes the fusion of his autobiographical experiments. Nothing is lost from the earlier narrative modes—no more than what is lost from the earlier experience—and in completing the climax of his narration, the narrator as well as the protagonist comes into his own, his story told.

The final indication that Dickens, as well as David, has come to be himself in the writing of *David Copperfield* is that this impressive text, no matter how highly one places it in the Dickens canon, is ascribed to the hand of its namesake.[14] Although the credit that attaches to writing an autobiography may differ from that attached to fiction, David the protagonist gains plausibility as a successful author by this evidence of his narrative skill. Pseudoautobiography has come round from the depiction of naïve incoherent self-reporters to the portrayal of highly self-conscious artists, as if by their own hand. There is less interest in distinguishing this autobiographical mode from the larger category of the *Künstlerroman* than in recognizing that in narrative sophistication and covert but determined self-manifestation, *David Copperfield* is surpassed in its kind only by *A Portrait of the Artist as a Young Man.* For it is this composite figure of the text—the outcast but mana-laden child, the master craftsman of realism and fabulism, and the idealist straining after religious significance and personal redemption—that constitutes the fullest version we have of the totality known as Charles Dickens.

14. See Patten, "Autobiography into Autobiography," p. 284; and Frank, "Charles Dickens," for a clear focus on David's—and Dickens's—achievement in writing his autobiography.

9

Villette

PILGRIM
OF THE
IMAGINATION

━━━

THE AUTOBIOGRAPHICAL PARALLELS between Charlotte Brontë's Brussels experience and the action of *Villette* (1853)
have never lacked for attention. Biographers from Mrs. Gas-
kell to the present have used the life to inform the work—
where they have refrained from using the work to adumbrate
the life—and biographical critics have barely avoided the
abuses of uncritical biographers.[1] Yet it may be ventured
that the plot and character resemblances in the story of a
young English teacher at a Continental school who falls in
love with an older master are not the most telling contribu-
tors to the autobiographical dimension of the novel. If here,
as in other autobiographical novels, the differences are as
significant as the similarities between art and life, we must
look to the figures of language to find the figure of the
author.

A cue may be taken from one critic's downplaying of
the autobiographical element because of the distinction be-

1. The standard work is still Winifred Gérin, *Charlotte Brontë: The
Evolution of Genius* (London, Oxford, and New York, 1967). More
recent, and heavily psychoanalytic, are Helene Moglen, *Charlotte
Brontë: The Self Conceived* (New York, 1976); and Robert Keefe,
Charlotte Brontë's World of Death (Austin, Tex., and London, 1979).

tween Brontë and her heroines (including Lucy Snowe): "Another highly important aspect of Charlotte's life is totally absent in those of her heroines: her art."[2] Yet Earl Knies goes on in his discussion of *Villette* to describe the subtle control of temporal perspective in the narration, which registers the heroine's efforts to relate her past as a meaningful whole; whereas in *Jane Eyre*, Knies says, "truth is something given, in *Villette* it is something to be discovered." This discovery takes place by the narrator as she goes through the process of writing her life, and the novel becomes a dramatic act of self-writing largely because it is an artfully fashioned pseudoautobiography.

To make a concerted narrative of a confused young woman's perception and feeling is no simple project; the older Lucy has as much difficulty—at times bewilderment—in ordering and giving point to events in her life as Charlotte Brontë might have had with her own. Beyond the obvious problem of the denouement—how to end a love story that points toward a fictional happiness not matched in the life of the creator—there is a succession of exotic characters, mores, and institutions that clamor for attention in the story of a naïf exposed to the social and cultural complexities of a foreign city. Just as David Copperfield moves from his outcast childhood through his progressive education to his teleological union with Agnes, adopting new modes of narration along the way, so Lucy opens with her English memories, recounts the anxieties of her voyage and introduction to Continental life before proceeding on a series of educative ventures in the Pensionnat Beck and in Villette. She only then undertakes to tell her grand passion, the slowly unfolding love affair with Paul Emanuel. One might elect a number of the abundant climactic moments as dividing points in Lucy's career, but I shall maintain that the original first volume, of fifteen chapters, records a youth of successive (and

2. Earl A. Knies, *The Art of Charlotte Brontë* (Athens, Ohio, 1969), p. 37; the quotation below is from p. 181.

ultimately unexplained) alienations; the next, of twelve, a period of rapid enlightenment in the ways of the world and the redirection of her affections; while the final one is almost exclusively devoted to her love affair and the lovers' mutual adjustment to each other—largely by filling in familial and cultural backgrounds. It will not be surprising that the opening chapters are written in variations of the heightened style associated with the romance, that the middle volume makes full use of the realistic and satiric conventions of the *Bildungsroman,* and that the final volume moves to fresh means of expression by gathering up and recycling the metaphoric and mimetic means earlier deployed.[3]

Lucy as narrator is aware that it is not only her status in life that changes but her attitude toward it and that her feeling shifts not only in the temporal realm of the older woman who writes (the only indication of her age is a reference to her white hair in Chapter 5) but also in the past, within the course of the experience described. Fully self-conscious of this disjunction in the narration itself, she declares: "Reader, if, in the course of this work, you find that my opinion of Dr. John undergoes modification, excuse the seeming inconsistency. I give the feeling as at the time I felt it; I describe the view of character as it appeared when discovered" (ch. 18, p. 172).[4] The novel's complexity derives, then, not merely from the narrator's divergence from the protagonist's point of view but from the protagonist's divergences from her own—at least insofar as the narrator is able to recover and

3. A similar division is proposed by E. D. H. Johnson, " 'Daring the Dread Glance': Charlotte Brontë's Treatment of the Supernatural in *Villette,*" *Nineteenth-Century Fiction,* 20 (1966): 326. For the romance elements in this and other Brontë novels, see Robert B. Heilman, "Charlotte Brontë's 'New' Gothic," in *From Jane Austen to Joseph Conrad,* ed. Martin Steinmann, Jr., and R. C. Rathburn (Minneapolis, 1958), pp. 118–32.

4. Citations are from the Everyman edition (London, 1909) while awaiting the definitive text promised by the Clarendon edition. Cf. ch. 19, p. 178, for the two narrative viewpoints on Graham Bretton (Dr. John is his alternative name).

separate her strata of feeling. Such perspectival sophistication is compatible with the autobiographer's versatility in tone, mode, and figuration at the several stages of her life story.

At the outset, Lucy renders her shadowy origins in the style and with the attributes associated with romance:

> My godmother lived in a handsome house in the clean and ancient town of Bretton. Her husband's family had been residents there for generations, and bore, indeed, the name of their birthplace—Bretton of Bretton: whether by coincidence, or because some remote ancestor had been a personage of sufficient importance to leave his name to his neighbourhood, I know not.
>
> When I was a girl I went to Bretton about twice a year, and well I liked the visit. The house and its inmates specially suited me. The large peaceful rooms, the well-arranged furniture, the clear wide windows, the balcony outside, looking down on a fine antique street, where Sundays and holidays seemed always to abide—so quiet was its atmosphere, so clean its pavement—these things pleased me well.
>
> (ch. 1, p. 1)

Any connection between this clean, quiet place, reserved from the workaday world, and the idylls of Blunderstone Rookery or a hundred other Edenic childhoods, is purely formal—it fills their place with a special content. The name chosen for this ancient town, with its antique street (later called St. Ann's) suggests that we have to do here with the national version of a universal myth of some great, good place of origin. Although there is little to connect Bretton with the Victorian literary and political mythologizing of medieval England—or with an earlier Anglo-French romance world connoted by the name—there is an indelible suggestion that this town is a utopian schema of England. As for its inhabitants, so "specially suited" to the narrator, there is some question whether their place is named for them or they for their place—their "remote ancestor" lying now beyond the range of myth as well as history.

How far these inhabitants and their world are from the knowable modern one is borne out in the novel itself when they later take part in a series of renewed renditions of early experience. Lucy awakes from her climactic breakdown with an uncanny sense of return to her origins but soon discovers the numerous differences not only between past and present surroundings but also between her idea of the Brettons and the reality. The Belgian country house is only superficially furnished with tokens of the ancient English ways; although called a "chateau," it is more appropriately described as a *manoir* built in the Baroque style of the town (ch. 17, p. 164)—exactly the kind of place to call forth copious compliments from Madame Beck. Even more telling, her bourgeois judgment of the Brettons—"tellement dignes, aimables, et respectables" (ch. 19, p. 175)—is borne out by Lucy's fresh observations. Imposing enough in their physical health and glossy appearance to humble Lucy into bitter comparisons with her own poor endowments, they also emerge as the kind of people who make crude jokes about each other's getting fat (ch. 17, p. 168). Although Lucy's admiration for Mrs. Bretton remains high, it is tinged by a note of resentment at her worldly survival power: "No, the *Louisa Bretton* never was out of harbour on such a night" as these which the *Lucy Snowe* is forced and determined to weather (ch. 18, p. 162). It is exactly this kind of perception of her spiritual distinction from the attractive but somewhat brassy masculinity of Graham Bretton that marks her gradual falling out of love with him. In the same process of transforming vision and feeling, Lucy observes his growing attachment to Pauline Home de Bassompierre—the "changeling" or fairylike creature she had tutored ten years before. That she is still naïvely romantic but very much an heiress is evident to Lucy as she sums them up: "I wished him success; and successful I knew he would be. He was born victor, as some are born vanquished" (ch. 37, p. 395). The chivalrous and rather courtly Graham—who instantly appears when Lucy is all but stranded at the Belgian port—will make a fit match with a starry-eyed heiress not quite of this world, but that match, that mode of being, is not Lucy Snowe's.

The demystification of the mode of perception employed in characterizing the Brettons early in the novel is also observable in the style of representing other elements of Lucy's world. The middle chapters of *Villette* are given over to a systematic exploration of the capital, which had been denied her as a sheltered pupil-teacher. She now takes in the entire social ladder, from the working-class quarters as she accompanies Dr. John in making his rounds, to the gala concert in which she sees the king, his court, and the full regalia of the aristocracy (ch. 20). There is plenty of time for aesthetic education as well, and as Lucy makes her tour of art gallery, theater, and other institutions, she develops habits of critically penetrating the cultural symbols that are purveyed in a country's arts (chs. 19 and 23). The tone throughout is one of sharp observation and satirical seeing through, altogether commensurate with this, the subject matter of a *Bildungsroman*.

It is otherwise in the chapters that open and close the novel; although learning may be said to be a lifelong affair—in the text as in life—the protagonist's way of responding to it and the narrator's of conveying it are far from the satirical realism of her cultural education. From the outset, a dual train of figuration is established, which draws on two primary resources of the spiritual autobiography tradition for the narrating of a life. "My visits to [Mrs. Bretton] resembled the sojourn of Christian and Hopeful beside a certain pleasant stream," the narrator offers, "with 'green trees on each bank, and meadows beautified with lilies all the year round' " (ch. 1, p. 2). This is Bunyan's River of the Water of Life, and in its Edenesque setting all the trees may be eaten of, but Lucy soon finds, as the Pilgrims do, that "they had not journied far, but the River and the way, for a time, parted."[5] From this initial sense of lost idyllic origins, Lucy derives her language of life as a pilgrimage, repeatedly reverting to Bunyanesque figures. She encourages herself in the style of Lightheart the Beggar (ch. 13, p. 106), regards the world as Vanity Fair (ch. 38, p. 419), and erects M. Paul in the image of Greatheart set to fight Apollyon (ch. 38, p. 405). Early and late in *Villette*, the individual life is conceived as a journey among the pitfalls of the world toward some better place or state.

Fully in keeping with this resort to Bunyan, as the guide for spiritual adventurers recounting their life stories, is the narrator's saturation of her text with the language of Scripture.[6] The use of biblical language begins early, at Lucy's vision of the aurora borealis after her second mistress, Miss Marchmont, dies: "A bold thought was sent to my mind; my mind was made strong to receive it. 'Leave this wilderness,' it was said to me, 'and go out hence' " (ch. 5, p. 36). Arriving in London, she finds it invigoratingly full of life but a "Babylon" and identifies herself with a skeptical prophet who in his wanderings is taught by a parable the mysterious ways of God: "In that morning my soul grew as fast as Jonah's gourd" (ch. 6, p. 39—re Jonah 4). Going out into the world is conceived as a descent into hell, with classical allusions to Charon and the Styx at her Channel crossing (ch. 6, p. 42), but the predominant note is still the hopeful

5. John Bunyan, *Grace Abounding to the Chief of Sinners and The Pilgrim's Progress*, ed. Roger Sharrock (London, New York, and Toronto, 1966), p. 229. On Brontë's use of Bunyan in "abstract personification," see the all-too-brief remarks in Margot Peters, *Charlotte Brontë: Style in the Novel* (Madison, Wis., and London, 1973), pp. 122–23.

6. On Brontë's increased use of the Bible during her Brussels period—and on her vividly imagined school essay, "La Mort de Moïse," which M. Heger corrected—see Enid L. Duthie, *The Foreign Vision of Charlotte Brontë* (New York, 1975), pp. 46–48. The anticipation of Brontë's eventual use of this typological material in her life story for this period seems preternatural; see below, on Moses's Nebo/Pisgah vision.

one framed in biblical symbols—at this juncture, the rainbow, "a God-bent bow, an arch of hope" (ch. 6, p. 48).

A summative moment in Lucy's narrative provides a measure of the strength of this language and its life conception. At a transitional moment of her Belgian-Labassecourienne experience, Lucy sits down to take stock of her progress:

> My mind, calmer and stronger now than last night, made for itself some imperious rules, prohibiting under deadly penalties all weak retrospect of happiness past; commanding a patient journeying through the wilderness of the present, enjoining a reliance on faith—a watching of the cloud and pillar which subdue while they guide, and awe while they illumine—hushing the impulse to fond idolatry, checking the longing outlook for a far-off promised land whose rivers are, perhaps, never to be reached save in dying dreams, whose sweet pastures are to be viewed but from the desolate and sepulchral summit of a Nebo.
>
> (ch. 21, p. 209)

This accumulation of allusions is typical not only of Lucy's prose but of her mental habits (the two are inextricably entwined); she comes to the imagining of her past and future life with a full supply of biblical quotations and allusions,[7]

7. A crescendo of such references indicates the extent to which Lucy—and Brontë—are steeped in Scripture. Speaking to herself while addressing her putative audience, she writes:

Tired wayfarer, gird up thy loins; look upward, march onward. Pilgrims and brother mourners, join in friendly company. Dark through the wilderness of this world stretches the way for most of us: equal and steady be our tread; be our cross our banner. For staff we have His promise, whose "word is tried, whose way perfect": for present hope His providence, "who gives the shield of salvation, whose gentleness makes great"; for final home His bosom, who "dwells in the height of Heaven"; for crowning prize a glory exceeding and eternal. (ch. 38, p. 398)

(The approximate citations are from Psalms 18, Job 22, I Corinthians 9, II Timothy 4, and Habakkuk 1.) These sentiments might smack of cant as coming from one whose Christian sentiment seems largely focused on disdain for Catholicism, but they cumulatively project a

which she subtly varies in the service of her strong wish fantasies and her even more powerful repression of desire. Their cumulative effect is to inspire her view of her life with a religious sense of destiny—but it is the vision of a Moses, destined to wander, to be guided, to endure, but not to enter.

This pilgrimage view of life plays its role in shaping the final movement of the novel's action, toward a union with Paul Emanuel that makes active the eschatological suggestions of both his names. This enactment of the possibility of a return to or recovery of a promised land is not, however, conducted entirely in the displaced language of Bunyan and the Bible. A further source of figuration is developed, from as early as the opening pages of the second part, in a series of references to a guardian spirit. How closely this bright angel is connected with the White Goddess archetype will be clear to readers of Robert Heilman's classic essay on Brontë's lunar imagery.[8] Certain points of characterization, however, distinguish this as an idealized image of the self rather than as a distinct, tutelary deity.

---

sensibility possessed of the spiritual significance of its experience and deeply committed—we may say, religiously devoted—to the vision of personal fulfillment. The secular displacement of religious belief and language can go no further than Brontë's creation of a heroine who *testifies to* her feelings with a devotional fervor usually reserved for higher powers.

8. Robert Heilman, "Charlotte Brontë, Reason, and the Moon," *Nineteenth-Century Fiction*, 14 (1960): 283–302. Heilman establishes a persistent structure in Brontë's imagination, evolving from her version of the moon/White Goddess archetype. The essay distinguishes the changes in Brontë's use of the figure in her major novels: in *Villette*, the moon is "identified now not with 'feeling' as in *Jane Eyre* but with that other challenger of Reason, Imagination." Drawing on some salient passages in the novel, Heilman establishes that Brontë "is restating in lunar imagery the problem with which she was always concerned—the distinction between an imagination which falsified reality by creating specious comfort or needless fear, and imagination which intuited truth. She rejects moonbeam mirages but never the moon." For the further personification of this positive (one might say, Coleridgean) imagination, see below.

In the passage recounting the period of unconsciousness that follows her nervous breakdown, Lucy gives her first in a series of essayistic accounts of the war of Reason and Feeling within her. These personified abstractions are less vivid than the angelic figure who emerges from the allegorical network:

> Certainly, at some hour, though perhaps not *your* hour, the waiting waters will stir; in *some* shape, though perhaps not the shape you dreamed, which your heart loved, and for which it bled, the healing herald will descend, the cripple and the blind, and the dumb, and the possessed, will be led to bathe. Herald, come quickly! . . . Long are the "times" of Heaven: the orbits of angel messengers seem wide to mortal vision; they may enring ages; the cycle of one departure and return may clasp unnumbered generations; and dust, kindling to brief suffering life, and, through pain, passing back to dust, may meanwhile perish out of memory again, and yet again. To how many maimed and mourning millions is the first and sole angel visitant, him easterns call Azrael.
>
> (ch. 17, p. 161)

Perhaps the most remarkable feature of this speculation is that, beginning in the language of the healing waters of Bethesda, it ends in an invocation of the Near Eastern angel of death. The monitory words on the long cycles of heavenly intervention into the course of human time are a self-rebuke for her peremptory calling on her angel to "come quickly!" The ministering spirit is called upon not so much for relief from earthly pangs as for personal contact with "*some* shape, though perhaps not the shape you dreamed, which your heart loved, and for which it bled." This idealized lover is, however, less likely to function as an object of sexual desire than he is as an ego ideal for the self—the complement of psychic integration that Jungians call the animus (to complete the female unconscious).

Support for such an interpretation is given in a passage following not long after the above. Lucy returns to her thesis on Reason and its related personifications but passes on to her angel again:

> Often has Reason turned me out by night, in midwinter, on cold snow. . . . Then, looking up, have I seen in the sky a head amidst circling stars, of which the midmost and the brightest lent a ray sympathetic and attent. A spirit, softer and better than Human Reason, has descended with quiet flight to the waste—bringing all round her a sphere of air borrowed of eternal summer; bringing perfume of flowers which cannot fade—fragrance of trees whose fruit is life; bringing breezes pure from a world whose day needs no sun to lighten it. My hunger has this good angel appeased with food. . . . Divine, compassionate, succourable influence! When I bend the knee to other than God, it shall be at thy white and winged feet, beautiful on mountain or on plain. Temples have been reared to the Sun—altars dedicated to the Moon. Oh, greater glory! . . .
> This daughter of Heaven remembered me tonight; she saw me weep, and she came with comfort: "Sleep," she said. "Sleep sweetly—I gild thy dreams!"
> (ch. 21, p. 208)

One cannot account for all the elements of this elaborate personal iconography though some negative conclusions may be drawn. This spirit is to be identified neither with the Christian God, pagan figures of Sun or Moon, or other traditional deity. It is heavenly and stellar but a creature of great intimacy, entering the mind as it does during sleep. Despite its present form, this spirit has no precise sex, being both motherly in its ministrations and masculine in its earlier heraldic bearing. Nor is the figure to be readily identified with Feeling, Imagination, or any of the other antitheses Lucy raises to her alternatively dominant master spirit, Rea-

son. The key word in this passage is "influence": "Divine,
compassionate, succourable influence!" We may recall Emily
Brontë's poem at this point:

> And thou art now a spirit pouring
> Thy presence into all—
> The essence of the Tempest's roaring
> And of the Tempest's fall—
>
> A universal influence
> From Thine own influence free;
> A principle of life, intense,
> Lost to mortality.[9]

In this great lyric, "Aye, there it is! . . ." Emily Brontë gives
the names "spirit," "presence," "essence," "influence," and
"principle of life" to the human vital force itself, which shall
escape its earthly prison and mingle "with the skies." For
Charlotte Brontë, this creative source and end takes the
form of a specific human faculty, the personal mythmaking
power that underwrites an individual's sense of his integrity
and destiny.

We do not, of course, know Lucy's ultimate destination,
but in perhaps the most evocative of the visionary passages
of this visionary novel, Lucy for a time enacts the role of
her guardian spirit on earth and in a social relationship. The
scene is the climactic fete at which she sees what seems the
entire populace of Villette gathered in the illuminated park.
She penetrates them all under the aegis of the moon goddess,
who now directs her power of vision by a special light:

> Imagination was roused from her rest, and she came
> forth impetuous and venturous. . . .
> "Look forth and view the night!" was her cry; and
> when I lifted the heavy blind from the casement close

9. *The Complete Poems of Emily Jane Brontë*, ed. C. W. Hatfield
(New York, 1941), poem no. 148.

at hand—with her own royal gesture, she showed me
a moon supreme, in an element deep and splendid.
(ch. 38, pp. 409–10)

Following these instructions from her guiding faculty, Lucy
looks on at the fete to see her friends—and her rival for
Graham—alike in a cool, detached review: "I saw the occu-
pants of that carriage well: me they could not see. . . . I saw
the Count de Bassompierre; I saw my godmother, handsomely apparelled, comely and cheerful; I saw, too, Paulina
Mary, compassed with the triple halo of her beauty, her
youth, and her happiness. . . . I saw Graham Bretton . . ."
(ch. 38, p. 412). It is Lucy who plays out the role of her
stellar spirit, observing all the scene with awe but equa-
nimity, "viewlessly," withdrawn from personal striving and
perhaps most intensely herself—the realization of her symbolic ideal.

If there is a threat to the possibility of seeing one's life
clearly in the final movement of *Villette*, it is the persistence
within Lucy's prose—and in her corresponding vision of
things—of many of the same hobgoblins which had popu-
lated her feverish state in earlier experience. Much of this
movement continues the demystification process of her
earlier *Bildung*. The mildly indulged hallucinations concerning the spectral nun of the school are finally put to rest, as
Lucy comes to share both good sense and religious sanity
with M. Paul. There is also an incitement to renewed speculation on revenants in the form of the lost betrothed of Paul,
Justine-Marie, but this ghost, too, is laid aside when she appears in the form of a buxom Belgian bourgeoise, the niece
and namesake of the early departed. Less easily dispersed by
the light of truth, however, are the figures associated with
Madame Walravens and Père Silas. In the "Malevola" chapter (34), the narrator's account employs figures drawn from
folklore (the sorceress Cunegonde), romantic literature
(J. W. Meinhold's *Sidonia von Bork: Die Klosterhexe*), and

mythology (the suggestions of bisexual prophets like Tiresias in Madame Walravens's bitter utterance, deep voice, and silver beard).[10] Brontë seems to have captured a strain of Flemish cultural imagination that has persisted from Bruegel and Bosch to Ensor and Ghelderode, but the allusions are more than renderings of the extraordinary spectacle: they also express Lucy's still mystified state of mind. She tries to shrug off the story of Paul, which Père Silas tells as "quite a little romantic narrative" (ch. 34, p. 356), but she has been threatened at a concrete point and tender place: her love for a man of different religion and complex family involvements.

Moving under the influence of an overdose of some tranquilizer (probably an opiate), Lucy experiences—and the narrator paints—the park fete in the lurid colors of surrealism. Yet she is not to fall victim to her predilection for the fantasy of romantic terror, not this time: "There, then, were Madame Walravens, Madame Beck, Père Silas—the whole conjuration, the secret junta. The sight of them thus assembled did me good. I cannot say that I felt weak before them, or abashed, or dismayed. They outnumbered me and I was worsted and under their feet; but, as yet, I was not dead" (ch. 38, pp. 419–20). Lucy's power to look steadily with the light of her imagination—even on the distortions of her fantasy, her romantic elaboration of her prosaic, though substantial enemies—falls into step here with the fatalistic and self-negating view of her life which she had earlier nurtured. She still conceives of herself as a born loser, a perennial pilgrim fated to wander without her inheritance, yet she takes on herself that destiny and asserts her will to suffer it and survive.

Given this power of holding her visions with some detachment and control, Lucy does enact, if only temporarily,

10. Her name derives from the *wal rabens* or slaughter birds sacred to Odin; see Georgia S. Dunbar, "Proper Names in *Villette*," *Nineteenth-Century Fiction*, 15 (1960): 79, for this and other onomastic lore.

her myth of inheriting a promised land. In her achieved understanding with Paul—and in the prospect of her own vocational fulfillment in the school which he establishes for her
to head—she finds a language adequate to her vision of earthly
happiness:

> We walked back to the Rue Fossette by moonlight—
> such moonlight as fell on Eden—shining through the
> shades of the Great Garden, and haply gilding a path
> glorious for a step divine—a Presence nameless. Once
> in their lives some men and women go back to these
> first fresh days of our great Sire and Mother—taste
> that grand morning's dew—bathe in its sunrise.
>
> (ch. 42, p. 447)

It is crucial to an appreciation of this passage that it be seen
not merely as an easy indulgence in paradisal images of
wedded bliss but as a creative fusion of the iconography of
the moon (which she consistently associates with her imagination) and the biblical-autobiographical language she has
employed to account for her destiny. She has pursued an
Eden of personal relationship, that is, winning her beloved,
but has found it under the moon, that is, within herself, a
paradise happier far. This self-fulfillment is, to be sure, dependent on Paul's love and cooperation, but his subsequent
departure and failure to return do not cancel out the promise
attained. Lucy writes these lines after the event, after the reported storm and apparent death of Paul, yet these disasters
are not sufficient to cancel them out in the book of her life.

It is not only Lucy who survives her loss and lives to
affirm the value of what was lost, but Charlotte Brontë. In
the act of tracing her narrative alter ego's passage through
her several modes of vision—which are her modes of being—
Brontë not only represents her own adjustment to the loss
of M. Heger but her command of the otherwise divided
elements of her identity. Recognizing both the strong self-
negating and fatalistic streak in herself—closely allied with
her religious heritage and the fund of biblical figuration that

it provided—and the imperative to affirm her imagination with a strength of commitment rarely seen after the Romantic period, Brontë manages to bring these apparently disparate elements of the self together in her art. For *Villette* is one of the great autobiographical novels by virtue of its power to fuse the sense of fated alienation and perpetual wandering with the assertion of the individual's imaginative capacity to see clearly and to create soundly. To that faith, the existence of *Villette* itself is a strong testament.

10

The Mill on the Floss

CONVERSION
TO TRAGEDY

━━━━

IN CONTRAST TO THE AMPLE ATTENTION that the autobiographical novels of Dickens and Brontë have received, George Eliot's has been approached from this standpoint only occasionally and with misgivings. Perhaps it was the censure of F. R. Leavis that accounts for this embarrassment at the prospect of catching Eliot in self-indulgent self-references in portraying Maggie Tulliver. Certainly the materials for biographical investigation have been plentifully available, yet Eliot's authoritative biographer approaches such references in her fiction with great circumspection, anxious perhaps to avoid the excesses of intuitive sympathy to which a more enthusiastic interpreter might be inspired.[1] Yet *The Mill on the Floss* (1860) is not only a characteristic Victorian autobiographical novel but marks a crucial turning in the use of traditional forms and figures in fictional self-conception. In the same years in which Darwin began to

---

1. Gordon S. Haight, *George Eliot: A Biography* (New York and Oxford, 1968); empathic restraint has been substantially overcome in Ruby V. Redinger, *George Eliot: The Emergent Self* (New York, 1975).

undermine the literal reading of the scriptural account of Creation, Eliot began a lesser but parallel transformation of the biblical figures of traditional autobiography, with their burden of typological promise and divine underwriting of a life.

It is important at the outset to specify how much of *The Mill* follows the general outlines of its literary forebears. The first volume (comprising the first two of seven parts) has often been apprehended as Wordsworthian in tone and substance, an idyll and elegy for an unrecoverable childhood in rural innocence. Later chapters have been mined for biographical references to personal originals but have only glancingly been connected with Eliot's own religious and spiritual promptings—never, to my knowledge, to the patterns of crisis and conversion in the spiritual autobiography line. The final phases of the novel have received perhaps most attention, mainly in derogation of the abrupt denouement in which Maggie and her brother are reunited at the moment of death in a flood. Yet this portion, too, has its creative motive in Eliot's appropriation of literary tradition for self-writing—in this case, the appropriation of tragedy. We should be prepared to find in this, as in all of Eliot's novels, a fundamental allegiance to realism which does not preclude but is derived from a sophisticated grasp of other formal and generic possibilities. Just as her other works are generated in a sustained reworking of comedy, pastoral, historical fiction, prophecy, etc., *The Mill* is at once an autobiographical novel and a critique of the entire canon of autobiographical writing as it descended into her own time.

To this subject, as to most others, Eliot devoted sustained reading and thought. I shall not review the full tally of her reflections and writing about the self but choose two texts to illustrate her views of such writing and of the concept of identity that underlies it. As for the latter, we may reflect on the unsettling implications of a verse fragment, probably of 1874:

I grant you ample leave
To use the hoary formula "I am"
Naming the emptiness where thought is not;
But fill the void with definition, "I"
Will be no more a datum than the words
You link false inference with, the "Since" & "so"
That, true or not, make up the atom-whirl.
Resolve your "Ego," it is all one web
With vibrant ether clotted into worlds:
Your subject, self, or self-assertive "I"
Turns nought but object, melts to molecules,
Is stripped from naked Being with the rest
Of those rag-garments named the Universe.
Or if, in strife to keep your "Ego" strong
You make it weaver of the etherial light,
Space, motion, solids & the dream of Time—
Why, still 'tis Being looking from the dark,
The core, the centre of your consciousness,
That notes your bubble-world: sense, pleasure,
                                        pain,
What are they but a shifting otherness,
Phantasmal flux of moments? [2]

The skepticism of personal identity exhibited here rivals Hume's and enters the tradition that descends from him into modern philosophy; from this standpoint, *I* is a term without a verifiable referent, a relational term like *since* and *so* (or what modern linguists have called a *shifter*). The other alternative envisaged—the Kantian one which identifies the self with the "ego" that synthesizes experience with its endowment of universal categories (space, time, etc.)—is equally suspect as a control over the flux of phenomena that it claims to transcend. Yet even this unsanguine view opens a possibility of selfhood. The power which looks from the

2. Quoted in Bernard J. Paris, "George Eliot's Unpublished Poetry," *Studies in Philology*, 56 (1959): 544–45; Paris's explanation of its original context in a philosophic dialogue does not invalidate its exploration of aspects of Eliot's thought.

empty center or dark core of consciousness is named "Being," and although it is also characterized as "naked Being" (with the suggestion of nonindividual, pure or mere existence), this Being is a universal with which the otherwise unlocalizable individual may be identified. The problem for autobiography written with such a concept of self and world is to find forms which acknowledge the spuriousness of identity and its "bubble-world" constructions, yet envisage the will to be and the fitful thought of man as twin manifestations of universal existence—"Being looking from the dark."

Another potential hindrance to mastering the obliquity of *The Mill on the Floss* as an autobiographical novel is George Eliot's reputation for straightforwardness. When a writer uses the omniscient author convention as she does, to intervene, evaluate, and expostulate, the assumption naturally follows that she is too fastidious to require masks and fictions in her self-presentation. This tacit conviction about an awesome authorial presence is the more remarkable in the light of the persistent pseudonymity that marks her career. Born Mary Ann Evans, she gives herself the names Marian Evans, George Eliot, and Mrs. George Henry Lewes before coming to rest as Mrs. John W. Cross. Nor is she averse to employing fictional personae of an elaborate and inventive kind. Her last book, *Impressions of Theophrastus Such* (1879), brings together a number of essays clearly expressing Eliot's point of view—like the proleptic affirmation of Zionism, "The Modern Hep! Hep! Hep!"—with framing essays in the voice of an eponymous pseudoauthor. Theophrastus Such—the character-writer of self (*sich*)—describes himself as a bachelor, a loner, a failed author, and an ugly duckling; Eliot was herself none of these four things but had come close enough to them to readily adopt such a grotesque as her persona. Nevertheless, we do not think of her as the Theophrastian ironist that he affects to be:

> Thus if I laugh at you, O fellow-men! if I trace with curious interest your labyrinthine self-delusions, note

the inconsistencies in your zealous adhesions, and smile at your helpless endeavours in a rashly chosen part, it is not that I feel myself aloof from you: the more intimately I seem to discern your weaknesses, the stronger to me is the proof that I share them. How otherwise could I get the discernment?[3]

It is this latter note of self-identification in character analysis that sounds the authentic Eliotic tone.

It is on this personal basis that the introduction to the volume, "Looking Inward," reaches an extended discussion of the art of autobiography, Eliot's most important statement on the subject:

Is it then possible to describe one's self at once faithfully and fully? In all autobiography there is, nay, ought to be, an incompleteness which may have the effect of falsity. We are each of us bound to reticence by the piety we owe to those who have been nearest to us and have had a mingled influence over our lives; by the fellow-feeling which should restrain us from turning our volunteered and picked confessions into an act of accusation against others, who have no chance of vindicating themselves; and most of all by that reverence for the higher efforts of our common nature, which commands us to bury its lowest fatalities, its invincible remnants of the brute, its most agonising struggles with temptation, in unbroken silence. But the incompleteness which comes of self-ignorance may be compensated by self-betrayal. A man who is affected to tears in dwelling on the generosity of his own sentiments makes me aware of several things not included under those terms. Who has sinned more against those three duteous reticences than Jean Jacques? Yet half our impressions of his character come not from what he means to convey, but from what he unconsciously enables us to discern.

3. The Cabinet edition of Eliot's works (Edinburgh and London, n.d.), p. 5; the quotation below is from pp. 6–7.

The passage marks an early and definite statement of a view of autobiography that I have characterized as the expression theory, whose chief tenets are touched on in references to unconscious self-revelation, "impressions" of personality, and the utility of "incompleteness" or other stylistic deviations in revealing essential traits. Yet the larger portion of the passage is given over not to unconscious but to conscious self-revelation, which is by no means highly valorized. Rousseau is singled out not only as a lachrymose self-pleader but as the chief sinner against the "three duteous reticences": silence about the harms done by those close to us, refraining from "accusations against others" (presumably in the larger world), and suppressing the defects of our own "common nature," which are best left unconfessed.

It is these reticences, particularly the first, that make *The Mill on the Floss* the especially evasive and expressive book it is. The situation in which Eliot found herself as she approached the writing may be briefly summarized. In 1854 she eloped with Lewes to the Continent (marking her steps with a letter reference to Brontë's Continental experience, as described in *Villette* and published the year before);[4] in 1857 she tried to communicate her situation to her brother and through him to her family—he replied by enforcing a complete break not only with himself but with their sisters; in 1859 her sister Chrissey (whom brother Isaac had shabbily treated in the midst of her adversities) died. One has only to read the relevant letters to sense the emotional depths beyond these hard facts. Writing *The Mill* was an exercise in conveying something of those truths about oneself to others while observing "the piety we owe to those who have been nearest to us and have had a mingled influence over our lives."

To create a fiction that would express her feelings of love and injury, shared relationship and bitter rejection, Eliot

4. *The George Eliot Letters*, ed. G. S. Haight, 7 vols. (New Haven and London, 1954–55), II, 165.

needed a plot that both paralleled and obscured the biographical one. For the conflict over her liaison with Lewes, she created the scenes of Tom's reproaches against Maggie's attachment to Philip Wakem—the most bitter in the novel and among the most wrenching in Eliot's *oeuvre*. But brother Tom's cruelty presupposed a motivation in the family history, and here Eliot had to develop an equivalent for the long tale of conflict and repression in her family—that involving her religious and intellectual development. The Wakem-Tulliver conflict, ostensibly a legal and economic one but manifestly fueled by neurotic will (Tulliver's alone at first, but later by Wakem's and Tom's as well), is the dramatic occasion for Eliot to review the compromises she had had to make in 1842 in behalf of her father's and brother's formalist orthodoxy and social conventionality.

The distance between the religious and intellectual tenor of this *donnée* and its humdrum vehicle of loans and leases is bridged by a set of otherwise unaccountable disquisitions on Protestantism, which frames the major part of this plot sequence. To begin, there is the cultural-historical essay on the town of St. Ogg's, which promises to account for the domestic milieu in which Tulliver's initial financial blunder is made but which turns into a broader critique: "The days were gone when people could be greatly wrought upon by their faith. . . . Protestantism sat at ease. . . . Public spirit was not held in high esteem at St. Ogg's . . ." (Bk. I, ch. 12, pp. 106–07).[5] The final essay is a sarcastic account of the "variation of Protestantism unknown to Bossuet," Tulliver's curse added to the family Bible (Bk. III, ch. 9), as elaborated in the following chapter under that title ("They were part of the Protestant population of Great Britain. . . . Their religion was of a simple, semi-pagan kind. . . . The religion of the Dodsons consisted in revering whatever was customary and respectable . . ."—Bk. IV, ch. 1, p. 239). The bitterness

5. Citations are from the Riverside edition of the novel (Boston, 1961), ed. G. S. Haight, but I have checked them against the Clarendon edition, also edited by Haight (Oxford, 1980).

against paternal religion and its repressive edge is only partly muted by the summary advice that Bob Jakin offers Maggie for her loneliness in the family's outcast condition: "Hev a dog, Miss!—they're better friends nor any Christian" (Bk. IV, ch. 3, p. 248).

Having found a plot correlative for personal experiences, Eliot needed a character to play a role equivalent to her own and perhaps inevitably opened a Pandora's box by creating Maggie Tulliver. Upon reflection, there is no wonder in the fact that Maggie has elicited the most extreme varieties of judgment accorded any Eliot character, for her fictive nature is to be ambiguous in line with Eliot's perceptible ambivalence about her own role in family relations. From the wholly sympathetic view of Maggie, which has been derided by Leavistite critics, we have been asked to shift to a clinical and covertly judgmental view of her neurotic self-destructiveness, and a third position has predictably been generated, in which her defects are explained by social determinism, malforming her by the limits on women's education and their larger claims for freedom.[6]

The indisputable truth of each of these positions is underscored by their explicit appearance in the narrator's prose. Chapter and verse can be cited for Eliot's sympathy, sentimentality, disapprobation, and explanation of her heroine's attributes. Even without Maggie's special claims on her author's multiple awareness, how could it be otherwise in a novel which states and follows the canons of realism about the mixture of character traits—even in so unprepossessing a figure as Mr. Tulliver (Bk. III, ch. 1, pp. 173–74)—and which requires that we draw on our reserves of imaginative sympathy even when witnessing Tom's sadistic incivility and Stephen Guest's sexual banality? Yet the sympathy and judg-

6. For a psychiatric analysis of Maggie's self-destructiveness, see Bernard J. Paris, *A Psychological Approach to Fiction* (Bloomington, Ind., and London, 1974), ch. 5; for a sympathetic woman's view of the same, see Elizabeth Ermarth, "Maggie Tulliver's Long Suicide," *Studies in English Literature*, 14 (1974): 587–601.

ment that we are asked to balance in our regard for Maggie are put under especially high obligation because they are enlisted in Eliot's project of self-manifestation and self-criticism in the text of her novel. In tracing Maggie's consciousness through the phases of her brief life, Eliot probed the roots of her own predilections toward renunciation, asceticism, and a religion of sorrow—and reaffirmed the rightness of her decisions to seize her opportunities for intellectual freedom, life affirmation, and personal love.

A third essential in Eliot's enterprise was the provision of a setting, preferably one in which the action and its significances could be closely correlated with the structural attributes of the landscape. Anticipating Kenneth Burke's concept of the act-scene ratio but fully aware of Coleridge's dicta on naïvely allegorical relations, Eliot placed her rural childhood in close proximity to an inveterately bourgeois provincial town and connected the two by a river and its tributary stream. It has been noted that Eliot, early in her writing, was looking up cases of flooding in the Midlands and shifted the location from her native Warwickshire to Lincolnshire, closer to wide rivers and the sea. The bearing of these choices falls not only on the plotting of the novel, designed clearly to end in disaster (although the closing flood and the "final rescue" have always been scorned as unanticipated manipulations of the plot), but more profoundly on the conception of personal existence and family fortunes writ large in the work.

For *The Mill* takes a potentially romantic tale of a *schöne Müllerin* and her disappointed suitors and turns it into a tragedy commensurate with, though on a different social register from, the *Antigone*.[7] In this modern revamping, the comic-realistic subject matter of rustic clowns and town-bred fools is transformed into a domestic tragedy of family

7. See David Moldstad, "*The Mill on the Floss* and *Antigone*," *PMLA*, 85 (1970): 527–31; and U. C. Knoepflmacher, *George Eliot's Early Novels: The Limits of Realism* (Los Angeles and Berkeley, 1968), pp. 164ff.

breakdown—on the order, let us say, of *Buddenbrooks* if not of *Hamlet*. In conceiving the scene and its natural activity—the river in idyllic nascence, ever-changing flow, and ultimate expiration, marked occasionally by violent debacle—Eliot found a symbolic equivalent for her sense of lost relationship with her family (although the family continued as a going concern under Isaac's firm hand). She also expressed a deep conviction about her personal fortunes, deeper than her self-congratulation in having made the right choice of a mate and embarking on an already successful and eventually illustrious literary career. This was her sense that personal life, including her own, was—in modern times, for men and women of great promise—under the sign of tragedy.

Given these large ambitions and wide designs for her autobiographical novel, Eliot's adaptation of traditional forms and figures of autobiography will be seen to develop an implicit critique of their efficacy. For Eliot's tragic sense of life was out of accord with the self-satisfied retrospects of one strain and the self-assured expectations of another strain in that tradition. The Edenic garden of childhood, formally closed at the end of the first volume by the family's economic fall (Book III, following, is titled "The Downfall"), betrays a self-conscious employment of familiar tropes:

> The two slight youthful figures soon grew indistinct on the distant road—were soon lost behind the projecting hedgerow.
> They had gone forth together into their new life of sorrow, and they would never more see the sunshine undimmed by remembered cares. They had entered the thorny wilderness, and the golden gates of their childhood had for ever closed behind them.
> (Bk. ii, ch. 7, pp. 170–71)

The passage is grandiloquent as a closural gesture, but it should be evident that its biblical figures of innocence and exile are not to be divorced from what precedes it. In that context, the tone cannot but tinge nostalgia with irony, for the scenes of childhood have consistently been shaped by the mixed qualities of realism. The rural idyll is punctuated by severe judgments of the social, educational, and other cultural forces that shape it. Two typical incidents, Maggie's fatal neglect of Tom's pet rabbits and her flight to the gypsies (following an outburst of resentment against Lucy), both detract from the idyllic by their pained awareness of children's emotional torments and of childish egoism, disabused of its illusions. Moreover, the loss of this barely protected state of childhood derives from no external, mysterious, or mythologizable force—as it is conceived by other novelists, like Dickens and Brontë—but from the inherent flaws of its participants. In this case, a father who chooses a mate on the worst of grounds, cherishes but hobbles his daughter in a most unhealthy way, and wagers the farm with egoistic competitiveness finally succeeds in bringing on their undoing.

In contrast with the somewhat tawdry realism in which this purportedly Wordsworthian pastoral is written, one might witness the sonnet sequence "Brother and Sister," which Eliot felt compelled to write ten years later.[8] The sentiment and nostalgia she undoubtedly felt but would not put directly into a fiction, she later safely disposed of in—for her—the lesser art of poetry:

> Thus rambling we were schooled in deepest lore,
> And learned the meanings that give words a soul,
> The fear, the love, the primal passionate store,
> Whose shaping impulses make manhood whole.

8. Written 1869; originally published in *The Spanish Gypsy and Other Poems* (1874), and quoted below from the corresponding volume of the Cabinet edition. Only Redinger, *George Eliot*, pp. 45–65, gives ample attention to the poems in relation to *The Mill* and Eliot's conflicting feelings about her brother, but the interpretation is diverted into speculations on the sources of Eliot's writing in childhood daydreaming—in line with Redinger's larger thesis. The parallels are uncanny and deserve further attention.

Those hours were seed to all my after good;
My infant gladness, through eye, ear, and touch,
Took easily as warmth a various food
To nourish the sweet skill of loving much.

Here is the Wordsworthian ethos of the permanent affective
influence of childhood, which is, indeed, written at length
into the novel. But after a plot *donnée* strikingly similar to
the novel's denouement, the sonnet sequence makes two
moves not to be found in *The Mill*: a nonironic figuration of
Edenic childhood as that "happy clime" and a professed
wish to repeat it with a brotherly companion:

Yet the twin habit of that early time
Lingered for long about the heart and tongue:
We had been natives of one happy clime,
And its dear accents to our utterance clung.

Till the dire years whose awful name is Change
Had grasped our souls still yearning in divorce,
And pitiless shaped them in two forms that range
Two elements which sever their life's course.

But were another childhood-world my share,
I would be born a little sister there.

In the novel, it is not some abstract change or impersonal
time that fixes the siblings' "divorce" but more specific impediments of character and circumstance, which more
closely resemble those of Eliot's family relations.

Just as Eliot follows the formulas of Edenic childhood
but fills them with realist content and complex attitudes, she
adapts the pattern of spiritual crisis and conversion to her
own fictional purposes. She might have modeled her self-
writing directly on the spiritual autobiographers to convey
her own period of evangelical enthusiasm; or she might have
been among the first to trace the loss of faith she experienced
in the 1840s. (F. W. Newman's autobiography, *Phases of
Faith*, 1850, and J. A. Froude's autobiographical novel, *The*

246

Nemesis of Faith, 1849, were close contemporaries.) Instead of making a direct representation of her experience, however, Eliot chose to explore an element in her character which never achieved doctrinal assent from her but which acted as a constant prompting throughout her life: the tendency toward self-doubt, self-suppression, and life denial whose concomitant in religious tradition is asceticism.

Reader responses to Maggie's adoption of Thomas à Kempis as a guide—and her subsequent use of his maxims in her persistent decisions to avoid personal happiness—vary from a grudging acknowledgment of their philosophical affinity to the positive version in Eliot's religion of humanity, to excoriation of them as rationalizations of Maggie's neurotic self-destructiveness. Both views are partial but consistent with Eliot's management of the quoted texts, for she is using a religious ideology as a stepping stone to her own demystified vision while revealing her capacity to avoid the emotional traps that her heroine sets for herself—affirming her decisions in faith and love and encouraging herself in face of continued promptings toward depression and self-denial.

Although Eliot sets up Thomas à Kempis's *The Imitation of Christ* as her paradigm for religious asceticism and quotes a number of its phrases to fill the text with the language of medieval piety, its autobiographical relevance is not restricted to the evocation of a favorite book of Eliot's youth. For the succeeding account of Maggie's conversion under its auspices is filled with the language of later pietistic movements, including the strains at work in England during Eliot's youth, both inside (evangelicalism) and outside (Methodism, etc.) the established church. To be sure, the heroine does not consciously employ this terminology—"She knew nothing of doctrines and systems—of mysticism or quietism . . ." (Bk. IV, ch. 3, p. 255)—but Eliot seizes the occasion to make a radical critique of their language as schemas for personal experience, including her own.

The phraseology of these movements is rife: "*ekstasis* or

outside standing-ground," "something that good society calls
'enthusiasm,' " "her long night-watchings," "the light of her
new faith," "that new inward life," "her own ascetic wish to
have no personal adornment" (Bk. IV, ch. 3, pp. 256–58).
Eliot places Maggie's experience firmly in the context of her
society, as well as in that of her own life, but she is not content to identify her heroine with the religious movement—
any more than she totally identifies herself with her heroine.
For Maggie's conversion is presented as a subjective version
of the real thing; not only are her conception of and motives
for renunciation exposed, but her religious experience itself
is described as only metaphorically resembling the claims of
divine inspiration:

> Maggie drew a long breath and pushed her heavy
> hair back, as if to see a sudden vision more clearly. . . .
> It flashed through her like the suddenly apprehended
> solution of a problem. . . . she sat in the deepening
> twilight forming plans of self-humiliation and entire
> devotedness; . . . Maggie was still panting for happi-
> ness, and was in ecstasy because she had found the
> key to it.   (Bk. IV, ch. 3, pp. 254–55)

The distance between mystical *ekstasis* and romantic "ec-
stacy" is clearly measured here.

What is perhaps most remarkable about Eliot's rewriting
of the spiritual autobiography tradition is her simultaneous
adaptation of another model of personal development in the
nineteenth century, the *Bildungsroman*. Much of *The Mill*
is, of course, devoted to discussion of education, and we are
given a detailed accounting and humorous critique of the
standard boys' schooling of the time. There is even a short
listing of the equivalent mental furnishing for girls, which
provides additional material for a subsidiary theme of the
novel, one that Eliot never tired of repeating throughout her
career but one which is only partially described as a com-
plaint against the condition of women. *The Mill* gives this
frustration a universal basis and a more profound level of

regret in describing the youthful potentialities and aspirations of every age that are left undernourished and unfulfilled; one might call this the provincial limits theme.

Maggie's education is pursued a step further than her schooling, and although—dying at nineteen—she cannot become the focus of an extended passage through and learning of the world, she is given some opportunities to explore the culture as well as the social relations of the bourgeoisie. This exploration is not allowed to become mere backgrounding of her milieu—any more than the autobiographical reference of these scenes is limited to Eliot's recollection of the enlightened circle of the Brays and Hennels, whom she encountered in her break from orthodoxy and her family. The spiritual development traced by Eliot in manipulating traditional autobiographical language is thoroughly interwoven with the *Bildung manqué* explored in sophisticated illustrations of the aesthetic culture of Maggie's world.

Even in this shift of subject matter, the favored figures of spiritual autobiography are repeatedly employed to structure the stages of Maggie's career. The brief central book of the novel's seven, in which the ascetic conversion occurs, is titled after Bunyan's Valley of Humiliation, the fifth book is called "Wheat and Tares" (Matthew 13) and the sixth, "The Great Temptation"—not by itself enough to link it to Genesis but, taken together with its first chapter title, "A Duet in Paradise," unmistakably self-conscious and ironic. The materials of Maggie's exiled state or wilderness condition are not, however, exclusively drawn from her reduced worldly fortunes or spiritual self-abasement. Instead—and consonant with Eliot's own experience—the withdrawal from childhood nurture and familial security is not to a desert but to a plentitude; Maggie's problem, like Eliot's, was how to make her selection among the advantages offered for personal growth and intellectual discovery.

Again, the novel operates by subtle deviation from tradition. The heroine, given her displaced conversion and self-destructive promptings, ensures that her exposure to the cultural advantages of the Deane and Guest households (satirized in their turn) will do her little good. When Philip leads her into the larger perspective of European literature, she reacts in a narrowly projective way, identifying the "dark, unhappy" heroine of Mme. de Staël's novel with herself (Bk. v, ch. 4, p. 290)—as she has already done with those of her favorite author, Scott. In the same way, her response to the mock-pastoral singing contest in which her twin suitors engage is to understand the reproach and the passion of Philip's Bellini aria but to lose herself in the "influence" (the word is used three times) of Stephen's Cavalier lyric in his "saucy" rendition (Bk. vi, ch. 7, p. 365). In the same process, she systematically derails any growth in her personal attachments, denying Philip's proposals on the grounds of her father's (and later, Tom's) prohibitions and denying Stephen's proposals on the grounds of Philip's (and Lucy's) prior claims. Eliot is not directly mirrored here, but we are made aware by contrast of her heroism in choosing the husband she did, against even more formidable impediments.

With these uses of tradition at work to reveal the heroine's heroic potentialities and fatal limitations, we gain a vantage for seeing the denouement not as a furtive expedient but as a mirror of tragedy. In this mirror, Eliot distinguishes her own experience from that of her heroine yet enables the creature to enact the larger self-conception of her creator.

The image of the river as the course of human life—from a slowly gathering stream at its sources, through its expanded movement in inhabited valleys, to its inevitable expiration in the sea, where it is mixed with the waters of innumerable other streams—this image has appeared so long and so often in literature that it claims the status of an archetypal symbol. From even a broad statement of its elements, it can be seen that the symbol has tragic implications. The movement of the stream is toward annihilation, its end is implied in its beginning, and there is an almost mocking irony in the contrast between its progressive expansion and its dissolution at the height of its powers. A number of recent critics of Eliot have studied her use of the river image and have connected it with her reading and thinking on the nature of tragedy. As we have seen in the case of Dickens, there is no necessary contradiction between autobiographical fiction and universal implication so that we may hope to find the river symbol in this novel to be both an identification of the self and a figure of human life.

From the opening chapter, we sense both references at work: "A wide plain, where the broadening Floss hurries on between its green banks to the sea, and the loving tide, rushing to meet it, checks its passage with an impetuous embrace." The implied course of life and the inevitable arrival at death are here presented with resonances of powerful human feelings—"loving," "impetuous," "embrace." Within this patterning of life in general, we find a specific application to the novel's heroine, the passionate and conflict-ridden Maggie, and to one strain in the author's personality as well. Even more personal are the memories voiced by the narrator (who makes no effort here to hide behind a mask of impersonality): "How lovely the little river is, with its dark, changing wavelets! It seems to me like a living companion while I wander along the bank and listen to its low placid voice, as to the voice of one who is deaf and loving. I remember those large dipping willows. I remember the stone bridge" (Bk. 1, ch. 1, p. 7). The pathos of this memory is heightened by Eliot's specific loss and alienation. The river is like a "living companion," but that companion is now lost; it murmurs like one "deaf and loving" who is gone and now communicates only in the imagination.

The poignancy of this effort to think oneself back into the past is heightened by Eliot's picture of her childhood self, which is first presented as indistinguishable from her heroine: "Now I can turn my eyes towards the mill again, and watch the unresting wheel sending out its diamond jets of water. That little girl is watching it too: she has been

standing on just the same spot at the edge of the water ever
since I paused on the bridge" (Bk. I, ch. I, p. 8). This identification by the author with her heroine has been found excessive by some critics, but the effect seems to me to be
more eerie than sentimental. We are given not simply an
author picturing herself as a girl but a complex scene in
which a woman watches a river and mill and places herself
next to a girl watching the same river and mill. The scene is
then turned into a dream, and the narrator awakes to find
herself pressing her arms on a chair and not on the cold stone
of the bridge. The past self is lost but remains living in the
dreams and sensations of the present self—equally transitory
and vulnerable.

The structuring value of the river throughout the novel
is obviously great. The crucial scenes of personal communion
and conflict are most often set on or near the river until the
climactic flood finally fulfills its dramatic potential in action.
But for present purposes it is most significant because it is a
symbol central to the author's conception of her heroine and
of herself. At the very center of the novel, midway in the
arrangement of its sections and at the turning point in the
fortunes of its characters, George Eliot develops an extended
metaphor of rivers as representing two types of human existence. Contrasting the swift, romantic, and storied Rhine
with the broad, sluggish, and prosaic Rhone, she associates
the atmosphere of the novel with the latter and apologizes
for telling such a humdrum tale of provincial life: "Perhaps
something akin to this oppressive feeling may have weighed
upon you in watching this old-fashioned family life on the
banks of the Floss, which even sorrow hardly suffices to lift
above the level of the tragi-comic" (Bk. IV, ch. I, p. 238).
The life of the Tulliver and Dodson families is Rhone-like,
and, by contrast, the aspiration of the heroine after the higher life of cultural enrichment and moral service is Rhine-like
in its heroic struggle and romantic impulsiveness. The author
knows how to value both the higher life and the lower, to
take seriously the personal tragedies of such Rhone dwellers

as Mr. Tulliver, and to acknowledge the frailty of Maggie's efforts to live the heroic life in modern times.

Yet when all accounts are cleared, there remains a dash of bitterness in Eliot's summary of her heroine's situation in the Rhone environment: "You could not live among such people; you are stifled for want of an outlet towards something beautiful, great, or noble; you are irritated with these dull men and women, as a kind of population out of keeping with the earth on which they live—with this rich plain where the great river flows for ever onward, and links the small pulse of the old English town with the beatings of the world's mighty heart" (Bk. IV, ch. 1, p. 238). Whom is the narrator addressing here? Ostensibly the reader, whom she has previously engaged in hypothetical dialogue. But the force of the conclusion—"You could not live among such people"— makes this seem the reassertion of a personal decision. Eliot could not live among such people, but she knew their importance in the lives of young men and women striving to lift themselves above the commonplace conditions of their lot. She goes on in the next paragraph to acknowledge the need to know and feel the "oppressive narrowness" of the humdrum life in order to understand and sympathize with the "suffering, whether of martyr or victim, which belongs to every historical advance of mankind" through the efforts of innovative youth.

If we ask, then, which image of the river Eliot makes central to her vision of human life, we must answer that both are necessary in the tragic condition. Rhine-like creativity fortunately arises in every generation but will inevitably be dissipated in the Rhone-like succession of men going their daily rounds. The author identifies with the energetic heroine in her tumultuous and swift passages through life; she also spends much of her time in the novel carefully painting the ripples and eddies of the broad stream of provincial life. Eliot's consciousness contains them both, and it is in the novelist's power to include both heroic young women and banal ordinary folk in the total impression of *The Mill on the*

Floss. This consciousness, uniting the Rhone and the Rhine, the past and the present, the personal and the universal, is expressed most prominently in the image of the river, which is always before us—"the great river [which] flows for ever onward, and links the small pulse of the old English town with the beatings of the world's mighty heart." Eliot has created an image of herself in this autobiographical novel, neither by recounting her life nor by mirroring herself in her heroine, but by establishing a symbol of the authorial consciousness, which flows through, absorbs, and embraces all.

With these complex interweavings of autobiographical tradition and self-critical feeling at work in *The Mill*, it is inevitable that its denouement will be difficult to accept as a total aesthetic or personal resolution. Friendly critics have tried to answer the charges of arbitrary plot manipulation and willed but unachieved reunion by pointing out the consistent anticipation of the flood throughout the work; or they have justified the reliance on an external calamity by the example of the *deus ex machina* in classical tragedy, which comes as often to clear the scene as to resolve it. Yet the resolution may also be found to be closely linked with Eliot's religion of humanity as it emerges in the novel through the displacement of traditional figures and symbols.

When Maggie reaches the end of her tether, having systematically renounced all her possibilities of relationship and survival, she gives a further twist to the ascetic language she has lived by. After quoting *The Imitation*—"I have received the Cross" and will "bear it till death"—she proceeds to a statement of self-dedication with a burden closer to Eliot's than to Thomas à Kempis's. Maggie's prayer is a formulation, still with religious overtones, of Eliot's nontheistic creed of living for others: "O God, if my life is to be long, let me live to bless and comfort—" (Bk. VII, ch. 5, p. 451). What follows directly is an apparently fortuitous circumstance, in a double sense: accidental in the course of nature and unmotivated by the train of events. Nothing can assuage our objections to the random course of nature—given the Aristotelian principle that the possible action must also appear probable—but the thematic motive for this event is firmly established by the immediately preceding one. The flood comes as the answer to Maggie's prayer: if not from the god whom she addresses, certainly from the network of reality which she confronts; if not as a gracious gift of redemption, at least as an ethical situation open for her will to heroism, her acting out of her tragedy.

It is instructive to compare this episode, the provision of a flood in which Maggie may display her willingness to live and die for others, with the formally similar legend of St. Ogg told early in the novel. From this standpoint, it may be read as Eliot's secular equivalent of an outworn mythos—although enacted in a demystified nature under the conventions of realism. With this displaced miracle, Eliot allows her heroine to fulfill the formulas of Christian asceticism in a personally communicative rather than life-denying role—although her moment of union with Tom cannot suspend the death that takes them. Maggie reenacts the role of St. Ogg in selflessly ferrying those in need across the self-same river; Eliot's revaluation of the human content of Christianity looked to just such popular legends as conveying its essential core of response to the needs and wisdom of the heart.

Having been raised in a theological culture (to use Comte's term), which interprets natural phenomena in the language of Scripture, Maggie finds the flood "that awful visitation which her father used to talk of" (Bk. VII, ch. 5, p. 452) and calls on God to show her "the way home." But this figural language has now been rendered literal by the action of natural forces, and she must return home by engaging "all her skill and power," not by faith alone. Maggie cannot herself perform miracles in this nontheistic world, and her action is not rewarded as Ogg's had been by the Virgin herself. Yet Maggie endows her own illumination, if not as a light on the water, then in the deeper reaches of her own and her brother's love. Thus is the universal burden of the naïve medieval legend fulfilled, not by supernatural showings but by the strength and passion of the human heart: "Yet it was witnessed in the floods of aftertime, that at the coming on of eventide, Ogg the son of Beorl was always seen with his boat upon the wide-spreading waters, and the Blessed Virgin sat in the prow, shedding a light around as of the moon in its brightness, so that the rowers in the gathering darkness took heart and pulled anew" (Bk. i, ch. 12, p. 105).

By the same token, the language of conversion is employed in a poignant but demystified way to describe Tom's sudden insight into the strength of his sister's love: "The full meaning of what had happened rushed upon his mind. . . . a new revelation to his spirit, of the depths in life, that had lain beyond his vision . . ." (Bk. vii, ch. 5, p. 455). It is in this manner that we are to interpret the final appropriation of scriptural language, the epitaph which forms the closing words of the novel: "In their death they were not divided" (II Sam. 1:23). The odor of sanctity wafted at the close does not dispel the bitter reflection that in life they *were* divided and that the serene resolution of the biblical text (with its Christian overtones of redemption) is not in full accord with the tragic condition of human life and death. As the accompanying maxims of Eliot declare: "Nature repairs her ravages —but not all. . . . To the eyes that have dwelt on the past, there is no thorough repair" (Conclusion, p. 457).

It is this critical reworking of traditional ideas and their language that marks George Eliot's art throughout her career, but we see her revisionary enterprise operating with a wrenching proximity to her personal situation in *The Mill on the Floss*. In the final scenes, as in the novel at large, we witness the author written into her work—in the characters, figures and scenic symbols by which she makes herself manifest. At the close, she is at one with the defeated heroine and with the survivors of the past—both united in feeling with her family and irrevocably apart.

11

The Way of All Flesh

DISFIGURING
THE FIGURES

THE RESTRAINT EXHIBITED by George Eliot in recounting her separation from her family seems to have been cast aside by Samuel Butler in his recrimination against the perpetrators of his upbringing. Its vitriolic hostility to presumptive loved ones, combined with the apparent simplicity of its fictional guise, has led to the novel's reputation as a sounding board rather than a work of art. Yet a careful weighing of Butler's use of autobiographical and fictional conventions and of his innovations within the figurative tradition makes a case for *Ernest Pontifex, or The Way of All Flesh* (1903) as standing among the most artful of autobiographical novels.

The turns of plot in the novel depart far from the course of Butler's life, to be sure, but the portrayal of the central characters is close to being an onslaught against actual persons, particularly the Butler family. And the impulse to write the book clearly derived from a need to establish the author's own identity, for when he was at peace with his family, he let it lie but took it up again after scenes of intense wrangling. Yet *The Way of All Flesh* may be seen not only as Butler's means of mercilessly satirizing his family's religious hypocrisy and crimes against himself as child but also as his way of objectifying the being that he struggled to make of himself against such odds.

Nowhere is this self-conscious artistry more evident than in Butler's manipulation of the pseudoautobiographical form, modifying it as a pseudobiography of the young protagonist by an older and wiser narrator. In autobiographies and pseudoautobiographies, there is always some embarrassment about the doubling of the author into his dual roles of naïve experiencer and sage commentator. The desire to slough off an outworn skin must imply some bad faith whereas the effort to show how all errors have conspired to make one what one is may create suspicions of ex post facto special pleading. But what if both the narrator and the protagonist are conceived with detachment, in the comic-ironic mode? Butler's erection of a biographical older friend to tell the story of a young man's suffered crimes and follies is not merely a way to exhibit himself twice over in his text, as his outworn self and as he is at the time of writing. It is also his way of reducing both the immature and the mature selves to aesthetic objects so as to direct the same ironic light on each and make their common existence as created objects the ground of their unity.

The doubling is not an accidental but an essential part of Butler's plan from the time he conceived a chronological outline for the action some pages into the composition. For the year 1802 he notes: "I [am] born p. 1, and Theobald [Pontifex, the protagonist's father] (my name is Edward [Overton] p. 7)."[1] For 1835 he writes: "Ernest born Sep. 6"—giving him the year if not the date of his own birth. And so the narrative proceeds, close enough to Butler's biography to give us clear indications of his self-scrutiny

1. Quoted in the Riverside edition of *Ernest Pontifex, or The Way of All Flesh*, ed. Daniel F. Howard (Boston, 1964), p. 364; this text, which restores Butler's manuscript intentions and radically differs from the bowdlerized version created by his first editor, will be cited parenthetically below (inserting the chapter numbers of the conventional version where these differ).

and strongly enough guided by Overton's worldly-wise tone to place the mature Butler in the foreground. The two are brought together in the plot by Overton's role as executor of Ernest's deferred inheritance, but the narrator is mainly occupied in noting the painful immaturity of his young friend and in congratulating himself on his cynical indifference to the wayward youth's self-mystifications—his continued belief in his family's honorableness in morals and religion.

When Ernest has been thoroughly whelped by experience, the two personae move toward a synthesis in thought and action; and when Ernest finally inherits his competence, the two go off together on a trip to the Continent, thoroughly enjoying their meeting of minds—as Butler must have done, since they represent aspects of himself. Almost immediately, their consciousnesses become identified: Ernest falls ill and Overton reports his own pleasurable feelings on a similar occasion (ch. 86 [80], p. 309). The two take to speaking the same lingo in their dialogues and sharing the same jokes against the Christian idols they have overthrown. Moreover, they establish a division of labor in making up the sum of Butler's activities. Ernest joins Overton as a writer and takes charge of Butler's nonfictional works whereas Overton does the satirical artistic writing at which Butler was also adept. To this final summing of the parts is added an ideal image of the whole. The minor character Towneley, who has been invoked only as a model of handsome survival power to contrast with Ernest's self-deluding and self-destructive behavior, is now added to the group as a friend and equal. So there emerges a happy society of the elect, according to the antithetical norms which the book has authenticated—and this society, rather than any one member of it, constitutes the total autobiographical image that Butler creates in *The Way of All Flesh*.

Given this operation of the novel's self-imaging, we must reconsider the title and its metaphoric reading of what passes under its heading. *The way* has a religious ring but by itself presents a neutral image of passage through the world, the linear model of experience that the novel takes up in its status as a *Bildungsroman*. *All flesh* brings an ascetic overtone with it, but we anticipate that Butler will turn this Christian pejorative into a biologically substantial subject matter, exploring the behavior of his characters as typical of the racial endowment. This displacement of the religious to the secular bearing of the terms gives way to another range of implication, already hinted at in the fusion of narrative personae described above. There is a covert religion at work in the text, which only the initiate presumably are to discover—although it lies exposed for all to see. This is the faith that all men are one, in the most literal sense of the phrase, which eighteenth-century rationalists and even Romantic organicists would blush to hear. We are all members of each other, Butler suggests, and all the positive figures of the text combine to constitute his self-image because he is in some way all these figures. He is even, in a disturbing recognition, all the negative figures as well and must strive manfully to differentiate the lower, sanctimonious Pontifex in himself from the higher strains which have flourished in the past and may still be selectable by proper husbandry. For an explanation of this new mystique in an apparently rationalistic and demystified text, we must look to the author's "scientific" writings and their bearing on his fiction.

Butler had in mind an image of humanity and a theory of the human species, something which is implied by his generalizing title. As a number of studies have shown, his series of books on the biological and social implications of evolution owes something to the Lamarckian hypothesis of the heritability of acquired characteristics. Though the theory was already being disavowed in biological science, it is none the weaker for that in Butler's works, where it takes on a strong ethical and almost theological force. Briefly, his theory ascribes much—and indeed the most effective part—of our behavior to the unconscious and innate in mind and body, and it ascribes the transmission of experience from generation to generation not to a racial memory or other carrier of the data but to the persistence of the organism itself. According to Butler, the earlier generation does not experience, learn, and modify its genetic material, transmitting this to the new generation, after which it dies. Rather he believes that there is a persistence of the being who learns from experience and modifies itself, for it establishes itself in a new body, thus dying in one form but continuing to live in the new. Each of us is "*actually* the primordial cell which never died nor dies, but has differentiated itself into the life of the world, all living beings whatever being one with it, and members one of another."[2]

It may readily be seen from this organic view of the human species in what sense the hero's career is the way of all flesh since not only fathers and sons but all men are literally one person—"one enormous individual ever in process of change and self-fulfillment."[3] It may, however, take some effort to receive the full force of Butler's view that not merely the germ plasm but the entire individual is continuous from generation to generation so that the embryo is identical to the child, to the mature man, and to the embryo that he generates. This being is constantly changing, of course, as experience and volition modify it, but it is reproduced as a whole in the next generation. What we have here is not so much an intelligible genetic theory as a revived doctrine of the transmigration of the soul. When Butler comes to apply his thesis to his own case, he is sketching a rationale for his own identity and, by extension, for the immortality of the human soul and body.

The mystifications of this biological speculation go far to account for the large measure of mystery that is generated

2. *Life and Habit*, in *The Shrewsbury Edition of the Works of Samuel Butler*, ed. H. F. Jones and A. T. Bartholomew, 20 vols. (London and New York, 1923–1926), IV, 70.
3. Claude T. Bissell, "A Study of *The Way of All Flesh*," in *Nineteenth-Century Studies*, ed. Herbert Davis et al. (Ithaca, 1940), p. 285.

by *The Way of All Flesh*. Far from rendering a coolly rational satire even more perspicuous by scientific principles, as some commentators have tried to make them do, Butler's ideas help to explain the reader's almost inevitable impression that something strange indeed is being said—or, rather, imagined—in the novel. The first hint of a mystery occurs in the portrait of the hero's great-grandfather, Old John Pontifex, who is celebrated as an eighteenth-century, prebourgeois craftsman of the yeoman tradition. The account of his death endows him with greater afflatus, however:

> The old man had a theory about sunsets and had had two steps built up against a wall in the kitchen garden on which he used to stand and watch the sun go down whenever it was clear. [The narrator's] father came on him in the afternoon, just as the sun was setting, and saw him with his arms resting on the top of the wall looking towards the sun over a field through which there was a path on which my father was. My father heard him say "Good bye sun, good bye sun" as the sun sank, and saw by his tone and manner that he was feeling very feeble. Before the next sunset he was gone. (ch. 3, p. 13)

The scene remains merely touching until a point about midway in the novel when Ernest Pontifex, the hero, is wearily leaving his public school after a full series of mental and moral castigations:

> There was a grey mist across the sun, so that the eye could bear its light, and Ernest . . . was looking right into the middle of the sun himself, as into the face of one whom he knew and was fond of. . . . Still looking into the eye of the sun and smiling dreamily, he thought how he had helped to burn his father in effigy, and his look grew merrier till at last he broke out into a laugh—exactly at this moment the light veil of cloud parted from the sun, and he was brought back to *terra firma* by the breaking forth of the sunshine. On this he became aware that he was being watched atten-

tively by a fellow traveler opposite to him, an elderly gentleman with a large head and iron-grey hair.

"My young friend," said he good-naturedly, "you really must not carry on conversations with people in the sun, while you are in a public railway carriage."

. . . The pair did not speak during the rest of the time they were in the carriage, but they eyed each other from time to time so that the face of each was impressed on the recollection of the other.

(ch. 44, pp. 170–71)

The effect of this passage is quite outside the major movement of the plot and the explicit thrust of the satire. It is only when Ernest is hauled before a magistrate for indecent advances to a fellow lodger that this note of the otherworldly and freely imaginative is again sounded. For the magistrate turns out to be the gentleman of the railway carriage; he deals with Ernest in character, that is, as a British judge might be expected to act, by sentencing him to six months' hard labor, but his reason for punishing him is the remarkable one that Ernest doesn't have sense enough to "distinguish between a respectable girl and a prostitute" (ch. 62, p. 238), that is, that he is criminally naïve. What is even more provoking about this coincidence is that it leads in the next chapter to a summary reversal of attitude to the hero by the narrator:

[The Pontifexes'] case was hopeless; it would be no use their even entering into their mothers' wombs and being born again. They must not only be born again but they must be born again each one of them of a new father and of a new mother and of a different line of ancestry for many generations before their minds could become supple enough to learn anew. . . . If a man is to enter into the kingdom of heaven he must do so not only as a little child but as a little embryo, or rather as a little zoösperm—and not only this but as one that has come of zoösperms who have entered into the kingdom of heaven before him for many generations. (ch. 63, pp. 240–41)

This gets as close to biological fatalism as we can go, even in an age of Social Darwinism, for it cuts the ground from under every effort of the individual to repair the damage done him by his parental endowment. But there is another side to this remorseless logic.

The subtler implication of the argument is that Ernest can look far back in his ancestry and find progenitors who have *not* traveled down the road of the Pontifexes, that there is an essential self or zoösperm at the outset of the individual's career that is somehow—Butler does not tell us how—recoverable. It is my contention that though Butler does not give us an arguable theory of the recovery, he shows this essential self in the images of the novel. Old John Pontifex is close to this originative seed and bears the marks of it; he relates himself to it in his attention to—or worship of—the sun. The association of this seminal source with the sun is nothing other than a late appearance of an archetypal myth, which many cultures have fostered. It carries the notion that we are children of the sun, that the sun is our father in heaven, and that looking into the sun we see a person—"the face of one he knew and was fond of," as Ernest discovers on the train. Recovery of this progenitor is a recovery of oneself. It brings us to laughter and a comic insight into our condition; it helps us to recognize the other men around us who are true kin; and it may even bring on a rebuke for carrying on "conversations with people in the sun."

This is perhaps the most subversive doctrine in Butler's outrageous repertoire. Certain men are not simply better but holier than others (quite different from those that British Christian culture would lead one to expect); they are closer to the sources of being and thereby more pure-bred incarnations of the human archetype. Butler's way of seizing such truths has as little to do with Darwin and science as it has to do with the Kingdom of Heaven and faith. The imagination behind such a world view would seem to be privy to a large fund of ancient myth and pagan learning, and Butler's own tastes ran to the classics (as can be seen in his remarkable study *The Authoress of The Odyssey*). The hidden suggestion of the text is that Butler is in on the secret because he is a child of the sun himself. And that is ultimately what is given in this autobiographical fable. It is a projected image of Butler himself as a sublime man of wisdom.

To conclude that Butler's achievement in *The Way of All Flesh* is not so much an accurate record nor a fictive exposition of his life as it is a manifestation of himself as a man of wisdom is not to ascribe to him more than usual autobiographical egoism. He artfully erects not only a pathetically naïve hero but a coldly skeptical narrator to control the reader's sympathies and avoid introducing himself directly into the tale. But the voices that echo in the novel are not only those of Butler's fledgling and mature selves but also that of his originating self or source. In a frequently quoted passage, Butler allows Ernest's "more real" and "true self" to address his "reasoning and reflecting self" as a "prig" and to insist on its obedience—"for I, Ernest, am the God who made you" (ch. 31, p. 116). This godly being is the eternal seed or source that Butler identifies with the sun, and by allowing it to speak in his novel, he brings to expression a part of himself that he seems to regard as his most impressive and mysterious. It is almost an anticlimax when Butler makes the hero of his last fictional work, *Erewhon Revisited*, a revised version of his early, naïve persona. The hero is taken in this never-never land to be a divine savior, who appeared briefly and then ascended to his father in heaven—and Butler names this ironic final image of himself "the Sun-child."

An element of the novel that gains added force by association with its covert but commanding self-myth is that of the *dea ex machina*, Ernest's aunt and godmother, Alethæa. Aside from her provision of a fortune that allows the hero, at the nadir of his career, to clear himself entirely of the social and economic constraints of his society and to adopt the detached self-cultivation that was the lifestyle of

Butler himself, Alethæa provides something more. As her name suggests, she is a standard of truth and clarity of vision, *in* but not *of* the world—involving herself only by communicating with the more directly implicated Overton but always seeing clearly the broad shape of Ernest's career. That Ernest is allowed to flounder in darkness while his fate is all the time secure might be thought an arrogant form of personal manipulation—if not a somewhat sadistic taste for watching worms wriggle—were it not for the reflection that this is the way the classical gods observe the toils of mortals, even when they are beneficently inclined. The Greekness of her name suggests that Alethæa is being made to carry some of the fruits of Butler's classical learning, and it thus invites interpretation of that name and her character at their root.

The Greek derivation in question is *a-lethe*—"without concealment"—a negation of the Lethean darkness that is the condition not only of our future but of our present lives. In the cave where Plato imagines us to live, we see only by artificial light, and only shadows at that; were we to convert, turn about, and face the sun directly, we should see truly and ideally. Alethæa stands for this possibility; as Jacques Derrida has pointed out,[4] the connection between the standard of truth and the light of the sun stands at the origin (if such a point were admissible) of Western philosophy. What must be added to Derrida's imaginative rendering of these philosophic roots is their strong feminine strain; although truth and the sun are arrogated by the philosophers to masculine power, they are endowed to mankind through the filter, as it were, of the eternal feminine. Zeus and the Sun may be light themselves, but it is Athena (like Alethæa) who mediates it for the human mind.

4. Jacques Derrida, "White Mythology: Metaphor in the Text of Philosophy," *New Literary History*, 6 (1974): 5–74; for another nineteenth-century artist struck by the sun into identification with it, see Ronald Paulson, "Turner's Graffiti: The Sun and Its Glosses," in *Images of Romanticism: Verbal and Visual Affinities*, ed. Karl Kroeber and William Walling (New Haven and London, 1978), pp. 167–88.

Since Butler's enterprise is one of projecting an alternative religion in which to identify himself, he makes primary use of classical and scientific language and thought in creating his new mythos. Yet Butler has also been called to account for the very Victorian earnestness with which he pursued his demolition job, and we will not be surprised to discover traces of the old dispensation in the temple of the new. Indeed, much of the energy of the humor which powers *The Way of All Flesh* derives from that simplest of ironic techniques, the pompous restatement of the enemy position (as Butler did in *The Fair Haven*, with near-disastrous results). An alternative mode of formulation is uniform inversion, that simplest of comic techniques for reducing the sacrosanct items in a system to materials of play. Instances of both types abound; I cite one of each for their flavor:

> For the embryo has already so often changed its form as to have died and been born anew a dozen times over before it reaches its full development . . . so that not only is it true that in the midst of life we are in death, but also that in the midst of death we are in life.
>
> Death indeed is being swallowed up in life. If the last enemy that shall be subdued is death then indeed is our Salvation nearer than what we thought, for death is being defeated at all points. True, we know no more about the end of our lives than about the beginning: we come up insensibly and go down insensibly. . . .
>
> (ch. 6, p. 27; references are to the
> Book of Common Prayer,
> I Corinthians 15, Romans 13, and Job 1)

> I said, "You cannot tell your father and mother [about your inheritance]—it would drive them mad."
>
> "No, No, No," said he, "it would be too cruel—it would be like Isaac offering up Abraham and no thicket with a ram in it near at hand."
>
> (ch. 87 [81], p. 318)

With the proliferation of these kinds of humor, a definitive text of the novel would cite biblical references as heavily as if it were a canonical work. At certain points, Butler seems to have been drawn into the spirit of this language, as in the hortatory rhetoric of the "real Ernest" quoted above, who speaks with the voice of Jehovah, only half-ironically: "And I will rend you in pieces even unto the third and fourth generation as one who has hated God; for I, Ernest, am the God who made you" (ch. 31, p. 116; the sentiment echoes Numbers 15, which Theobald reads for his sermon in Chapter 23). Similarly, biblical allusions come aptly to hand in establishing the true nature of the hero and his kind, as when the liberated Ernest declares: "I am an Ishmael by instinct as much as by accident of circumstances, but if I keep out of society I shall be less vulnerable than Ishmaels generally are" (ch. 90 [84], p. 336).

Even more significant than this tendency not merely to devastate but to appropriate goods from the enemy camp is Butler's provision within the text itself of a brief manual on how to proceed. The passage may not immediately recommend itself as a guide to linguistic appropriation, for it takes the form of a comment on Handel's musical setting of a Miltonic text, but the lessons are easily transferred to Butler's own proceedings with biblical and other traditional idioms. Willfully misreading a passage of *Samson Agonistes*, in which Manoah's paternalism may be easily mocked, Butler intercalates a paragraph typical of his own notebooks:

I have never been able to understand how Handel failed to see and point the humour of this passage with that exquisitely playful irony which he has elsewhere displayed in Samson [i.e., the oratorio], and which no one has so inimitably translated into music as he. Handel has treated these two lines with the utmost pathos, and I have looked in vain for the slightest hint of his having smelt a rat anywhere in their vicinity. I suppose the explanation lies in the fact that he lost his own father when he was six years old, was independent at the age of fifteen, if not earlier, and never married—so that his ideas of family life were drawn mainly from what the poets told him about it. So again in the air "Such tears as tender fathers shed," he lays no emphasis on the word "such." From all of which we conclude that even a Handel cannot be trusted to write about things which he does not understand. (ch. 38, p. 144)

The self-indulgently arch manner and apparently tacked-on rationale of this passage do not obscure its relevance to Butler's own enterprise in *The Way of All Flesh*. Applying the free spirit and the ironic wit of a Handel to an area in which the master was inexperienced, Butler attempts to make himself the Handel of family life. In doing so, he erects the composer as the type of the comic artist and identifies him with the small band of the elect established at the end of the novel.[5] (Overton is, as a writer of stage burlesque, after all a lesser successor of Handel, that West End impresario.) It remains to see whether the figure of the artist is raised even higher, to a deific role which would replace the outworn transcendental gods with an immanent human power.

Ernest very early shows an inclination both toward Handel's music and to the creative craftsman ethos of his great-grandfather, expressed in his instinctive drive not only to play organs but to make them. It is precisely these innate traits that lead his demystified fairy godmother, Alethæa, to prefer him: " 'He likes the best music,' she thought, 'and he hates Dr. Skinner; this is a very fair beginning' " (ch. 32, p. 121)—and she immediately sets him up in organ building.

5. In this interpretation of Handel as humanistic dramatist, opera impresario, and inheritor of the classical spirit in comedy and tragedy by turns, Butler anticipates the recent demythologizing of the domestic-Christian author of *The Messiah*; see Winton Dean, *Handel's Dramatic Oratorios and Masques* (London, New York, and Toronto, 1959); and Paul Henry Lang, *George Frederic Handel* (New York, 1966).

Ernest reveals his inherent knowledge of his racial and personal nature by writing his aunt's epitaph in the musical language of Handel (ch. 36, p. 136), pointing out that it might also serve as his own epitaph.

He pursues his devotion to oratorio music even after his father stops the organ building and at school singles out the organist of the local church as a kindred spirit. The old man's life goes back to the eighteenth century, and he claims to have known the musical historian Charles Burney. Through him Ernest can construct a chain of vision back to the source and origin: "He knew that Dr. Burney, when a boy at school at Chester, used to break bounds that he might watch Handel smoking his pipe in the Exchange coffee house—and now he was in the presence of one who if he had not seen Handel himself had at least seen those who had seen him" (ch. 37, p. 140). In our gesture consigning these reflections to boyish fondness, we may reflect that the logic of the procedure closely resembles the authentications of canonical texts and witnessed epiphanies.

The pursuit of his racial endowment to its sources leads Ernest relentlessly back to the eighteenth century, but it is not so easily demonstrated that it puts him in touch with his great-grandfather. Unfortunately, Butler deleted from his manuscript a passage that would have made their common link to Handel definite:

> [Old John] worshipped Handel whom as a young man he had seen when he was on his way to Dublin, and for whom, if I mistake not he had executed some small errand or commission; this fact had perhaps intensified the old man's admiration, but at any rate he was as certain that Handel was the greatest of all musicians, past present and to come as that Shakespeare was the prince of all possible writers. I myself [i.e., Overton] took to Handel at a very early age and old Mr. Pontifex found it out and became partial to me at once, for there is nothing that goes so straight

home to the heart of a good Handelian, as to observe
an instinctive love for Handel's music in a child.

(ch. 1, p. 4n.)

As important as Ernest's linkage to his great-grandfather in
this passage—with its emphasis on the "instinctive" in the
child, which is later perceived and nourished by his aunt—is
the suggestion that the predilection for Handel sets up a
community that crosses family lines. The phrase, "a good
Handelian," is colloquial and casual here, but as the novel
proceeds, it sets up two camps, roughly corresponding to
the elect and unredeemed in Butler's biological eschatology,
and these camps may well be called the Handelians and the
anti-Handelians.

Members of the latter camp are enlisted early on. Ernest's
mother, during Theobald's courtship of her, is witheringly
described as having a "very beautiful contralto voice" but
with an extremely limited range: "She had transposed 'Angels ever bright and fair' into a lower key so as to make it
suit her voice. . . . at every pause she added an embellishment
of arpeggios from one end to the other of the keyboard, on
a principle which her governess had taught her; she thus
added life and interest to an air which all—so she said—must
feel to be rather heavy in the form in which Handel left it"
(ch. 11, p. 42). Butler's contempt may be understood by
anyone who shares his feeling for the little-known masterpiece, *Theodora*, in which the sublime aria in question appears.

A more general kind of discrimination between musical
sheep and goats is made by the narrator as he surveys the
"fat, very well-to-do folk" who make up Theobald's con-
gregation: "Somehow or other I find the strain which Handel has wedded to the words 'There the ploughman near at
hand' [from *L'Allegro*] has got into my head and there is no
getting it out again. How marvellously old Handel understood these people!" (ch. 14, p. 56). This is snobbish, of

271

course, but not social snobbism; "these people" are not merely apt subjects for musical penetration but lie beyond the pale of participation in that music. Instead, they have their own, and Overton launches into a mock-historical divagation on their hymns—their "Wesleyan symphony."

With the establishment of these antithetical groups and the shaping of a plot that carries the hero from one affiliation to the other, we may be prepared to rethink the shape of Ernest's career as a revised edition of the conversion process. It is well established that the form of his story is that of the *Bildungsroman* as he passes in review through the several religious varieties available in mid-Victorian England and travels through the lower and lower-middle classes in his descent into prison and tailoring, before passing beyond his natal class to genteel affluence. Yet it is not only the conversions of the loss of faith and of social reaffiliation that Ernest passes through; he also enacts a progressive accession to higher powers, ultimately discovering them within himself—or, as himself. This enactment is shaped by demystified forms of the traditional conversion scenes.

Ernest has his first intimation of his kinship with the sun during his journey from school, in which he encounters the old gentleman who becomes his judge but in whom we may also detect the marks of his eighteenth-century progenitor. It should now be noted that Ernest has prepared himself for this revelation. Leaving his school at Roughborough with mixed emotions, he assuages his anxieties by going to church, but by means of music: "He walked up and down the aisle for a while in meditative mood, and then settling down to the organ played 'They loathed to drink of the river' about six times over, after which he felt more composed and happier; then, tearing himself away from the instrument he loved so well, he hurried to the station" (ch. 64, p. 170). It is, ironically, a chorus from *Israel in Egypt* that Ernest favors but divested of its theological context (an account of one of the plagues). Instead, Ernest mingles himself with the complex contrapuntal composition and feels "more com-

posed" in consequence. This, together with his growing
comic insight during his meditation in the train, marks the
start of his progress toward solar illumination and personal
identification with his heroic lineage.

Whatever indecision we may have in seeing Ernest's experience in the displaced forms of the conversion process
should be dispelled by his later meditation on his descent
into prison:

> As he thought further he remembered that all things
> work together for good to them that love God; was it
> possible, he asked himself, that he too however im-
> perfectly had been trying to love him? He dared not
> answer yes, but he would try hard that it should be
> so. Then there came into his mind that noble air of
> Handel's, "Great God who yet but darkly known,"
> and he felt it as he had never felt it before. He had
> lost his faith in Christianity, but his faith in some-
> thing—he knew not what—but that there was a some-
> thing as yet but darkly known which made right
> right, and wrong wrong—his faith in this grew strong-
> er and stronger daily.
>
> (ch. 69 [68], pp. 259-60)

Lest there be any temptation to see Ernest as still operating
within the confines of Christianity, despite his disclaimer, it
should be evident that the opening sentence repeats the epigraph of the novel (from Romans 8:28) and that the effect
of these allusions is roughly equivalent to the famous line
in *Erewhon*: "As luck would have it, Providence was on my
side."[6] By the same token, Cyrus's air in *Belshazzar's Feast*
does not convey a gospel message but an awe of universal
forces closer akin to that of the Greek tragic chorus. This
great god, darkly known, is not some eternal not-ourselves
which makes for righteousness, in Arnoldian phrasing, but
precisely the eternal *ourselves* that Ernest is well on his way
to discovering.

From this meditation in prison, akin to Bunyan's and

6. *Shrewsbury Edition of the Works*, ch. 4, p. 23.

Fox's in the martyrological subspecies of autobiography, Ernest passes directly to his newly redeemed condition:

> He lit his pipe and sat down to the piano. He played Handel for an hour or so, and then set himself to the table to read and write. He took all his sermons and all the theological works he had begun to compose during the time he had been a clergyman and put them in the fire; as he saw them consume he felt as though he had got rid of another incubus. Then he took up some of the little pieces he had begun to write during the latter part of his undergraduate life at Cambridge, and began to cut them about and rewrite them.
>
> (ch. 76 [72], p. 281)

Among these essays is, no doubt, the one quoted in Chapter 46 on the higher standing of comedy over tragedy.

Although it may be too much to say that Handel is the deity whom Ernest converts to—although Overton's assertion that "he worshipped Handel" (ch. 83 [73], p. 284) is no mere hyperbole—it is clear that his music has recurrent epiphanic effect in the growth of the hero's mind. His is the accent of the divine element in humanity, if not biologically identifiable with the immortal germ plasm of Butler's theorizing, then historically identifiable with the comic spirit that breathes in Handel's music and that is readily convertible into the tragic sublime when the occasion demands. In choosing this creative figure as his equivalent for a theological antitype or salvific deity, Butler makes a new form of cultural model available for modern autobiography and fiction—the artist.

Yet in his musical preferences, Butler and his hero are not quite in the modernist swing; Ernest explains to his headmaster's arty daughter that he's trying hard to like modern music but hasn't quite succeeded:

> "And pray where do you consider modern music to begin?"
> "With Sebastian Bach."
>
> (ch. 93 [86], p. 354)

12
Turning
Figures

SOME CONFIRMATION for the widely shared view that secular autobiography rose with the rise of the individual comes from the dramatic proliferation of self-writing toward the end of the nineteenth century, at the inception of what Lukàcs called "the permanent carnival of fetishized interiority." The evidence is impressive, especially if one considers quantity rather than quality and even if one ranges no farther than the intellectual and artistic sphere. Nothing like the present-day barrage of lives by socialites, politicians, and theatrical folk, yet professionals of all kinds were talking shop. Industrious stories of quest and discovery are told by scientists (A. R. Wallace, Francis Galton, T. H. Huxley), following Darwin's example in his self-writings. There are meticulous records of careers in the fine arts (William M. Rossetti, William Holman Hunt, Frederick Locker-Lampson) and close reporting of their intellectual milieus by T. A. Trollope, Mrs. Humphrey Ward, and Augustus Hare. And there are histories of the self-cum-history of ideas by Herbert Spencer, Harriet Martineau, and Frederick Harrison, marshals in the march of mind.

Yet at a time when almost every writer had a life story to tell, only a smaller number seized upon the available language in which to tell it. The self-writings we recall as especially readable are those which venture more than a dignified statement of the facts—which become memorable by the mediation of their prose. Despite their avoidance of the norms of historical narration, these works come into an exemplary status for their period, becoming more representative than the historically minute memoirs. And by a delicate irony, these writings of the iconoclasts—or, failing that, of the experimental artists and freer spirits of the time—are those which more fully utilize the traditional figures of autobiography, even in the act of casting off the weight of inherited religious and social commitments.

The spectacle of unbelievers preaching to the converted in their own tongue has not gone unmarked by students of the period. Richard Ellmann, a close observer of the emergent modern spirit, has commented on this aspect of fin-de-siècle art:

> What strikes us at once about Edwardian literature is that it is thoroughly secular, yet so earnest that secularism does not describe it. . . . Almost to a man, Edwardian writers rejected Christianity, and having done so, they felt free to *use* it, for while they did not need religion they did need religious metaphors. . . . In creative writers, this new temper appears not in discussion of religion, which does not interest them, but in vocabulary. Religious terms are suddenly in vogue among unbelievers.[1]

And Ellmann follows out these changes in metaphor and diction among Joyce, Yeats, Lawrence, and other builders of the temple of modernism on the displaced foundations of Christianity. We shall find much the same to be true of their self-writings as of their poetry and fiction.

Among the varieties of turn-of-the-century experimentation with the traditional forms and terms of self-writing, not all were motivated by a principled desire to found the

1. Richard Ellmann, "Two Faces of Edward," in *Edwardians and Late Victorians: English Institute Essays, 1959,* ed. Richard Ellmann (New York and London, 1960), pp. 191–92.

secular self on the ruins of an outworn religion. Some writers pursued the aestheticist conversion of content into style in a purely formal way so that the figures they employ become fully detached from their tradition. Thus, George Moore begins his lifelong series of books about himself with *Confessions of a Young Man* (1888),[2] but his figure of confession is so sharply divorced from religion that it now connotes self-advertisement rather than self-correction. When Moore goes on in *Hail and Farewell* (1911–1914) to associate himself with Siegfried and with St. Patrick in his mission to bring culture to Ireland,[3] the saint's life and the Nordic myth have reached an abstractness in which the inversion of traditional content borders on self-parody. Much of the writing in this period enjoys a carnival spirit of mockery and misrule, and autobiography is no exception. The finer spirits, however, inhabit a borderland between the satirizing of conventions and the fall into conventionality.

Pater's "*The Child in the House*"

Walter Pater's autobiographical essay, "The Child in the House" (1878), has been heartily praised for its anticipations of modern writing—its depiction of the forming of personality through close attention to childhood sensibility. This "imaginary portrait" has not yet received its due as a veritable anthology of autobiographical figures, a summation of the old that fosters a turning to the new. In taking up so many of the terms in which previous nineteenth-century writers had shaped their accounts of themselves, Pater shows clear signs of being aware of these devices as fictional constructs. His self-conscious use of the figurative code suggests

2. For a summary of this series, see the introduction to Susan Dick's edition of *Confessions of a Young Man* (Montreal and London, 1972).

3. See Herbert Zirker, *George Moore: Realismus und autobiographische Fiktion: Versuch zur Form der Autobiographie* (Cologne and Graz, 1968), pp. 221ff.

that the code was becoming reified and artificial through wide repetition, making this autobiographical essay a crucial transition from Victorian to modern self-writing.

Pater is often thought of as a classical hedonist, if not an iconoclastic materialist (both terms might serve as a fair philosophical description), as remote from biblical textualism, Puritan morality, and typological thought as it is possible to be in the nineteenth century. But conscientious editions alert us that his language is shot through with biblical allusions,[4] and closer inquiry reveals a network of figures echoing Christian conceptions of personal life. It is true that the root metaphor of "The Child in the House"—the notion of the house as a mental space, a structure of associations linked to specific topoi, literal places—is not a distinctly religious one. Yet the larger space mapped by the essay places the house in relation to garden and road and thereby relates it to two of the favored figures of Victorian autobiographical writing.

It is initially important to grasp the vitality and interest of the root metaphor, only broadly described in commentaries on the essay. From the first paragraph, the house is mentioned as "that half-spiritualized house [where] he could watch the better, over again, the gradual expansion of the soul which had come to be there. . . ." By the fifth paragraph, this half-spiritualization has become total, as the root metaphor is given its fullest elaboration:

> How insignificant, at the moment, seem the influences of the sensible things which are tossed and fall and lie about us, so, or so, in the environment of early childhood. How indelibly, as we afterwards discover, they affect us; with what capricious attractions and associations they figure themselves on the white paper, the smooth wax, of our ingenuous souls, as "with lead in

4. See *Selected Writings of Walter Pater*, ed. Harold Bloom (New York, 1974), pp. 15–16; I have compared this text with that of the Macmillan Library edition of Pater's works and cite it by paragraph number (a convenience possible with a brief work).

the rock for ever," giving form and feature, and as it were assigned house-room in our memory, to early experiences of feeling and thought, which abide with us ever afterwards, thus, and not otherwise. The realities and passions, the rumours of the greater world without, steal in upon us, each by its own special little passageway, through the wall of custom about us. . . . manifold experiences—our various experiences of the coming and going of bodily pain, for instance—belong to this or the other well-remembered place in the material habitation—that little white room with the window across which the heavy blossoms could beat so peevishly in the wind, [for example]; and the early habitation thus gradually becomes a sort of material shrine or sanctuary of sentiment; a system of visible symbolism interweaves itself through all our thoughts and passions; and irresistibly, little shapes, voices, accidents—the angle at which the sun in the morning fell on the pillow—become parts of the great chain wherewith we are bound.

Moving quickly past the atomic bombardment of "sensible things" and the tabula rasa, two well-established philosophical metaphors of the mind—and with a passing allusion to Job 19 for another image of our fixed character—the text reaches its root metaphor somewhat self-consciously ("as it were") and only partially ("house-room in our memory"). The next sentence, however, makes the metaphor active and dramatic: realities of the outer world steal by special passageways through the wall of custom and make their entrance to the mind's inner space. Each experience is connected in the storehouse of memory with a place in the "material habitation"—the literal house in which the child lived, now become a "well-remembered" memory structure itself—so that the order of remembered experiences is homologous to the order of remembered rooms. In the final clauses of the long last sentence, the house of mind has become not merely a free-standing structure but another kind of dwelling: it is a "system of visible symbolism" and also a "shrine or sanctuary of sentiment," a house of some holiness. Beyond worshipping in this temple of the self, however, Pater acknowledges its confining and determining limitations or "great chain."[5] Subsequently, a philosophical formulation of this genetic epistemology is given, and the metaphor is made explicit: "Such [later] metaphysical speculation did but reinforce what was instinctive in his way of receiving the world, and for him, everywhere, that sensible vehicle or occasion became, perhaps only too surely, the necessary concomitant of any perception of things, real enough to be of any weight or reckoning, in his house of thought" (¶13).

The figure of the house is from the first accompanied by the literal and metaphorical appendages of garden and road: "In the house and garden of his dream he saw a child moving, and could divide the main streams at least of the winds that had played on him, and study so the first stage in that mental journey" (¶1). The following paragraphs provide further details of the literal garden, its high wall, varied flowers and trees, and a gate. This latter, when found open, reveals the spectacle of a red hawthorn tree in blossom—"the beginning of a revelation" of aesthetic color, which he is eventually to find "still alive in the works of old Venetian masters or old Flemish tapestries" (¶12). We are well prepared, therefore, to find the child's life figured in the language of the enclosed garden: "And the sense of security could hardly have been deeper, the quiet of the child's soul being one with the quiet of its home, a place 'inclosed' and 'sealed'" (¶9; referring to Canticles 4, as in Ruskin's use of the figure). In the next breath, however, the enclosure is found porous and temporary: "But upon this assured place, upon the child's assured soul which resembled it, there came floating in from the larger world without, as at windows left ajar unknowingly, or over the high garden walls, two streams

5. For a Lacanian reading of similar mental structures in another of Pater's autobiographical fictions, see Michael Ryan, "Narcissus Autobiographer: *Marius the Epicurean*," *English Literary History*, 43 (1976): 184–208.

of impressions, the sentiments of beauty and pain . . ." (¶9). As in the previously analyzed passage, the garden figure invites a double emotion. House and garden make an enclosure of security, pleasure and first things; but they are also a high-walled prison (associated with "the great chain" of material determinism), a reclusive separation like the Lady of Shalott's closed tower, and an especially vulnerable place in admitting the temptations and anxieties of beauty and pain.

The other autobiographical figure established at both the literal and metaphoric levels leads just as directly to a statement about the child's mind and its subsequent course in life. The house stands near "a great city" (it was at Enfield, near London), and it is connected with other places by a road:

> The coming and going of travellers to the town along the way, the shadow of the streets, the sudden breath of the neighbouring gardens, the singular brightness of bright weather there, its singular darknesses which linked themselves in his mind to certain engraved illustrations in the old big Bible at home . . . all this acted on his childish fancy, so that ever afterwards the like aspects and incidents never failed to throw him into a well-recognised imaginative mood, seeming actually to have become a part of the texture of his mind.   (¶4)

A number of associations are mingled here, but I would single out the latent force of "along the way," to be developed in a number of formulations on the passage of life: "his way through the world" (¶4), "the weariness of the way" (¶9), "Angels might be met by the way" (¶18), etc. Indeed, the essay begins and ends with wayside scenes; the opening incident reports the meeting of the adult Florian Deleal with a Wordsworthian "poor aged man," who speaks of his natal place and provokes a dream and the essay, whereas the closing narrative is of leaving the house and traveling down "that favourite country-road" (¶19). For all the dominance of his static images of house and garden, Pater conceives of his life equally in terms of movement, change, and leave-taking.

It would be excessive to say that such references are restrictively allegorical, for example, in shaping life like *The Pilgrim's Progress*,[6] for the autobiographical figure of life as a journey is strongly marked in this essay by broader undertones of spiritual pilgrimage. The Wordsworthian catalyst of memory is himself such a figure: "He seemed weary with the road, [and Florian] helped him on with the burden which he carried, a certain distance. . . . the story told, [he] went forward on his journey comforted" (¶1). Later, describing Florian's "singularly intense" "sense of home"—in a passage bristling with combinations of the word ("home-like," "home-counties," "home-life")—the prose shows further marks of theological language:

> And so for Florian that general human instinct was reinforced by this special home-likeness in the place his wandering soul had happened to light on, as, in the second degree, its body and earthly tabernacle. . . . The wistful yearning towards home, in absence from it, . . . interpreted to him much of a yearning and regret he experienced afterwards, towards he knew not what, out of strange ways of feeling and thought in which, from time to time, his spirit found itself alone. . . .   (¶8)

6. Cf. Gerald C. Monsman, *Pater's Portraits: Mythic Pattern in the Fiction of Walter Pater* (Baltimore, 1967), pp. 40–51, which relates the "archetypal" figures of life journey, road, house, etc., to Bunyan's and establishes them as the "central allegory" of the piece. For a more schematic statement, see Monsman's *Walter Pater* (Boston, 1977), pp. 75–80, which emphasizes the Wordsworthian antecedents of "Edenic garden," "aged man," and "moment of vision." Monsman has made a further extension of his long studies in *Walter Pater's Art of Autobiography* (New Haven and London, 1980), which treats the entire *oeuvre* as an autobiographical project—by an argument which I find difficult to follow.

From this standpoint, we are all "pilgrims and wayfarers," to whom "final banishment from home is a thing bitterer still" (¶6).

A secondary association of the passage in which the road of life is introduced is with dark illustrations in the family Bible, and these associations are brought to the foreground in a later paragraph:

> He pored over the pictures in religious books, and knew by heart the exact mode in which the wrestling angel grasped Jacob, how Jacob looked in his mysterious sleep, how the bells and pomegranates were attached to the hem of Aaron's vestment, sounding sweetly as he glided over the turf of the holy place. His way of conceiving religion came then to be in effect what it ever afterwards remained—a sacred history indeed, but still more a sacred ideal, a transcendent version or representation, under intenser and more expressive light and shade, of human life. . . . A place adumbrated itself in his thoughts, wherein those sacred personalities, which are at once the reflex and the pattern of our nobler phases of life, housed themselves. . . . Some ideal, hieratic persons he would always need to occupy it and keep a warmth there.
>
> (¶17)

It would be too much to say that this formulation is an aesthetic version of religious typology, for Pater's metaphorical language prevents our taking this habit of mind as a disciplined system of thought. But when he goes on to speak of "a constant substitution of the typical for the actual" (¶18), we must conclude that he is playing on the language of typology in the same way in which he transforms "sacred personalities" into patterns of "our nobler phases of life" and literal "sacred history" into a loosely personal "sacred ideal."

We may watch this process of symbol making, of self-conscious appropriation of traditional language, at work in

Pater's biblical allusions. He misquotes I John 2 on the "lust of the eyes" but reverses the valence of John's disapprobation to make this an attractive attribute—"the activity in him of a more than customary sensuousness, 'the lust of the eye,' as the Preacher says, which might lead him, one day, how far!" (¶9). He entertains the "lively hope" of II Peter 1, but not in connection with the resurrection of Christ, rather in association with "a melancholy already deeply settled in him" (¶17). And his anticipation of the recompense vouchsafed at the "resurrection of the just" (Luke 14) leads him to think of his dead father "like the figure in the picture of Joshua's Vision" (¶16; concerning Joshua 5). But this "benign, grave figure in beautiful soldier's things" gives way to nocturnal fears of revenants, "a certain sort of figure he hoped not to see" (¶16). In the service of Pater's aestheticism, the sacramental system of traditional religion acquires a set of personal associations and sentimental valuations. Ultimately, religious language is reduced to incidental metaphor for the expression of taste: "All the acts and accidents of daily life borrowed a sacred colour and significance; the very colours of things became themselves weighty with meanings like the sacred stuffs of Moses' tabernacle, full of penitence or peace" (¶18). In "The Child in the House," Pater ends by turning biblical associations into enhancements of the value of aesthetic experience in the phenomenal world. No account of his sensibility and its formation could more precisely define him..

Wilde's *De Profundis*

Recent critics have taught us to attend closely to the autobiographical strain in Oscar Wilde, which reaches a peak in *The Picture of Dorian Gray*. Richard Ellmann has linked this strain not merely with the Decadent nineties but with a confessional impulse particularly deep-seated in the author:

In Wilde the interest does not lie in the aesthetic theory [of the mask] which is perhaps no more than a taste for stylization, but rather in that for him the doctrine of the mask is itself a mask. . . . Wilde's creative works almost invariably end with a ceremonial unmasking. . . . The ultimate virtue in his essays is pretence, but the denouement of his dramas and narratives, no matter from what varied sources he borrows their plots, is always the same: pretence is thrown to the winds. . . . Salomé strips the veils from her body. . . . We burn to show what we are.[7]

As Ellmann suggests, this tendency toward self-exposure, even to the point of self-immolation, is carried out in Wilde's life as well as in his art so that Wilde's legal persecutor, the Marquis of Queensberry, "instead of being his villain, appears in retrospect as the mere agent of much of Wilde's mind." If this pattern of self-destruction preceded or followed by self-exposure can be traced in Wilde's life as well as in his fictions, we should not be surprised to discover it in his main autobiographical narrative, the extended letter called *De Profundis* (1905; written 1897).

Ellmann's remarks provide a clue to the linkage between two elements of Wilde's letter that might otherwise remain obscure or seem merely mannered: his religious preoccupation and his urgent masochism. Reading *De Profundis*, we may be prepared to wade through the so-called "religious digression," in which Wilde reports on his biblical reading in prison and offers to reinterpret Christ in terms of his newly moralized version of aestheticism. But we are unprepared—even after several readings, in my own case—to believe our eyes when Wilde closes the long litany of Alfred

7. Richard Ellmann, Introduction to Oscar Wilde, *Selected Writings* (London, New York, and Toronto, 1961), pp. x–xi. For the text of *De Profundis*, I cite from *Selected Letters of Oscar Wilde*, ed. Rupert Hart-Davis (London, 1962)—the authoritative text of Hart-Davis's *Letters of Wilde* and more widely available.

Douglas's abuses of him with detailed plans for their meeting again after his release from Reading jail. It is an unlooked-for implication of Christian love that Wilde applies to reunion with his destroyer: "To Humility there is nothing that is impossible, and to Love all things are easy" (p. 238). This is not enough to cancel the expressions of sexual degradation, addiction to pain as inflicted by a perfectly heartless youth, and powerlessness to foreswear the addiction: "My friendship with you . . . was intellectually degrading to me" (p. 155); "Having made your own of my genius, my will-power, and my fortune, you required, in blindness of an inexhaustible greed, my entire existence. You took it" (p. 158); "The basis of character is will-power, and my will-power became absolutely subject to yours" (p. 157). If indeed *De Profundis* turns out to be a protracted love letter, it is also a painful exhibition of the self-abasing tendency in Wilde, which is the basic dynamic of his ruination.

The conclusion of Wilde's effort to strip away all pretence by writing out his painful degradations in love and in law might therefore seem yet another layer of pretence—this time adopting the pseudo-Christian mask of forgiveness or yet another layer of self-deception with respect to his self-destructive impulses. But there exists a formula that connects these psychological postures of provocative self-abasement with certain age-old patterns of religious experience. It is a formula derived from the archetypes of penitent sinner and innocent scapegoat that Wilde himself invokes and from a set of heroic figures with whom he shares his deep-dug cell.[8]

De Profundis, as its title (although it is not Wilde's) suggests, is an exercise in biblical rewriting and in a typological

8. Cf. Jan B. Gordon, "Wilde and Newman: The Confessional Mode," *Renascence*, 22 (1970): 183-91, for additional figures of wandering, conversion, and sacramental redemption. George Landow has suggested to me that a precedent for Wilde's strategy—in which an imprisoned character modifies his image by typological expansion of himself as a Christ figure—exists in the dramatic monologues of Guido in Browning's *The Ring and the Book.*

redaction of personal experience. The language of typology appears throughout: "Sorrow is the ultimate type both in life and Art" (p. 201); "Of course all this [interpretation of his experience] is foreshadowed and prefigured in my art" (p. 203); "The song of Isaiah . . . seemed to [Christ] to be a prefiguring of himself, and in him the prophecy was fulfilled" (p. 210). The work establishes an Old-Testament-type figure, David—presumed author of the psalm from which the title is taken—along with the antitype of Christ as models for the man of sorrows whom Wilde sets up to be.

Although Wilde early places himself "in the lowest mire of Malebolge . . . between Gilles de Retz and the Marquis de Sade" (p. 159; repeated on p. 185 and alluded to on p. 226), the same passage ranks Alfred Douglas with the infant Samuel and thus directs us to the biblical book in which David's tale is begun. Although Wilde's reference is explicit only with regard to Douglas's unmerited exemption from the expected punishment of his family's iniquities, it invites attention to other Davidic proceedings. Especially relevant is the tale of David and Jonathan in which the naïve David, like Wilde, is persecuted by the maddened father of his friend, anticipating Wilde's relations with Queensberry. When Wilde speaks *de profundis*, he echoes, of course, Psalm 130: "Out of the depths have I cried unto thee, O Lord. Lord, hear my voice." This is the voice of the chastened old king calling on God not for redress of grievances but to confess the depths of his own sins—sexual and familial in David's case, as in Wilde's. The peculiar pathos of Wilde's Davidic call is, however, that it is directed not to a divine but to a human ear; as an earlier letter addresses Douglas: "Even covered with mud I shall praise you, from the deepest abysses I shall cry to you" (p. 137; May 20, 1895).

But Wilde's stance as David typologically links him with that descendant of David who came to suffer and redeem mankind, and Wilde is not loath to pursue this interpretation of his own fate. Although they are quoted only once and briefly in the letter (p. 210), the text repeatedly borders on the language of the "servant songs" of Isaiah 53: "He is despised and rejected of men; a man of sorrows, and acquainted with grief: and we hid as it were our faces from him; he was despised and we esteemed him not. . . . He was oppressed, and he was afflicted, yet he opened not his mouth: he is brought as a lamb to the slaughter. . . . He was taken from prison and from judgment: and who shall declare his generation?" In these terms, the "religious digression" becomes the interpretive crux if not the dramatic center of the entire work. Not only does Wilde here engage in a protracted exercise in self-analysis by the standards of Christian ethics, but he makes an extended character study of the Savior himself, as man and hero—antitype of his own type.

It would be simplistic to say that this modern aesthete is donning the trappings of the god or prophet here as he had done in identifying himself with John the Baptist in *Salomé*. Rather, the essential patterns enacted by these figures—the martyred herald of the Savior, the slaughtered lamb, and the latter-day incarnation—are equally assumed in a religious archetype to which all of Wilde's mythologizing of himself tends. *De Profundis* is perhaps the most remarkable projection (barring Kafka) of the modern hero in his role as scapegoat or *pharmakos*. As such it stands near the inception of the theme of ritual immolation that runs through the heart of modern letters, from "The Love Song of J. Alfred Prufrock" through Yeats's theater and on to Pound's Pisan cantos.

The tableau of the public spectacle—the malign mockery, public scourging, and protracted punishment of the sacrificial victim—is given in the famous scene of Wilde's transfer to prison:

> From two o'clock till half-past two on that day I had to stand on the centre platform of Clapham Junction in convict dress and handcuffed, for the world to look at. I had been taken out of the Hospital Ward without a moment's notice being given to me. Of all possible objects I was the most grotesque. When people

saw me they laughed. Each train as it came up swelled
the audience. Nothing could exceed their amusement.
That was of course before they knew who I was. As
soon as they had been informed they laughed still
more. For half an hour I stood there in the grey November rain surrounded by a jeering mob.

(p. 219)

After this, it is but a short step from Clapham Junction to
Golgotha.

Wilde's response to his scourging is, given the circumstances, remarkably restrained: "For a year after that was
done to me I wept every day at the same hour and for the
same space of time. That is not such a tragic thing as possibly it sounds to you." Without excessive sentimentality
and in a measured prose, Wilde solemnly ritualizes the hour,
the tears, and the tragedy. He reflects that the experience "is
not such a tragic thing" perhaps because the ritual, whatever
its psychological efficacy, has transformed him into the after-
type of the redeemer. In place of the image of a "*flâneur*, a
dandy, a man of fashion" (p. 194), which he had carefully
established, Wilde seeks out a new way of standing "in symbolic relations to the art and culture of my age" (p. 194).
His new image is as a devotee of the religion of sorrow if
not the incarnation of the Man of Sorrows himself: "Sorrow,
then and all that it teaches one, is my new world. . . . I now
see that sorrow, being the supreme emotion of which man is
capable, is at once the type and test of all great Art. . . . There
are times when Sorrow seems to me to be the only truth. . . .
For the secret of life is suffering. It is what is hidden behind
everything" (pp. 200–02).

Indeed, Wilde's considerable power in establishing this
myth of himself is derived from his ability to view such
scenes not only as participant but as spectator; like every
good dramatist, he is both on the stage and in the stalls. Another passage suggests the self-consciousness with which he
views his life as a performance, his confession as a public
ritual:

289

> I remember as I was sitting in the dock on the occasion of my last trial listening to [Prosecutor] Lockwood's appalling denunciation of me . . . and being sickened with horror at what I heard. Suddenly it occurred to me, *"How splendid it would be, if I was saying all this about myself!"* I saw then at once that what is said of a man is nothing. The point is, who says it. A man's very highest moment is, I have no doubt at all, when he kneels in the dust, and beats his breast, and tells all the sins of his life.
>
> (p. 230)

It would be easy to confuse this with the exhibitionism of enthusiastic religious cults, with the sado-masochistic violence of the "theater of the absurd," or with the therapeutic group confessions encouraged by recent psychiatric schools. Unlike these, the tendency to see oneself as scapegoat and the impulse to make one's own declaration of it are linked here by a previously unused potentiality in Wilde's theater: his tragic dimension. As so much of *De Profundis* runs through a succession of historical and literary models for Wilde's career as sinner, victim, and hero, it appropriately concludes with Hamlet: "Instead of trying to be the hero of his own history, he seeks to be the spectator of his own tragedy" (p. 233). Wilde identifies himself with Hamlet in his capacity to tell his own story with tragic irony, flagellating himself but not denying himself the role. The tragic hero is, after all, the successor of both the *pharmakos* and the dying-and-reviving god in the literary displacement effected by classical tragedy, and both his degradation and his glory suit Wilde.

Tragic self-knowledge, not only that of the hero within a play but that of the author writing the drama of his life, is recommended by Wilde as the distinguishing mark of the truly elect. On the level of the suffering sinner, this knowledge is the hallmark of personal redemption: "Of course the sinner must repent. But why? Simply because otherwise he would be unable to realise what he had done. The moment of repentance is the moment of initiation" (p. 215). The passage from suffering through knowledge leads, then, to a special kind of redemption, which Wilde names "initiation." This may mean simply the beginning of a *new life*—and Wilde borrows the term (and much else) from Dante to describe his present condition—or it may refer to his entry into a new fraternity, a fellowship with men of another cast from those with whom Wilde has been identified. The long list of heroes and martyrs that Wilde assembles is complemented by a list of poets of the tribe of Marsyas, who sing of their immolation in a peculiarly modern timbre: "I hear in much modern Art the cry of Marsyas. It is bitter in Baudelaire, sweet and plaintive in Lamartine, mystic in Verlaine. It is in the deferred resolutions of Chopin's music. It is in the discontent that haunts the recurrent faces of Burne-Jones's women. Even Matthew Arnold, . . ." etc. (p. 218). It is with this entourage that Wilde identifies himself as artist and hero, nowhere more vividly than in what is perhaps his greatest work of art, not a poem or play but a prosaic letter.

The main obstacle to such a conclusion, no matter what the degree of our adherence to the theory of literary displacement—and irrespective of our religious persuasions—is likely to be Wilde's identification of himself with Christ or of Christ with himself. We might be prepared to accept a measure of compensatory self-glorification in one so cruelly used, but we are less inclined to see a religious figure turned into an aesthetic object. Yet Wilde's portrait of Christ as Aesthete has a certain probity, for it expands beyond his somewhat fanatical literary afflatus to ethical qualities of mind and heart. It is not the artist-god but the human ideal that Wilde feels he now can emulate:

> I see a far more intimate and immediate connection
> between the true life of Christ and the true life of the
> artist. . . . Christ [is] the true precursor of the roman-
> tic movement in life, but the very basis of his nature
> was the same as that of the nature of the artist, an in-
> tense and flamelike imagination. . . . And, above all,

> Christ is the most supreme of Individualists. . . . It is
> man's soul that Christ is always looking for. . . . His
> chief war was against the Philistines. . . . In opposition
> to their tithing of each separate day into its fixed rou-
> tine of prescribed duties, as they tithed mint and rue,
> he preached the enormous importance of living com-
> pletely for the moment. (pp. 204–14 *passim*)

That Wilde can make these identifications come to seem
plausible is the measure not of his outrageous wit but of his
expanded vision. Christ's imagination is defined at its moral
rather than its aesthetic base: "He realised in the entire sphere
of human relations that imaginative sympathy which in the
sphere of Art is the sole secret of creation" (p. 205).

By a similar movement from accidentals to essences,
Christ's literary connections are shifted away from the Romantic artists and toward the broader autobiographical tradition: "And it is the imaginative quality of Christ's own
nature that makes him this palpitating centre of romance.
The strange figures of poetic drama and ballad are made by
the imagination of others, but out of his own imagination
entirely did Jesus of Nazareth create himself" (p. 211). By
making Christ the ideal not only of imaginative sympathy
with others but of imaginative self-creation, Wilde is perhaps at his most fanciful in reinterpreting the biblical text
but also at his most striking in fleshing out his own self-
image: "His last word when he cried out 'My life has been
completed, has reached its fulfillment, has been perfected,'
was exactly as St. John tells us it was: τετέλεσται: no more"
(p. 212). "It is finished" becomes not the Creator's eternal
commentary on the historical event but the self-creator's fiat
in completing his greatest work of art, himself.

Yet for all his ethical expansion of aestheticism and his
profound identification with Christ, Wilde's appropriation
of religious language for his secular concerns cannot fail to
seem bathetic. Bathos usually attends his capitalized nouns,
whether referring to traditional or other figures: "That
something hidden away in my nature, like a treasure in a

field, is Humility" (p. 195); "I would like to found an order for those who cannot believe: the Confraternity of the Fatherless one might call it . . ." (p. 195); "Yet I must . . . be filled with joy if my feet are on the right road, and my face set towards the 'gate which is called Beautiful' " (p. 203). Such appropriation of religious formulas, whatever the degree of sincerity in a recent and intense reader of the Gospels, must seem another Wildean mask, another exercise in style. Although Wilde may have been more transiently drawn toward Christian faith and expression than others in the autobiographical tradition, *De Profundis* forms part of the late-Victorian movement toward secular versions of Christianity. In preference to a Nietzschean nay-saying to the life-denying basis of Christian ethics, the voices in this movement affirmed and reprojected Christianity's human core of suffering and sacrifice.[9] In this modern tradition, linking the sacrificial heroes and heroines of Dickens and George Eliot to certain contemporary versions of the eternal victim, like Faulkner's *Fable* and Barth's *Giles Goat-Boy*, Oscar Wilde modestly demands his place.

Gissing's *Henry Ryecroft*

The Private Papers of Henry Ryecroft (1903) is another turn-of-the-century work that overturns conventional notions of autobiography by means of traditional forms and figures. George Gissing was hardly as sweeping an iconoclast as Oscar Wilde, yet his career shows some of the same traits of self-destructiveness and self-promulgation, of outcast and martyr—if not of redemptive *pharmakos*. Although Gissing's novels contain an admixture of self-reference in tracing the careers of victimized hack writers and battered husbands,[10]

9. For modern literary versions of the iconography of Christ's advent and passion, see Theodore Ziolkowski, *Fictional Transfigurations of Jesus* (Princeton, 1972).

10. See Jacob Korg, *George Gissing: A Critical Biography* (Seattle, 1963), pp. 158–59, for autobiographical parallels in *New Grub Street*; less convincing associations are the stock in trade of other biographers.

his distaste for visibility was in control of his habitually downplayed prose style. It was only in *Ryecroft* that he allowed himself to create a full autobiographical image although this required the invention of a persona and an ideal set of circumstances—an aging writer who becomes financially independent through an inheritance. It is in this sense that Gissing's disclaimer of historical self-reference is to be taken: "The thing is much more an aspiration than a memory."[11] Yet if the conditions are utopian, they are there to show forth the man. In place of the narrative form of the *Bildungsroman* or the successive stages of spiritual autobiography, the author's image is manifested as a whole, at a single time, that of the elderly man writing, having come into serene retirement.

Yet *Ryecroft* is no wish-fulfilling fantasy of distantiation from the world. The work as a whole is a gathering place for the sum of Gissing's attributes and incorporates the memory and the pain of much of his experience. There is evidence that the text grew out of writing his own commonplace book and that it reports his cherished opinions on the world and summary views of himself. If fiction there be, it goes less into disguises than into the creation of an adequate form in which to embody the whole life, without retracing it step by step in a narrative sequence. For this purpose, Gissing has recourse to a well-thumbed formula of the classical tradition, the seasonal cycle, by which he divides the text into four sections corresponding to the seasons. This is no writerly convenience but a determining choice, answering to the structure of Gissing's imagination. What the autobiographer here accomplishes is not so much to dissect his own nature as to allow it to live through its natural phases.

Jackson Cope has observed, in one of the few available

11. Quoted in Jacob Korg, "The Main Source of *The Ryecroft Papers*," in *Collected Articles on George Gissing*, ed. Pierre Coustillas (New York and London, 1968), p. 173; this essay is the introduction to Korg's edition of Gissing's *Commonplace Book* (New York, 1962).

studies commensurate with Gissing's learned mind,[12] a number of classical topoi rather than the traditional figures employed by Victorian autobiographers. These images of the *locus amoenus* prepare us to recognize in the work a late appearance of the classical ideal of retirement. Gissing's persona inherits an annuity and, like the author, retires to a Devon cottage after a life of New Grub Street drudgery. The image of this universally desired condition is, of course, a widely varied and historically changing one, but it achieves a remarkable coherence when linked to a natural setting for the retirement. Pastoral, utopian, and horticultural traditions are deeply involved in the so-called "retirement myth," and all enter into Gissing's account. Another element frequently associated with the complex of topoi mentioned here is the seasonal cycle. The retired man summing up his life, the utopian gardener setting out his ideal realm, the pastoralist imagining himself back to the childhood of the race— all are attentive to the season. Pope claimed that his use of the seasonal tetrad was an innovation in the tradition of the pastoral, but modern scholarship has adduced an enormous body of learning and poetic imagery of the seasons, from which, for example, Spenser had already drawn for his (albeit monthly) calendar.[13] Not all the traditional applications of the tetrad are made much of by Gissing, but one of its chief parallels—to the four ages of man or stages of an individual life—is at the forefront of his work.

12. Jackson I. Cope, "Definition as Structure in *The Ryecroft Papers*," in *Collected Articles*, pp. 152–67. A fuller treatment of Gissing's learning is Samuel V. Gapp, *George Gissing: Classicist* (Philadelphia, 1936). Another work by Gissing which combines his classical and autobiographical predilections is the travel book *By the Ionian Sea* (1901).

13. For the fourfold numerology, see S. K. Heninger, Jr., "The Implications of Form for the Shepheardes Calendar," *Studies in the Renaissance*, 9 (1962): 309–21. On pastoral, retirement, and other conventions with a strong similarity to Gissing's figures, there is a substantial literature by Maren-Sofie Røstvig, E. M. W. Tillyard, Maynard Mack, et al.

In setting out the course of Ryecroft's year, Gissing reveals that the themes and conventions in *Ryecroft* are related to a traditional philosophic attitude that upholds the norms of nature above mechanism, affirms common sense and moderation as pillars of a natural ethic, and proclaims a stoical acceptance of the course of life with all its imperfections. The ideas are generally traceable to the Stoic philosophers, and *Ryecroft* may have taken the form of a collection of meditative passages in imitation of the writings of that school. Gissing was a trained classicist and a lifelong devotee of late Roman culture particularly, to which several of his works, including his last novel, are devoted. At the heart of this literary taste are a number of attitudes to life, which Gissing shared with his Latin exemplars; his is the classical-conservative mentality, which includes a resigned pessimism, an antidemocratic politics, an assertion of national and other traditional virtues, and a skepticism of the so-called progressive trends in one's society, but does not preclude a hearty contempt for many features of the status quo. All these attitudes show up in *Ryecroft* and supply the book's range of opinions on a wide variety of subjects—from deity to cooking, approximately.

The book opens with "Spring" (the title of the first part), and the first notes are those of the renewal of the old man by fresh breezes and the revival of his memory of youth: "Spring has restored to me something of the long-forgotten vigour of youth; I walk without weariness; I sing to myself like a boy, and the song is one I knew in boyhood" (sec. 3, p. 27).[14] The recovery of the force and the image of youth is extended by memories of occasions in the course of his later life when the impulse to return to innocence and nature was expressed in flights to the countryside: "At the end of March I escaped from my grim lodgings, and

14. I quote from the Signet paperback of *The Ryecroft Papers* (New York, 1961) in the absence of a definitive edition. There is a scholarly apparatus for the French translation, ed. Pierre Coustillas (Paris, 1966).

before I had time to reflect on the details of my undertaking, I found myself sitting in sunshine at a spot very near to where I now dwell. . . . That was one of the moments of my life when I have tasted exquisite joy. . . . Then first did I know myself for a sun-worshipper" (sec. 9, p. 35). He is said to step into a "new life," but it is established that this is a fulfillment of his own youthful powers as they have "been developing unknown to me" (sec. 9, p. 35). Yet the old man's synthetic reconstruction of his youthful sensibilities from several stages of life carries with it an awareness of youth's fated place in the cycle of life and death. Even the surge of vitality has its *memento mori*: "I enjoy with something of sadness remembering that this melodious silence is but the prelude of that deeper stillness which waits to enfold us all" (sec. 23, p. 62); and again: "Walking in a favourite lane to-day, I found it covered with shed blossoms of the hawthorn. Creamy white, fragrant even in ruin, lay scattered the glory of the May. It told me that spring is over" (sec. 25, p. 63).

The qualities of "Summer" are put forward in terms almost too stark for interpretation: "In this hot weather I like to walk at times amid the full glow of the sun. . . . there is a magnificence in the triumph of high summer which exalts one's mind" (sec. 8, p. 74). Height, triumph, exaltation— these are the physical expressions of the fullness and maturity of the growing self. But even this moment of fulfillment is rendered equivocal, not only by an implicit knowledge of the whole cycle of life and death but also by the peculiarities of English weather: "July this year is clouded and windy, very cheerless even here in Devon. . . . Can I not have patience? Do I not know that some morning the east will open like a bursting bud into warmth and splendour . . . ?" (sec. 14, p. 85). Instead of worrying about the end of summer, the Englishman waits for it fully to arrive; his time of enjoyment is not only transient but insufficiently achieved.

More certain than this prophecy, "Autumn" comes on.

Its first appearance is not a physical but a metaphorically moral one: "Boy and man, I blundered into every ditch and bog which lay within sight of my way. Never did silly mortal reap such harvest of experience . . ." (sec. 6, p. 113). If the harvest is bitter, the autumn develops its own special beauty: "Never, I could fancy, did autumn clothe in such magnificence the elms and beeches; never, I should think, did the leafage on my walls blaze in such royal crimson" (sec. 18, p. 133). The influence of the declining year on the declining man is to lead him toward an acceptance of his failings and a grim satisfaction in his life, even though it is diminishing: "As I walked to-day in the golden sunlight—this warm, still day on the far verge of autumn—there suddenly came to me a thought which checked my step and for the moment half bewildered me. I said to myself: My life is over" (sec. 23, pp. 140–41). In true stoical fashion, Ryecroft convinces himself that he can be grateful that he has "suffered no intolerable wrong," and his dominant wish is to be attuned to the rhythm of the seasons and thereby to the rhythm of his life: "To-night the wind is loud, and rain dashes against my casement; to-morrow I shall awake to a sky of winter" (sec. 25, p. 144).

The effect of "Winter" is to stimulate the memory and create a summing up of the dark side of Ryecroft-Gissing's life—one which counterbalances the gathering of forces that had occurred in the spring:

> In the middle years of my life—those years that were the worst of all—I used to dread the sound of a winter storm which woke me in the night. . . . I lay thinking of the savage struggle of man with man, and often saw before me no better fate than to be trampled down into the mud of life. . . . But nowadays I can lie and listen to a night-storm with no intolerable thoughts; at worst, I fall into a compassionate sadness as I remember those I loved and whom I shall see no more.
> (sec. 12, pp. 160–61)

The gathering of darker thoughts and dying impulses in a winter polarity is not, however, allowed to act as a neat completion of the seasonal tetrad. The cycle begins anew with the quite natural corollary of the winter mood: anticipation of spring. This hope is not permitted to become sanguine in the aging man, and Gissing deftly balances the hope of life and the fact of death:

> All through the morning the air was held in an ominous stillness. . . . I saw nothing but the broad, grey sky, a featureless expanse, cold, melancholy. . . . A few minutes more, and all was hidden with a descending veil of silent snow. It was a disappointment. Yesterday I half believed that the winter drew to its end; . . . I began to long for the days of light and warmth. My fancy wandered, leading me far and wide in a dream of summer England.   (sec. 23, p. 177)

The dream of renewal and the chill touch of snow mingle in a complex winter stance.

At the close, Gissing expresses his balance of attitudes toward the cycle of life: "So, once more, the year has come full circle. . . . Now my life is rounded; it began with the natural irreflective happiness of childhood, it will close in the reasoned tranquillity of the mature mind" (sec. 26, pp. 182–83). But this sense of formal completion is accompanied by another trope that has all along been near to hand but not explicit in *Ryecroft*: the notion of one's life as a book and the related notion of writing as the realization of a life:

> How many a time after long labour on some piece of writing, brought at length to its conclusion, have I laid down the pen with a sigh of thankfulness; the work was full of faults, but I had wrought sincerely, had done what time and circumstance and my own nature permitted. Even so may it be with me in my last hour. May I look back on life as a long task duly completed— a piece of biography; faulty enough, but good as I could make it. . . .   (sec. 26, p. 183)

So Gissing completes his self-writing—and he does so by the metaphor of living as the writing of a work of literature. How appropriate that he should specify in his metaphor of life not a book of any kind but precisely a work of biography! Although his resources are somewhat different from those exploited by other late-Victorian autobiographers, Gissing joins them in the imaginative freedom with which he recasts traditional lore in the enterprise of inventing a novel literary form to convey an adequate figure of himself.

Gosse's *Father and Son*

The most comprehensive rewriting of traditional autobiography at the turn of the century is Edmund Gosse's *Father and Son: A Study of Two Temperaments* (1907). Most of the elements of the standard English autobiography are to be found here, though not necessarily in their original distribution: high endowment and loss, crisis and epiphany, journey and return. But there is from the outset a literary self-consciousness in Gosse's proceedings—signaled by the appearance of dozens of verse and other quotations in the text—that might open him to the charge of exploitativeness or artificiality were it not for the palpable emotion with which he writes. Gosse's sophistication is not only literary; he is aware of the cultural-historical significance of his writing and presents it as a "document" of a "dying Puritanism" (Preface).[15] Although his tone is at times arch, he usually avoids the sprightly vilifications of the Lytton Strachey school of biography, which his work may be said to anticipate, in favor of a droll but sympathetic evocation of habits of mind he can only with difficulty recall as his own. The work lies somewhere between historical reportage

15. I quote from the Norton paperback edition, as most readily available (New York, 1963). There is a useful apparatus in the edition by James Hepburn (London, New York, and Toronto, 1974), with an introduction keenly comparing the intellectual habits of the father and the son.

and self-justifying propaganda. It is also a generically comic transformation of its often somber material[16]—though Gosse claims in his preface that "the comedy was superficial and the tragedy essential." Despite the seriousness with which he recalls his adolescent conflicts and eventual estrangement, Gosse succeeds in distancing himself sufficiently to recount his religious struggles with ironic amusement. Not only does his change of heart represent an exactly opposite shift from those of spiritual autobiography, but his rendering of that change is conducted by a precise inversion of the figures employed in that tradition. *Father and Son* is not merely a comic and ironic work but approaches the status of literary parody—which at its best is a form of literary and cultural criticism.

Gosse's parody of spiritual autobiography is empowered largely by the fact that the origin from which he struggles to emerge is itself a travesty of religious orthodoxy. Taking up with a powerful will the literalism of Protestant bibliolatry and the independent spirit of the self-convinced elect, Gosse's parents create their own church, or at least communion, and all but their own theology and ethics. They claim, of course, to derive directly from Scripture: "At last they met only with a few extreme Calvinists like themselves, on terms of what may almost be called negation—with no priest, no ritual, no festivals, no ornament of any kind, nothing but the Lord's Supper and the exposition of Holy Scripture drawing these austere spirits into any sort of cohesion" (ch. 1, p. 11). Gosse is somewhat at a loss to give a name to this sect—"They called themselves 'the Brethren,' simply; a title enlarged by the world outside into 'Plymouth Brethren' "—and at other points calls them evangelical either with a small or a capital letter. But the word he applies to his mother has a more precise ring: "My Mother was a Puritan in grain . . ." (ch. 1, p. 17). Although Gosse was not aware

16. Cf. R. Victoria Arana, "Sir Edmund Gosse's *Father and Son*: Autobiography in the Shape of Comedy," *Genre*, 10 (1977): 63–76.

of the fact until late in life, his mother was indeed a New England by birth, and there is an element of the uncanny in his father's choice of the original Plymouth for a home and religious base after his wife's death.

In such a cultural environment, the language of an Eden-esque original provision is readily replaced with images of the rocky soil of an inhospitable land: "This, then, was the scene in which the soul of a little child was planted, not as in an ordinary open flower-border or carefully tended social parterre, but as on a ledge split in the granite of some mountain" (ch. 1, p. 19). But the dour scenes of parental negativity very quickly give way to signs of growth, rebellion, and fall. The fall is, however, as much connected with the father's status as it is with the son's; when the elder Gosse makes a trivial error of fact, the event "meant an epoch. Here was the appalling discovery, never suspected before, that my Father was not as God, and did not know everything" (ch. 2, p. 33).

The more significant fall is, however, the son's although he recognizes it not as loss but as gain:

> My Father, as a deity, as a natural force of immense prestige, fell in my eyes to a human level. . . . But of all the thoughts which rushed upon my savage and undeveloped little brain at this crisis, the most curious was that I had found a companion and a confidant in myself. There was a secret in this world and it belonged to me and to a somebody who lived in the same body with me. There were two of us, and we could talk with one another.   (ch. 2, p. 35)

This genetic development, which modern psychologists and social scientists have studied with close attention, was known to an earlier age as the fall into self-division. In its attenuated forms in adult personality, it can lead to the duality of will and identity that is featured in so many late nineteenth-century works about the double. Gosse's account of his self-multiplication reproduces the pleasant curiosity with

which the child must have experienced the verbal equivalent
of the "mirror stage" rather than the wrenching drama in
which the Romantic poets, for example, rendered similar
scenes of passage from innocent at-homeness in the world to
self-conscious recognition of separation and limitation.

The immediate result of the drop in paternal prestige and
infantine complacency is the testing of divine authority, in
this case of the scriptural prohibitions on idolatry. Although
the narrator's language is that of the modern man of skeptical science—"to test the matter for myself," "my experiment"—the scene is rendered as a child's version of Exodus:

> I knelt down on the carpet in front of the table and
> looking up I said my daily prayer in a loud voice, only
> substituting the address "O Chair!" for the habitual
> one.
>
> Having carried this act of idolatry safely through,
> I waited to see what would happen. . . . God would
> certainly exhibit his anger in some terrible form, and
> would chastise my impious and wilful action. . . . But
> nothing happened; there was not a cloud in the sky,
> not an unusual sound in the street. Presently I was
> quite sure that nothing would happen. I had com-
> mitted idolatry, flagrantly and deliberately, and God
> did not care.
>
> The result of this ridiculous act was not to make me
> question the existence and power of God; those were
> forces which I did not dream of ignoring. But what
> it did was to lessen still further my confidence in my
> Father's knowledge of the Divine mind. My Father
> had said, positively, that if I worshipped a thing made
> of wood, God would manifest his anger.
>
> (ch. 2, p. 44–45)

We shall return to this careful acting out of canonical scenes
at a later point, but what is evident early on is the power of
Gosse's prose to reproduce the language of traditional texts
and heightened autobiographical moments in a superb comic
reduction.

The tragic side of the fall is registered only in the next

chapter, with the loss of the mother. As she dies of cancer, the child is made the intimate witness of pain and death: "The experiences upon which I presently entered were of a nature in which childhood rarely takes a part. I was now my Mother's sole and ceaseless companion; the silent witness of her suffering, of her patience, of her vain and delusive attempts to obtain alleviation of her anguish. For nearly three months I breathed the atmosphere of pain ..." (ch. 3, p. 51). At the final moments, "language cannot utter what they suffered," and Gosse is led to quote Newman on "the tranquillity and the intensity with which faith gazes at the Divine Majesty" (ch. 3, p. 61). But the heightened spirituality of the spectacle of serene martyrdom is mitigated for the child by the enormous burden placed upon him:

> She repeated two or three times, "Take our lamb, and walk with me!" Then my Father comprehended, and pressed me forward; her hand fell softly upon mine and she seemed content. Thus was my dedication, that had begun in my cradle, sealed with the most solemn, the most poignant and irresistible insistence, at the death-bed of the holiest and purest of women. But what a weight, intolerable as the burden of Atlas, to lay on the shoulders of a little fragile child! (ch. 3, pp. 61–62)

If this account portrays the sufferings of the mother and the loss felt by the child with complete conviction, it also expresses the indignation of the mature Gosse at the emotional bondage into which he had been cast. The scene is thus converted, by its final sentence, into a parody of the biblical scenes of dedication which lie behind it. It becomes less a point of apocalypse or transcendence by the faithful than a point of *akedah* or binding to the lower realm—in which the Prometheus-like Atlas emerges as the figure of the burdened child and of man fallen under the sway of a heavy god.

Having been provided only with the wilderness and the fall up to this point in his life, the child is now belatedly offered a time in Eden. The move to Plymouth is also a move

to the Devon seacoast, and the elder Gosse—a marine biolo-
gist of some distinction, and of even greater opprobrium[17]—
makes a companion of his son in his researches. This accession is not merely to the freedom of the outdoors but to
natural innocence:

> The antiquity of these rock-pools, and the infinite
> succession of the soft and radiant forms, sea-anem-
> ones, sea-weeds, shells, fishes, which had inhabited
> them undisturbed since the creation of the world, used
> to occupy my Father's fancy. We burst in, he used
> to say, where no one had ever thought of intruding
> before; and if the Garden of Eden had been situate
> in Devonshire, Adam and Eve, stepping lightly down
> to bathe in the rainbow-coloured spray, would have
> seen the identical sights that we now saw. . . .
>
> (ch. 6, pp. 110–11)

Although Gosse quotes Keats and Flaubert to complement
his father's mode of apprehending natural values, the latter's
biblical figure is even more evocative of the Edenic vision—
even capturing a sense of innocent sexuality in the image of
the bathing Adam and Eve. The social life of the community
of Brethren gave the boy much to contend with, and his
contention with the father was only partly mitigated by
their mutual absorption in scientific observation and drawing, but this maritime Eden is nonetheless painted in the
strongest colors in the work, shining still more vividly for
the author than any other aspect of his life.

What is perhaps most curious in Gosse's reversion to
traditional figures of childhood bliss is his taking up a debate
with Wordsworth in the same breath. The Devonshire account begins with an effort to establish the precise age of his
coming into his Romantic inheritance:

> A new element now entered into my life, a fresh rival
> arose to compete for me with my Father's dogmatic

17. See Edmund Gosse's filial but backhanded biography, *The Life of
Philip Henry Gosse, F.R.S.* (London, 1890), which bears close comparison with the portrait in *Father and Son.*

theology. This rival was the Sea. When Wordsworth was a little child, the presence of the mountains and the clouds lighted up his spirit with gleams that were like the flashing of a shield. He has described, in the marvellous pages of the "Prelude," the impact of nature upon the infant soul, but he has described it vaguely and faintly, with some "infirmity of love for days disowned by memory." . . . It was at the age of twice five summers, he thought, that he began to hold unconscious intercourse with nature, "drinking in a pure organic pleasure" from the floating mists and winding waters. Perhaps, in his anxiety to be truthful, and in the absence of any record, he put the date of this conscious rapture too late rather than too early. Certainly my own impregnation with the obscurely-defined but keenly-felt loveliness of the open sea dates from the first week of my ninth year.

(ch. 5, p. 81)

The evident purpose of this quibble is to provide an occasion for inserting a number of key autobiographical locutions into his own text,[18] and by their intertextual weaving, Gosse aligns his experience with the paradigm of childhood access to the mysteries of being, available in unreflective—but eventually highly reflected-upon—experience in relatively untrammeled nature.

Having achieved his Eden at Plymouth, the child is less inclined to the stony path of his religion's wilderness view of life, and when the ritual of baptism is to be fulfilled, he treats it with appropriate solemnity and some comic malice. The brethren practised total immersion upon adults, and a special case had to be argued for this "Infant Samuel"; the father "admitted the absence in my case of a sudden, apparent act of conversion resulting upon conviction of sin. But he stated the grounds of his belief that I had, in still earlier infancy, been converted . . ." (ch. 8, p. 143). The language of spiritual autobiography is here brought to book along with the specialized eschatology of this Baptist sect. If any

18. There are further Wordsworthian allusions in ch. 12, p. 211.

doubt about his tone remains after Gosse's narrative of the event, his summing up removes it: "My public baptism was the central event of my whole childhood. Everything, since the earliest dawn of consciousness, seemed to have been leading up to it. Everything, afterwards, seemed to be leading down and away from it" (ch. 8, p. 145).

The decisive conversion occurs not under these formal auspices but by the firm and sensible decision of his stepmother (a religious woman but not a sectarian) that he is old enough to be sent to boarding school. It is as much a crisis for the father as it is for the boy: "The Great Scheme (I cannot resist giving it the mortuary of capital letters) had been, as my readers know, that I should be exclusively and consecutively dedicated through the whole of my life, to the manifest and uninterrupted and uncompromised 'service of the Lord.' That had been the aspiration of my Mother, and at her death she had bequeathed that desire to my Father, like a dream of the Promised Land" (ch. 12, p. 207). That this is no stray biblical allusion is made clear as Gosse goes on to cite the dedication of Samuel to similar service, giving a full listing of biblical names and phrases. It is the parents' dream of a promised land and their intended shaping of a life according to the model of the prophets that are dashed here whereas the rubrics of conversion are employed in behalf of the apostate: "The great scheme, so long caressed, so passionately fostered, must in its primitive bigness be now dropped" (ch. 12, p. 207).

In place of this life scheme and without a sharp crisis of conscience, the boy has his own "revelation" and a change of heart. Buying a volume of the poetry of Jonson and Marlowe, he reads while walking in an achetypal setting for conversion:

> I carried it with me to devour as I trod the desolate road that brought me along the edge of the cliff on Saturday afternoons. Of Ben Jonson I could make nothing, but when I turned to "Hero and Leander," I was lifted to a heaven of passion and music. It was a

> marvellous revelation of romantic beauty to me, and
> as I paced along that lonely and exquisite highway,
> ... I lifted up my voice, singing the verses, as I strolled
> along. . . .   (ch. 12, pp. 223–24)

Thus, the scenic elements and common expressions of conversion scenes are marshaled for the benefit of a secular epiphany, the dedication of the youth to the worship of profane beauty and a career in poetry and humane letters. It is but a short step to the "bird-girl" epiphany in *A Portrait of the Artist as a Young Man.* We sense now that all the quotations of verse—from the banal songs of childhood to the repeated soundings of a mighty line of Virgil—which have competed in *Father and Son* with the formulas of religious tradition, have been carefully placed to prepare the work as a narrative of vocation. Gosse was unaware of their import as a child and leaves the reader unaware of their determinative power until the moment of choice is sealed. Although he went on to no great career as a poet and only a transient centrality as a man of letters, Gosse is here decisively committed to an aesthetic rather than an ascetic higher life.

This epiphany and conversion are rendered without irony although inverting the values traditional in such scenes. Irony and deliberate parody are reserved for another scene, in which the experimental method earlier employed on the language of Scripture is now employed on the central text of autobiographical tradition, Augustine's *Confessions.* The boy is moved by his incipient change of vocation to a new searching of the Scriptures and a new questioning of the tenets of his parental faith. In this mood of impatient questing for an answer to his religious doubts, he opens himself to inspiration from without. Although he is placed not in a garden but in a room looking down on gardens, the setting and its anxious tones are familiar enough:

> There was an absolute silence below and around me;
> a magic of suspense seemed to keep every topmost
> twig from waving.

Over my soul there swept an immense wave of
emotion. Now, surely, now the great final change
must be approaching. I gazed up into the tenderly-
coloured sky, and I broke irresistibly into speech.
"Come now, Lord Jesus," I cried, "come now and
take me to be for ever with Thee in Thy Paradise. I
am ready to come. My heart is purged from sin, there
is nothing to keep me rooted to this wicked world. Oh,
come now, now, and take me before I have known
the temptations of life, before I have to go to London
and all the dreadful things that happen there!" And
I raised myself on the sofa, and leaned upon the win-
dow-sill, and waited for the glorious apparition.

This was the highest moment of my religious life,
the apex of my striving after holiness. I waited awhile,
watching. . . . Then a little breeze sprang up and the
branches danced. Sounds began to rise from the road
beneath me. Presently the colour deepened, the evening came on. From far below there rose to me the
chatter of the boys returning home. The tea-bell rang,
—last word of prose to shatter my mystical poetry.
"The Lord has not come, the Lord will never come,"
I muttered, and in my heart the artificial edifice of
extravagant faith began to totter and crumble.

(ch. 12, pp. 231–32)

If this carefully constructed scene were merely a parodic
reduction of the "Tolle, lege" to "the chatter of the boys returning home," it would lose much of its independent force
as an autobiographical creation. Despite its wry tone, the
narrative betrays a genuine flow of spiritual experience. But
in place of palmary words or other vocal utterance, Gosse
is filled with the sounds of the living world, the passage of
mankind on the road, the movement of the wind in the
branches, the measuring of ordinary life by tea bells. This
is prosaic and deflating, but it attests to the human and natural world as a worthy successor to the religious realm—the
world in which the boy and man will find their identity and
their authority.

PART IV

The
Lifelong
Autobiography

—

IN THE EIGHTEENTH CENTURY, the truism runs, a gentleman had to apologize for writing his autobiography; in the nineteenth, apology was still necessary, but the indiscretion was all the more widely committed. Although the imperatives of truth telling were still strong and although they tended to clash with equally strong sanctions against self-revelation, the nineteenth-century writer had recourse to a number of expedients.[1] Full-scale prose autobiographies there were in abundance, but there were also withheld fragments, fictional disguises, and experiments in other forms, like letters and *pensées*, as we have seen. Although workers in other fields, like science and statecraft, showed signs of overcoming the critical prejudice against self-writing—by now, perhaps merely a conventional formula masking an active desire for them—literary artists still showed unwonted diffidence. Anthony Trollope's temerity in revealing his personal motives and working methods—and the derision his *Autobiography* met with, not to speak of declining sales of his fiction—may have served as a warning. Thus, we have the elaborate charades of other Victorian writers, for example, the scheme by which Thomas Hardy passed off his autobiography as a biography written by his wife.[2] The more usual stratagems

1. See Howard Helsinger, "Credence and Credibility: The Concern for Honesty in Victorian Autobiography," in *Approaches to Victorian Autobiography*, ed. G. P. Landow (Athens, Ohio, 1979), pp. 39–63.
2. Hardy is quoted on this plan in Cyril Clemens, *My Chat with Thomas Hardy* (London, 1944), p. 26; other materials pertaining to

were those of the novelist's fictionalization or the poet's symbolic transformation, and writers of enormous reticence from Matthew Arnold to T. S. Eliot have managed to recount crucial episodes in their lives in lyrical or other fragmented sequences.

Yet from the first decades of this century, major writers have dedicated themselves to lifelong feats of self-accounting —as in the sixty years of André Gide's *Journal*—or to sustained acts of total literaturization of a life, as in Marcel Proust's *A la Recherche du temps perdu.* With the grand shift in culture that is called modernism, the new valuation of and curiosity about (not necessarily understanding of or respect for) the interior life, the growth of the mass market, and the journalistic industry of literature, the publishing of an autobiography by a literary man became an expected event. In our own day it is assumed, particularly in England, that a writer of a certain magnitude of sales—the minimum figure is known only to the publishers and seems to be decreasing though the market fluctuates—will produce an autobiography or at least a set of memoirs or reflections. What works once may be done again, and many of these self-writings are followed by a second and a third volume, either on a different period of life or in a different format. There are, of course, autobiographies in four volumes (John Masefield and, cumulatively, Alec Waugh) and five (Osbert Sitwell, Leonard Woolf), but the normal *littérateur* is content to add one book to his original effort (Brendan Behan, Norman Douglas, Storm Jameson, Patrick Kavanagh, T. E. Lawrence,[3] Laurie Lee, Hugh MacDiarmid, Dom Moraes, Frank

the autobiography are collected in *The Personal Notebooks of Thomas Hardy with an appendix including the unpublished passages in the original typescripts of The Life of Thomas Hardy,* ed. Richard H. Taylor (New York, 1979).

3. With the appearance of Thomas J. O'Donnell, *The Confessions of T. E. Lawrence: The Romantic Hero's Presentation of Self* (Athens, Ohio, 1979), it is now established that *Seven Pillars of Wisdom* (with *The Mint*) is one of the pillars in the house of self-writing, if not in its declared temple. O'Donnell's efforts in his opening chapter to place

Part IV

O'Connor, Sean O'Faolain, William Plomer, V. S. Pritchett, Herbert Read), or at most two (H. E. Bates, Oliver Gogarty, Liam O'Flaherty, J. B. Priestley).[4]

Yet few of these publishing enterprises match the intensity and persistence shown by the truly committed autobiographical writers of this century. Not necessarily the foremost of authors or the finest of self-writers, a number of men have returned so often to the subject of their own lives as to suggest their pursuit of a perpetual autobiography. George Moore was the first of these, beginning with the fictional *Confessions of a Young Man* (1888) and closing with *A Communication to My Friends*, which he was writing at the time of his death in 1933. In this sequence, the major work, *Hail and Farewell* (1911–1914), becomes merely the centerpiece in a continual reflection on one's life and on the writing of autobiography—as conducted in the books themselves, even *en train de se faire*.[5]

these works in "the confessional tradition" are, however, typical of the somewhat self-evident results to be obtained by treating confessions from Augustine, Bunyan, and Rousseau to modern times by way of their religious or lack of religious content; their "private myth," "analogous in function to the earlier Christian myth of conversion" (p. 13); and their movement from a "young Romantic," expansive stage, through a self-contraction "to the point of annihilation," to an eventual (though in Lawrence's case, unconvincing) absorption in society (pp. 18–19). It is illuminating to find that "*Seven Pillars* and *The Mint* are in the English Puritan confessional tradition" (p. 16), but this has more to do with Lawrence's sexual itches than it has with the general form of modern autobiography.

4. These numerical summaries are subject to modification according to the definition of autobiography employed and, of course, continued production by still-living authors; the bibliography of this tangled subject will be improved with the publication of a study of modern autobiography by Brian Finney, in progress. Anthony Powell currently promises to set new standards for the doling out of memoirs, having reached three slim volumes at present writing.

5. See Susan Dick's introduction to her edition of *Confessions of a Young Man* (Montreal and London, 1972) for an account of Moore's seven autobiographical publications (counting the trilogy, *Ave*, *Salve*, and *Vale* as one work); for the writing-to-the moment experiment in autobiography, see Moore's *Conversations in Ebury Street*, ch. 5.

Moore's forty-five-year meditation on his life as he went about the business of living it was unlikely to be equaled by later autobiographers, and he seemed secure of his position as the laureate of self-writers. Ford Madox Ford did, to be sure, so often return to phases of his career[6] in novels and memoirs that he seemed to replace the Romantic proposition that a man's life is a continual allegory by the notion that it is a continual autobiography. Yet his span of self-writing—some twenty-six years—came nowhere near challenging Moore's long dedication. Then a late flowering by an octogenarian highly endowed in years and words revised all ideas of what it is to be a lifelong autobiographer.

As early as 1913, Compton Mackenzie had drawn on his early experience at school and after to focus a novel of lower-depths crime and passion, *Sinister Street*.[7] Mackenzie bided his time, however, until 1961 when he began the incredible project of devoting a year to write each of the ten "octaves" or eight-year periods of his life, "each one to be published on as many birthdays as I am left to keep in this world."[8] The successful issue of this program hardly in doubt, from the outset Mackenzie laid plans for what was to follow: "On my eightieth birthday [i.e., in 1963, when the first volume was to be published] I shall start a diary which will stop when my end comes. If by God's grace I should

6. Ford's wellspring of reflection begins with *Ancient Lights and Certain New Reflections* (1911), peaks with the autobiographical elements of *Parade's End* in the twenties, and runs out in the sands of the five memoirs and *obiter dicta* of the thirties; there is a convenient anthology of the entire canon, *Your Mirror to My Times: The Selected Autobiographies and Impressions of F. M. Ford*, ed. Michael Killegrew (New York, Chicago, and San Francisco, 1971).

7. W. Somerset Maugham quickly followed him into the field, using his medical student days as similar quarry for *Of Human Bondage* (1915), then turning to another mode in the series of reflections on life and art beginning with *The Summing Up* (1938). Mackenzie also published three volumes of memoirs of his World War I experiences.

8. Compton Mackenzie, *My Life and Times: Octave One: 1883–1891* (London, 1963), "Prologue and Apologia," p. 13; the quotation that follows is from p. 16.

succeed in keeping what many will think is a presumptuous time-table, I shall be eighty-nine when the tenth octave is published in January 1972, and I shall leave the diary of an octogenarian for posthumous publication." Mackenzie beat his deadline by a year, publishing *Octave Ten* in 1971; plans for the diary await a further dispensation.[9]

By comparison with Mackenzie's longevity and assiduity, the autobiographical bouts of other modern writers might seem to dwindle to brief outbursts. A number of autobiographies have, however, been written over several decades and, together with the authors' self-writings in other modes, may rank them among the devoted exponents of the art. Neither volume nor enthusiasm are guarantors of achievement in this, as in other enterprises, but it seems no accident that Yeats, Sassoon, O'Casey, and Muir realized their persistent efforts in the splendid works they produced.

9. A lifelong autobiography still in the making is Christopher Isherwood's, beginning with the linked stories and personal commentary of *Lions and Shadows* (1938), growing by indirection in the memoir of his parents, *Kathleen and Frank* (1971), and becoming explicit in *Christopher and His Kind* (1976) and *My Guru and His Disciple* (1980).

13

The Autobiography of William Butler Yeats

PERFECTION OF THE LIFE

YEATS DID NOT WORK at his autobiography in all the years between the journal of 1909, which became one of its quarries, and the final stabilization of the text in 1938, four months before his death.[1] Yet he may rank with the most dedicated of self-writers and self-inventors. From the outset of his career, there is a painful urgency to fashion or find the self, which shows up in the early autobiographical novels *John Sherman* and *The Speckled Bird*,[2] and which issues in highly finished personal expressions in the volumes of poetry of the first decade of this century. The major phase, which begins with *Responsibilities* (1914) and reaches an eminence

1. For pertinent biographical data and the publishing history of the work, I follow Joseph Ronsley, *Yeats's Autobiography: Life as Symbolic Pattern* (Cambridge, Mass., 1968), esp. ch. 2, which synthesizes the research of numerous biographers.

2. These have recently been edited: *John Sherman and Dhoya*, ed. R. J. Finneran (Detroit, 1969 [1891]); and *The Speckled Bird*, ed. W. H. O'Donnell, 2 vols. (Dublin, 1973–1974).

in *The Tower* (1928), is marked throughout not only by philosophic system building and violent political challenge and response but also by an effort to bring both those "primary" concerns into relation with the "antithetical" promptings of the subjective self. And the last decade, in which the poet's final mask, "Old Rocky Face," is forged, is made heroic not only by the continued energy and invention of the poetry but by the persistence of his quest. In the last of his collected letters, Yeats writes: " 'Man can embody truth but he cannot know it.' I must embody it in the completion of my life."[3]

Yeats's great project of self-creation is so manifold in its execution and so spectacular in its results that his autobiography has been regarded as entirely unprecedented or as entirely contained within the special terms of his life and thought. Among the few English self-writings that have had numerous monographs devoted to them,[4] the *Autobiography* has been carefully linked with the system of *A Vision* so as to relate its numerous portraits of his contemporaries with the highly original manner in which Yeats portrays the cultural world. Alternatively—yet with a similar regard for the uniqueness posited in a phrase from the *Autobiography*, "the tradition of myself"[5]—the appropriate context for studying this work has been deemed to be the body of his poetry. Thus, Marjorie Perloff treats it as a typically Yeatsian work of art, representing both the source of the autobiographical inquiries pursued in the poems and the equivalent in prose of the symbolic techniques employed in them.[6]

3. *The Letters of W. B. Yeats*, ed. Allan Wade (New York, 1955), p. 922.

4. In addition to Ronsley, *Yeats's Autobiography*, see Daniel T. O'Hara, *Tragic Knowledge: Yeats's Autobiography and Hermeneutics* (New York, 1981).

5. *The Autobiography of William Butler Yeats* (New York, 1969 [1938]), p. 312; I quote this Macmillan/Collier paperback edition, as most readily available.

6. Marjorie Perloff, "The Tradition of Myself: The Autobiographical Mode of Yeats," *Journal of Modern Literature*, 4 (1975): 529–73.

These studies have had the salutary effect of rooting the *Autobiography* firmly in the *oeuvre*, the lifework of a man who could dedicate one of its volumes "to those . . . who have read all that I have written." The inevitable concomitant of such approaches has been to separate the work from the tradition of self-writing, in which a number of writers almost of Yeats's stature have engaged with equal commitment in the imaginative creation of a literary equivalent of their towering and ramified personalities.[7] In taking as context not, for the moment, the Yeats canon but the autobiographical tradition, it will be seen that the distinctiveness of his mask and the distinction of his autobiography are only intensified by association with similar projects and equivalent verbal experiments.

There is nothing to suggest the strong influence of any particular autobiographer on Yeats. He scrupulously omits from the final text the sexual activities set down in an initial draft—the materials of confession in which, for example, a Rousseau would have indulged. Yet the first installment of the *Autobiography*, *Reveries over Childhood and Youth* (1916), promises by its title the mode of approaching early memories—especially as set within a verdant landscape—which Rousseau established as the norm of poetic retrospection.[8] It is the fragmentariness of the images, the randomness of their recall, and the wide range in clarity among them that places these reveries in the Romantic tradition, as Joseph Ronsley has urged. Moreover, as he remarks in passing, they are employed in a recovery of origins: "Yeats begins . . . as if he were writing about the beginning of the world . . . and in this way unfolds an Edenic view of his own beginnings."[9]

7. One such connection has been developed in Marjorie Perloff, "Yeats and Goethe," *Comparative Literature*, 23 (1971): 125–40; but see Yeats's rejection of the deliberate educational program of *Wilhelm Meister* (*Autobiography*, p. 235).

8. The parallel between Rousseau's sheltered island and "The Lake Isle of Innisfree" comes to mind, but Yeats gives *Walden* as his provocation in *Reveries*, sec. 17, p. 47.

9. Ronsley, *Yeats's Autobiography*, p. 34.

Yet just as in earlier idylls of youth amid relatively unspoiled nature, there are anxieties or losses which mark this as an eminently traditional Eden.

"There was a large garden behind the house full of apple trees" (*Reveries*, sec. 2, p. 7) in this prosperous West Country Ireland of Yeats's mercantile and land-owning forebears. It is, moreover, a plentitude denied by no religious or familial constraints: "My uncle, Mat Yeats, the Land Agent, had once waited up every night for a week to catch some boys who stole his apples and when he caught them had given them sixpence and told them not to do it again. Perhaps it is only fancy or the softening touch of the miniaturist that makes me discover in [the family] faces some courtesy and much gentleness" (sec. 3, p. 13). Yeats is at pains to portray his country origins amid simple folk in a way that will underwrite their charm and goodness, and these pages make a winning accompaniment to the better-known images of the flamboyantly active and passionate forebears in his poems.

Yet there is a serpent in this "miniaturist" picture of the child's childlike environment: the evil not of sin but of sensibility.[10] "It is further away than it used to be" (sec. 1, p. 1): these first remembered words express the boy's reaction to a scratch on a mastless toy boat, but they might well have been applied to all the joys of life, which are from the first invested with melancholy or with terror. The roots of the difficulty lie neither in temporal nor in spatial distance but in subjectivity: "Indeed I remember little of childhood but its pain. I have grown happier with every year of life as though gradually conquering something in myself, for certainly my miseries were not made by others but were a part of my own mind" (sec. 1, p. 5). This decisively inverted view of the pleasures of childhood is based on Yeats's version

10. Yeats has no myth of the Fall but shows himself aware of its poetic language at his first séance: "I tried to pray, and because I could not remember a prayer, repeated in a loud voice—'Of Man's first disobedience and the fruit / Of that forbidden tree whose mortal taste / Brought death into the world and all our woe ... Sing heavenly muse' " (*Reveries*, sec. 31, p. 70).

of established notions of the origins of human misery in our bondage to our "own mind." As Yeats grows, he does not lose but learns to value and use his heightened imagination, though it will cost him further pain and intellectual challenges as he comes upon other subjectivities and larger primary facts. This early stage is set down as a period of latency, one which persists even up to the time at which Yeats writes of it: "All life weighed in the scales of my own life seems to me a preparation for something that never happens" (sec. 33, p. 71).

By this time, Yeats's distinctive method is clear. While following out the stages of autobiographical writing, he inverts the values and sentiments traditionally attached to them so as to render himself racially representative and uniquely subjective at the same time. Already anticipated in *Reveries* and emerging in full force in *The Trembling of the Veil* (1922), the conflict with paternal orthodoxy looms as an inevitable late-Victorian conflict. But in place of the son's apostasy against the father's Christian dogmas, we find John Butler Yeats a freethinker and William a hungering dogmatist:

> I was unlike others of my generation in one thing only. I am very religious, and deprived by Huxley and Tyndall, whom I detested, of the simple-minded religion of my childhood, I had made a new religion, almost an infallible church of poetic tradition, of a fardel of stories, and of personages, and of emotions, inseparable from their first expression, passed on from generation to generation by poets and painters with some help from philosophers and theologians. I wished for a world, where I could discover this tradition perpetually, and not in pictures and in poems only, but in tiles round the chimney-piece and in the hangings that kept out the draft.
>
> (*Trembling*, Bk. 1, sec. 2, p. 77)

This satiric account—deftly catching his penchant for an "infallible church" and the attendant taste for appropriate tiles and hangings—leaves out some of the vehemence of his rebellion against the father's libertarian authority. In the first draft, blows are invited if not struck, but even here the tone is wry, the postures theatrical.[11] In the version he chose to publish, the irony is directed against his own artsy-craftsy inclinations ("I was in all things pre-Raphaelite") and adolescent enthusiasm: "At seventeen years old I was already an old-fashioned brass cannon full of shot, and nothing had kept me from going off but a doubt as to my capacity to shoot straight."

The comic portrayal in *Trembling* of the Bedford Park community where he grew up in the eighties begins to turn sour as he meets the band of poets who are to become the tragic generation of the nineties. Yeats's insistence on a generic tag for the period—"tragic in the history of literature" —is undercut by his awareness, even at the time, of the movement's merely modish aspects: "I remember saying one night at The Cheshire Cheese, [where The Rhymers' Club met] when more poets than usual had come, 'None of us can say who will succeed, or even who has or has not talent. The only thing certain about us is that we are too many' " (Bk. 1, sec. 17, p. 115). After his accounts of Oscar Wilde, Ernest Henley, and other inspiring but evidently doomed mentors, he begins to recognize their pattern of directing themselves by self-images "always opposite to the natural self or the natural world" (Bk. 1, sec. 18, p. 115). In consequence, Yeats begins to think of such images for himself and so begins to evolve his doctrine of the Mask. (It is remarkable that he immediately hits upon two of the leading images of his after years: a young man "studying philosophy in some lonely tower"

11. W. B. Yeats, *Memoirs: Autobiography—First Draft; Journal*, ed. Denis Donoghue (London and Basingstoke, 1972), p. 19; this text may also be consulted for the sexual affairs omitted from the finished autobiography and for the original journal entries from which *Estrangement* and *The Death of Synge* are drawn.

and an old man "hidden from human sight in some shell-strewn cavern."[12]) But these reflections upon others and upon himself do not satisfy, and he pursues a circuit of psychical researches with Madame Blavatsky and other sages (Macgregor Mathers, for example, was "a necessary extravagance"—Bk. I, sec. 20, p. 126), of political talk and projects of cultural action with a series of Irish personalities ("I should have kept myself apart and alone"—Bk. II, sec. 10, p. 154), and of theatrical ventures ("I had surrendered myself to the chief temptation of the artist, creation without toil"—Bk. II, sec. 1, p. 135). The succession of personalities encountered and roles played begins to take a figurative form—a road not going somewhere but meandering in disorder and dissipation; and Yeats, with characteristic mythologizing power, gives this, the time of his wandering, a name: "I was . . . astray upon the Path of the Chameleon, upon *Hodos Chameliontos*" (Bk. I, sec. 7, p. 181).

Although the protracted agony of his relations with Maud Gonne scarcely reaches the pages of the *Autobiography*, it is evident that the wanderings of this chameleon were not merely aimless but conscience-ridden. "It was to me a time [of] great pain and disquiet . . . an undiscerned self-loathing," Yeats wrote in a preliminary draft, but his self-reproach for masturbation shows itself in the final text only by reference to intellectual vices: "I generalised a great deal and was ashamed of it. . . . I began to pray that my imagination might somehow be rescued from abstraction and become as preoccupied with life as had been the imagination of Chaucer. For ten or twelve years more I suffered continual remorse, and only became content when my abstractions had com-

12. *Trembling*, Bk. I, sec. 18, pp. 115–16; for the latter figure and its autobiographical significance, see Dillon Johnson, "The Perpetual Self of Yeats's *Autobiographies*," *Eire-Ireland*, 9 (1974): 69–85. James Olney identifies other figures which I shall discuss: "Some Versions of Memory/Some Versions of *Bios*: The Ontology of Autobiography," in *Autobiography: Essays Theoretical and Critical* (Princeton, 1980), pp. 259–67.

posed themselves into picture and dramatisation" (*Trembling*, Bk. i, sec. 21, p. 127). This way of redeeming abstraction and generalization was to be enacted in Yeats's conception of a tragic theater; it also became the guiding principle in his sense of his own life. Although the revelation was not vivid at the time, Yeats does not refrain from anticipating it at this point in his text: "We begin to live when we have conceived life as tragedy" (Bk. i, sec. 21, p. 128).

Along with this dawning intuition comes the first formulation of the doctrine of the Mask and, shortly after, the initial statements of the personal ideal, Unity of Being, and the cultural ideal, Unity of Image—method and goal, respectively, of the new model of his life that Yeats had begun to construct. His accession to this world view cannot be fixed at a single moment of crisis or epiphany, yet it makes *Trembling*—and with it the *Autobiography*—a narrative of conversion: "I know now that revelation is from the self, but from that age-long memoried self . . . and that genius is a crisis that joins that buried self for certain moments to our trivial daily mind" (Bk. iii, sec. 9, p. 182). Like the Augustinian discovering his true rest in God or the Wordsworthian discovering his continued connection with the power that flows through all things, this non-Christian late Romantic discovers the source of "revelation" already within himself. The "age-long memoried self," however much Yeats later bolsters it with philosophical and theosophical speculations, plays the same role of liberating intuition in his conversion process as similar ideas connecting the individual with the race had played for Christian and Romantic autobiographers before him.

No one would wish to cut away the inventive nomenclature and instructive mythology with which Yeats surrounds his root perception—"Anima Mundi," "Gates and Gatekeepers," "Mask and Image," terms which he brings into play at this stage. Yet the climactic power of this summative passage does not depend on new terminology but on older notions of human fate and freedom. Speaking of the "supreme mas-

ters of tragedy," like Dante and Villon, who become his
heroic models for the artist, Yeats writes:

> The two halves of their nature are so completely
> joined that they seem to labour for their objects, and
> yet to desire whatever happens, being at the same
> instant predestinate and free, creation's very self. We
> gaze at such men in awe, because we gaze not at a work
> of art, but at the re-creation of the man through that
> art, the birth of a new species of man, and, it may even
> seem that the hairs of our heads stand up, because that
> birth, that re-creation is from terror.
>
> (Bk. iii, sec. 9, p. 183)

The extravagance of the language is moderated not merely
by the familiarity of certain phrases and concepts in Yeats's
poetry and plays but also by its translatability into the language of rebirth, of free will and predestination, and of
tragic apotheosis that has come down from both Greek and
Christian tradition. Yeats rewrites the languages of classical
tragedy and of Christian apocalypse in terms that seem disarmingly his own but that craftily reveal their provenance
in the act of asserting triumphant discovery.

This key passage in *Trembling* was probably written in
the early twenties when *A Vision* was in process of formulation, when the great poems related to the system were coming into being, when Yeats's stature as "king of the cats" was
shortly to be acknowledged by the Nobel Prize. In order to
convey both the error and confusion of his youthful experience and the subsequent assurance of his illuminated mind,
Yeats carefully manipulates the autobiographer's dual perspective, recounting the past with great immediacy and yet
reminding the reader of how far he has come. "I know now,
. . ." the passage begins, and others vary the formula: "I now
know, . . ." "I did not yet know, . . ." etc. At the time, in the
middle nineties, Yeats was in no position to maintain this
dual perspective, and yet he urgently pursued autobiographical writing, in the form of a novel, *The Speckled Bird*—"a
novel that I could neither write nor cease to write which had

Hodos Chameliontos for its theme" (Bk. v, sec. 6, p. 250).
But he was still on that way, with only the name of it as a
figure, and with no sure grasp of its form and end.

Looking back on the period while writing *Trembling*,
Yeats was aware of the series of crises suffered by his friends
and of his own method in surrounding his self-portrait with
the portraits of men in crisis: "I study every man I meet at
some moment of crisis—I alone have no crisis."[13] Yet while
reciting the litany of Henley, Dowson, Johnson, Davidson,
Beardsley—as well as the more public aspects of Maud
Gonne's bizarre life—*Trembling* builds to a second climax at
the close of Book IV. After watching the embattled first
performance of *Ubu Roi*: "I am very sad, for comedy, ob-
jectivity, has displayed its growing power once more. I say,
'After Stephane Mallarmé, after Paul Verlaine, after Gustave Moreau, after Puvis de Chavannes, after our own verse,
after all our subtle colour and nervous rhythm, after the
faint mixed tints of Conder, what more is possible? After
us the Savage God'" (Bk. iv, sec. 20, p. 234). Thus, the
form of his life had taken him from disturbed innocence,
through embattled self-assertion, to protracted wandering
and momentary illumination, but to no clear way in art and
thought—no crisis, no conversion, but only a modern world
dominated by a "Savage God."

The final book of *Trembling* builds waywardly to a third
climax; as its title, "The Stirring of the Bones," suggests, the
movement is irregular and ghostly—or merely sleepy. After
further mingling in Irish politics—in which the best, or worst,
sight is that of Maud Gonne on the hustings—Yeats begins
experimenting with some of the techniques and symbols
picked up from adept friends like Mathers. His first vision
follows a well-planned invocation of the moon: "I saw between sleeping and waking, as in a kinematograph, a gallop-
ing centaur, and a moment later a naked woman of incredible beauty, standing upon a pedestal and shooting an arrow

13. *Letters*, p. 675; Dec. 22, 1921.

at a star" (Bk. v, sec. 6, p. 248). Its mystery is enhanced by reports of other people's similar visions, but the varied commentaries leave him in the dark: "I came to no conclusion, but I was sure there was some symbolic meaning could I but find it" (Bk. v, sec. 6, p. 249). The interpretation of a learned cabbalist opens up connections with a larger fund of symbolism, but when Yeats ventures a literary interpretation, "he could not throw light on the other symbols except that the shot arrow must symbolise effort, nor did I get any further light" (Bk. v, sec. 6, p. 250).

Yeats's next vision—which occurs at Lady Gregory's Coole House, a fact of enormous significance to him—is less striking in content and briefer in the telling, yet it seems the decisive point of entry into the realm of speculation that was to absorb him for the rest of his life: "It was at Coole that the first few simple thoughts that now, grown complex through their contact with other thoughts, explain the world, came to me from beyond my own mind. I practised meditations, and these, as I think, so affected my sleep that I began to have dreams that differed from ordinary dreams in seeming to take place amid brilliant light . . ." (Bk. v, sec. 6, p. 252). The account reaches this heightened claim abruptly and comes down from it almost as swiftly; the end of *Trembling* comes after another page, and Yeats does not even tell us what the visions were. The epiphanic moment is reached, it seems, as a possession at last claimed, a fate at last fulfilled, and loses something of its drama only to gain in assurance and finality.

What is perhaps most unlikely in the entire account is its series of reflections—ascribed to the time of the vision and not to the time of writing—on the Christian parallels to his vision:

> I was crossing a little stream near Inchy Wood and actually in the middle of a stride from bank to bank, when an emotion never experienced before swept down upon me. I said, "That is what the devout Christian feels, that is how he surrenders his will to the will

329

of God." I felt an extreme surprise for my whole
imagination was preoccupied with the pagan mythology of ancient Ireland. . . . The next morning I awoke
near dawn, to hear a voice saying, "The love of God is
infinite for every human soul because every human
soul is unique, no other can satisfy the same need in
God."   (Bk. v, sec. 6, p. 252)

The initial reflection may simply have been that of a man
without a church-going upbringing who remembers reading
somewhere about Christian mysticism; it is almost amusingly
detached and naïve. But the report of a voice in a waking
dream pronouncing on the love of God—although describing
God's desires and needs with a most unascetic flavor—suggests that Yeats was actively conforming his experience with
others in the mystical tradition and that his self-writing is
pervaded by the forms of a long history of epiphanies and
conversions, for all its highly individual language.

Another nocturnal visitation is mentioned only in passing
in the final pages of *Trembling*, but it leads to an insertion of
experience into the text at precisely the juncture where previous autobiographers had positioned the confirming *sortes*
of textual authority. "I woke one night," Yeats recalls, "to
hear a ceremonial measured voice, which did not seem to be
mine, speaking through my lips[.] 'We make an image of
him who sleeps,' it said, 'and it is not him who sleeps, and we
call it Emmanuel' " (Bk. v, sec. 6, p. 252). The mingled
provenances of this phenomenon might have been obscure
to the novice, but in later years the autobiographer pursues
the memory and its sources:

A few months ago at Oxford I was asking myself why
it should be "An image of him who sleeps," and took
down from the shelf, not knowing what I did, Bur-
kitt's *Early Eastern Christianity*, and opened it at
random. I had opened it at a Gnostic Hymn that told
of a certain King's son who being exiled, slept in
Egypt—a symbol of the natural state—and how an
Angel while he slept brought him a royal mantle. . . .
                              (Bk. v, sec. 6, pp. 252–53)

Unlikely as the text is for this *sortes*, it provides eschatological materials entirely commensurate with those of more orthodox texts. If the "image of him who sleeps" is only tentatively to be identified as the king's son or Emmanuel, it is surely the soul awaiting resurrection, just as the angelic gift of a higher form of clothing is clearly redemptive. Yeats adds his own autobiographical content to this archetypal vision, however, as he continues: "At the bottom of the page I found a footnote saying that the word mantle did not represent the meaning properly for that which the Angel gave had the exile's own form and likeness" (Bk. v, sec. 6, p. 253). The divine gift is, then, none other than the exiled soul's essential identity, the long-sought goal of many an autobiographical striving, here defined as the promised end by an extremely wayward route yet with a decisive closure.

Yeats published *Reveries* and *Trembling* together in 1926 as *Autobiographies*, adding in final revision the passages on his wandering in the condition of *Hodos Chameliontos* and on his epiphanic visions.[14] This state of publication left him at the point of embarking on a life to be spent adding confirmations of those "first few simple thoughts that now . . . explain the world"—an autobiographical structure of proven utility in establishing a life without drama but with steady expansion in a governing faith. Beyond this, Yeats's autobiographical ventures were limited in this period to the publishing of two sets of extracts from his journal of 1909: the one, *Estrangement* (1926), giving testimony of his continued state of alienation well into the new century; the other, *The Death of Synge* (1928), offering an example of his heroic model, the tragic artist.

In the first of these, the anguished cry of the exile is heard, protesting his dissipation in political activities: "I cry continually against my life. I have sleepless nights, thinking of the time that I must take from poetry . . ." (*Estrange-*

14. Ronsley, *Yeats's Autobiography*, pp. 29ff.; on the centrality of these visions, see also pp. 103–06.

ment, sec. 50, p. 333). At the same time, there is growing clarity about the requirements for a tragic theater and, one might argue, for the tragic dimension of his poetry as well: "Tragedy is passion alone, and rejecting character, it gets form from motives, from the wandering of passion. . . . A poet creates tragedy from his own soul, that soul which is alike in all men" (sec. 24, pp. 318–19). Similarly, in the second set of extracts, Synge is raised to the paradigm of total dedication of life to art: "Can a man of genius make that complete renunciation of the world necessary to the full expression of himself without some vice or some deficiency? You were happy or at least blessed, 'blind old man of Scio's rocky isle' " (*Death of Synge*, sec. 18, p. 347)—applying to Synge, poet of the islands, Byron's epithets for Homer.[15]

For Yeats, the price in "perfection of the life" that was to be paid for "perfection of the work" was clear enough.[16] Though he continues to chafe at the self-sacrifice, he bolsters his resolve in markedly traditional language: "Am I going against nature in my constant attempt to fill my life with work? . . . Can one reach God by toil? He gives Himself to the pure in heart. He asks nothing but attention" (*Death of Synge*, sec. 35, p. 354). These further autobiographical fragments, then, made available to Yeats the materials for a further narrative of his career in the years following his accession to vision. The continued exactions but also the renewed affirmation of his vocation are both dropped in amid the *disjecta membra*, the daily notations of passing experience.

Yeats did not proceed directly to write the continuation of his narrative. His visions and researches were adumbrating each other; his struggles with himself and with the world were carrying him forward but as yet to no clear end. At a moment of well-earned pause for stock-taking, however, Yeats had written a brief text which supplied some pointers toward that end. In his Nobel Prize lecture to the Swedish Academy—and in the narrative of his visit which he pub-

15. Byron, *The Bride of Abydos*, Canto II, sec. 2.
16. The terms are codified in his poem "The Choice."

lished in 1924—there was an opportunity for summarizing his career, which he did not fail to seize. In these texts, "The Irish Dramatic Movement" and "The Bounty of Sweden"— both to be included in the collected edition of the *Autobiography*—he created composite images of himself in order to focalize the several stages or relationships of his career.

In the former, the composite is of three persons: "When I received from the hands of your King the great honour your Academy has conferred upon me, I felt that a young man's ghost should have stood upon one side of me and at the other a living woman sinking into the infirmity of age" ("Irish Dramatic Movement," p. 387). In the other, the composite is made with other figures, these more clearly aspects of himself; looking at his medal, he muses: "It shows a young man listening to a Muse, who stands young and beautiful with a great lyre in her hand, and I think as I examine it, 'I was good-looking once like that young man, but my unpractised verse was full of infirmity, my Muse old as it were; and now I am old and rheumatic, and nothing to look at, but my Muse is young" ("Bounty of Sweden," sec. 7, p. 365). It would be facile to fuse the elements of these two constructs, for the young man of the first is named as Synge and marked by other traits than good looks and poetic immaturity. Similarly, the aging woman of the first is Lady Gregory and not—except in a broadly figurative sense—the young or old aspect of the Muse. Yet the two constructs work similarly for more sanguine visions of himself and his career than Yeats had previously allowed himself to entertain. The sight of his medal and the analysis of his Muse generate a cautious claim of personal rebirth: "I am even persuaded that she is like those Angels in Swedenborg's vision, and moves perpetually 'towards the day-spring of her youth' " ("Bounty of Sweden," sec. 7, p. 365). From his association with Synge and Lady Gregory, moreover, he anticipates another form of survival in political and cultural history, in times when their names will be spoken together by future generations ("Bounty of Sweden," sec. 12, p. 374).

These composite images must have been in Yeats's mind for some time, but it was the death of Lady Gregory in 1932 that set him to self-writing again. *Dramatis Personae* (1935), the last installment of the *Autobiography*, declares itself by the years given in the subtitle a record of the Irish dramatic movement for 1896–1902. It will be seen, however, that the cast of characters assembled under its title is less a crowd of theatrical folk than the figures of a personal myth, one which Yeats was at last able to complete.

Dramatis Personae begins precisely at the points in time and space where Yeats had set the two visions that conclude *The Trembling of the Veil*: the country estates of Edward Martyn and of Lady Gregory where he had, respectively, his dream of centaur and archer and his dreams "amid brilliant light." After his visit to Tullyra Castle with Arthur Symons, Lady Gregory calls to invite him to Coole House. The visit seems momentous from the first:

> A glimpse of a long vista of trees, over an undergrowth of clipped laurels, seen for a moment as the outside car approached her house on my first visit, is a vivid memory. Coole House, though it has lost its great park full of ancient trees, is still set in the midst of a thick wood, which spreads out behind the house in two directions, in one along the edges of a lake. . . . In later years I was to know the edges of that lake better than any spot on earth, to know it in all the changes of the seasons, to find there always some new beauty. . . . years were to pass before I came to understand the earlier nineteenth and later eighteenth century, and to love that house more than all other houses. (sec. 3, pp. 259–60)

The house and its setting are bounteous not only in natural and historical values—in all the qualities of an aristocratic culture that Yeats was later to celebrate in some of his greatest poems—but in its proprietress as well. Worn out by his tormented pursuit of Maud Gonne, he summers at Coole House and is given doses of nature and culture by their local custodian: "Finding that I could not work, and thinking the open air salutary, Lady Gregory brought me from cottage to cottage collecting folklore. . . . My object was to find actual experience of the supernatural . . ." (sec. 6, p. 267). And so Yeats continues his education in the mental realms to which his visions have led him, under the aegis of the matriarchal figure who dominates the land and who plays the role of nourishing mother for the careworn exile come home to a folkloric landscape very like his youth's.

Lady Gregory's ministering hand continues to protect and further Yeats's career; by infusions of money—which he only after a struggle can bring himself to record—and by providing a home: "For twenty years I spent two or three months there in every year. Because of those summers, because of that money, I was able through the greater part of my working life to write without thought of anything but the beauty or the utility of what I wrote" (sec. 9, p. 273). Most of the text of *Dramatis Personae* is given to the somewhat nasty, somewhat comic report of the early days of the Irish National Theater, in which Lady Gregory was his stalwart against the inanities of Edward Martyn and George Moore and against the prejudice of public and Church. But her central role in the text, as in the life, is not as woman of action or even as literary collaborator but as a living matriarch of the visionary realm and the poetic vocation to which he was dedicated.

In order to establish Lady Gregory at that symbolic level, Yeats makes her not only a maternal "centre of peace" for himself (sec. 23, p. 305)—much like Monica's place in Augustine's career—but also an avatar of his own self-realization through art. To her work as "founder of modern Irish dialect literature," the final pages of *Dramatis Personae* and the *Autobiography* are directed. After listing her equipment ("her inherited sense of caste, her knowledge of that top of the world where men and women are valued for their manhood and their charm, not for their opinions"—sec. 23, p. 306) and her motives ("'We work to add dignity to

Ireland' was a favourite phrase of hers"—sec. 23, p. 306),
Yeats sketches quickly but with telling strokes the self-
transcendence she had achieved in art:

> Sometimes in her letters, in her books when she wrote
> ordinary English, she was the late-Victorian woman
> turning aside from reality to what seems pleasing, . . .
> but in her last years, when speaking in her own char-
> acter, she seemed always her greater self. A writer
> must die every day he lives, be reborn, as it is said in
> the Burial Service, an incorruptible self, that self op-
> posite of all that he has named "himself." . . . Lady
> Gregory, in her life much artifice, in her nature much
> pride, was born to see the glory of the world in a
> peasant mirror.   (sec. 23, pp. 306–07)

Her artistic self-transformation, her transcendence of personal limitations, her heroic annulment of ordinary personality in favor of her "greater self," are expressed here, it
comes as no surprise, in the traditional language of the burial
service and the figures of death and rebirth. In giving his
final pages to his friend and in taking up what might seem
an extraneous sanctity for a non-Christian, Yeats was actually writing his finest formulation of the artist figure, whose
daily death and renewal as opposite of "himself" he identified as his own self-image.

To conclude this portrait of his lady, so carefully modeled on and standing for his portrait of himself, Yeats quotes
some fine passages of Lady Gregory's prose, including the
lullabye of Grania over the sleeping Diarmuid: "The parting of us two will be the parting of two children of the one
house; it will be the parting of life from the body" (sec. 23,
p. 308). These lines speak not only to the intimacy of Lady
Gregory's and Yeats's spiritual relationship but sound the
note of separation, which is death—the death she had come
to and the death that he had now to anticipate.

14

The Memoirs of George Sherston

SASSOON'S PERPETUAL PILGRIMAGE

———

"I TOLD HIM that I was a Pilgrim going to the Celestial City." When the reader of the *Complete Memoirs*[1] reaches the epigraph to the final volume, *Sherston's Progress*, the impression is confirmed that he has been accompanying a spiritual wayfarer. All his long, meditative life, Siegfried Sassoon maintained the dual role of action and rumination[2] under the aspect of pilgrim allegory. Throughout his extended autobiographical career—from *The Heart's Journey* poems of

---

1. Siegfried Sassoon, *The Complete Memoirs of George Sherston* (London, 1972 [1937]); I quote from the Faber paper edition. The volumes were first published separately: *Memoirs of a Fox-Hunting Man* (1928), *Memoirs of an Infantry Officer* (1930), and *Sherston's Progress* (1936).

2. Declaring himself a "professional ruminator," Sherston/Sassoon writes: "A ruminator really needs two lives; one for experiencing and another for thinking it over. . . . My own idea is that it is better to carry the best part of one's life about in one's head for future reference" (*Sherston's Progress*, Pt. II, sec. 2, p. 563). Other remarks on the autobiographer and on self-writing are to be found in this volume at Pt. I, sec. 4, p. 543; Pt. I, sec. 5, pp. 546–57; and Pt. IV, sec. 2, p. 636.

1927 to the final volume of his *propria persona* autobiographical trilogy, *Siegfried's Journey* (1945)—Sassoon was
governed by the figure of quest, though his active life diminished and his ruminations increased in inverse proportion. With the benefit of hindsight and with varied degrees
of satisfaction in his conversion to Catholicism in 1957, his
critics have mapped his religious path in closed or handsome
curves, but the view from the road his books report is un-
encumbered by claims to distance and direction. To apply
the phrase with which another long-lived contemporary concluded his autobiography, "the journey not the arrival
matters."[3]

The absence of religious conversion and formal completion in Sassoon's self-writings does not, however, bar them
from full use of the figures with which spiritual autobiographers have given pattern and meaning to their lives. Sassoon
habitually uses the terms *spiritual autobiography* and *private
pilgrimage* for his career,[4] and he exhibits a long-standing
obligation to Bunyan that goes well beyond the choice of
epigraph.[5] Perhaps more significantly, his poetry gives frequent indications of a typological habit of mind in confronting the otherwise unassimilable spectacle of the Great War.
"The Redeemer," for one, creates a typological image closely resembling those of other war poets, such as David Jones,
that superimpose the sufferings of the human-all-too-human
Tommy and the paradigmatic martyrdom:

> He faced me, reeling in his weariness,
> Shouldering his load of planks, so hard to bear.

3. Leonard Woolf, *The Journey Not the Arrival Matters* (London,
1969).

4. Diary entries for March 29, 1951, and March 6, 1954; quoted in
Siegfried Sassoon: Poet's Pilgrimage, ed. Felicitas Corrigan (London,
1973), pp. 140, 165; see also the letter of March 26, 1966, quoted on
p. 242: "I just go on being told that I am a war poet, when all I want is
to be told that I am only a pilgrim and a stranger on earth, utterly
dependent on the idea of God's providence to my spiritual being."

5. See *Poet's Pilgrimage*, p. 32, and note for the editor's commentary
on the epigraph and diary references to Sassoon's readings of Bunyan.

I say that He was Christ, who wrought to bless
All groping things with freedom bright as air,
And with His mercy washed and made them fair.
Then the flame sank, and all grew black as pitch,
While we began to struggle along the ditch;
And someone flung his burden in the muck,
Mumbling: "O Christ Almighty, now I'm stuck!"[6]

Other Sassoon war poems take up biblical models for less agonized yet more alarming identifications with their modern instances. Adam becomes "the gaunt wild man whose lovely sons were dead" whereas the modern king sending troops to the slaughter for his selfish purposes stands revealed as another David, quick to exploit the death of Uriah.[7] Some of these identifications are made for their topical, satirical thrust, but the long-standing practice of Sassoon's poetry confirms his autobiographical tendency to apply to the Bible for the figures of life. We may trace the habit to his sense of his Jewish heritage—"as a poetic spirit I have always felt myself—or wanted to be—a kind of minor prophet"[8]—or to his favoring of the devotional and mystical poets of the seventeenth century, especially Herbert and Vaughan.[9]

For all Sassoon's ample provision of biblical analogies with which to piece together the fragments of his war-shattered life, the first volume of the *Complete Memoirs—Memoirs of a Fox-Hunting Man*—is relatively free of figuration. This is the book that made him a venerated relic of the social world he set out to decently bury—the Cranford-Barset-"sceptered isle" world he continued to relish and recall while undertaking to show its limitations and its passing. Sassoon later took his opportunities for mythologizing the

6. Sassoon, *Collected Poems: 1908–1956* (London, 1961); cf. the non-typological but epiphanic poem "Christ and the Soldier" quoted in *Poet's Pilgrimage*, pp. 81–82.

7. "Ancient History" and "Devotion to Duty," respectively.

8. Letter of June 25, 1965, quoted in *Poet's Pilgrimage*, p. 47.

9. See the poem "At the Grave of Henry Vaughan" and the discussion in Sassoon's lecture "On Poetry," both quoted in *Poet's Pilgrimage*, pp. 104–05.

idyll of the turn-of-the-century home counties; in the second trilogy, *The Old Century* and *The Weald of Youth* move easily into symbolic ascriptions for childhood scenes, for example, the "half-hour's pilgrimage" to Watercress Well, which becomes a "symbol of life" and the "source of all my journeyings."[10] But in *Memoirs of a Fox-Hunting Man* (*MFM*), the landscape and his activities within it are held to the level of physical density and rich psychological impression: "With a sense of abiding strangeness I see myself looking down from an upper window on a confusion of green branches shaken by the summer breeze. In an endless variety of dream-distorted versions the garden persists as the background of my unconscious existence" (Pt. I, sec. 4, p. 23).

Sassoon wishes to maintain his native scenes—for all their numinousness in the memory—at the literal level, in preparation for the violent contrast he will draw between them and the war spectacle. Even in these early scenes, the descriptions are set up for pointed contrast with larger landscapes and other realms of experience. An extended passage on the expanding perceptions of waking follows the boy out beyond his window and garden to the valley, the town, and the historical world behind them: "How little I knew of the enormous world beyond that valley and those low green hills. From over the fields and orchards Butley Church struck five in mellow tones. . . . I inspected the village grocer's calendar which was hanging from a nail. On it there was a picture of 'The Relief of Ladysmith.' . . . Old Kruger and the Boers. I never could make up my mind what it was all about, that Boer War, and it seemed such a long way off" (*MFM*, Pt. II, sec. 1, pp. 48–49).

The literal prevails in all the prose on his youthful love affair with horses, which takes up the major part of this first volume. But in these detailed accounts as well, a contrast is effected with another level of consciousness that stands out-

10. Siegfried Sassoon, *The Old Century and Seven More Years* (London, 1938), p. 12.

side and judges the vigorous physical activity. At a climactic moment of the young rider's career, his winning of the "Colonel's Cup" at "Dumbridge," the cup is placed next to another treasured object in his room:

> Everything led back to the talisman; while I gazed and gazed on its lustre I said to myself, aloud, "It can't be true that it's really there on the table!" The photograph of Watts's "Love and Death" was there on the wall; but it meant no more to me than the strangeness of the stars which I had seen without question, out in the quiet spring night. I was secure in a cozy little universe of my own, and it had rewarded me with the Colonel's Cup. My last thought before I fell asleep was, "Next season I'll come out in a pink coat."
>
> (*MFM*, Pt. VI, sec. 4, p. 173)

The contrast of the cup and the reproduction seems at first casual, but when the "strangeness of the stars" is brought into the equation, it reveals the young man's lack of curiosity about the truly mysterious and his banal awe at the presence of the apparently numinous and merely fatuous symbol of sporting success. The Watts painting has come up at other summary junctures, we now recall (Pt. I, sec. 4, p. 22; Pt. II, sec. 1, p. 48), to suggest the realm of artistic depth and spiritual mystery to which the youth is vaguely sensitive but not as yet committed.[11]

Memoirs of a Fox-Hunting Man does not end with this contrast but with the more primitive one between peace and war. As the part titles indicate, the first volume leaves Sherston "At the Front" whereas *Memoirs of an Infantry Officer* takes up the tale much later, with a 1916 scene, "At the Army School." The form of the opening volume, then, already encompasses the full range of the transition from the idyll of gardens and race courses to the mud of trench life

---

11. An inspiring boyhood visit to the Watts Exhibition of 1897 is recounted in *The Old Century*.

and the clay of death. As the third in a succession of friends troops to the grave, the narrator baldly reports: "A sack was lowered into a hole in the ground. The sack was Dick. I knew Death then" (*MFM*, Pt. X, sec. 5, p. 274).

The movement downward to this low place begins early, even in the midst of fox-hunting larks. Quick to enlist and proudly mounted, Sherston tries to extend his prewar "picnic in perfect weather" in the mounted infantry: "My notion of acting as ground scout was to go several hundred yards ahead of the troop and look for jumpable fences. But the ground was still hard and the hedges were blind with summer vegetation, and when I put the farrier-sergeant's horse at a lush-looking obstacle I failed to observe that there was a strand of wire in it" (*MFM*, Pt. IX, sec. 1, pp. 225–26). The resulting fall is figurative as well as literal: its consequence is not merely a broken arm but an alertness to strands of wire impeding movement, freedom, and life. There will be much ado with wire cutters purchased at the army and navy stores and pressed into service at the Battle of Mametz Wood, but already the mortal bonds of the soldier—and with him, man—are laid on.

As Sassoon's commentators observe—and as he himself discloses in one of his frequent chats in the autobiographer's workshop[12]—his creation of a pseudonymous persona to tell an authentic but selective tale allows him to exaggerate the ingenue in his early self-portrait. Yet it is not the young romantic Sherston who is raised as the figure of innocence led to the slaughter but the brother officer who becomes the contents of that sack, "Dick Tiltwood":

> His was the bright countenance of truth; ignorant and undoubting; incapable of concealment but strong in reticence and modesty. . . . he had arrived at manhood in the nick of time to serve his country in what

12. *The Weald of Youth* (London, 1942), pp. 66–67, 132–33. See Michael Thorpe, *Siegfried Sassoon: A Critical Study* (Leiden and London, 1966), *passim*, for the differences in perspective and detail between the two trilogies.

he naturally assumed to be a just and glorious war.
Everyone told him so; and when he came to Clither-
land Camp he was a shining epitome of his unembit-
tered generation which gladly gave itself to the German shells and machine-guns. . . .

(*MFM*, Pt. IX, sec. 4, p. 241)

The language inclines here not only toward indignation at
outraged innocence but also toward universal finality: this
"bright countenance of truth" becomes the "shining epitome" not only for his historical generation but for an eternal pattern of human experience. It is this larger burden of
the narrator's slowly growing political awareness that begins
to emerge in his anticipation of the debacle: "To him, as to
me, the War was inevitable and justifiable. Courage remained
a virtue. And that exploitation of courage, if I may be allowed to say a thing so obvious, was the essential tragedy of
the War, which, as everyone now agrees, was a crime against
humanity" (Pt. IX, sec. 2, p. 230).

The story of Sherston's first years at war is briefly told
by comparison with the close attention that will be given
the final years in the next volumes. Moving to the Front is
to pass a traditional threshold, not merely beyond the familiar world at peace but beyond an insular culture: "For
the first time in our lives we had crossed the Channel"
(*MFM*, Pt. X, sec. 1, p. 244). The specific boundary in time
and place is marked—and remarked upon—by the line, "We
got to Béthune by half-past ten" (Pt. X, sec. 1, p. 245).
From this point, an accretion of baleful events begins to
separate the fox-hunting man from his old self: "Everything
I had known before the War seemed to be withering away
and falling to pieces . . ." (Pt. X, sec. 4, p. 265). With the
loss of his riding friend, "Stephen Colwood," his former
groom, "Dixon," and then "Dick Tiltwood," a point is
reached well known to less naïve but equally spiritual autobiographers: "Somewhere out of sight beyond the splintered
tree-tops of Hidden Wood a bird had begun to sing. Without knowing why, I remembered that it was Easter Sunday.

Standing in that dismal ditch, I could find no consolation in the thought that Christ was risen" (Pt. X, sec. 6, p. 282). The pilgrim now embarked on his ways of exile experiences the blankness of despair: "As for me, I had more or less made up my mind to die: the idea made things easier" (Pt. X, sec. 6, p. 280).

From the point where *Memoirs of an Infantry Officer* (*MIO*) begins, the language of the lower world rises by steady increments to sweeping asseveration: "I remember waiting there in the gloom and watching an unearthly little conflagration caused by some phosphorous bombs up the hill on our right" (Pt. IV, sec. 2, p. 327); "I am staring at a sun-lit picture of Hell, and still the breeze shakes the yellow weeds, and the poppies glow under Crawley Ridge where some shells fell a few minutes ago" (Pt. IV, sec. 2, p. 333); "Our own occupation of Quadrangle Trench was only a prelude to that pandemonium which converted the green thickets of Mametz Wood to a desolation of skeleton trees and blackening bodies" (Pt. IV, sec. 3, p. 348); "Low in the west, pale orange beams were streaming down on the country that receded with a sort of rich regretful beauty, like the background of a painted masterpiece. For me that evening expressed the indeterminate tragedy which was moving, with agony on agony, toward the autumn. . . . altogether, I concluded, Armageddon was too immense for my solitary understanding" (Pt. IV, sec. 4, pp. 360–61).

A brief leave at an Oxford college gives him a wary taste of "Paradise"—"Had I earned it? I was too grateful to care" (*MIO*, Pt. V, sec. 1, p. 369). Here, and on his return to the captured Hindenburg Line, Sherston begins to contrast his knowledge-without-forgiveness with the stolid incomprehension of the "people at home who couldn't understand." The effort to make sense of the inchoate leaves him in spiritual dryness: "But my mind was in a muddle; the War was too big an event for one man to stand alone in. All I knew was that I'd lost my faith in it and there was nothing left to believe in except 'the Battalion spirit' " (Pt. VIII, sec. 2, p.

421). This last faith proves equally difficult to maintain: "Last summer the First Battalion had been part of my life; by the middle of September it had been almost obliterated." One last hope remains, in the human spirit and the heroic principle:

> I, a single human being with my little stock of earthly experience in my head, was entering once again the veritable gloom and disaster of the thing called Armageddon. And I saw it then, as I see it now—a dreadful place, a place of horror and desolation which no imagination could have invented. Also it was a place where a man of strong spirit might know himself utterly powerless against death and destruction, and yet stand up and defy gross darkness and stupefying shell-fire, discovering in himself the invincible resistance of an animal or an insect, and an endurance which he might, in after days, forget or disbelieve.
>
> (Pt. VIII, sec. 4, p. 431)

These last defiances of the *néant* avail him nothing as he descends into the abyss of the tunnel under the Hindenburg Trench: "The earthy smell of that triumph of Teutonic military engineering was strongly suggestive of appearing in the Roll of Honour and being buried until the Day of Judgment" (Pt. VIII, sec. 4, p. 433). There is only one further point of exile, the Outpost Trench:

> wherever we looked the mangled effigies of the dead were our *memento mori*. Shell-twisted and dismembered, the Germans maintained the violent attitudes in which they had died. The British had mostly been killed by bullets or bombs, so they looked more resigned. But I can remember a pair of hands (nationality unknown) which protruded from the soaked ashen soil like the roots of a tree turned upside down; one hand seemed to be pointing at the sky with an accusing gesture. Each time I passed that place the protest of those fingers became more expressive of an appeal to God in defiance of those who made the War.

Who made the War? . . . the dead were the dead; this was no time to be pitying them or asking silly questions about their outraged lives. Such sights must be taken for granted, I thought, as I gasped and slithered and stumbled with my disconsolate crew. Floating on the surface of the flooded trench was the mask of a human face which had detached itself from the skull.
(Pt. VIII, sec. 4, p. 435)

At this point, Sherston is wounded in the shoulder and is withdrawn to England for convalescence, but his illness is more radical than a tearing of flesh. In company with the other survivors, he feels "estrangement from everyone except the troops in the Front Line": "I couldn't be free from the War; even this hospital ward was full of it, and every day the oppression increased" (*MIO*, Pt. IX, sec. 1, p. 452). The oppression and bondage express themselves in the characteristic visions of combat neurosis: "Shapes of mutilated soldiers came crawling across the floor; the floor seemed to be littered with fragments of mangled flesh. Faces glared upward; hands clutched at neck and belly; a livid grinning face with bristly moustache peered at me above the edge of my bed; his hands clawed at the sheets" (Pt. IX, sec. 1, p. 453).

At once, at the point of crisis, a sign is given, though in a medium oddly different from the usual organs of revelation. It is the *"Unconservative Weekly"* (*The Nation*): "The omniscience of this ably written journal had become the basis of my provocative views on world affairs. . . . an article in the *Unconservative Weekly* was for me a sort of divine revelation. It told me what I'd never known but now needed to believe . . ." (*MIO*, Pt. IX, sec. 2, p. 455). It is true that Sherston goes on to belittle his ability to comprehend and retain the political acumen of the journal, but his comic reduction of his rational response only enhances the power of his faith. This faith is further bolstered by its contention with the traditional beliefs of "Lady Asterisk," who likes having "serious helpful little talks with her officers": "When

I had blurted out my opinion that life was preferable to the Roll of Honour she put aside her reticence like a rich cloak. 'But death is nothing,' she said. 'Life, after all, is only the beginning. And those who are killed in the War—they help us from up there. They are helping us to win' " (Pt. IX, sec. 3, p. 465). With this travesty of Christian consolation and the news that all but one of the officers of his Second Battalion have become casualties, Sherston writes to consult the editor of his journal of revelation, "Mr. Markington" (H. V. Massingham).

Their first meeting is a luncheon at the editor's club, "the mecca of the Liberal Party," under the visible aegis and spiritual example of Richard Cobden. Markington provides historical perspective on past antiwar campaigns and political insight into one of the chief impediments to a negotiated peace—the Allies' refusal to publish their war aims and secret treaties. He also, almost in passing, provides the idea of moral protest and witnessing resistance to the war: "He told me that I should find the same sort of things described in Tolstoy's *War and Peace*, adding that if once the common soldier became articulate the War couldn't last a month" (*MIO*, Pt. X, sec. 1, p. 474). Sherston takes the idea home and returns, the following week, to the editorial office: "It was a case of direct inspiration; I had, so to speak, received the call, and the editor of the *Unconservative Weekly* seemed the most likely man to put me on the shortest road to martyrdom" (Pt. X, sec. 1, p. 476).

Markington spells out the broad lines of a proclamation of protest, and the unpolitical Sherston is led beyond his characteristic diffidence: "His words caused me an uncomfortable feeling that perhaps I was only making a fool of myself; but this was soon mitigated by a glowing sense of martyrdom. I saw myself 'attired with sudden brightness, like a man inspired' . . ." (*MIO*, Pt. X, sec. 1, p. 477).[13] Lit-

13. The internal quotation is from Wordsworth's "Character of the Happy Warrior."

347

erary as well as religious conventions are here put subtly to the test of simultaneous renewal and satire.

To counteract the excessive afflatus of the newly dedicated spirit, Markington also provides contact with the best rational mind—and the most vigorous antiwar protester—of the time, Bertrand Russell ("Thornton Tyrrell"). The philosopher's discourse is clipped and pragmatic, shifting focus quickly from the large political issues to the scale of the man before him and his spiritual crisis: " 'It amounts to this, doesn't it—that you have ceased to believe what you are told about the objects for which you supposed yourself to be fighting? . . . Now that you have lost your faith in what you enlisted for, I am certain that you should go on and let the consequences take care of themselves. . . . But I hadn't intended to speak as definitely as this. You must decide by your own feeling and not by what anyone else says' " (Pt. X, sec. 2, pp. 478–49). The act of protest on which they collaborate takes the form of a traditional religious protest-cum-profession of faith. Sassoon/Sherston's famous declaration begins:

> *I am making this statement as an act of wilful defiance of military authority, because I believe that the War is being deliberately prolonged by those who have the power to end it. . . . I believe that this War, upon which I entered as a war of defence and liberation, has now become a war of aggression and conquest. . . . I have seen and endured the sufferings of the troops, and I can no longer be a party to prolong these sufferings for ends which I believe to be evil and unjust.*
> (Pt. X, sec. 5, p. 496)

In difficulty at the unwonted bravado of his position and his prose, Sherston seeks inspiration where he can find it. He goes to Cambridge, drawing mingled sustenance from his alma mater: "Sitting in King's [College] Chapel I tried to recover my conviction of the nobility of my enterprise and to believe that the pen which wrote my statement had 'dropped from an angel's wing.' I also reminded myself that Cambridge had dismissed Tyrrell from his lectureship because he disbelieved in the War" (*MIO*, Pt. X, sec. 3, p. 488).[14] With these mixed influences, Sherston finds himself in "purgatory" (Pt. X, sec. 4, p. 488) and returns to his home town to suffer through his condition. There follows one of the classic scenes of autobiographical writing, an ascent of a hill to the point of epiphany, in which a vision of history and of oneself in history enables the divided mind to resolve itself and make its central choice in life:

> Late on a sultry afternoon, when returning from a mutinous-minded walk, I stopped to sit in Butley Churchyard. From Butley Hill one looks across a narrow winding valley, and that afternoon the woods and orchards suddenly made me feel almost as fond of them as I'd been when I was in France. While I was resting on a flat-topped old tombstone I recovered something approximate to peace of mind. Gazing at my immediate surroundings, I felt that "joining the great majority" was a homely—almost a comforting—idea. Here death differed from extinction in modern warfare. I ascertained from the nearest headstone that *Thomas Welfare, of this Parish, had died on October 20th, 1843, aged 72. "Respected by all who knew him." Also Sarah, wife of the above. "Not changed but glorified."* Such facts were resignedly acceptable. They were in harmony with the simple annals of this quiet corner of Kent. . . . And Butley Church, with its big-buttressed square tower, was protectively permanent. One could visualize it there for the last 599 years, measuring out the unambitious local chronology with its bells, while English history unrolled itself along the horizon with coronations and rebellions and stubbornly disputed charters and covenants. Beyond all that, the "foreign parts" of the world widened incredibly toward regions reported by travellers' tales.

14. The internal quotation is from Wordsworth's *Ecclesiastical Sonnets*, pt. III, no. 5.

And so outward to the windy universe of astronomers and theologians. . . .

Meanwhile my meditations had dispelled my heavy heartedness, and as I went home I recovered something of the exultation I'd felt when first forming my resolution. I knew that no right-minded Butley man could take it upon himself to affirm that a European war was being needlessly prolonged by those who had the power to end it. They would tap their foreheads and sympathetically assume that I'd seen more of the fighting than was good for me. But I felt the desire to suffer, and once again I had a glimpse of something beyond and above my present troubles—as though I could, by cutting myself off from my previous existence, gain some new spiritual freedom and live as I had never lived before.   (Pt. X, sec. 4, pp. 492–94)

———

Coming down from this exalted vision and gritty determination, Sherston's final volume of memoirs might be expected to record a steady progress in pacifist activity and spiritual enlightenment. Indeed, that is what he anticipates; when shunted back to the Front, he suffers pangs of doubt as to his course but accepts them as "an inevitable conjuncture in my progress" (*MIO*, Pt. X, sec. 7, p. 506). And there is the monitory epigraph to *Sherston's Progress*, indicating movement toward the Celestial City, to lay out the path of the denouement. But the form and content of this last volume are by no means so clear, and Sherston's return to the Front only to suffer a near-fatal wound offers no easy moral or aesthetic resolution—it simply brings his war service to an end and closes the *Memoirs*. It was some such awareness of this inconclusive ending—along with the pressure of other aspects of his life that required telling—that must have led Sassoon to write three further volumes of autobiography in his own name.

Yet running through *Sherston's Progress* there is a figure of life that gives point to his further experiences in battle and hospital. By its very nature, this figure is unlikely to suggest full resolution as it opens the future to possibility rather than resting at a determinate place. Although Sherston's narrative of his treatment by Dr. W. H. R. Rivers is readily reducible to a psychiatric revelation of his fundamental immaturity and new dependence on a father figure, the human figure that emerges is of a less easily grasped kind. The terms of Sassoon's later poem on Rivers cast him in an archetypal form:

> What voice revisits me this night? What face
> To my heart's room returns?
> From that perpetual silence where the grace
> Of human sainthood burns
> Hastes he once more to harmonize and heal?
>
> . . .
>
> O fathering friend and scientist of good. . . .[15]

In *Sherston's Progress* (*SP*), this image is scaled down to that of an "alert and earnest" face with the "half-shy look of a middle-aged person intruding on the segregative amusements of the young," steadily regarding one with an "unreprimanding smile" (Pt. I, sec. 2, pp. 533–34). Given this dual image of the universal healer and the vividly human friend, suggestions of Christological displacement arise, but Sherston urges no certainty about the good doctor or his cure: "In later years, while muddling on toward maturity, I have made it my business to find out all I can about the mechanism of my spontaneous behaviour; but I cannot be sure how far I had advanced in that art—or science—in 1917. I can only suggest that my definite approach to mental maturity began with my contact with the mind of Rivers" (Pt. I, sec. 3, p. 534).

Whether or not Sherston's condition is a rebirth and his activity a progress, the further pages of the volume infuse doses of expansive experience. Sherston even makes a jour-

15. "Revisitation: Dr. W. H. R. Rivers"; the poem was first published in *Vigils* (1934).

ney to Jerusalem as part of a military force, but the occasion is not one for racial identification or postexilic return; it is instead an encounter with another learned doctor, who provides a running commentary on the flora and fauna of the land. Similarly, Sherston's reading provides no telling insights but a deepening of his response to long-familiar writers like Hardy. Yet he is still trapped inside the war: "And I felt a great longing to be liberated from these few hundred yards of ant-like activity—to travel all the way along the Western Front—to learn through my eyes and with my heart the organism of the monstrous drama which my mind had not the power to envision as a whole. But my mind could see no further than the walls of that dug-out with its one wobbling candle which now burnt low" (*SP*, Pt. IV, sec. 2, p. 640).

From this antlike limitation he is released with a violence that almost destroys him. He is sent home and decisively begins his lifelong career of trying to make sense of the war and his transformation by it. Back in the hospital, he tries to take stock of his life but is not impressed with the sums; of course, Sherston is prevented from reckoning in the war poetry that Sassoon had published and that was to provide a vocation and a means of establishing his identity. Summing up his faith in his vision and his protest: "I had no conviction about anything except that the War was a dirty trick which had been played on me and my generation" (*SP*, Pt. IV, sec. 3, p. 655). But at this stage of renewed *accidie*, the good doctor returns:

> And then, unexpected and unannounced, Rivers came in and closed the door behind him. Quiet and alert, purposeful and unhesitating, he seemed to empty the room of everything that had needed exorcising.
>
> My futile demons fled him—for his presence was a refutation of wrong-headedness. . . .
>
> He did not tell me that I had done my best to justify his belief in me. He merely made me feel that

he took all that for granted, and now we must go on to something better still. And this was the beginning of the new life toward which he had shown me the way.   (Pt. IV, sec. 3, pp. 655–56)

15

Mirror in My House

A LION AMONG
THE CHRISTIANS

ANYONE WHO HAD SEEN an early production of a Sean O'Casey play might have predicted what his autobiography would be like. It would break out in sudden outbursts of invective, eruptions of song and dance, rhetorical set pieces in "Flutherian" brogue, pathos and farce laid on side by side and tending to become one. These traits all showed themselves in turn in the six volumes of *Mirror in My House*, which O'Casey published between 1939 and 1954,[1] and have been lovingly quoted by faithful critics or roundly condemned by impassive ones.[2] What no one could have fore-

1. *Mirror in My House: The Autobiographies of Sean O'Casey*, 2 vols. (New York, 1956); this cited edition is not numbered consecutively, so location will be indicated by O'Casey's volume titles. The original six volumes were published in 1939, 1942, 1946, 1949, 1952, and 1954.

2. The best summary of the autobiography and its historical situation is David Krause, *Sean O'Casey: The Man and His Work* (London, 1960), chs. 1, 7. A fair statement of the objections to the later volumes is Lawrence J. Dessner, "Art and Anger in the *Autobiographies* of Sean O'Casey," *Eire-Ireland*, 10, no. 3 (1975): 46–61. See also James R. Scrimgeour, *Sean O'Casey* (Boston, 1978), esp. pp. 39–40. I regret not being able to make use of the collection *Essays on Sean O'Casey's Autobiographies*, ed. Robert G. Lowery (Totowa, N.J., and London, 1981).

seen was the degree of dependence by this religious iconoclast on the language of the Scriptures to tell the story of his
life.

The use of biblical language in *Mirror* is also an abuse of
it, to be sure. Although the title of the first volume, *I Knock
at the Door*, issues an invitation to life, the epigraph—"Knock,
and it shall be opened unto you" (Matthew 7; Luke 11)—
sounds a bitter note to begin a tale of myriad exclusions. Although the protagonist (called Johnny Casside at this stage)
does not suffer the exclusion from life itself that his two
namesakes do, he is successively shut out of a decent home
life, healthy boyhood, and even minimal schooling by the
bad breaks and human derelictions that plague him. The first
chapter, "A Child Is Born," sets the tone of biblical reference
throughout. O'Casey's megalomania does not extend to identification with the messianic child promised by Isaiah, but he
appropriates the sentiment called up by the phrase to reveal
how little children are suffered to come unto him in a nominally Christian society.

Other broadly scriptural chapter titles—"The Hill of
Healing," "A Child of God," "The Lord Loveth Judgement"
—point up similar inhumanities clothed in sanctimony. Perhaps the most painful is a sexton's turning the boy from the
church porch into the rain, after which he contracts a severe
bronchial illness. But this bitterness is passing by comparison
with the lasting effects of his minimal treatment for eye cata-
racts at a charity hospital and his expulsion from school after
retaliating in kind for a teacher's unjustified corporal punishment. By the end of the volume, the ten-year-old has been
effectively excluded from most of the goods of life, and only
his first fumbling acquaintance with literature—"Who the
hell's Tennyson? he asked himself, as he slowly recited . . ."
("I Knock at the Door")—holds any promise of the life to
come.

It is, perhaps, inevitable that the language of a Christian
culture will be employed with scornful irony to point out
its wide divergence from its own professions. And it comes

as no surprise to learn that O'Casey was well prepared—especially in his Protestant subculture—to see the world and himself in scriptural terms. When his most industrious critic, David Krause, asked him about his "childhood proficiency in Holy Scripture," O'Casey late in life replied: "I remember it as through a glass lightly. . . . The Bible was the important book in our house, and full of fine stories and mysterious words for a curious kid to imitate. I liked the sound of the words long before I knew what they meant, and it gave me a feeling of power to spout them in the house and in front of the other kids."[3] The larger implications of this childhood stance may be drawn by those who would characterize O'Casey's dramatic rhetoric as prophecy or bombast, but its narrower relevance to the child's self-conception and the formation of his enduring self-image is yet more evident.

If the stylistic technique of inverting biblical language for satirical or polemical purposes were O'Casey's only appropriation of religious tradition in his autobiography, its interest would be limited to matters of rhetoric and politics. But *Mirror in My House* is shot through with the major figures of the autobiographical tradition, and the conjunction of rhetoric and figuration suggests a self-conception that runs deeper than its local outbursts. No large design or firm consistency can be anticipated in a six-volume prose work by a dramatist who amply demonstrated his scorn for conventional unities and moderate stylistic registers. O'Casey wrote his autobiography with the freedom to intercalate vignettes or short stories, dramatic dialogue and choruses, and political essays ad libitum so that no student of its half-million words will ever discover a formal principle that will take it all in. But there are frequent moments, especially in the early volumes, of direct emulation of the major scenes and stages that we have noted among the autobiographers studied here. A line can be drawn—and a semblance of aes-

---

3. Quoted in Krause, p. 296. Krause is editing *The Letters of Sean O'Casey* (New York and London, 1975-).

thetic unity discovered—among some of the set pieces, which seem to claim their unmotivated reasons for being.

After the eight-paragraph overture, which attunes us to the historical moment in Dublin of the 1880s,[4] the prose of *I Knock at the Door* shifts to the rhythms of physical gestation:

> And the woman in child-pain clenched her teeth, dug her knees home into the bed, became a tense living mass of agony and effort, sweated and panted, pressed and groaned, and pressed and pressed till a man child dropped from her womb down into the world; down into a world that was filled up with the needs, ambitions, desires, and ignorances of others, to be shoved aside, pressed back, beaten down by privileges carrying godwarrants of superiority because they had dropped down into the world a couple of hours earlier. The privileges were angry and irritable; but the round-bellied, waggle-headed, lanky-legged newborn late-comer kicked against the ambitions, needs, and desires of the others, cleared a patch of room for itself . . . and so grew gradually, and gathered to itself the power, the ignorance, the desire, and the ambition of man.   (Vol. I, pp. 3–4)

As the language shifts again from the peristaltic repetitions of childbirth to the thumping sounds of the conflict of life, another theme is faintly heard: the logistics of the Fall. "Down into the world; down into a world," "dropped down into the world," "pressed back, beaten down"—the universal condition is proclaimed a radically, if not ethically, fallen one. To this downward drift (from a prior state that remains

---

4. This brief passage has been studied as a key to the whole work in Bernard Benstock, "Chronology and Narratology in Sean O'Casey's Beginnings," *Genre*, 12 (1979): 551–64. Benstock has also written a series of books and articles on the character types who populate O'Casey's autobiography as well as his plays; of direct bearing on the birth-creation scene is "The Mother-Madonna-Matriarch in O'Casey," *Southern Review*, 6 (1970): 603–23.

merely a logical premise), a contrary movement is opposed: the upward, expansive energy of fleshly growth and spiritual aspiration. Here in the opening pages, as he will again later, O'Casey makes an overt identification of his individual case and humanity's; his claim is to incarnate "the power, the ignorance, the desire, and the ambition of man."

The fall into life is rendered more poignant when it becomes more literal and personal. The child's father enacts the human aspiration upward in maintaining high literary pursuits on a clerk's income, but his amassing of a large library opens the way to a prosaic decline: "A ladder on which he stood, it was said, had slipped from under him, and, in falling, his back had struck a chair, and his spine had been injured. . . . There was one comfort that, if he died, he would die in the midst of his books" (Vol. I, pp. 41–42). And die he does, leaving the family to another palpable fall, into poverty. As his two brothers go off to the army—with physical and moral consequences that will later be brought home—and as his sister drifts into a disastrous marriage, the boy begins to sink further down in his tenuous place on the ladder of life.

Yet a contrary force is found to be at work, at least potentially, in the grim environment of the Dublin slums. In "The Tired Cow," the first of the intercalated chapters, which recall the stories of *Dubliners*, a reluctant animal being led to slaughter is made to stand for the larger life around. In the midst of this vignette, the boy has a vision which combines up-to-date techniques of Joycean epiphany with the materials of the first book of the Bible:

> How 'ud it be, thought Johnny, if God opened the windows of heaven, an' let it rain, rain like hell, for forty days an' forty nights, like it did when the earth was filled with violence, an' it repented the Lord that He hath made man. . . . But that could never happen now, for God had promised Noah, a just man and perfect in his generation, there'd never be anything like a flood any more; and as proof positive, set His bow

in the cloud as a token of a covenant between Him
and the earth. . . .

There was the very rainbow, now, sparklin' fine,
one end restin' on the roof of Mrs. Mullally's house,
and the other end leanin' on the top of one of the
Dublin Mountains, with the centre touchin' the edge
of the firmament; an', if only our eyes were a little
brighter, we'd see millions an' millions of burnished
angels standin' on it from one end to the other, havin'
a long gawk at all that was goin' on in the earth that
God made in the beginnin', an' that had to make a
fresh start the time that Noah an' his wife, an' his sons,
an' his sons' wives came outa the ark with the ele-
phants, the lions, the horses, and the cows that musta
given Noah the milk he needed when he was shut off
from everything, till the dove came back with the
olive branch stuck in her gob.

(Vol. I, pp. 116–17)

But no manifestation of the divine is apparent in the scene;
Johnny assists the drovers in their brutal attempts to get the
reluctant cow moving with the herd and then is left "to watch
the cow starin' straight out in front of her as if she saw
nothin', while the rain, made golden by the shinin' sun, still
kept softly fallin'." By the end of the chapter, in this conjunction of visionary promise and everyday unfulfillment,
the cow is still staring straight ahead, the boy is still watching
the cow, "but the sun had stopped her shinin', and the rain
was no longer golden."

Yet there is a place of pleasure and bountifulness available
to Johnny, though it is only in the imagination. In two dream
chapters ("The Dream School" and "The Dream Review"),
he can have his fill of the Edenic things which other self-
writers have celebrated: "The sky above was a far deeper
blue than the blue on the wing of the blue-dotted butterfly,
while through the deep blue of the sky sailed white clouds
so low down that some of them shone with the reflected
gold from the blossoms of the daffodils. Many beautiful trees
lined the road that Johnny walked on, and from some came

the smell of thyme and from others the smell of cinnamon" (Vol. I, p. 149). That this is not merely a private fantasy but a cultural endowment is borne out by the rhythms of the prose and the choice of spices; we are in the presence of a biblical paradise, and the mature author joins the hungry boy in his submission to the master figures of the autobiographical tradition.

This is the only taste of a natural childhood the young O'Casey is to have, for his prevailing contact with nature is the pain of his diseased eyes whereas his consistent contact with human nature takes the form of hostility and humiliation. There is also a fall into sin—the primal one of stealing food—but this autobiography is not troubled by the traditional response to an early theft: "Johnny didn't bother much about food or raiment. There wasn't much of either to be had, so he took what was given, and forgot to thank God" ("Life Is More Than Meat"). He is learning to survive in an alien world, even though it is his own world, and the first volume concludes on a note of some satisfaction: "Well, he'd learned poethry and had kissed a girl. If he hadn' gone to school, he'd met the scholars; if he hadn' gone into the house, he had knocked at the door" (Vol. I, p. 294).

The pattern of the second volume repeats the major turnings of the first although the admixture of material on other phases of life—the decline of the family, the introduction to Irish politics, first pratfalls in the theater—may serve to obscure it. The longest continuous section of *Pictures in the Hallway* is the story of Johnny's first job, as a shipping clerk with a true-blue Protestant firm. Each of the seven chapters is concluded with a punning allusion to the days of Creation: "And Johnny felt that it was good; and the morning and the evening were the fair'st day"; "but Johnny felt uneasy, and saw that it was not good; and the morning and the evening were the sicken'd day"; etc. O'Casey's ironic use of biblical language is not as convincing here as it is elsewhere, for the association of the budding youth with the creation of the world is tenuous at best. Indeed, it is not long before the emphasis shifts to the pattern of rebellion through theft as the clerk makes use of his opportunities in the stock room. But the irony is heavy when the boy is expelled after an act of insubordination and refusal to accept his boss's heavy fine: the chapter title "To Him That Hath Shall Be Given" (conflating Matthew 5 and Luke 6) can be taken only as bitter sarcasm rather than a revelatory adaptation of traditional motifs.[5]

The consequence of this renewed cycle of creation and expulsion is, however, to confirm the outcast in his role of rebel and prophetic voice against the world's iniquities. At his expulsion from the firm, a copy of Milton, which he has also stolen, is sent flying after him, and he takes the occasion to identify himself with the bardic voice, if not with his chief antihero:

> I leave th' pair of you [his bosses] with your god-
> liness and go;
> And when th' ending day comes, day of wrath, I hope
> You two may catch a glimpse of heaven's glory;
> Then sink down, sudden, down, deep down to hell,
> Amazed and sightless!   (Vol. I, p. 200)

This isn't quite up to the role of Miltonic imitation, but it makes its point about the budding poet-prophet wih humor and economy.

A more immediate avenue to express the confirmed rebel's protest lay open in politics, particularly of the mass action variety. As early as the nationalist demonstrations in support of the Boers against British imperialism, O'Casey took up his lifelong political commitment, but in this early scene he could play out the role of violent rebellion as well. After knocking from his horse a sabre-wielding policeman among the troop breaking up the riot, Johnny takes shelter with a

---

5. The same is true of the Carlyle allusion in another chapter title, "Work While It Is Not Yet Day" as well as in other biblical takeoffs like "Work Made Manifest."

fetching and rewarding young woman straight out of one of his plays and improbably but rightly named "Daisy Battles" ("I Strike a Blow for You, Dear Land").

Fast becoming not merely a rebel but a revolutionary hero, the young man is vouchsafed an epiphanic vision. Standing by the Liffey at sunset, he gazes at "Dublin in the grip of God":

> He resolved to be strong; to stand out among many; to quit himself like a man; he wouldn't give even a backward look at the withering things that lived by currying favour with stronger things; no busy moving hand to the hat for him. . . . His treasures would be simple things, like those gathered together by St. MacCua, who had a cock who served his owner by crying lustily at midnight to warn the saint it was time to greet the day with his first devotions; a mouse that saw the saint wasted no more than five hours a day in sleep, . . . and a fly that strolled along the lines of the psalter as it was being read aloud by MacCua. . . . So, something like MacCua, he would seek the things that endured; his treasures would be books, bought by the careful gathering of widely scattered pence. From life he had learned much; and from books he would learn more of the wisdom thought out, and the loveliness imagined, by the wiser and greater brethren of the human family.
>
> (Vol. I, pp. 337–38)

And the scene of dedication ends with the O'Casey ritual of a wild dance with a life-force colleen, renewed scorn of the mass's opium as he watches the churches fill, and a snatch from a passing conversation showing the limited ideals of his compatriots.

O'Casey succeeded in bringing much of this high-sounding program to pass. The middle two volumes of *Mirror in My House*, spanning the decades from 1906 to 1926, record the twin struggles of Ireland to become Eire and of Johnny Casside to become Sean O'Casey. The two processes are linked not only by the protagonist's involvement in the independence struggle but also by the linguistic rededication in which they mutually participate. *Drums Under the Window* is much occupied with the language question; as the protagonist enters into the social movement, his identity—even at the level of his name—becomes more complex: "He had three names: to his mother he was Johnny; his Gaelic friends knew him as Sean; to his workmates he was Jack, and when they wished to distinguish him from another Jack, they added the title of Irish, so Irish Jack he became . . ." (Vol. I, p. 64). But his affiliation with this cultural cause is also the occasion of one of his most bitter defeats. With the clerical campaign to suppress the teaching of Irish at the National University by muzzling its leading advocate, Dr. Michael O'Hickey, the protagonist gains a new awareness of the Church's conservative role ("Lost Leader" and "Gaelstroem"). A comic finale for this phase of his disaffiliation comes in the form of a parody of Genesis. As a mealymouthed Catholic apologist named "Jeecaysee" (G. K. Chesterton) spreads his flattering unctions, Adam and Eve in their Ireland paradise decide that the price of the envisioned new order is too high to pay. Anticipating O'Casey's own decision, Eve declares they will leave Ireland: "To where things may be better. . . . I've a child coming, and he won't be born here. There will be others too; and in higher ground and purer air they can start to build a Paradise of their own, safer, firmer, and more lovely than anything even a God can give" (Vol. I, p. 274).

A similar pattern of affiliation and withdrawal governs the next phase of O'Casey's political career: his role in the labor movement under the leadership of Jim Larkin. This movement, too, suffers its defeats at the hands of the bourgeoisie, staunchly backed by the Church, in the eight-month lockout of 1913, but here, too, the autobiographer can muster his comic verve to round off the episode with a splendid pastiche. From the top of the procathedral, St. Patrick shouts encouragement to a "Bishop Eblananus" in his efforts to suppress the working class's rise; but when Lord Nelson from his pillar adds his opinions on Irish recalcitrance, they turn on him with nationalistic fervor and copious brogue ("Prometheus Hibernica"). A more severe defeat of O'Casey's political efforts comes with the shift of dominance from his labor-oriented Irish Citizen Army to the more crudely nationalistic Irish Volunteer Army so that by the time of the Easter Rising of 1916 he is on the sidelines, one of those passed over in the clash of more elemental forces.

These are also the years of the Casside family's last gasps, and the grand public themes and personal aspirations of the protagonist are told above a steady ground bass of illness and death. In *Drums Under the Window* it is his brother Tom and sister Ella who decline; in *Inishfallen, Fare Thee Well*, it is his mother and another brother, Michael—the latter into a state of moral degeneration rather than death. It would be too much to say that these years are a continual state of crisis for the protagonist, for he is rewarded with small successes along the way to becoming a major dramatist. But the anguish of his memories comes through on every page of these volumes and makes them even more excruciating reading than the tale of crimes against the child in *I Knock at the Door*. The mark of this agony is the appearance in the prose of the first signs of the uncontrolled vituperation and political naïveté that overwhelm the later volumes of the autobiography. At his mother's death, for example, the simple pathos of the fact is disfigured by the strainings of symbolism:

> Over the white shroud, over the coffin, he draped the red cloth that had covered the box on which she had so often sat. It would be her red flag, ignorant as she was of all things political . . . ; but she was, in her bravery, her irreducible and quiet endurance, her fearless and cheery battle with a hard, and often brutal, life, the soul of Socialism; and the red symbol, draping her coffin, honoured itself in warming the dead-cold breast of an indomitable woman.   (Vol. II, p. 36)

As this sort of figuration takes over *Mirror in My House*, it eddies from the broad stream of the autobiographical tradition and becomes a more specialized, and lesser, form of prose.

After the succession of crises, personal and social, which climax in the Civil War that followed independence in 1922, it was inevitable that a survivor would feel that a threshold had been crossed, a new life embarked upon. But the prevailing note of O'Casey's record of the twenties—which saw his emergence as a recognized literary figure—is one of bathos. What is true of the nation is at least partly true for the dramatist: nothing fails like success. To liven his spirits at the sight of a revolution led into compromise and propriety by a new leader, he attempts a light touch: "Looksee, said De Valera, hooking an arm into one of [Lloyd] George's, you're a Kelt and I'm another; so we'd better have a stroll, and talk of the first four things first, before we decide everything in the discourse of time" (Vol. II, p. 213). And with the founding of the Irish Free State, he bursts into gay but mocking song:

> A terrible beauty is borneo,
> Republicans once so forlorneo,
> Subjected to all kinds of scorneo,
> Top-hatted, frock-coated, with manifest skill,
> Are well away now on St. Patrick's steep hill,
> Directing the labour of Jack and of Jill,
> In the dawn of a wonderful morneo.
> (Vol. II, p. 213)

Similarly, to mark his accession to the rank of accomplished dramatist, he asserts his independent stance when his first play is produced at the Abbey Theater:

> He felt, though, as he stood quiet in the vestibule, that he had crossed the border of a little, but a great, new kingdom of life, and so another illusion was born in his poor susceptible soul. He didn't know enough then that it was no great thing to be an Abbey playwright;

and, afterwards, when he knew a lot more, he was glad
he had suffered himself to feel no jubilation to mar his
future by thinking too much of a tiny success: life
remained a mystery to him.   (Vol. II, p. 164)

When his later play *The Plough and the Stars* suffers slings
and arrows from the prudery of critics, actors, and part of
the Abbey directorate, he is only confirmed in his resolve
to stand aloof even from mixed acclaim.

Inishfallen, Fare Thee Well is, as its title declares,
O'Casey's declaration of independence from Ireland. Its final
chapter, under the same title, is an extended leave-taking, a
set of variations on the theme of exile:

> It was time for Sean to go. He had had enough of it.
> He would be no more of an exile in another land than
> he was in his own. He was a voluntary and settled
> exile from every creed, from every party, and from
> every literary clique. . . . He would stay no longer to
> view life through a stained-glass window, a Sinn Fein
> spy-glass, from a prie-dieu, or through the thigh bone
> of a hare [an allusion to Yeats's mysticism]. He would
> go beyond these, and view life through his own eyes.
> (Vol. II, p. 370)

And the closing pages become a kaleidoscopic review of his
experience—almost a topographical synopsis of the autobiography—as his cab takes him to the boat for England:

> The car turned down Abbey Street and swung into
> Beresford Place, trotting past Liberty Hall, once the
> sweltering, weltering university of the Dublin work-
> ers, now a dead tomb held by an enemy, with Ichabod
> written all over it, for Larkin had gone, and its glory
> had departed; . . . passing the Queen's Theatre where
> Sean had seen his first play, *The Shaughraun*. . . . It was
> this street that had been Sean's via dolorosa, through
> which he had passed, three times a week, year after
> year, for fifteen or more of them, with his mother
> first, then on his own, to the Ophthalmic Hospital to

seek ease for aching eyeballs. Ah, here was Westland Row Station—the last spot of Dublin that would feel his footfall. It was from this sad site that the coffin holding Parnell came slowly out, borne by strenuous, tearful men, hesitating to part even with the dead body of their persecuted Chieftain. Oh, God Almighty, the life he was living now had almost all been spun from what he had felt, had seen, had touched in these few Dublin streets! (Vol. II, p. 395)

And so this fourth volume of *Mirror in My House* comes to a temporary closure with the binding down of O'Casey's worldly goods as he sets out for lifelong exile—his goods the portable and durable provision of memories, passions, and determined independence.

———

The formal structure of a work so extended as the six-volume autobiography does not emerge apart from its natural divisions into the three phases of O'Casey's career: the miseries of childhood and youth, triumph and defeat as a playwright, theatrical paper wars and nondramatic literary activity in protracted old age. The first two volumes, I would maintain, are incomparable classics of our prose; the second pair, *Drums* and *Inishfallen*, mark a falling off as O'Casey fights his way through the mundanities of political factions, the literary milieu, and the religion-shackled public; the last pair, *Rose and Crown* and *Sunset and Evening Star*, are severely disfigured, the one by bitterness at his treatment by Yeats in the *Silver Tassie* controversy, the other by traces of the megalomania and paranoia that are long-standing threats to the great man abused. Yet the early established pattern of innocence, abuse, and rebellion continues to structure these later volumes so that the created self survives, flagging but still vital, in the writings of O'Casey's last years. They exhibit the same determined independence in discovering for himself the proper style for his self-writing—the independence, if not the style, that he exercised in order to stay alive at all. In this sense, his autobiography is as much an effort of regeneration—even of self-birth—as was his life; and when his energies become crude or his vision blurred by passion, we still recognize these as the forces from which he fashioned his remarkable identity.

16

Muir's
Autobiography

TWICE MORE
IN EDEN

———

WITH EDWIN MUIR'S *An Autobiography* (1954), the self-awareness of the self-writer in foregrounding the traditional autobiographical figures reaches a moment of fulfillment. It is only one such moment, to be sure, for in the years between Muir's first and his expanded versions of the text, other autobiographers were conducting formal experiments in full awareness of living in an age after the fall into generic self-consciousness. Muir's work is the distillation of a tradition rather than the founding of a new one—for all its copious use of dream materials from the age of Freud to enlarge upon conscious experience. Its exercises in Freudian interpretation now have an air of early modernist mustiness about them, but its array of biblical figures, archetypal patterns and prophetic—though winningly modest—rhetoric continues to give *An Autobiography* the kind of luminous power we associate with *The Prelude* as a definitive autobiography.

That this power exerts itself on most of Muir's critics is, however, something of an irony, for their rendition of the work—a *de rigueur* synopsis opens most studies of his poetry[1]—captures only its sequence as a story without straining

1. E.g., Elizabeth Huberman, *The Poetry of Edwin Muir: The Field*

369

to discover the pattern or fable to which Muir himself aspired. The terms of this distinction are those of the first version, *The Story and the Fable* (1940), and are set out at several places in *An Autobiography*:

> It is clear that no autobiography can begin with a man's birth, that we extend far beyond any boundary line which we can set for ourselves in the past or the future, and that the life of every man is an endlessly repeated performance of the life of man. It is clear for the same reason that no autobiography can confine itself to conscious life, and that sleep, in which we pass a third of our existence, is a mode of experience, and our dreams a part of reality. In themselves our conscious lives may not be particularly interesting. But what we are not and can never be, our fable, seems to me inconceivably interesting. I should like to write that fable, but I cannot even live it; and all I could do if I related the outward course of my life would be to show how I have deviated from it; though even that is impossible, since I do not know the fable or anybody who knows it. One or two stages in it I can recognize: the age of innocence and the Fall and all the dramatic consequences which issue from the Fall. But these lie behind experience, not on its surface; they are not historical events; they are stages in the fable.[2]

This approach to the autobiographical project carries echoes of Jungian archetypalism and has been so interpreted, but Muir's psychological thinking reveals no theoretical ties to Jung's and is rather of the classical, literary variety—more germane to Muir's highly productive career as a literary

---

of Good and Ill (New York, 1971), ch. 1; or Christopher Wiseman, *Beyond the Labyrinth: A Study of Edwin Muir's Poetry* (Victoria, Can., 1978), ch. 1.

2. Edwin Muir, *An Autobiography* (New York, 1968 [1954]), ch. 1, pp. 48–49; I quote the American paperback edition in the text. Cf. another summative passage on the fable and the Fall at ch. 3, p. 114.

critic. There is, nonetheless, an aporia of intellectual fuzziness or genuine mystery—it is hard to tell which it is—in Muir's theory of the fable, one which may be filled by Jungian interpretation as well as by others. In speaking of the shape of his life, the above passage distinguishes between the universal fable and the individual's deviations from it, suggesting that the underlying pattern of one's personal experience constitutes *another* fable, departing significantly and apparently balefully from the universal one. I shall call this personal arrangement Muir's myth and distinguish it from the fable—a religious truth about human destiny, which neither Muir nor the present writer has been able to discover —as well as from the story, the specific enactments of the myth that make up the narrative of the autobiography. For in expanding his work from its first version, Muir not only filled in the events of his biography from 1922 to the time of writing but also ran through the myth or pattern of his early years at least twice over. *An Autobiography* is not merely an extension of *The Story and the Fable* but a codification of it as the perennial myth of Muir's life, and it deserves to be treated in some detail as a formal construct in order to grasp the full measure of his achievement.

Muir's story of his early childhood in the unspoiled landscape and folk community of the Orkney Islands has been so often recounted that I shall content myself with only a brief excerpt to stress its figural mode of presentation. Speaking of his parents, he declares:

> I never thought that they were like other men and women; to me they were fixed allegorical figures in a timeless landscape. Their allegorical changelessness made them more, not less, solid, as if they were condensed into something more real than humanity; as if the image "mother" meant more than "woman," and the image "father" more than "man." . . . That world was a perfectly solid world, for the days did not under-

mine it but merely rounded it, or rather repeated it, as if there were only one day endlessly rising and setting. Our first childhood is the only time in our lives when we exist within immortality, and perhaps all our ideas of immortality are influenced by it.

(ch. 1, pp. 24–25)

Although these ideas have been expressed in many languages and explained by many theories, the terms employed here insist on the child's repetition of the conditions of Eden—with father and mother as generic Adam and Eve—even in these rocky and sea-swept northern isles.

So, too, with the events of later childhood:

I have often fancied, too, that in a child's mind there is at moments a divination of a hidden tragedy taking place around him, that tragedy being the life which he will not live for some years still, though it is there, invisible to him, already. And a child has also a picture of human existence peculiar to himself, which he probably never remembers after he has lost it: the original vision of the world. I think of this picture or vision as that of a state in which the earth, the houses on the earth, and the life of every human being are related to the sky overarching them; as if the sky fitted the earth and the earth the sky. Certain dreams convince me that a child has this vision, in which there is a completer harmony of all things with each other than he will ever know again. There comes a moment (the moment at which childhood passes into boyhood or girlhood) when this image is broken and contradiction enters life.

(ch. 1, p. 33)

The fall into division and self-consciousness, after an "original vision of the world" in which "the sky fitted the earth and the earth the sky," is here psychogenetically reported and plausibly explained, yet it is clearly a latter-day version of the philosophical and religious fables on which autobiographers have long modeled their personal sense of loss. Without bombast and, at this stage, without elaborate use of biblical terminology, Muir writes the story of his early years in terms of the Platonic-Christian fable of human life, before going on in his further pages to personalize it as myth.

The more palpable forms in which the fall occurs are registered as "childish guilt" (at touching a prohibited sack of dangerous sheep dip), unwilling submission to the regimentation of school ("I disliked school from the start"), and the threat of violence—told in the account of "the day when Freddie Sinclair chased me home" and immortalized in the poem "Ballad of Hector in Hades."[3] But the full scope of the fall is felt only when the family is driven from its farm by a "bad landlord" and sinks steadily to the Glasgow slums:

> My first years in Glasgow were wretched. The feeling of degradation continued, but it became more and more blind; I did not know what made me unhappy, nor that I had come into chaos. We had lived comfortably enough in Orkney, mainly on what we grew; but here everything had to be bought and paid for. . . . My elder brothers had already grasped the principle of this new society, which was competition, not cooperation, as it had been in Orkney. . . . Though we imagined that we had risen in some way, without knowing it we had sunk into another class. . . . We were members of the proletariat, though at that time we had never heard the name. Happily my brothers kept their jobs, and we did not have to become acquainted with the abyss over which we lived.
>
> (ch. 3, pp. 92–93)

But the abyss is there, if not that of unemployment and destitution, that of illness and death. Mother, father, and two brothers are dead within two years.

Although Muir survives his illnesses, he reaches another depth of his exile when he takes a clerk's job in a plant processing charcoal from waste bones:

3. Edwin Muir, *Collected Poems: 1921–1958* (London, 1960); the poem appeared originally in *First Poems* (1925).

When I left the office in Glasgow I had no picture of the job I was going to. . . . As I stood there [at "Fairport" station] I became aware of a faint insinuating smell. I paid no attention to it. I should have done so. . . . It was a gentle, clinging, sweet stench, suggesting dissolution and hospitals and slaughter-houses, the odour of drains, and the rancid stink of bad, roasting meat. On hot summer days it stood round the factory like a wall of glass.   (ch. 4, pp. 130–31)

Though rendered with naturalistic detail and disarming simplicity, the account moves through scenes resembling a medieval dance of death: "There were old, faithful hands in the place who had spent their lives among the bones. . . . They made free with the bones, humorously flinging them at one another as they sat at their midday meal in the bone-yard; the older ones cynically stirred their tea with a pointed dry bone" (ch. 4, p. 131). From this hellish scene it is a short step to a sense of general depravity and of one's own implication in it: "I had nothing to do with the stuff out of which the firm ground its profits. Yet I could not stave off a feeling of degradation" (ch. 4, p. 132). Trying to do his work with strict accuracy and "cleanliness," he is put constantly in the wrong by the incompetence of others: "I ended by acquiring a habitual bad conscience, a constant expectation of being accused" (ch. 4, p. 133). Thus was formed the English translator of Kafka—of novels about the unreasonable workings of a castle and a trial dooming man to alienation and condemnation, about a system of life in which some universal fault puts every man in the "constant expectation of being accused."[4]

After these elementary structures of the child in an uncorrupted nature, his fall into personal guilt and insecurity,

4. Muir's long bout of translating and writing about Kafka has been well summarized in Elgin W. Mellown, *Edwin Muir* (Boston, 1979), pp. 39–44; it is tempting to find parallels between Muir's changing views of Kafka's narrative and allegory and his performance in narrating and allegorizing his own life.

and exile to infernal realms of social life, the succeeding phases of Muir's early career become considerably more complex. As a prototypic modern intellectual, his philosophical and political questing takes in a fair number of the ideologies prevailing early in this century: Nietzscheanism, socialism, Freudianism, etc. Though he receives intellectual and emotional support from his wife—"My marriage was the most fortunate event in my life" (ch. 4, p. 154)—and from his editor, A. R. Orage, his mental state can readily be compared with the long-gathering crises that spiritual autobiographers have recounted. Even some of the terms are the same, as Muir experiences the "Methodist" conversion stage, which Mill also named "conviction of sin" (ch. 5, p. 158).

At this critical point Muir undergoes psychoanalysis, a phase of his development that has been badly overestimated by his critics. Far from providing him with clarification and serenity, the analysis is shown in *An Autobiography* to fall far short of his native insight. In a typical situation, Muir's analyst "indicated the sexual symbolism of the dream, which by this time I could read for myself. . . . Yet these things, though obvious enough, did not seem applicable to the dream, which was unearthly, or rather unhuman, and so in a sense unsexual" (ch. 5, p. 163). In a similar case, the disparity between the figures of psychological health and the biblical fable is even more heavily stressed: "The longing to fling myself down from a height (which comes into both dreams) is immediately associated with the analyst's exhortations to come down to earth, to accept reality; but it also brings to my mind images of the Fall and of the first incarnation, that of Adam, and another image as well, which is my image of timeless human life as the intersection and interpenetration of a stationary beam falling from heaven and the craving, aspiring dust rising for ever to meet it . . ." (ch. 5, p. 166).

It is not through Freud that Muir comes into self-possession but through the traditional language of the seventeenth-century poets, recounting their spiritual travail and triumph. In this process of conversion—Muir uses the term

375

in its verb form—the mediator is no psychoanalyst but a rather strange and otherwise little known friend, John Holms, "the most remarkable man I ever met" (ch. 5, p. 180). Although he is always quoting Wordsworth at Muir, sometimes to apply to his own mental distress and sometimes to Muir's, Holms's affinities lie in an earlier century; the plebeian Muir is careful to point out that "he was descended from John Ferrar, the brother of Nicholas Ferrar, who founded the religious community of Little Gidding" (ch. 5, p. 177). In Holms's company, Muir has what can surely be classed as an epiphanic experience, though it comes in the medium of poetry:

> The very first day that I met him he started to quote Donne (whom I did not know at that time) as we returned from our long summer day in the country. . . . he went on to the opening verse of *The Relic*, stopping in delight over "the last busy day" and the picture of the resurrected soul waiting by the lover's grave to "make a little stay." For the last half-hour we had been meeting a long line of courting couples moving in the opposite direction: as we leaned on the gate they went on passing us, a millennial procession in the calm evening light. Perhaps it was this that recalled to Holms Traherne's "orient and immortal wheat, which never should be reaped, nor was ever sown," for he began to recite the passage, which moved me more deeply than Donne. He held Traherne's and Vaughan's and Wordsworth's theory of childhood, which was bound up with his belief in immortality; in time he converted me to it, or rather made me realize that my own belief was the same as his.   (ch. 5, p. 179)

Following on this epiphany, a sense of renewal and return to origins is not long in coming: "These good hours [with Holms] always brought a sense of abundance, or numerous herds, rich fields, full streams, endless food and drink —all things gladly fulfilling the law of their nature—and was like a return to Adam's world" (ch. 5, p. 180). It is only in the following years, when the Muirs begin to make the most of their first Continental adventures, that the renewal is portrayed as a psychological recovery as well as a return to the bounties of childhood:

> We left for Dresden about the end of March [1922], and from the start loved the fine, spacious city. There during the hot, idle summer I seemed at last to recover from the long illness that had seized me when, at fourteen, I came to Glasgow. I realized that I must live over again the years which I had lived wrongly, and that every one should live his life twice, for the first attempt is always blind. . . . In turning my head and looking *against* the direction in which time was hurrying me I won a new kind of experience; for now that I no longer marched in step with time I could see life timelessly, and with that in terms of the imagination. . . . I did not feel so much that I was rediscovering the world of life as that I was discovering it for the first time.   (ch. 6, pp. 192–93)

But as his citation of Proust suggests (in a number of sentences I have omitted), this "first time" feeling is connected with the sense of liberation "from the order of time." The past is not retrieved for its own sake but is seen as the focus of a new vision—"*against* the direction" of time. The transformation of the familiar but forgotten into the uncanny and newly discovered is an act of the imagination, and Muir here joins not only Proust but also Wordsworth among the high exemplars of a special form of transformative power, the imagination of the past.

What the traditional language of Muir's recuperation does not reveal is the extent to which he was experiencing the entire process over again at the time he wrote of it. Completed in 1939, *The Story and the Fable* follows in the wake of an intense religious experience that Muir had in February of that year and that he reports in its place in the final text

(ch. 11, pp. 246–47). The special feature of this event is its
Christian burden, and although Muir's conversion was never
of an orthodox kind, his later writings are as much imbued
with New Testament figures as with those of the Old. Perhaps even more decisive for the form that the completed autobiography eventually took, in 1946 he read Augustine's
Confessions "with intense attraction and repulsion: it seems
to me one of the greatest of books; the description of the
ecstasy [the leave-taking at Ostia] unsurpassed by anything
else I know."[5] By the following year, he had made the *Confessions* into an encompassing norm for autobiography. Comparing his own subjective and particularist method with
Herbert Read's objective and generalizing one, he concludes:
"Both methods are equally good, I think; when they are
combined, as in Augustine's *Confessions*, they produce something terrifically impressive."

The model autobiography is made to stand for yet another norm in an article Muir published in 1940, "Yesterday's
Mirror: Afterthoughts to an Autobiography." Here three
ways of looking into one's memory are described. They are
the three modes of vision set out in the poem "The Three
Mirrors." Beyond the realist's way—he sees only the world's
wrongs because he has forgotten childhood—and the way of
the man who remembers childhood and sees "an indefeasible
rightness beneath the wrongness of things," there is another
vision:

> The world which the mystical poet sees is a world in
> which both good and evil have their place legitimately;
> in which the king on his throne and the rebel raising
> his standard in the market place, the tyrant and the
> slave, the assassin and the victim, each plays a part
> in a supertemporal drama which at every moment, in
> its totality, issues in glory and meaning and fulfillment.
> . . . St. Augustine saw it and so did Blake; it is the

5. *Selected Letters of Edwin Muir*, ed. P. H. Butter (London, 1974),
p. 127 (Nov. 15, 1940); the quotation that follows is from p. 128 (April
16, 1940).

supreme vision of human life, because it reconciles all opposites; but it transcends our moral struggle, for in life we are ourselves the opposites and must act as best we can.[6]

This mode of vision is presumably the one Muir found himself winning through to; it is an advance on the despair and the naïve optimism of his earlier mirrors. It is an Augustinian-Blakean-mystical viewpoint, according to his essay, but the special qualities Muir attaches to it seem more distinctly those of a personal myth that he was evolving for himself. Without reference to a Christian dispensation, the myth reconciles all the conflicting and random experiences of a life in a "supertemporal drama"—neither a theodicy nor a rationale but a formal narrative that hangs together as all one story, one's own.

The apparent "bottom line" of *The Story and the Fable* is its concluding sentence; although complaining about his late start as a poet, Muir announces that in the year of his recovery (1922) he began to write poetry. But the continuation of the autobiography as he composed it in the 1950s does not hew to this line of professional or visionary vocation. Having been stirred by his religious experience in 1939—and by later experiences which *An Autobiography* will recount—he described the further stages of life in the twenties and after in terms similar to those with which he began: lost and recovered Edenic scenes.

The new milieu is vastly different, to be sure: Central Europe during a period of violent social change rather than the remote and timeless Orkneys. But here, too, his imagination of the past is fully in control:

> We lived there [Dresden] in ignorance, not looking ahead. In spring we watched the sweet-smelling lime blossom coming out on the trees bordering the streets,

6. Quoted in P. H. Butter, *Edwin Muir: Man and Poet* (New York, 1967), pp. 186–87.

and in summer spent a great deal of time on the banks
of the river, sun-bathing among the seal-like Saxons
whose skin was tanned to a Red Indian brown: a
pleasant, vacant life without a trace of boredom, for
everything round us was strange. . . . All this was thirty
years ago, and with one half of my mind I can look at
it historically, while the other half still sees it as I saw
it then, wrapped in its own illusions. We lived, it seems
to me now, in a climate of "new ideas," and looked
forward to a "new life" which would be brought
about by the simple exercise of freedom, a freedom
such as had never been formulated before in any terms,
since it too was new.   (ch. 8, pp. 198-99)

With handsight, Muir can see that the Weimar period's en-
thusiasms—like the Dalcroze eurhythmics in which he joined
at Hellerau—were not so novel as claimed and that the appeal
to primal innocence in bodily movement and personal relations was a latter-day variant of a perennial human urging.
The "new life" to be fostered by "new ideas" of self-
congratulation and heavy sunbathing was ignorant and illusory but nonetheless effective:

The German landscape, as I have said, helped to foster
it. There was something in the appearance of the
woods which seemed to invite nature-worship, and
from nature-worship to worship of our own nature,
which we were modestly practising, was an easy step.
The trees solicited us to be natural, since they were
natural, to be young, since they renewed their youth
every year, to be child-like, since we could easily feel
as we wandered among them that we were children of
nature.   (ch. 8, p. 202)

In this unlikely setting, Muir renews not merely his childhood insouciance but his fable of it, and we are told on successive pages about Vaughan and Traherne and the *Wan-
dervögel* balladeers.

After a stay in Italy with Holms—an unsatisfactory one, as the English mystic is off his form as a *cicerone* of Latin culture—Muir returns to *Mitteleuropa* and receives his first foretaste of the coming fall. At Salzburg, he is impressed enough by the beauty and strangeness of the scene to store up impressions for a novel, *The Marionette*, a surrealistic fantasy about an idiot boy who falls in love with such an object.[7] But the more surrealistic fantasies in this city are those which are published in the local newspapers: "We read with astonishment of ritual murders still happening, and of curious Jewish perversions, described in detail, of which we had never heard. A little time afterwards we met some intelligent Austrians who maintained against all we could say that Ramsay Macdonald and Bernard Shaw were Jews: they must be, for they were subverters of society" (ch. 8, p. 214). Returning to Vienna, they find the first signs of the coming debacle: "The misery in Vienna created its own nightmare. We did not know that the nightmare would end in the slaughter of a people" (ch. 8, p. 218). But there are already strong indications that this is a society in disintegration.

Returning to England after four years of innocence and experience, the Muirs gradually achieve a measure of literary success, though without financial security, and in the thirties they come to lead the literary life of Hampstead. These pages are condensed and only half-attentive to the inner life, but when the family suffers a near-disaster the original urgency and weight return to Muir's prose. After their son, an only child, is hit by a car, he suffers longer from his psychological than from his physical trauma, and the parents decide to remove to a quieter place. Without explaining his thought process, the autobiographer makes clear the significance of his decision:

7. In addition to this fiction, Muir wrote an autobiographical novel, *Poor Tom* (1932), with a Glasgow setting of illness and death; Mellown, *Edwin Muir*, pp. 70–80, treats these and the novel *The Three Brothers* (1931) as autobiographical in varying ways.

> A friend got a furnished house for us in St. Andrews.
> But first we went to Orkney, so that our son should
> have a complete rest. . . . I had not been back to Ork-
> ney for many years; few of the people I had known
> were there still; but the beauty of the light showered
> from the wide sky and reflected from the spreading
> waters, and diffused, a double radiance, over the bright
> fields, was the same beauty I had known as a child; and
> the loneliness of every shape rising from the treeless
> land, the farm houses and the moving outlines of men
> and women against the sky, had, as then, the simplicity
> of an early world. The peace helped to still Gavin's
> fears.   (ch. 10, pp. 241–42)

Whatever fears are being stilled here are not the son's alone
as Muir clearly creates or seizes the opportunity to relive
and rewrite his childhood once again. It is not only a pattern
of psychic repetition that is being formed here but a pattern
of narrative and lyrical writing. This practice becomes the
myth of which Muir makes his poetry over the last decades
of his life, reaching a grand finale in his last volume, *One
Foot in Eden* (1956).

Despite Muir's satisfaction in finding himself once more
in Eden, his myth became so compelling that he had to make
the cycle of exile and return all over again after the war.[8] If
his version of the Christian fable was fueling his poetry during these years, his created myth of childhood, fall, and return was dominant over his personal fortunes—or at least
over his conception of them. In adding these later episodes

8. For a contrary view of the later chapters, see Roger J. Porter,
"Edwin Muir and Autobiography: Arch of a Redemptive Memory,"
South Atlantic Quarterly, 87 (1978): 521–22; *An Autobiography* "surrenders that pervasive structure which earlier saw *all* Muir's experience
unified in the dialectic of innocence and Fall, and it covers over the
darker elements to resolve everything too neatly."

to the final pages of his autobiography, Muir followed the myth pattern that he had used twice over in telling of his earlier losses and recoveries.

After spending the war years with the British Council in Edinburgh, Muir was appointed director of the British Institute in Prague in 1945. As the chapter title "Prague Again" suggests, his sense of the voyage is one of uncanny repetition. But the conditions of an occupied city in a war-torn continent make difficult a recovery of earlier days of liberated innocence: "The new impression was more vivid and less agreeable than I had expected; it was as if whole series of familiar objects were presenting themselves a second time and asking to be digested again. During my first few weeks in Prague I felt I was in a strange place, and was teased by the fancy of another city, the same and yet not the same, whose streets I or someone very like me had walked many years before" (ch. 12, p. 255). It soon emerges that the city has not merely been changed by time but has suffered a range of experiences known only to sermons on hell and records of the holocaust. Looking at pictures of the former German overlords with friends, the widow of a resistance leader "pointed at one young man and said without expression: 'That is the one who strangled my husband.' But it might have been any of the others. They stared out from the photographs with the confidence of the worthless who find power left in their hands like a tip hastily dropped by a frightened world. Though they had done so many things to satisfy their revenge on mankind there was no satisfaction in their faces, and no hope" (ch. 12, p. 261).

Yet worse is to come, for the brief hopes raised by the withdrawal of the Russian troops come to an end when the Communist party enacts a classic coup d'état. Muir finds that the narratives of Kafka, which he had been translating as existential allegories, were close to becoming literal histories: "We heard of the attempt of the students to reach the President. The police had blocked the main street to the

Castle, and the students took another route. When they reached the Castle they found it shut and soldiers on guard. An officer raised his sword as a warning to them to keep back" (ch. 12, p. 266; cf. p. 270). Powerless to do more than look on at the extinction of liberty, Muir deepens his identification with individuals suffering the moral equivalent of the national crisis. A Czech acquaintance is given the choice of keeping her job by becoming a Communist or asserting her Catholic faith and losing her means of supporting her invalid father and mother. He is never to learn the outcome of this paradigmatic situation, for conditions at Charles University become so repressive as to force his departure. As soon as he arrives back in England, he suffers a breakdown "and fell plumb into a dead pocket of life which I had never guessed at before" (ch. 13, p. 274). His depression may be reduced to a psychiatric regression, but given its moral and political inducements, it seems better to view it as Muir's renewed apprehension of the fallen human estate.

Fortunately, there is Edenesque relief at hand, if not return to Scotland (until a later time), at least a sojourn in a cultural paradise. Muir is assigned to direct the British Institute in Rome and finds both the city and the workplace immensely congenial:

> it was a new experience to know people who spoke from the heart, simply and naturally, without awkwardness, and put all of themselves, heart and soul, into what they said. I had known fresh and natural speech among Orkney farmers living close to the cattle and the soil, but not till now among men and women moulded by city life. . . . The humanity was perfectly natural, but I knew that naturalness does not come easily to the awkward human race, and that this was an achievement of life.
>   . . . I felt, the first morning I called at the Institute that I was breaking into an Eden. . . . The Institute remained a sort of talkative Eden and was the most friendly, kind, busy place imaginable.
>
> (ch. 13, pp. 275–76)

It is not only his Italian co-workers and the office cama-
raderie that give the exhausted Muir the impulse to resort
again to his archetypes but the larger culture in which they
are placed. Even Roman history becomes adaptable to the
Edenic vision: "The history of Rome is drenched in blood
and blackened with crime; yet all that seemed to be left now
was the peace of memory. . . . The grass in the courtyard of
the Temple of the Vestals seemed to be drenched in peace
down to the very root, and it was easy to imagine gods and
men still in friendly talk together there" (ch. 13, p. 277). It
is evidently easy for Muir, in his relieved state of mind and
with its controlling structures, to imagine this Hölderlinian
conclave (Muir's poem on the Romantic-classicist poet
comes readily to mind). More difficult to assimilate—because
more sketchily articulated—is the sudden reverence Muir
feels for the images of Catholicism that mark the city. The
pull toward Christian spirituality continues to draw Muir
steadily, but he never commits himself to a religious conversion, preferring the articles of his private faith, though they
draw on the tradition for their images.

Returning to Scotland at last, as warden of an experimental workingmen's college, Muir has leisure to write the
continuation of his autobiography, but his embarrassment or
diffidence in promulgating his myth shows up at the close:

> Some kind of development, I suppose, should be ex-
> pected to emerge, but I am very doubtful of such
> things, for I cannot bring life into a neat pattern. If
> there is a development in my life—and it seems an idle
> supposition—then it has been brought about more by
> things outside than by any conscious intention of my
> own. I was lucky to spend my first fourteen years in
> Orkney; I was unlucky to live afterwards in Glasgow
> as a Displaced Person. . . . In my middle thirties I
> became aware of immortality, and realized that it gave
> me a truer knowledge of myself and my neighbors.
> Years later in St. Andrews I discovered that I had
> been a Christian without knowing it. I saw in Czecho-

slovakia a whole people lost by one of the cruel turns of
history, and exiled from themselves in the heart of their
own country. I discovered in Italy that Christ had
walked on the earth, and also that things truly made
preserve themselves through time in the first freshness
of their nature. . . . As I look back on the part of the
mystery which is my own life, my own fable, what
I am most aware of is that we receive more than we
can ever give; we receive it from the past, on which
we draw with every breath, but also—and this is a
point of faith—from the Source of the mystery itself,
by the means which religious people call Grace.

(ch. 13, pp. 280–81)

Although Muir's religious meditations and personal version
of Christianity have come up in the autobiography, they
have not been allowed to shape his "development"—certainly
no decisive conversion pattern or pilgrimage has been suggested, even in displaced form. At the final sentence, an
enormous weight is placed on the unanticipated and un-
earned, on the fable of Christian redemption, and the term
Grace is appropriated for it.

Yet *An Autobiography* has seen the formal reenactment
of a pattern—twice over again, after the first and most telling
sequence—in a personal life interpretation, which I have
called Muir's myth. For this pattern, Muir has employed a
Judeo-Christian mythos of a more elementary kind: the fable
of Eden and the Fall, of lost innocence and diminished powers. He fills this abstract space with various sources of creative energy: the love and care of wife and child, the imagination of the past, the islands of human civility and rich
culture, which occasionally survive the horrors of modern
politics. In returning to primary values, deeply imagined and
at least temporarily realized, Muir has renewed a universal
fable that comes earlier than Christianity, lies deeper perhaps
than religion, and comprehends the endemic autobiographi-

cal drift to recapitulate one's origins and end—to make one-self whole again and at last.[9]

9. "The expulsion from Paradise is in its main significance eternal: Consequently the expulsion from Paradise is final, and life in this world irrevocable, but the eternal nature of the occurrence (or, temporally expressed, the eternal recapitulation of the occurrence) makes it never-theless possible that not only could we live continuously in Paradise, but that we are continuously there in actual fact, no matter whether we know it here or not." The words are not Muir's but Kafka's, in the translation by Muir and his wife, Willa Muir, *Parables* (New York, 1947), p. 25.

PART V

Modern Autobiographical Fiction

———

Samuel Butler began writing *The Way of All Flesh* in 1873 at the turn of the tide in Victorian sensibility but still at its high water mark; James Joyce published *A Portrait of the Artist as a Young Man* as a book in 1916, well into the formative period for modern writing and thinking. The distance of generations between these events would be enough to explain their differences as autobiographical novels, but their deeper resemblances are more specifically accountable. Butler would not or could not publish his self-writing in his lifetime; after it was published in 1903, one of its early readers was Joyce, who in 1904 began the series of portraits of his early life that was to take him some eighteen years to complete.[1] The delay in both these ground-breaking ventures is perhaps as significant as their juncture: one does not revolutionize fictional style and self-conception without long and careful preparation. But during the years in which *A Portrait* was taking shape, other major novelists were charting the direction of their careers in autobiographical novels we scarcely think of as personal stories because they have become paradigmatic of modern fiction and its attendant forms of self-consciousness.

1. Joyce owned a copy of the 1911 edition of Butler's novel, though an owner's stamp suggests that he acquired it in Zurich, where he moved in 1915: Richard Ellmann, *The Consciousness of Joyce* (Toronto and New York, 1977), pp. 104, 6. For the chronology of the writing of *A Portrait of the Artist as a Young Man*, see Chester G. Anderson's edition (New York, 1968), pp. 551ff.

Virginia Woolf declared, with mock-historical precision, that the date on which modernity began was December 1910[2] with the showing of Post-Impressionist art in London, but a better case might be made for 1915, when a cluster of novels was published bearing a cumulative weight that came to be decisive. These were *The Rainbow*, *The Voyage Out*, *Pointed Roofs* (the first volume of Dorothy Richardson's *Pilgrimage*), and the final installments of Joyce's *Portrait* in the *Egoist* magazine. Of these, only two may be considered distinctly autobiographical novels, but *The Rainbow* and *The Voyage Out* are of a piece with the others although they recast their authors' personal probings onto characters not their equivalent in external characteristics or narrative fortunes.

Dorothy Richardson offers a somewhat different and longer chronology of this historical conjunction, but her words are definitive, given her high degree of self-consciousness about the changes in which she was participating. She specifies 1911 as the date by which "every form of conventionalized human association is being arraigned by biographical and autobiographical novelists"; she gives 1913—the date of Lawrence's first contribution to autobiographical fiction and of Proust's beginning to publish his life's research—as the starting point for her own lifework, "written to the accompaniment of a sense of being upon a fresh pathway, an adventure so searching and, sometimes, so joyous as to produce a longing for participation"; and she settles on 1915, the year of her novel's publication, as her moment of union with Woolf and Joyce:

> The lonely track, meanwhile, had turned out to be a populous highway. Amongst those who had simultaneously entered it, two figures stood out. One a

2. For the full background of this historic dating—which has itself become an historic event—see Samuel Hynes, "The Whole Contention Between Mr. Bennett and Mrs. Woolf," in his *Edwardian Occasions: Essays on English Writing in the Early Twentieth Century* (New York, 1972).

woman mounted upon a magnificently caparisoned charger, the other a man walking, with eyes devoutly closed, weaving as he went a rich garment of new words wherewith to clothe the antique dark material of his engrossment.[3]

Although Richardson's figure for Woolf retains a measure of derision despite its striking appropriateness, her characterization of Joyce meets his enterprise in self-writing head-on. The "fresh pathway," already marked by *Sons and Lovers* and *Swann's Way*, was soon to become a general meeting ground as psychological novelists of all makes availed themselves of its wide opportunities. The list of novelists who advert to a portion of their life stories for one or more tales would constitute a bibliography of modern fiction; I select here only the first and founding marchers on the "populous highway" of fictional self-writing.

3. Dorothy Richardson, *Pilgrimage*, 4 vols. (New York, 1967 [1938]), I, 10; this foreword was extracted from Richardson by her publishers for what they took to be the complete edition of the work.

17

Sons
and Lovers

A PROPHET
IN THE MAKING

D. H. Lawrence is one of the "makers of the modern mind"
who conducted that undertaking as an autobiographical activity. From his earliest poems—"secret sins," as he described
them[1]—to his last accounts of sexuality and apocalypse,
the presence of the master is never far to seek. Among his
most explicit self-portraits are Birkin in *Women in Love*,
Somers in *Kangaroo*, and the risen Christ in *The Man Who
Died*. In addition, there are the four travel books, the criticism—which Lawrence used, as he used his poetry and fiction, to work out problems in his theory and practice of
living—and the paintings, which regularly portray the lover
and the martyr with his own features. If to these are added
the voluminous correspondence, the induced images of himself in biographies and autobiographies by friends and hang-
ers-on, and the body of criticism that prefers to focus on the

1. For the phrase, its context, and autobiographical significance, see
Evelyn Shakir, " 'Secret Sin': Lawrence's Early Verse," *D. H. Lawrence Review*, 8 (1975): 155–75. A sustained study of Lawrence's poetry
touching its autobiographical concerns is Sandra M. Gilbert, *Acts of
Attention: The Poems of D. H. Lawrence* (Ithaca and London, 1972).

man rather than his work, there emerges a copious literature of Lawrencian self-portrayal.

Not even the most partisan Lawrencian would assign all of these writings an equal standing in the canon. Beyond the fact that the self-portraits in *Women in Love* and *The Man Who Died* are assimilated into works of art that go well beyond the scope of autobiography, many of the self-writings are too occasional or fragmentary to achieve more than documentary—or in *Kangaroo* journalistic—value. The one novel in which Lawrence is primarily engaged in a narrative of his own experience and by which his performance in autobiographical fiction must be judged is *Sons and Lovers*.

Sons and Lovers (1913) is so much an autobiographical novel that our knowledge of its roots in the author's life threatens to overwhelm our critical appreciation of the book. So powerful are these links between life and art that its composition was influenced by Lawrence's (and others') concern for its autobiographical accuracy so that, for example, the girl who provided the model for Miriam in the novel could read an early draft and suggest changes in characterization (including her own) to make it more true to life—a rare instance of an aesthetic object debating about itself with its creator.[2] There has been a commendable effort in recent criticism to get away from assessing the novel on the sole ground of its psychological penetration and to grasp its vision of love and growth in symbolic terms.

Sons and Lovers has been seen as structured by a symbolic pattern that runs throughout Lawrence's work: the simultaneous attraction and repulsion between a fair, sexually repressed girl and a dark, sexually virile man—often recalling the seduction and divided conquest of Persephone by Pluto

2. Jessie Chambers, *D. H. Lawrence: A Personal Record, by "E. T."* (New York, 1965); excerpted in the Viking Critical Library edition of *Sons and Lovers*, ed. Julian Moynahan (New York, 1968), pp. 478–85; this edition will be cited in the text.

in the classical myth.[3] Lawrence is by now recognized not
only as a student of mythologies from a wide variety of cultures but also as a mythmaker in his own right, and it is no
longer surprising that he portrayed the members of his own
family and the ordinary folk of Midlands England in his own
versions of well-known psychological types or archetypes.

It is also widely acknowledged that Lawrence was a student of the Bible from his youth to his last days and owes a
greater debt to scriptural style and figuration than any major artist in England since Blake.[4] The presence of patriarchal and prophetic figures from the Bible is less obvious
but no less significant in *Sons and Lovers* than it is in *The
Rainbow* or *The Man Who Died*. There is no surprise in
the idea that the self-writing of a mighty individualist and
iconoclast may have an elaborate religious background, for
Lawrence's preoccupation with the cycle of the generations,
sibling rivalries, and parental preferences for younger and
older sons finds a seedbed in the stories with which Genesis,
especially, is filled. The groundwork for scriptural reference
is well prepared by the fact that the characters—particularly
the hero's mother, Mrs. Morel—are themselves imbued with
the Bible-centered, "low-church" Protestant tradition in
which Lawrence grew up. This community of culture allows Lawrence to find images of his own early years in the
narrative patterns of the Bible and to place these analogies
not only in the situations of the story but in the speech of
the characters who enact them.

———

From birth, Paul Morel, Lawrence's surrogate in the
novel, is conceived as a biblical hero of continuing fascina-

3. See George H. Ford, *Double Measure: A Study of the Novels
and Stories of D. H. Lawrence* (New York, 1965), pp. 28–47.

4. See, e.g., Frank Kermode, "Lawrence and the Apocalyptic Types,"
in *Word in the Desert*, ed. C. B. Cox and A. E. Dyson (London, New
York, and Toronto, 1968), pp. 14–38.

tion: Joseph. Mrs. Morel establishes the younger son as her favorite in the struggle against her husband, and we are invited to see the family romance as a modern instance of the succession of younger sons, like Jacob and Isaac, who are preferred to the elder. Mrs. Morel herself is conscious of the tradition as she walks in the fields with the newly born Paul: "A few shocks of corn in a corner of the fallow stood up as if alive; she imagined them bowing; perhaps her son would be a Joseph" (ch. 2, p. 36). The preference for the younger in the novel takes the form not of conflict between the brothers but rather of alliance between the mother and the favorite son: "She felt as if the navel string that had connected its frail little body with hers had not been broken. . . . She thrust the infant forward to the crimson, throbbing sun, almost with relief. She saw him lift his little fist. Then she put him to her bosom again, ashamed almost of her impulse to give him back again whence he came" (ch. 2, p. 37). The child is established as a specially favored, perhaps a divinely endowed one, and in his gesture of raising his fist toward the sun one can sense that he is born for struggle and competitive success—as Freud noted about intensely mother-loved sons.

The figure of Joseph with its burden of favored standing, high intellectual aptitude, and power to control large forces—rulers and brothers, father if not mother—is not allowed to stand alone as the type for Lawrence's protagonist and self-image. He was inordinately self-aware and honest in acknowledging the strong repressive and life-denying impulses in himself and etched these into his portrait by allusions to the hero's namesake, Paul. Mrs. Morel names him for her father's favorite apostle; just as her father is for her "the type of all men," so George Coppard "drew near in sympathy only to one man, the Apostle Paul; who was harsh in government, and in familiarity ironic; who ignored all sensuous pleasure . . ." (ch. 1, p. 10). It is this aspect of the Pauline heritage that seems at work in Mrs. Morel when she names her child; it involves the "impulse to give him back again whence he came," the shame at such an impulse, and the anxiety generated by conflicting feelings:

> "If he lives," she thought to herself, "what will become of him—what will he be?"
> Her heart was anxious.
> "I will call him Paul," she said suddenly; she knew not why. (ch. 2, p. 37)

It was part of Lawrence's genius to recognize that this nexus of thought and feeling was not merely present in his culture and at work in his origins but that it remained a potent force in his own life and work. The Whitmanesque paeans to death that regularly emerge in both, in tandem with even stronger life assertions, the physical and psychic aggression that he practiced on others and on himself, the apocalyptic stance that seems to preach a utopian future but more urgently relishes a nihilistic clean sweep, all may be traced to a familial and cultural heritage like Paul's. The mother "was puritan, like her father, high-minded, and really stern" (ch. 1, p. 10).

If the figurative composition of the protagonist were restricted to his Joseph and Paul components, his Old Testament competence and his New Testament restraints, he could be understood by reduction to the dual principles represented by his parents. But Paul is not merely the sum of the Pauline, puritan mother and the "sensuous flame of life"—emerging from the dark Plutonian or Dionysian figure that is, or originally was, his father. He is also, in a sum that is greater than its parts, an artist, and this is an essential, though largely potential, aspect of Paul—neglected in most criticism probably because the work does not announce itself as a *Künstlerroman*. The budding painter has been somewhat slighted in most readings of the novel, and the figure adapted for that role is even more easily overlooked as it is, on its face, an unlikely one. Yet there it stands:

> Another day [Miriam] sat at sunset whilst he was
> painting some pine-trees which caught the red glare
> from the west. He had been quiet.
> "There you are!" he said suddenly. "I wanted that.
> Now, look at them and tell me, are they pine trunks
> or are they red coals, standing-up pieces of fire in that
> darkness? There's God's burning bush for you, that
> burned not away." (ch. 7, p. 152)

By itself, this allusion—even with its precise verbal citation—
is not enough to associate Paul with Moses or Moses with art,
but the seed has been planted for a sustained identification.

Paul is able to see and to reveal the life force in the trees,
issuing from the sun and never failing, because he has from
an early age connected it with its sources under the earth,
with the father, and with the realm of darkness. Walking
with his third lover, Clara, he rejects her rejection of the coal
mines marring the landscape:

> "You see, I am so used to it I should miss it. No; and I
> like the pits here and there. I like the rows of trucks,
> and the headstocks, and the steam in the daytime, and
> the lights at night. When I was a boy, I always thought
> a pillar of cloud by day and a pillar of fire by night was
> a pit, with its steam, and its lights, and the burning
> bank,—and I thought the Lord was always at the pit-
> top." (ch. 12, p. 320)

Knowing and valuing the destructive-constructive forces of
the mine and the divine aegis over earthly resources—the
upper-world life of plants and animals and the lower-world
realm of demonic knowledge—Paul is prepared to embark
on his artistic career with an equipment comparable with
Lawrence's own impressive endowment. He will follow the
pillars of fire and cloud as attentively by day and night as
had his biblical avatar. Whether he will be able to maintain
the balance and mutual dependence of these symbolic structures more consistently than Lawrence himself did—this was

the perpetual challenge that both the writer and his protagonist had to face—the one at novel's end, the other
throughout his life.

The typological dimensions of Lawrence's Mosaic image
of himself are enforced by his relationship with Miriam.
The figure of Miriam in Numbers 12, who as Moses's sister
is both an adjunct and a competitor to him in his prophetic
role—and who is partially protected from divine displeasure
by the magnanimous hero—informs Lawrence's conception
of Paul's sisterly lover. But he does not allow her female
hero stature to outweigh her symbolic value as a figure of
repression and life denial. She is presented mainly in terms
of virginal heroines: St. Catherine, Mary at the annunciation,
and cloistered nuns in general. But in contact with Paul she
plays a role in another Mosaic scene, a revelation of the
virile force in nature as focused in a wild rose bush: "In
bosses of ivory and in large splashed stars the roses gleamed
on the darkness of foliage and stems and grass. Paul and
Miriam stood close together, silent, and watched. Point after
point the steady roses shone out to them, seeming to kindle
something in their souls. The dusk came like smoke around
and still did not put out the roses" (ch. 7, p. 160). Their responses to this burning bush are indicative of their differing
spiritual energies. Miriam wants "communion" with Paul in
a shared emotional relationship whereas Paul is absorbed less
by tender emotions and more by the manifestation of power: "It was the communion she wanted. He turned aside, as
if pained. He turned to the bush" (ch. 7, p. 160). In contrast
to Paul's burning bush, Miriam has her own moment of
epiphany, expressed in another figure of biblical manifestation: "She always regarded that sudden coming upon him in
the lane as a revelation. And this conversation remained
graven in her mind as one of the letters of the law" (ch. 7,
pp. 166–67). Although the Moses figure does not achieve
as much prominence in *Sons and Lovers* as it does later in
Aaron's Rod, there is enough linguistic heightening in these

scenes to afford the hero the stature of an isolated but energetic prophet in touch with the mysteries of the universe.

Lawrence superimposes these three biblical figures to blend the most salient aspects of his created self-image: Joseph for his masterly and combative streak, Paul for his underlying Puritanism and pull toward negation, Moses for his power to communicate with the sources of being and to make them manifest in art. But, conscious novelist as he was, Lawrence still faced the task of narrative, just as—self-writer and not merely self-portraitist as he was—he had to seek out a plot in the matter of his early life. The most available plot forms are those implied by the novel's title: the succession of sons—favored status passing from the elder William to Paul—and the series of lovers, from mother to mother surrogate to mature sexual mate (although the latter is not the final term in the series). To accomplish the imperatives of plotting, a writer of Lawrence's breeding would readily fall in with autobiographical tradition in appropriating biblical stories to shape his personal experience. But the special features of Lawrence's childhood, together with the relentlessly individualist cast of his mind, ensured that *Sons and Lovers* would make significant revisions in the sequence and content of the traditional stages of a life.

The novel begins in hell: " 'The Bottoms' succeeded to 'Hell Row' " (ch. 1, p. 1). Indeed, the Morels' working-class housing is not merely linguistically abased and socioeconomically low, but it is fallen from a prior condition that the opening pages lightly but unmistakably sketch in. "Hell Row was a block of thatched, bulging cottages that stood by the brook-side on Greenhill Lane"; like the mine, it is "on the edge of Sherwood Forest," in the vicinity of a "ruined priory of the Carthusians and . . . Robin Hood's Well" (ch. 1, p. 1). The symbols of the lost English past, dear to the mythology of Tory conservatism and Morrisite socialism alike, are here deployed without indignation or hope of resurgence.

Indeed, the Edenic time is not only mythologically remote but its decadence continues, though in modern forms. There is a place below Hell Row, the Bottoms: "The notorious Hell Row, which through growing old had acquired an evil reputation, was burned down, and much dirt was cleansed away"; the mining company builds the Bottoms on its site, "substantial and very decent" houses, but the insider's view is more subtly attuned to its decadence: "So, the actual conditions of living in the Bottoms, that was so well built and that looked so nice, were quite unsavoury because people must live in the kitchen, and the kitchens opened on to that nasty alley of ash-pits" (ch. 1, p. 2). Here, Mrs. Morel steadily declines: "She descended to it from Bestwood"; "She came down in the July, and in the September expected her third baby" (ch. 1, p. 2). Thus is Paul Morel brought into a world not only long fallen but much resembling hell in its family relationships as well as in its domestic arrangements.

In the absence of the conventional setting for a natural childhood, country pleasures are still available close by, and Lawrence can play on surviving elements of the traditional idyll of origins. In place of the garden and its associated theme of expulsion, there is a bitter parody of the figure when Morel puts his wife out during an argument: "I should laugh, laugh, my lord, if I could get away from you," Mrs. Morel says to her husband, satanic in his rage and drunkenness. "He came up to her, his red face, with its bloodshot eyes, thrust forward. . . . he pushed her roughly to the outer door, and thrust her forth" (ch. 1, p. 23).

The expulsion motifs quickly give way to the language of annunciation; under the light of a moon laden with a White Goddess aura, Mrs. Morel smears her face with the golden pollen of tall white lilies and experiences an ecstatic moment not only for herself but for her unborn child:

> Mrs. Morel leaned on the garden gate, looking out, and she lost herself awhile. She did not know what she

thought. Except for a slight feeling of sickness, and her consciousness of the child, herself melted out like scent into the shiny, pale air. After a time the child, too, melted with her in the mixing-pot of moonlight, and she rested with the hills and lilies and houses, all swum together in a kind of swoon.

(ch. 1, p. 24)

There is the same ambiguity here as exists about any moment of conception, but we may surmise that this is the true point of insemination and irradiation of the hero's life. It is the moment in which his mother takes into herself the maternal powers of the moon and the vital forces of vegetative reproduction—fusing herself with the external scene and merging into her nascent life. Despite the harried events that lead to this postlapsarian scene and the "forlorn" feeling the mother experiences in their wake, the language underscores the dual life of mother and son, one which is to become as much a fatal curse as a vital source in his career.

As if to seal this fate, another traditional action is performed in a shockingly distorted form. Morel throws a drawer at his wife in a fit of rage and wounds her brow: "With the catastrophe he had lost all balance. . . . he saw a drop of blood fall from the averted wound into the baby's fragile, glistening hair. . . . then, finally, his manhood broke" (ch. 2, pp. 39–40). The baptism in blood is not only a dire portent for the child and one of the indignities that cause the mother to bind the boy to herself, but it is also the final mark of the father's degradation and unmanning. Thereafter, he becomes less a Dionysian symbol and slice-of-life sketch of a miner and more a pathetic husk of a man—with even more baleful consequences for the protagonist's psychic development.

From these both promising and unpromising beginnings, Paul's lot is cast in a state of bondage to his mother—the equivalent in modern psychological terms of the exiled fate of the fallen or the wilderness condition of the outcast or prodigal. Much of Part I of *Sons and Lovers* is taken up with

the exemplary growth, marriage, and death of the elder
brother, William. The talons of the motherly embrace are
not far to seek in his poor choice of a mate although they
are less patently responsible for William's poor health and
early demise. Mrs. Morel's response to the loss confirms her
in her vocation and seals Paul's fate: "I should have watched
the living, not the dead" (ch. 6, p. 140). When Paul comes
down with pneumonia, the language waxes eschatological:

> She lifted him up, crying in a small voice: "Oh, my
> son—my son!"
> That brought him to. He realised her. His whole
> will rose up and arrested him. He put his head on her
> breast, and took ease of her for love.
> "For some things," said his aunt, "it was a good
> thing Paul was ill that Christmas. I believe it saved his
> mother." (ch. 6, p. 141)

The salvific effect on Paul is less clear as "the two knitted
together in perfect intimacy. Mrs. Morel's life now rooted
itself in Paul" (ch. 6, p. 141).

Under the constraints of this first lover, Paul's youthful
friendship with his second love stands condemned to failure.
Much can be—and has been—said on either side for the part-
ners in this long process of falling out of love, but it is clear
to Miriam, if not to Paul, that his mother is the bar. In a
passage framed from Miriam's point of view: "He had come
back to his mother. Hers was the strongest tie in his life. . . .
And nobody else mattered. There was one place in the world
that stood solid and did not melt into unreality: the place
where his mother was" (ch. 9, p. 222).

What Miriam and Paul are less aware of is the degree to
which she is cast in the same mold as Mrs. Morel. Yet Paul's
decisive letter to her bears out his general awareness of the
resemblance: "You see, I can give you a spirit love. I have
given it you this long, long time; but not embodied passion.
See, you are a nun. I have given you what I would give a
holy nun—as a mystic monk to a mystic nun. Surely you

esteem it best" (ch. 9, p. 251). Miriam chafes under the imputation of her nun's estate; but she tends to see the mother as the impediment rather than her own similarity to Mrs. Morel's Puritanism, which affects Paul in the same life-negating way. She therefore mythologizes the maternal intruder in an overly simple figure: "But there was a serpent in her Eden" (ch. 7, p. 171). This is Miriam's response to Paul's refusal to accept her spiritualized sexuality as the dominant bond of their love. She imagines a love imbued with secularized Christianity: "She fell into that rapture of self-sacrifice, identifying herself with a God who was sacrificed, which gives to so many human souls their deepest bliss" (ch. 7, p. 172). Despite her tendency to identify him with Jesus, Paul affirms a religion not of spirituality but of power: "I don't believe God knows such a lot about Himself. . . . God doesn't *know* things. He *is* things. And I'm sure He's not soulful" (ch. 9, p. 251). The serpent in Miriam's Eden is, of course, her own repressed and converted sexuality, and the mythos developed in *Sons and Lovers* transvaluates biblical values and sees her aversion to natural sexuality as original sin.

In place of her fastidiousness, Clara Dawes provides the full response of mature womanhood: "And after such an evening they both were very still, having known the immensity of passion. They felt small, half-afraid, childish and wondering, like Adam and Eve when they lost their innocence and realised the magnificence of the power which drove them out of Paradise and across the great night and the great day of humanity. It was for each of them an initiation and a satisfaction" (ch. 13, pp. 353–54; cf. ch. 12, p. 313). So the loss of sexual innocence is depicted in Lawrencian mythology as the dawn of full humanity; and the unblushing sexuality of Clara-Eve makes a new Adam of Paul.[5]

5. Lawrence frequently employed these biblical figures during the period in which the novel was written but often in contexts stressing

Yet Paul still lies in bondage, in the exile of the maternal embrace. For one thing, he cannot join this side of his life with the new vitality flowing from Clara: "Paul would have died rather than his mother should get to know of this affair. He suffered tortures of humiliation and self-consciousness. . . . He had a life apart from her—his sexual life. The rest she still kept" (ch. 13, p. 345). For another, there is at work in him the same tendency toward extinction of consciousness in which he. participated in the prenatal state and which parallels his mother's strong death wish: "To him now, life seemed a shadow, day a white shadow; night, and death, and stillness, and inaction, this seemed like *being*. To be alive, to be urgent and insistent—that was *not-to-be*. The highest of all was to melt out into the darkness and sway there, identified with the great Being" (ch. 11, p. 287). It is such an impulse—which Lawrence never lost and which crops up frequently in the entire *oeuvre*—that underlies the winding down of his affair with Clara, the sympathy-cum-blood rivalry he develops with her derelict husband, Baxter Dawes, and his general drift out of life in the final third of the novel.

Yet Paul's emulation of his mother is not perfect, for she makes a strong claim on life, which comes to seem unwarranted if not ghoulish. As she succumbs to cancer, her hold on Paul only intensifies: "It's the living I want, not the dead," she declares in an echo of her determination to fasten on Paul after William's death. Indeed, when Paul reports: "She wants to live even now," Clara appropriately responds: "Oh, how horrible!" (ch. 14, p. 388). In this depraved condition, Paul is sucked into the ghastly business of euthanasia to relieve her from agony; the immediate results are equally

---

temptation and sexual conflict, e.g., the short story "New Eve and Old Adam." It is this negative side of the paradisal or apocalyptic figures—fully enshrined within Judeo-Christian exegesis—which touches Lawrence's "sexual eschatology" (the term is Kermode's in "Lawrence and the Apocalyptic Types") even at its most enthusiastic preachings. This aspect also emerges in the denouement of Paul's affair with Clara.

ghastly: "Her mouth had fallen open, and she breathed with great, hoarse breaths, like snoring, and there were long intervals between" (ch. 14, p. 396).

This is the crisis not only in the mother's illness but in the son's hold on life. She succumbs, and he very nearly does: "Paul felt crumpled up and lonely. His mother had really supported his life. He had loved her; they two had, in fact, faced the world together. Now she was gone, and for ever behind him was the gap in life, the tear in the veil, through which his life seemed to drift slowly, as if he were drawn towards death" (ch. 14, p. 407). At this lowest point in his career, a sudden turn is given. It is not clear from where, inside or outside Paul, the epiphany comes, but it is undoubtedly delivered in the language of religious revelation:

> In the country all was dead still. Little stars shone high up; little stars spread far away in the flood-waters, a firmament below. Everywhere the vastness and terror of the immense night which is roused and stirred for a brief while by the day, but which returns, and will remain at last eternal, holding everything in its silence and its living gloom. There was no Time, only Space. . . . Where was he?—one tiny upright speck of flesh, less than an ear of wheat lost in the field. He could not bear it. On every side the immense dark silence seemed pressing him, so tiny a spark, into extinction, and yet, almost nothing, he could not be extinct. Night, in which everything was lost, went reaching out, beyond stars and sun. Stars and sun, a few bright grains, went spinning round for terror, and holding each other in embrace, there in a darkness that outpassed them all, and left them tiny and daunted. So much, and himself, infinitesimal, at the core a nothingness, and yet not nothing. . . . But no, he would not give in. Turning sharply, he walked towards the city's gold phosphorescence. His fists were shut, his mouth set fast. He would not take that

direction, to the darkness, to follow her. He walked
towards the faintly humming, glowing town, quickly.
(ch. 15, p. 420)

Paul's vision of the starry night is a return to the scene of
biblical creation when the heavens and the earth, the sun
and moon and the lesser lights, the day and the night, all
found their respective places and time began in the act.
In this awesome context, the individual is as nothing—in the
biblical image, an "ear of wheat lost in the field." But his
will to live is revived by the cosmic spectacle; life is breathed
into him, and he is created, too. In the course of *Sons and
Lovers*, and especially in its final scene, we are shown a process of self-creation in which the individual emerges distinct
from the forces that go into his making. At the close, Lawrence's hero stands like a prophet on a hill, ready to come
down and lead his people.

This sublime finale provides some justification for the
indeterminacy in which the hero's future is left. He finds no
parabolic formula, no clear explanation, nor even a firm grasp
of his identity in this spectacle, but he does derive an intuition of the universe's life that carries the seeds of personal
religion.[6] It is apparent that the epiphany involves a new hold
on life, amounting to a rebirth, but it is less evident that this
renewal involves a return to origins or first things. Lawrence
shifts the implications of Paul's turning toward his city to
suggest not a future domesticity but a protracted journey.
That Paul Morel derives from this epiphany the impetus to
live and work suggests that he can become a culture bearer
for a Lawrencian gospel—although his artistic vocation is
not specified here. That this apostolic imitation may well
begin a career of missionary travels, haranguing the established culture with doctrines of sexual liberation, neopagan

6. For another evaluation of the parallels between Paul and his
namesake, see Jerome H. Buckley, *Season of Youth: The Bildungsroman from Dickens to Golding* (Cambridge, Mass., 1974), p. 214.

vitalism, and tragic apocalypticism, completes the picture of a Paul displaced and transvalued for modern times. "And the Lord said unto him, Arise, and go into the city, and it shall be told thee what thou must do" (Acts 9).

18

A Portrait of the Artist

THE CONVENTIONS CONVENED

———

So MUCH—and so much of interest and genuine explanation —has been written about *A Portrait of the Artist as a Young Man* (1914–1915) that another such exercise hardly seems required. Yet in the critical canon on its style and symbolism and even in the biographical studies that have established its point-to-point correspondences with Joyce's early life, there has been none to my knowledge that considers *A Portrait* as an autobiographical novel, that is, as a fiction of a special breed. This omission is the more striking as the tradition-grounded character of even Joyce's most experimental works has become the accepted basis of their interpretation. Although it would be too much to claim that the autobiographical tradition stands to *A Portrait* in the same way as the *Odyssey* to *Ulysses* or Ibsen's dramas to *Exiles*, it would be surprising if the workshop in which Stephen Dedalus was made did not show the debris of literary transmutation on its floors.

A partial explanation for the scholarly omission noted

above is the subtle difference between Joyce's literary tradition and that of the other self-writers we have considered. Just as the *Bildungsromane* he would have in mind for models and departures would be French as well as English ones,[1] so his favored autobiographical texts, ranging from Augustine to Newman, would be those in which the symbols of religious rite are placed at the disposal of the writer seeking the formal significance of his life. These need not be Catholic, to be sure, but Joyce's origins in a Catholic culture provided special advantages for the autobiographical novelist—though his theme is his divestiture of that very culture.

In his first essay in autobiography, the brief "A Portrait" written in 1904, Joyce's conception of the task is couched in the Scholastic language he went on to write into the finished *Portrait*:

> The features of infancy are not commonly reproduced in the adolescent portrait for, so capricious are we, that we cannot or will not conceive the past in any other than its iron, memorial aspect. Yet the past assuredly implies a fluid succession of presents, the development of an entity of which our actual present is a phase only. Our world, again, recognises its acquaintance chiefly by the characters of beard and inches and is, for the most part, estranged from those of its members who seek through some art, by some process of the mind as yet untabulated, to liberate from the personalised lumps of matter that which is their individuating rhythm, the first or formal relation of their parts. But for such as these a portrait is not an identificative paper but rather the curve of an emotion.[2]   (pp. 257–58)

1. Joyce's adaptation of Flaubert's and Balzac's young-men-from-the-provinces en route to Paris, art, and fortune has yet, to my knowledge, to be fully assessed.

2. "A Portrait" is conveniently included in the Viking Critical Library edition of *A Portrait of the Artist as a Young Man*, ed. Chester G. Anderson (New York, 1968), which I cite in the text.

The new-model autobiographer will, then, scorn the characteristic details of "beard and inches"—"personalised lumps of matter"—in favor of a Thomistic (or is it Scotist?) principle of individuation. Joyce's terms for this personal essence—"individuating rhythm" and "curve of an emotion"—are transformations of Scholastic terminology into the working nomenclature of the fictional artist whose stylistic enterprise is to produce a linguistic rhythm in the tempo of that existential one and whose formal design is to be congruent with the dominant curve of the individual sense of life.

It has come increasingly to be recognized that the process of personal growth traced in *A Portrait* is largely a linguistic one, as is appropriate to the portrait of an artist whose art is writing.[3] Our general awareness of the centrality of language in the process of becoming human leads us to accept this story of a writer's verbal experience as a heightened instance of a universal story so that we readily follow Stephen from his baby talk on the first page to a sample of his mature prose (a journal) on the closing pages. In supplying the personal as well as the universal element of autobiographical fiction, the narrative of Stephen's absorption in words poignantly expresses the sensations of Joyce's early orientation in the world as a visually handicapped child—a condition impeding the hero's social relationships and psychosexual security in this and other works of the Joyce canon. The preponderance of aural sensation over visual in the novel and the distortions in the reporting of observed phenomena (intensifications alternating with dimnesses that make many passages of the novel so moving) are the records of a child aware of the threat of losing his eyes. But Stephen's handicap is also the wound that has been associated with the will to art in Freud-

3. See R. B. Kershner, Jr., "Time and Language in Joyce's *Portrait of the Artist*," *English Literary History*, 43 (1976): 604-19.

ian aesthetics and the symbolic mark of a potential Promethean rebel, tormented but defiant.

Before it comes to provide possibilities of individuality, language learning is a socializing process. As the child grows, he is furnished with a code carrying heavy rhetorical burdens designed to attach him to the dominant institutions of his society. The most explicit drama in *A Portrait* is Stephen's self-liberation from these "high-sounding" words of religion, nationalism, and gentility. The climax of this drama of language comes when he turns to words of his own, that is, words to which he has given his own significance, and when he begins using them to create works of art, which order words into forms and rhythms and give them independent value. From the first pages, with their refrains of nursery rhymes, cradle songs, and childish chants, the child is surrounded by words that have the force of things but have little verbalizable meaning. Eventually, the artist will endow them with meanings, and they will stand for units of himself.

At school, Stephen begins to learn words and meanings ("That was a belt round his pocket. And belt was also to give a fellow a belt"—ch. 1, p. 9), to hear words laden with mannalike significance ("Is [your father] a magistrate?"—ch. 1, p. 9), and to examine words for their onomatopoeic or purely aesthetic value ("Suck was a queer word"—ch. 1, p. 11). One of the problems connected with words is the question raised by one's own name; when a boy named Nasty Roche asks: "What is your name?" Stephen answers: "Stephen Dedalus." "Then Nasty Roche had said: What kind of a name is that? And . . . Stephen had not been able to answer . . ." (ch. 1, p. 9). The difficulty lies, of course, not in the child's imperfect knowledge of the myth and ritual behind his symbolic name but in the challenge to distinguish one's name from oneself—a name is, after all, to the child his only possible designation, as much a part of himself as his body and equivalent to his sense of identity.

The distinction between his name and himself begins to

dawn on Stephen when he engages in the formative experiment of placing himself within the geographical and cosmic frames provided by his advancing knowledge: "He turned to the flyleaf of the geography and read what he had written there: himself, his name and where he was. / *Stephen Dedalus / Class of Elements / Clongowes Wood College / Sallins / County Kildare / Ireland / Europe / The World / The Universe*" (ch. 1, p. 15). This placement of oneself in larger spatial contexts is the consequence of a prior discrimination of three aspects of one's being: "himself, his name and where he was." Stephen draws the appropriate correlations from his universal mailing address: "Then he read the flyleaf from the bottom to the top till he came to his own name. That was he. . . ." But he does not know enough to relate these three aspects to each other, to see how his name is a function of himself and where he is in Ireland, Europe, and the Universe. (In the same passage, he anticipates but does not yet grasp the relativity of human conceptions of God implied in the varied names by which he is called; for him, "God was God's name just as his name was Stephen.")

Yet the words that Stephen is given as absolutes begin to lose their hold on his mind perhaps simply because the words are given before the things are experienced: "Words which he did not understand he said over and over to himself till he had learned them by heart: and through them he had glimpses of the real world about him" (ch. 2, p. 62). Words are a preparation for experience but are not trustworthy keys to reality, as Stephen gradually discovers. The sacramental language of his religious education masks the grubbiness of the boys' life at his school, and the gentility of his father's standards comes into contrast with gross behavior at home (for example, the Christmas dinner scene) and with the family's social decline: "While his mind had been pursuing its intangible phantoms and turning in irresolution from such pursuit he had heard about him the constant voices of his father and of his masters, urging him to be a gentleman above all things and urging him to be a good catholic above all things. These voices had now come to be hollowsounding in his ears" (ch. 2, p. 83). So that Stephen, on a trip with his father to sell off family property (tantamount to Stephen's "dispossession"—ch. 2, p. 87), can sum up his education with a gesture of disdain for its merely verbal content: "I am Stephen Dedalus. I am walking beside my father whose name is Simon Dedalus. We are in Cork, in Ireland. Cork is a city. Our room is in the Victoria Hotel. Victoria and Stephen and Simon. Simon and Stephen and Victoria. Names" (ch. 2, p. 92). Yet these mere names will provide the materials out of which Stephen will create meaning in his life by endowing them with symbolic force in expressing the patterns of his own and mankind's life.

Having distanced his urban, contentious, heavily educated childhood about as far as can be from the natural idyll enjoyed by other autobiographers, Joyce turns to the language of tradition for his subsequent narrative. Two lines of force happily converge here: the liturgical rhetoric of Catholic Ireland and the redemptive figures of spiritual autobiography. As Part I of the novel has been occupied with the acquisition of language and Part II with its reduction to empty shibboleths, the growing boy must seek out a new language in undergoing age-old patterns of sexual and emotional development.

Astonishingly, it is in terms of language that the fall into sexuality is expressed:

> He wanted to sin with another of his kind, to force another being to sin with him and to exult with her in sin. . . . the cry that he had strangled for so long in his throat issued from his lips. It broke from him like a wail of despair from a hell of sufferers and died in a wail of furious entreaty, a cry for an iniquitous abandonment, a cry which was but the echo of an obscene scrawl which he had read on the oozing wall of a urinal. (ch. 2, pp. 99–100)

Although the ensuing initiation with a pink-gowned prostitute sets no marks for verbal eloquence, it is patently conceived as a form of communication, a language of gesture (to use another Joycean term). The woman's lips "pressed upon his brain as upon his lips as though they were the vehicle of a vague speech; and between them he felt an unknown and timid pressure, darker than the swoon of sin, softer than sound or odour" (ch. 2, p. 101).

But this lingual contact cannot firmly expunge the rich religious language that he has been acquiring throughout life. Oddly, for a time, the two languages, of sensuality and of sacramental purity, merge as Stephen recalls the lusher passages in the symbolic-erotic poetry of the Apocrypha:

> The glories of Mary held his soul captive: spikenard and myrrh and frankincense, symbolising the preciousness of God's gifts to her soul, rich garments, symbolising her royal lineage, her emblems; the late-flowering plant and lateblossoming tree, symbolising the agelong gradual growth of her cultus among men. When it fell to him to read the lesson towards the close of the office he read it in a veiled voice, lulling his conscience to its music:
> *Quasi cedrus exaltata sum in Libanon et quasi cupressus in monte Sion. . . . Sicut cinnamomum et balsamum aromatizans odorem dedi. . . .*
> (ch. 3, pp. 104–05; quoting Ecclesiasticus 24)

For a time this fusion of sensuality and sanctity in the adoration of Mary provides a resting place, but the rector announces a retreat as a time for drawing up accounts. Now a benevolent mentor of his boyhood—Father Arnall of Clongowes—comes on to deliver a full course in theological language, closely examining and defining a series of words central to the culture in which Stephen is to be confirmed.

So much attention has been paid to the elaborate sermon on hell and its demonstrable models in Jesuit instructional literature[4] that the finer points of Father Arnall's rhetorical style have been overlooked. For Arnall is a master of aesthetic as well as rhetoric, and the rhythms of his delivery come to strike deeper than the scarifying impact of the words:

> Adam and Eve, my dear boys, were, as you know, our first parents and you will remember that they were created by God in order that the seats in heaven left vacant by the fall of Lucifer and his rebellious angels might be filled again. Lucifer, we are told, was a son of the morning, a radiant and mighty angel; yet he fell: he fell and there fell with him a third part of the host of heaven: he fell and was hurled with his rebellious angels into hell. What his sin was we cannot say. Theologians consider that it was the sin of pride, the sinful thought conceived in an instant: *non serviam: I will not serve.* That instant was his ruin. He offended the majesty of God by the sinful thought of one instant and God cast him out of heaven into hell for ever. (ch. 3, p. 117)

The consequences of this speech are almost as manifold and determinant—at least for Stephen—as those of the events it describes. The immediate effect, of course, is to generalize his sin in that of the race and to lead him to apply the appropriate antidotes to the fallen state that his religion offers. But by a curious lapse in rhetorical technique, Arnall succeeds also in presenting vividly to Stephen's imagination the figure—and the formulaic essence—of the divine antagonist so that Stephen's eventual self-image as Luciferian rebel, mouthing his *non serviam* and flying from all restraints, is founded here. Moreover, the poetic style in which the bad example is described—a prose drenched in repetition, allitera-

4. For references to these sources and the critical discussion of them, see Anderson's editorial notes in *A Portrait*, p. 512.

tion, strong cadence, rhyme, etc.⁵—makes the heroic image
of Lucifer and the tragic nobility of his fall the most striking
effect of the oratory.

The roots of this self-image have already been prepared
in Stephen's education—particularly in association with
Byron. At Belvedere College he has suffered an enactment of
the persecution fantasies of childhood as his classmates mock
and beat him to the rhythm of "Admit that Byron was no
good. . . . Admit. . . . Admit" (ch. 2, p. 82; echoing *"Apolo-
gise, Pull out his eyes . . ."*). Stephen's approval of Byron's
poetry and the ascription of heresy, not only to the poet but
to his devotee, by the English master and the boys, is never
fully explained, nor is a specific poem brought into account
—presumably the boys are acting on the reputation not the
text. But beside all the Byron poems of libertarian defiance
of political and cultural authorities (in which the Church
need not but may find itself implicated) and among the
group of poems in which a rebellious *damnée* is made the
hero, one stands out: the visionary drama *Cain*. The chief
figure in this poem about a primal human apostate and outcast is not, indeed, its eponymous subject but Lucifer, the
prototype of Cain and, following in the train of identifications, of Byron himself. (The poet is strongly present in
passages concerning Cain's relations with his sister Adah.)
In the first scene of the second act of this closet drama Lucifer conducts Cain on a flight over the earth, giving him a
bird's eye view of the terrestrial condition in a language of
appropriate magniloquence. In the second scene, there follows a descent into hell, which neatly couples the darker
side of the apostate's condition with his soaring advantages.
It is my contention that Stephen's self-concept as Dedalus-
Icarus, Lucifer, Thoth, and other winged masters is derived

5. Some of these tropes are already present in the biblical text
from which the sermon is derived: "God spared not the angels that
sinned, but cast them down to hell, and delivered them into chains of
darkness, to be reserved unto judgment"—II Peter 2 (cf. Jude 6).

from literary as much as it is from theological and mythological sources and that Byron's poem is one of the chief
models for an art that expresses personal impulses and experiences in the figures of biblical or exegetic tradition.[6]

The immediate impact of the Lucifer figure on Stephen
is, however, neither a poetic nor a conceptual but a visceral
one: he has hell scared into him and makes a hasty retreat
from his sexual explorations. This finale of Part III corresponds to the crisis so often found in spiritual autobiographies, in which the sinner is overwhelmed by the magnitude
of his sin and his own dereliction. In *A Portrait*, conviction
of sin is conveyed in a parody of formulaic language: "We
knew perfectly well of course that although it was bound to
come to the light he would find considerable difficulty in
endeavouring to try to induce himself to try to endeavour to
ascertain the spiritual plenipotentiary and so we knew of
course perfectly well . . ." (ch. 3, p. 136). The words come
apparently from the faces and voices that "watched and
waited"—the ministers of conscience of ancient lineage and
perpetual internalization. Stephen tries to criticize their language by telling himself "calmly that those words had absolutely no sense which had seemed to rise murmurously
from the dark" (ch. 3, p. 136). But the power of their incantation is sufficient to submit him to the penances and
affirmations of the cult.

After goatish hallucinations, dreary confession, and an-
tiphonal prayers, he is fully reabsorbed in his linguistic-
cultural community: "His daily life was laid out in devotional areas. By means of ejaculations and prayers he stored
up ungrudgingly for the souls in purgatory centuries of days
and quarantines and years; yet the spiritual triumph which
he felt in achieving with ease so many fabulous ages of
canonical penances did not wholly reward his zeal of prayer . . ." (ch. 4, p. 147). The problem lies not only in the

6. Joyce was interested enough in the poem, at least at a later time,
to propose creating an opera from it with George Antheil; see Richard
Ellmann, *James Joyce* (New York, 1965), pp. 640–41.

mathematical uncertainties created by the mixture of literalism and indefiniteness in the "canonical penances" code but
in the limitations of this laying out of one's life in "devotional areas." He returns to his conflation of sensuality and religious mystery in a book by St. Alphonsus Liguori (who
also helped Newman on his way), "in which the imagery of
the canticles was interwoven with the communicant's prayers" (ch. 4, p. 152). These recollections of *Inter ubera mea
commorabitur* (Canticles 1) do little to bolster his efforts to
convince himself that "Frequent and violent temptations
were a proof that the citadel of the soul had not fallen and
that the devil raged to make it fall." The passage closes equiv-
ocally: "I have amended my life, have I not?" (ch. 4, p. 153).

Given this appearance of rededication and with the approach of his graduation, proposals for his vocation from
family and Church begin to press Stephen. Bolstering his
earlier tendency to "conceive himself as a being apart in
every order" are memories of Clongowes: "The chill and
order of the life repelled him" (ch. 4, p. 161). He tries to
imagine himself as "The Reverend Stephen Dedalus, S.J."
but has some difficulty bringing the image to his mind's eye:
"His name in that new life leaped into characters before his
eyes and to it there followed a mental sensation of an unde-
fined face or colour of a face" (ch. 4, p. 161). In his unde-
cided state, the rhythms of the sermon come back to him:
"The snares of the world were its ways of sin. He would
fall. He had not yet fallen but he would fall silently, in an
instant. Not to fall was too hard, too hard: and he felt the
silent lapse of his soul, as it would be at some instant to
come, falling, falling but not yet fallen, still unfallen but
about to fall" (ch. 4, p. 162). Just as Part III has traced the
protagonist's wilderness condition after the fall, his spiritual
crisis and ineffectual conversion, Part IV narrates the novel's
critical event. This might be taken as the climax of a five-
act dramatic structure, but, so closely linked to the autobiographical pattern with which we are familiar, it may be

seen as the epiphany not only in Joyce's but in the traditional sense of the term.

The scene begins without undue urgency as a "squad of christian brothers" crossing a bridge suggests the regimentation Stephen's "instinct" resists. He mouths a favorite line from his "treasure" of *mots justes* and pursues aesthetic speculations on the virtues of a "lucid supple periodic prose" perfectly mirroring the "inner world of individual emotions" (ch. 4, p. 167). There follows a "confused music within him" and from it "one longdrawn calling note, piercing like a star the dusk of silence." It is only the sound of boys' voices, but it comes with overtones of Lucifer, who is identified with the evening as well as the morning star, piercing "the dusk of silence." Moreover, the rowdy boys' voices hardly seem like the medium for an angel's call, but Augustine heard his in a children's game! Indeed, Joyce writes: "A voice from beyond the world was calling" (ch. 4, p. 167), and the identification of the voice as Lucifer's hardly makes it less angelic. We need to refocus our apprehension of this familiar scene to seize upon its reenactment of an even more familiar prototype, the inspiration to a redirected life through the seemingly random promptings of children's voices, urging renewed attention to a familiar text or, in this case, set of words.

The first phase of Stephen's epiphanic transformation is his discovery of the meaning of his own name. While walking along the beach, he is addressed by friends in the playful style of boys sporting their classical education: "Hello. Stephanos! Here comes The Dedalus! . . . Come along, Dedalus! Bous Stephenoumenos! Bous Stephaneforos!" (ch. 4, pp. 167–68). These mysterious words seem even stranger when translated: crowned or garlanded bull (or ox); wreath-bearing bull (or ox). They are explained by the language of Greek religious ceremonies, suggesting that Stephen is being alternately described in the terms used for sacrificial animals offered to the gods and in those used for priests and heroes receiving public acclaim. What unites these extremely different beings and underlies the common floral decoration of both victims and victors is their role as *pharmakoi* in social rituals of regeneration. The complexities of Joyce's thoughts on oxen, sacrificial heroes, and the artist in his double role of scapegoat and savior were to be enlarged in *Ulysses* and *Finnegans Wake*, but we may find here the origin of Stephen's awareness of his problematic but committed fate as artist.

Equally important in the boys' harangue is the locution of Stephen's name as "The Dedalus." The abstract form serves to place him under the type of the artist who serves his people but who is also outcast from them, as was Dedalus. The name metonymically connotes Dedalus's son Icarus, the young novice who learns his father's art but not so well as to escape injury from it. Both craftsman and apprentice, both master builder and self-destructive overreacher against authority's injunctions are joined in the name.

This symbolic language generates imaginative vision and urgent self-conception:

> Now, at the name of the fabulous artificer [i.e., Dedalus], he seemed to hear the noise of dim waves and to see a winged form flying above the waves and slowing climbing the air [i.e., Icarus]. What did it mean? Was it a quaint device opening a page of some medieval book of prophecies and symbols, a hawk-like man flying sunward above the sea, a prophecy of the end he had been born to serve and had been following through the mists of childhood and boyhood, a symbol of the artist forging anew in his workshop out of the sluggish matter of the earth a new soaring impalpable imperishable being?
>
> (ch. 4, p. 169)

Stephen recognizes in the name, then, his own nature and destiny, both the pattern that gives meaning to his previous groping development and the myth that serves as the model on which he will shape his future.

The second and major climax of the epiphany is yet to

come. Taking the boys' palmary words as "the call of life to his soul" (ch. 4, p. 169), Stephen repeats in an incantation the language of his vocation and its mythological figure (ch. 4, p. 170). He is now prepared for the full revelation in his mystery initiation, standing emptied and opened for the onset of a new deity. She will be crystallized in a natural being, ready to be imaginatively converted into an aesthetic object: "A girl stood before him in midstream, alone and still, gazing out to sea. She seemed like one whom magic had changed into the likeness of a strange and beautiful seabird. . . . Heavenly God! cried Stephen's soul, in an outburst of profane joy" (ch. 4, p. 171). The well-known passages of Stephen/Joyce's heightened prose, which I have refrained from transcribing in full, confirm the epiphanic vision as a manifestation of godhead in a human figure: the bird-girl is the living embodiment of Venus Pandemos—the "Heavenly God" of "profane" beauty later called "the angel of mortal youth and beauty" (ch. 4, p. 172). This—not the villanelle he struggles to write in Part V—is the moment of Stephen's confirmation as an artist; he has still some way to go before being master of a prose style like Joyce's, but he is here dedicated, as surely as any religious novice, to his calling—"Her eyes had called him and his soul had leaped at the call" (ch. 4, p. 172).

Although it is known that Joyce had some such experience of his own, with effects powerful enough to be recalled some twenty years afterward,[7] the fact does not exhaust the autobiographical significance of this epiphany. In autobiographers from Augustine to modern times, we have learned to see the co-presence of personal experience and literary convention as no contradiction but a confirmation of the ways in which autobiography transforms experience into art. It should come as no surprise, then—although the

7. The discovery of certain letters has induced this assumption, but the evidence is not conclusive, being derived from an interview with a Swiss lady once admired by Joyce, who reported his allusion to an earlier vision of a girl on a beach; see *Letters of James Joyce*, ed. Stuart Gilbert and Richard Ellmann, 3 vols. (New York, 1966), II, 428.

fact has not been noted in the scholarship of which I am aware—that the bird-girl epiphany occurs in a Romantic autobiography with which Joyce could well have been familiar, Leigh Hunt's. Here is Hunt's account:

> My strolls about the fields with a book were full of happiness: only my dress [as a Christ Hospital schoolboy] used to get me stared at by the villagers. Walking one day by the little River Wandle, I came upon one of the loveliest girls I ever beheld, standing in the water with bare legs, washing some linen. She turned as she was stooping, and showed a blooming oval face with blue eyes, on either side of which flowed a profusion of flaxen locks. With the exception of the colour of the hair, it was like Raphael's own head turned into a peasant girl's. The eyes were full of gentle astonishment at the sight of me; and mine must have wondered no less. However, I was prepared for such wonders. It was only one of my poetical visions realized, and I expected to find the world full of them.[8]

Hunt's rendering is more circumstantial and psychological—there is some indication of how the girl regarded her observer as there is not in *A Portrait*, but common to both accounts are the aesthetic properties of the figure. Although Hunt's figure, like Joyce's, is touched with sexuality and the natural realm, these traces are quickly assimilated in a larger aesthetic vision. For Hunt, it is the "wonders" of his "poetical visions" that allow him to superimpose the type of the artist, Raphael, on the girl's face; for Joyce, it is the human-animal forms of the girl's body which allow him to envision her not merely as a bird but as an angel: "A wild angel had appeared to him, the angel of mortal youth and beauty, an envoy from the fair courts of life, to throw open before him in an instant of ecstasy the gates of all the ways of error and

8. *The Autobiography of Leigh Hunt*, ed. J. E Morpurgo (London, 1949 [1850]), p. 96. Other similarities between the two protagonists include a scene of insubordination at school, absorption in Milton, Homer, and Ovid, and phrases like "Sir, I never eat apples" (p. 73).

glory" (ch. 4, p. 172). The extravagance of the language and the preciosity of certain phrases—"the fair courts of life," especially—should not blind us to the claims that are advanced here. Both Joyce and Hunt see these girlish figures as guarantors of their future career as artist—of their finding the world full of poetical visions which throw open the gates of error and glory. It is in this sense that these girls are Muse figures, not as lunar inspirations but as living figures of art.

Stephen must, however, not only know what his vocation is but also perfect it. To do so, he must work in the medium of language, but his language has already been infected by the words—religious, national, and cultural—in which he has been raised: "He walked on in a lane among heaps of dead language" (ch. 5, p. 179). We see him struggle to find fresh words for a poem—not very successfully; we see him working out a set of aesthetic principles by defining and modifying the Scholastic terminology in which he has been trained. But we do not reach with him the new language which he—or his creator—will develop in *Ulysses* and *Finnegans Wake* to embody himself as totally as any artist has in his own works.

A Portrait ends with a *nego* instead of a *credo*, both a negation of the claims of family, church, and nation that are laid on him and a declaration of self-exile—not a wandering after the fall but a purposeful rejection of the world offered for his inheritance. Stephen takes on himself the devil's sin of refusing to serve his cultural masters, employing the Luciferian *non serviam*: "I will not serve that in which I no longer believe whether it call itself my home, my fatherland or my church . . ." (ch. 5, pp. 246–47). He declares again, that is, his refusal to take things by the names he has been given for them, and his three weapons, "silence, exile, and cunning," are to be dedicated to finding new words "to express myself." Eventually, he will do so in that composite autobiographical fiction, *Ulysses*, which unites both sides of

Joyce, the father and the son, the "practical" and the "artistic," the scapegoat and the potentially regenerative artist, in the dual figures of Bloom and Stephen.

Although Stephen takes off on the final pages of *A Portrait*—soaring into flight like Icarus-Thoth-Lucifer—the shape of his career is not traced within the confines of this novel. Unlike many a *Künstlerroman*—the final volume of Proust's is the paradigm—*A Portrait* does not contain a resolution to write an autobiographical novel remarkably like itself. We need a sequel, *Ulysses*, to follow out his project, learning there that it is to Paris Stephen goes and to Dublin, at his mother's death, that he returns. Yet neither in *A Portrait* nor its greater sequel does Stephen give firm assurances of what's to come; the endless debate on his career as artist or aesthete will never be resolved, for it is genuinely ambiguous in these open-ended fictions.

Joyce's own brief return in 1903, after four months in bohemia, was neither—or not solely—to Stephen's dissipations nor to a passing encounter with a benevolent Jew (at least, none that can be proved).[9] Instead, this was the period in which *A Portrait* was begun; although the text does not explicitly predict its own genesis, this was the actual outcome of the parallel experience of the author as begun within it. The autobiographical "return" phase is omitted from *A Portrait* but was enacted by Joyce in the process of writing that text itself. The writing of this autobiographical novel must have been liberating for its creator, for when, some eleven years later, he finished *A Portrait* and fixed his identity in words, he was ready to begin his masterpiece, *Ulysses*.

9. The best evidence for this encounter is the eerie first-person voice—which can be assigned only to the author—that breaks into the "Aeolus" section of *Ulysses* to say, presumably of Bloom: "I have often thought since on looking back over that strange time it was that small act, trivial in itself, that striking of that match, that determined the whole aftercourse of both our lives"—*Ulysses* (New York, 1934 [1922]), p. 138. The vagaries and motivations of *A Portrait*'s chronology for Stephen's departure, measured against Joyce's own moves, are spelled out in Hugh Kenner, *Ulysses* (London, Boston, and Sydney, 1980), pp. 161–62.

19

Pilgrimage

THE ETERNAL
AUTOBIOGRAPHICAL
MOMENT

—

THE THIRTEEN NOVELS, or volumes, or "chapters" of Dorothy M. Richardson's *Pilgrimage* make so extraordinary an appearance that it would seem impossible to treat them as exemplary for autobiographical fiction. In sheer length (longer than O'Casey's autobiography, longer than Anaïs Nin's published diary), in homogeneous subject matter—largely restricted to the contents of consciousness—in virtuoso narrative technique, ranging from the so-called stream of consciousness (in direct discourse) to free indirect style, Richardson's dedication to her lifelong task resulted in one of the landmark achievements, but also one of the craggy monadnocks, of modern fiction. Yet as exceptional as *Pilgrimage* is among novels, it is firmly in place in the autobiographical tradition and forges stronger ties with its predecessors than any other modern self-writing. Indeed, from its title to its frequent references to spiritual autobiographers like Bunyan and Fox, the work declares its preoccupation with the religious searchings and moments of vision that have animated Western autobiography and that continue to do so even when the writer is unorthodox in her creed, staunchly combative in her version of feminism, and iconoclastically individualist, if not bohemian, as an artist.

428

Viewing *Pilgrimage* in the autobiographical tradition allows us to make some headway in the most pressing problem
for Richardson criticism, the problem of form. That this is
no narrowly formalist issue is attested by the severe limits
that its length and apparent amorphousness have placed on
the novel's popularity, leading to the author's continued benign neglect among the masters of modern literature. A work
published over three (or five) decades and pursuing a lonely
conception of itself will, like Pound's *Cantos*, put strains on
the reader trying to assimilate its bulky parts while remaining aware of its grand design. Richardson added thorns on
the path by her principled refusal to build up to finales at
the close of the separately published parts, in line with her
sense of life's fluidity and lack of dramatic finality. She also
added a trap for critics by her refusal to regard the work as
"complete" even after she had grudgingly given permission
to market it as such when twelve parts were published together in 1938. I shall pursue the problem of the thirteenth
volume, the uncompleted and posthumously published
March Moonlight (1967), in its place but call attention here
only to the added unsettlement created by this late arrival
and the interpretive revisions to which it led. In numerologi-
cal terms, the situation is symbolized by the switch from a
twelve-part conception to a twelve-and-a-tilly measure;
whatever comfort could be taken from the dozen neatly arranged—but never clearly related—parts was removed by the
thirteenth participant. By sketchily bringing her narrative
up to 1915, the year of her first novel's publication and by
adding some theorizing on fiction and her own first efforts
to write, Richardson seemed to be urging a *Künstlerroman*
upon us, with a Proustian loop of time and form that would
bring the tail of the novel's action into the mouth of its origin
—the decision to write a novel like itself. We shall see, however, that this vocational reading—probably deliberate but
not fully achieved in Richardson's sporadic efforts to finish
March Moonlight—pales by comparison with Proust's elaborate execution of the ouroboros form whereas her work's

best claims for formal coherence, if not tailored beauty, lie in another sphere.

Dorothy Richardson is the custodian of the figures of autobiography—Edenic childhood and its loss, aimless wandering and hellish torment, vision and conversion, if not return to origins. She is, in fact, so much their master that she employs them again and again to structure the individual parts of her work as well as the larger whole. With Richardson the figures of autobiography come to mark not singular and decisive stages but repetitive patterns of living, for she undergoes and describes them over and over in her more than two thousand pages.

Although Richardson suffered more than her share of the neglect meted out to the great innovators of modern art, she has developed a respectful reputation. She did not live to enjoy her polite investiture among the safely dead progenitors of modernism, and it was still possible for a biography published in 1973, the centenary of her birth, to be subtitled *The Genius They Forgot*.[1] With the appearance of a fuller biography by Gloria Fromm, it is now established not only that *Pilgrimage* is a detailed autobiographical novel but that it is an elaborate record of subjective as well as objective experience.[2] There is even a likelihood that the novel's text is reworked or partly transcribed from a notebook or diary although that does not seem to have survived.[3] The subtleties

1. John Rosenberg, *Dorothy Richardson: The Genius They Forgot* (London, 1973); it is unclear who "they" may be, given the attention, restricted though it is, in most surveys of modern fiction to her stream of consciousness experiments. The broad subject of female self-writing has been pursued in *Women's Autobiography: Essays in Criticism*, ed. Estelle C. Jelinek (Bloomington, Ind., and London, 1980), containing studies of Victorian and Colonial American works and close treatments of Martineau, Stein, Hellman, Nin, and others. It would be a pity if "they" forgot Richardson.

2. Gloria G. Fromm, *Dorothy Richardson: A Biography* (Urbana, Ill., Chicago, and London, 1977); this study, first reported in an article in 1963, becomes the definitive treatment of the parallels and divergences between the novel and the career.

3. At one point, on arrival in *Oberland*, the protagonist, Miriam

of the transaction between fact and fiction, between self-conscious experience and writing about it, between the life of ongoing sensation and the death entailed in art making have been so well explored by Fromm that they need not be repeated here. Meanwhile both her biographers and the relatively few attentive critics omit all but passing mention of the major current in Richardson's intellectual development, her study of the Quakers and publication of two books by or about them in the year preceding the first part of *Pilgrimage*, in 1914.

The foreword to *The Quakers: Past and Present* succinctly plots the angle at which Richardson approached her subject:

> The following chapters are primarily an attempt at showing the position of the Quakers in the family to which they belong—the family of the mystics.
>
> In the second place comes a consideration of the method of worship and of corporate living laid down by the founder of Quakerism, as best calculated to foster mystical gifts and to strengthen in the community as a whole that sense of the Divine, indwelling and accessible, to which some few of his followers had already attained. . . .
>
> The famous "peculiarities" of the Quakers fall into place as following inevitably from their central belief.[4]

While Richardson's doctrinal emphases and her historical survey will not find universal acceptance among Quakers or

---

Henderson, "was presently at the table in négligé and again ecstatically telling it her news" (*O*, ch. 2, p 35); although a number of nouns may be urged as the antecedent of the pronoun here, none makes as much sense as the unnamed "diary." The employment of a diary by the novelist would help explain the otherwise startling shifts into first-person narrative experience and also the summative passages where Richardson seems to be speaking in her own voice. All quotations are from *Pilgrimage*, 4 vols. (New York, 1967 [1938]).

4. Dorothy Richardson, *The Quakers: Past and Present* (London, 1914), p. v; the quotation below is from p. 35.

professional scholars, her clearly stated goals sufficiently reveal her own spiritual and personal interests. The three key
words of these paragraphs—"mystics," "corporate living,"
and " 'peculiarities' " (in a defensive posture)—are concerns
which will be readily recognized by readers of *Pilgrimage*.
The word more easily passed over is the figurative use of
"family"; on the pervasive importance of this concern in
Richardson's psychological make-up, all will agree but perhaps only a trained analyst should properly comment.

Beyond providing a focus for her spiritual interests and
her emotional needs, Richardson's study of the Quakers gave
her (or reinforced) the pattern of living and its appropriate
figure which are writ large in *Pilgrimage*. Her account of
Fox brings out its underlying but essential irony:

> The religious genius, as represented pre-eminently by
> the great mystics—those in whom the sense of an ulti-
> mate and essential goodness, beauty, and truth, is the
> dominant characteristic—have [*sic*] consciously bent
> all their energies to breaking through the veil of sense,
> to making a journey to the heart of reality, to win-
> ning the freedom of the very citadel of Life itself.
> Their method has invariably included what—again
> borrowing from psychology—we must call the delib-
> erate control of all external stimuli, . . . as we have
> seen with Fox, a setting forth to seek something al-
> ready found—something whose presence is in some
> way independent of the normal thinking and acting
> creature, something which has already proclaimed
> itself in moments of heightened consciousness—in the
> case of the religious temperament at "conversion."

Setting aside the question of the dynamics of mystical experience and its presumed explanation by "psychology," we
find Richardson focusing on the conscious and willed effort
to further those states of "heightened consciousness." Her
emphasis falls on the fact that such states have already come
of their own accord—"something which has already proclaimed itself"—in a prior "conversion" or its nontheological

equivalent. Richardson's splendid phrase for this kind of life is "a setting forth to seek something already found," and in that phrase lies the formal pattern and controlling figuration of her enormous novel. For *Pilgrimage* is distinguished among autobiographical writings not merely by its consistent figure of "making a journey to the heart of reality" but by its repeated testimony to the central irony of religious experience, that the journey is always to where one already is, that the quest is for what is already possessed if not firmly grasped, that the discovery is always a rediscovery and the illumination a repetition.

Just as Richardson's insight into the mystic journey reveals its ironic circularity, her own accession to this view was a harvest planted long before. Although she came upon a family of Quakers in 1907 and lived among them for longer periods in 1908–1911—in episodes recorded in her final volumes—she had long thought of her "Puritan" ancestry with curiosity as to its determinant influence on her life.[5] She made application, moreover, to *The Pilgrim's Progress* in a way distinctive even in the long tale of its influence upon English writers, particularly self-writers.[6] These delvings into her religious stock went in tandem with her acquisitions among the larger field of mystical and meditative writers, like Thomas à Kempis (*Honeycomb*, ch. 10) and Jacob Boehme (*Tunnel*, ch. 32). Taken together with the Bible, Dante (see below), and such recorders of religious experience as Newman (*Deadlock*, ch. 3), these writings establish for Richardson a cultural heritage roughly comparable with that of autobiographers in earlier centuries and perhaps exceptional among modern writers with an urbane, freethinking upbringing. Her protagonist, Miriam (Henderson), is cast

5. Extended discussions of the Puritans and other dissenting sects occur in *The Tunnel* (ch. 15), *Revolving Lights* (ch. 1), and *March Moonlight* (ch. 3).

6. Direct reference to Bunyan and his work (though not to *Grace Abounding*) is made in *Pointed Roofs* (ch. 12), *Backwater* (ch. 4), and *Honeycomb* (ch. 3).

in the mold not of a prophetess but of a spiritual pilgrim, and despite the independence of mind that caused her work to be proscribed by Spanish censorship during the Franco regime,[7] *Pilgrimage* remains one of the few modern self-writings dedicated to probing ultimate religious truths—despite the vagaries of its complex awareness.

It is this heritage, or a personalized version of it, that Miriam discovers in her *Germanische Reise*, the year spent as a pupil-teacher in Hannover as described in *Pointed Roofs* (*PR*). Although her first impressions are guardedly skeptical of the popular image of Germany, "das deutsche Vaterland—Germany, all woods and mountains and tenderness—Hermann and Dorothea in the dusk of a happy village" (ch. 1, p. 21)—she soon finds its authentic values well preserved. As her school directress reads from the Bible, "her ear was charmed by Fräulein's slow clear enunciation, her pure unaspirated North German. It seemed to suit the narrative—and the narrative was new, vivid and real in this new tongue" (ch. 3, p. 49). Similarly, when a well-known hymn is sung, "It did not sound like a 'proclamation' or an order. It was . . . somehow . . . everyday. The notes seemed to hold her up. This was—Luther—Germany—the Reformation—solid and quiet" (ch. 5, p. 76).

Yet these and other religious treasures associated with Germany and symbolized by the Gothic gables of the title are insufficient to dispel the predominant sense of the loss that has led Miriam to find herself there. The family's declining fortune under the poor stewardship of her would-be-gentleman father has forced her to take the post as a way of cutting the expenses of her maintenance. In her prevailing distress, even her memories of earlier religious experiences are clouded with guilt and despair. Recalling another hymn, "a hymn that even pater liked," she thinks also of her illustrated

7. See the introduction to Richardson's autobiographical "Data for Spanish Publisher," *London Magazine*, 6 (June 1959): 14–19.

Pilgrim's Progress and focuses on its terrors: "I belong to Apollyon . . . a horror with expressionless eyes . . . darting out little spiky flames . . . if only it would come now . . . instead of waiting until the end. . . . 'It's physically impossible' someone had said . . . the only hell thinkable is remorse . . . remorse . . ." (*PR*, ch. 12, pp. 170–71). Yet there are compensations even in the disturbed mind: the memory of a mill wheel seen "somewhere as a child" brought on by a piano piece played by one of the German pupils (ch. 3, p. 44); and the nostalgia evoked by a poem in which her longing for the green wood she has lost is echoed by "Wie grün der Wald den ich durchtritt" (ch. 4, p. 68).

If *Pointed Roofs* is a novel of remembered and partially restored heritage, if not of an Edenic childhood, its moments of anxiety anticipate the predominant sense of loss that suffuses *Backwater*. From apprentice in a Continental school, Miriam turns teacher in a drab North London one—and she will run the full course downward by becoming a governess in *Honeycomb*. We will later be told explicitly what is already evident, that Miriam relates herself to the heroines of Charlotte Brontë. She has acquired a copy of *Villette* when fifteen, and, at certain periods at least, "When I've finished it, I begin again" (*Tunnel*, ch. 30, p. 259).[8] In a full tide of Brontean anguish, the narrative of *Backwater* (*B*) makes its title seem more than colloquial—this is a decadent, swampy place. There are compensations, to be sure, in the kindness of her employers and the friendship of certain pupils, but Miriam's angst is not from the drabness of the conditions or the unfamiliarity of the scene. There is a separation between her and her cherished world:[9] "The reality she had found was leaving her again. Looking up uneasily into the forest of leaves above her head, she found them strange. . . . There

8. Other allusions to *Villette* occur in *Pointed Roofs* (chs. 1, 4) and *Deadlock* (ch. 2).
9. Rosenberg, *Dorothy Richardson*, pp. 78ff., employs such terms as "paradise lost," "fall from grace," and "journey towards redemption" in characterizing the novel.

they were as she had always known them; but between them and herself was her governess's veil, close drawn, holding them sternly away from her" (ch. 6, p. 279).

In this state of mind, Miriam's thoughts turn to suicidal despair of her prospects as a teacher, mixed with a tenacious reassertion of her own identity (*B*, ch. 3, pp. 244–45), to loss of religious faith—and her boss's seriocomic efforts to redeem her (ch. 4, pp. 259ff.), and to feelings both of isolation from others and of strong desire to isolate herself (ch. 8, pp. 317–18). Yet her friend Grace Broom's intense conviction of eternal life during an illness exerts a vital influence on her (ch. 6, pp. 291–92), providing the basis of a long-sustained friendship. Nevertheless, the prevailing anxiety is for the declining fortunes of her family, despite the appearance of suitors for some of her sisters (she loses two herself): "Things had reached their worst, the house going to be sold, pater and mother and Sarah going into lodgings in September, and the maddening helpless worry about mother and all the money for that" (ch. 6, p. 305).

"That" is her mother's derangement, and all through her next instructional venture in *Honeycomb* (*H*) the anxieties of a deeper loss weigh heavily. There are compensations in this job, as well, with its more gracious living conditions, its opportunities to observe the professional bourgeoisie in the suburbs and in the West End, and even the chance to shine—being careful not to shine too much—in society. It is a world whose members self-consciously refer to Bunyan's vision of themselves: "The vagaries of the Fair" (ch. 7, p. 422; ch. 10, p. 446). Called upon to display her cultural assets, Miriam sings Schumann's setting of Heine's "Ich grolle nicht" (ch. 3, p. 374) and can feel up to this refusal of recrimination against her lot. She can savor and take the measure of both "feminine worldliness" and "masculine worldliness" (ch. 3, p. 388). But these sweets of the honeycomb pall with the final break-up of her family (Richardson's father went bankrupt and her mother committed suicide at this point, in

1895).[10] Both facts are omitted from *Honeycomb*, but their impact is fully registered: "Disgrace had closed round her, stifling. 'It's *us*—we're doomed,' she thought, feeling the stigma of her family in her flesh. . . . 'I want to live, even if I slink through life. I will. I don't care, inside. I shall always have myself to be with.' . . . Deeper down was something cool and fresh—endless garden. In happiness it came up and made everything in the world into a garden" (ch. 8, p. 425).

Or almost everything; her mother's death is presented without reference to suicide but with painful details of her religious hysteria and self-destructive despair, and Richardson's own guilt at leaving her mother alone at the time of her death is also recorded obliquely in sibylline advice not to blame herself for what happened (*H*, ch. 11, p. 489). These last pages shift the tenor of the prose toward the mother's Bible-oriented religion as Miriam tries to reassure her with the happier visions of the Old Testament in place of the "dreadful" "reproachfulness" of St. Paul (ch. 11, p. 486). Failing to cheer her mother, Miriam falls into the very same slough of despond as the volume closes: "I am in eternity . . . where their worm dieth not and their fire is not quenched" (ch. 11, p. 490). It is the eternity of hell that is here disclosed, in the language of Isaiah 66, which Jesus repeats three times in Mark 9. From the loss of childhood bliss and the fall into worldliness and its fair, the protagonist here descends into hell.

Miriam enters the workaday world in a way even less protected than Brontë's heroines—or nineteenth-century heroines in general—enjoy. It is the way of the working girl, more specifically, the secretary to an office of Wimpole Street dentists, at a pound per week—rising to twenty-five

10. Beyond summarizing the newspaper accounts, Richardson's biographers have not been able to supply as much insight as one would desire on this central space in Richardson's world; the very lack of available detail testifies to the completeness of the psychic repression.

shillings when she proves more than satisfactory (at times more than they can handle). The life is grim, despite its lighter moments of office by-play and despite the protagonist's more frequent withdrawals into moments of ecstatic joy at the miracle of being, moments which Richardson's readers recognize as her special brand of mysticism.

Common to the middle portions of *Pilgrimage*, particularly in chapter openings, are images of journeying. The working girl making her way through the world is represented time and again in biblical figures of exile, Bunyanesque allusions to pilgrimage, and the Dantesque language of a journey through stratified layers of reality. *Honeycomb* had opened with repeated references to Miriam's reaching the end of her journey, on arriving at the Corries' mansion, though this turned out to be little more than a way station. *The Tunnel* (*Tu*) covers no spacious ground as Miriam's movements are restricted to the short distance from her Bloomsbury room to her nearby office. In place of outdoor movement, this part begins with Miriam's arrival at her rooming house and adds small gestures of locomotion as it proceeds. Indeed, Miriam takes up cycling to further her progress (for 1896 this is a bold stride) and she is almost killed in an accident. She begins making walks through London that will become progressively larger, both in territory covered and prose devoted to them, in later volumes. And she is able self-consciously to proclaim the style and significance of her movements as "wanderyahre" (ch. 4, p. 92). It is her equivalent of the male romantic's assertion of freedom: "I am going to lead a man's life, always getting away" (ch. 26, p. 230).

Yet this is also the period of her torment after the loss of her mother, and *The Tunnel* has been shown to be rife with images of the Dantean *nekuia* or descent into hell.[11] One particularly powerful torment occurs at a definite place in

11. See Fromm, *Dorothy Richardson*, pp. 128–30, for the Dantean allusions and psychic geography of the novel.

the London streets, in Chapter 7, which I quote in its entirety:

> Why must I always think of her in this place? . . . It is always worst just along here. . . . Why do I always forget there's this piece . . . always be hurrying along seeing nothing and then, suddenly, Teetgen's Teas and this row of shops? I can't bear it. I don't know what it is. It's always the same. I always feel the same. It is sending me mad. One day it will be worse. If it gets any worse I shall be mad. Just here. Certainly. Something is wearing out of me. I am meant to go mad. If not, I should not always be coming along this piece without knowing it, whichever street I take. Other people would know the streets apart. I don't know where this bit is or how I get to it. I come every day because I am meant to go mad here. Something that knows brings me here and is making me go mad because I am myself and nothing changes me.
>
> (*Tu*, ch. 7, p. 136)

This is the place of no thoroughfare where Miriam is, psychologically and literally, blocked; she isn't always at this by-street, transfixed before the terrible verbal formula and its mnemonic burden of associations with mother and with guilt, but she will be stuck there again from time to time. To anticipate: Miriam later remembers "the little unlocated street that had haunted her first London years," which draws her "willingly back and back through the intervening spaces of her life to some deserved destruction of mind and body," but she becomes aware of the necessity to get beyond it: "She asked nothing of life but to stay where she was, to go on. . . . London was her pillar of cloud and fire, undeserved, but unsolicited, life's free gift" (*Deadlock*, ch. 3, p. 107). Changing the biblical figure, Miriam will emerge from her Golgotha by a divine sign of directed movement.

Meanwhile, there are other byways down which Miriam lets herself meander for a time: moments of mystic bliss distinctly charged with memories of childhood yet weighted

439

with apocalyptic figures. On a seaside excursion reminiscent of Stephen Dedalus's, she falls asleep and is wakened by boys' voices: "Waking in the daytime is *perfect* happiness. To wake suddenly and fully, nowhere; in paradise. . . . the moment she had just lived was the same, it was exactly the *same* as the first one she could remember, the moment of standing, alone, in bright sunlight on a narrow gravel path in the garden at Babington [her childhood home] between two banks of flowers . . ." (*Tu*, ch. 23, pp. 212–13). Such revenant interludes, too, sustain Miriam on life's way.

The next volume is called an interlude by title, and while it opens with the busyness of journeying to visit her friend Grace Broom, it is largely taken up with moments of marking time. "One would [like to] move like the wind always, a steady human south-west wind, alive, without personality or speech" (*Interim*, ch. 2, p. 321), but her movements are the furtive ones of a boarder—furthered only by the generosity of a mother surrogate, Mrs. Bailey, the proprietress of her boarding house. Yet the world passes through its halls and rooms, and she meets mysterious, cosmopolitan Jews like Mr. Mendizabal, Canadian doctors like von Heber, and bohemian musicians like Mr. Bowdoin. With the world crowding in and her lengthier walks through London wearing her out, what she needs is an oasis, and she discovers one on the Euston Road in the form of Donizetti's, where she is treated decently though she can order only a roll and cocoa.

The result of these movements into the marginal intellectual world on the fringes of Bloomsbury is to take her a step up in her fortunes—whether these are measured psychologically, socially, figuratively, or spiritually. She attends a Dante lecture, which has great impact on her, encouraging her preference for the purgatorial path: "Purgatory. The waters of Lethe and Eunoe, 'forgetfulness and sweet memory'; and then heaven. . . . If life contains moments of paradise you must be in purgatory looking across the vale of asphodel. You can't be in hell. . . . Yet hell would not be hell without a knowledge of heaven. If once you've been in heaven you can never escape. Yet Dante believed in everlasting punishment" (*Interim*, ch. 8, p. 402). Faced with these symbols and conundrums, she takes her redemption where she finds it, in city streets: "Between the houses and the park the road glared wooden grey, dark, baked grey, edged with the shadowless stone grey of the pavement. Summer. Eternity *showing* . . ." (*Interim*, ch. 8, p. 403).

"Miriam ran upstairs narrowly ahead of her thoughts" (*D*, ch. 1, p. 11): *Deadlock* (*D*) begins with this note of movement, and there are indications of ascent out of the depths of psychic despair and marginal socioeconomic existence. Even the deadlock of the title is no fixed bondage but one of the most complex and important relationships of Miriam's life, her friendship with and courtship by a fellow boarder, Michael Shatov. His Russian-Jewish culture both enriches and alienates her, yet the emergence of another major character does wonders for the novel—at last there is a sense that Miriam can conceive an interpersonal world instead of subsuming others in her own. Eventually there is a confession scene reminiscent of the Dostoyevskian novels, which Shatov's name and traits recall, and Miriam reverts to the narrower lines of her religion in rejecting him because of his youthful debaucheries.

Yet Shatov works a wonderful effect on her: "During the last three months [the walls of her room] had not troubled her. They had become transparent, while . . . the figure of Michael Shatov, with Europe stretching wide behind him, had forced them into companionship with all the walls in the world" (*D*, ch. 3, p. 87). And Miriam reciprocates by leading Shatov through her London space with unwonted gusto; after her first beer, taken in a Continental-style *Stube*: "She passed, talking emphatically out into the wide dimly-lit sky-filled East End street, and walked unconscious of fatigue, carrying Mr. Shatov along at his swiftest plunge, mile after mile, in a straight line westward along the opening avenue of her new permanent freedom from occasions" (ch. 3, p. 129). Her sense of journeying becomes fully articulate, as she grasps this period as her *rites de passage*.[12] At one point she is tempted to conclude: "Love *was* the secret of things" (ch. 10, p. 195); at another, her defensive hostility to men leads her to ask: "Why was God in league only with women?" (ch. 11, p. 213). But pervading all her movements, terrestrial and emotional, is her protectiveness of her inner core of self: "The power of London to obliterate personal affairs depended upon unlimited freedom to be still" (ch. 9, p. 188).

Revolving Lights (*RL*) returns the protagonist, as its title suggests, to a multiplicity of experiences in the social world and an intensification of her reflections upon them. The grand opening chapter begins quietly with Miriam at a meeting of the Lycurgan (read: Fabian) Society but then follows her on a mighty progress through London as she thinks over the intellectual influences acting upon her (ch. 1, pp. 240–89). It is a tour de force of the journeying theme, uniting the stream of consciousness with the sequence of movements through an urban network of associations. Foremost among the influences she must sort out is the one that will dominate her sexual life—and a later volume—her relations with Hypo Wilson (read: H. G. Wells). His impact is by force of artistic personality, and he sets her mind working on matters of signal concern to her eventual vocation: speculations on fiction—especially on Conrad, whose powers Wilson/Wells cannot touch (ch. 1, pp. 275–76); affirmation of the Puritan element in her heritage ("Their roots in life were deeper and harder and the light from the Heavenly City fell upon their foreheads *because* they struggled in the gloom"—(ch. 1, p. 249); opinions on sex, politics, and the personal relationships that are filling up her life. Yet at the close of her ambulatory meditation she comes upon the Woolfian figure of an old crone who returns her to herself: "It was herself, set in her path and waiting through all the

12. The language of journeying occurs throughout *Deadlock*, e.g., in chs. 2, 9, 11.

years. Her beloved hated secret self, known to this old woman" (ch. 1, p. 289).

Another of the cultural enlargements that Miriam undertakes during this period is a visit to a Quaker meeting house. The experience is disappointing, the people she meets are marked by ordinary human flaws, and the event makes no sharp impact on the form of the novel or the course of her life. But it provides a first inkling of what she is to discover: "To have been born amongst these people; to know at home and in the church a *shared* religious life. They were in heaven already" (*RL*, ch. 2, p. 326).

Again there is movement to open the next volume, *The Trap* (*Tr*), but as the title proclaims, it is to a place of no movement. Specifically, Miriam moves to Flaxman's Court or, as Richardson did, to Woburn Buildings, now charmingly restored but then a slum. She moves in, to make matters worse, with a barely known acquaintance, who makes a poor companion, especially for one herself so uncompanionable. The only compensation she can find amid the din and squalor is the sight of William Butler Yeats framed in his window across the way—for Yeats did live there during these years. There is also a forceful encounter with the prose of Henry James as she reads *The Ambassadors* with admiration and disdain. Though a discussion of Schopenhauer leads her to conclude that "nothing can ever be expressed in words" (ch. 4, p. 463), her "pride in discovering the secrets of [James's] technique" leads her to see that "style was something beyond good and evil" (ch. 4, pp. 409–10). Intellectual currents flow swiftly through her cul-de-sac, but her affirmation of self remains the same, though touched by frustration: "The shadow of Nietzsche, the problem of free-love, . . . the triple tangle of art, sex, and religion. . . . But she was out in the dance of youth. . . . She was ready now to drop all props and wander forth. . . . But the kingdom of heaven is within. Communist colonies were not a solution of anything. Yet the kingdom within is a little grey and lonely. Marriage is no solution, only a postponement" (ch. 6, p.

482). She feels the flight of time in the vanishing of another spring but has an intimation of her power to arrest it, though at present only by memory: "Every one had had those moments of reality in forgetfulness. Quickly passing. Growing afterwards longer than other moments, spreading out over the whole season; representing it in memory" (ch. 8, p. 498). At present all she can determine on is the need to leave Flaxman's Court, using Stephen Dedalus's words: "Away. Away . . ." (ch. 9, p. 509). She will not, however, make even this short flight until a later volume.

Oberland (*O*) opens, like the other volumes, with a scene of traveling, but new images enter on this, Miriam's second, Continental voyage. A new register of language takes over when she reaches Switzerland and prepares to take leave of her traveling companions: "And she liked them, was attached to them as fellow adventurers, fellow survivors of the journey. The falling into the trap of travellers' freemasonry was inevitable: a fatal desire to know the whence and the whither. . . . The station was in a wilderness. . . . There was no sign from where she stood of any upward track. Sheds, dumped upon a waste of snow beyond which mountains filled the sky and barred the way" (ch. 1, p. 23). In such a setting and with such a figurative sense of her surroundings, both the protagonist and the reader are prepared for the event that follows her first night at her hotel: "From which she awoke in light that seemed for a moment to be beyond the confines of earth. It was as if all her life she had travelled towards this radiance, and was now within it, clear of the past, at an ultimate destination" (ch. 3, p. 49).

The vision is comparable with other mystic moments of joy in the light that have brightened Miriam's life all through *Pilgrimage*; the conviction of having reached a resting place at a heavenly level is "for a moment" and "as if." Yet the event marks a turning point in the life of the heroine and in the form of the novel. The point of epiphany at a high place carries not only trains of mythic significance but an invigorating infusion of health. From this point, Miriam will have her descents and her further wanderings, but she will carry on with greater emotional fortitude if not yet spiritual conviction: "And this miracle of renewal was the work of a single night" (*O*, ch. 3, p. 58). The reason is not far to seek; she has been restored to her past: "The dawn had wakened to remind her. Watching the coming of the light, she had been restored to her first communion with it. . . . this winter paradise would go forward, brightening her days with the possibility of reunion" (ch. 5, p. 98). We dare not be sure of Richardson's meaning here, but it seems that the epiphany is not only a return to childhood and an integration of scattered moments of a life, nor only a renewed "first communion" of mystical contact, if not religious ritual, but also an opening to communication with the departed—"the possibility of reunion." Miriam, who has never doubted eternity because of her severe misgivings about the reality of time, has always faced it as a lonely pleasure, an indulgence in the bliss of subjectivity. Now it shadows forth the prospect of shared existence, perhaps with her mother. Although salvation is not assured, Miriam has no doubts about "her health that was restored for evermore since she had seen the light on the mountains. . . . 'I could remember anything I wanted to, and see *into* things'" (*Dawn's Left Hand* [*DLH*], ch. 3, p. 149).

By the time she came to write *Dawn's Left Hand* (1931), Richardson was empowered to deal with her own obsessive repetition, in art if not in life. Her protagonist returns from Switzerland with the determination to marry neither of the men who have absorbed her: "In Hypo there was no sense of eternity; nor in Michael, except for [his Jewish] race, an endless succession of people made in God's image, all dead or dying" (ch. 3, p. 155). As she walks from her doctor-friend's office, she comes again to the uncanny place:

> Teetgen's Teas, she noted, in grimed, gilt lettering above a dark and dingy little shop. . . .

Teetgen's Teas. And behind, two turnings back,
was a main thoroughfare. And just ahead was another.
And the streets of this particular district arranged
themselves in her mind, each stating its name, making
a neat map.

And *this* street, still foul and dust-filled, but full
now also of the light flooding down upon and the air
flowing through the larger streets with which in her
mind it was clearly linked, was the place where in the
early years she would suddenly find herself lost and
helplessly aware of what was waiting for her eyes the
moment before it appeared: the grimed gilt lettering
that *forced me to gaze into the darkest moment of my
life and to remember that I had forfeited my share in
humanity for ever and must go quietly and alone until
the end.*

*And now their power has gone. They can bring
back only the memory of a darkness and horror, to
which, then, something has happened, begun to hap-*
(ch. 3, pp. 155–56; emphasis in original)

This is the most distinctive of the growing indications
that "*something has happened, begun to happen,*" but other
transcriptions of the by-now-familiar magical moments also
suggest a new tonality in Miriam's mental life. She visits
friends and recalls "that morning when I first noticed a
shadow lying on the *wrong side* of a gable. Across the silent
early freshness of the square, feeling the remains of night
and dawn in the deep scent and colour of its leaves, drinking
its strange rich lonely air that seemed in the heart of London
to come from a paradise as deep as any to be found in distant
country lanes and woods" (*DLH*, ch. 8, p. 209). Not only
natural but domestic sights provoke hyperbole: "She stood
looking into heaven. On the hearth . . . stood a copper kettle,
quiet and bright and beautiful, telling, more plainly than a
voice could speak, of the world surrounding the uncertainties of nursery life, kind and careful and peaceful and full
of love and forgiveness, now, when no one was there, and
making her know that this was what it really was when

every one was there" (ch. 10, pp. 249–50). She sees another fireplace in "the heaven of downstairs life" and continues:

> Only these two; glowing eternally. From the un-
> desired effort of recalling more than these spontaneous
> offerings of memory, that promised if she lingered
> with them, to recall in perfect fullness the years lying
> beyond the barrier raised by the horror that had
> wrenched her life in twain. . . . To-night, for the
> first time, her separate existence was consciously pre-
> vailing against its glamour, reaching forward away
> from it to something that would set it in the past.

Finally, there are further excursions to such splendid scenes as a ruined abbey in Yorkshire:

> Rievaulx suddenly there below us, on the floor of the
> green valley. Heartmelting love and gratitude . . . for
> seeing this left message, and seeing at different angles
> the oblong of crumbling stone, arch beside arch, in
> each of its different perfections, towards those who
> long ago had expressed in this perfection their own
> perfect certainties and their enduring joy, and to
> those, in whom deep down these certainties and this
> joy were still persisting, who had brought me to see
> it. . . .   (ch. 10, pp. 255–56)

Yet though *Dawn's Left Hand* closes with another of Miriam's sweeping seizures of the totality of her London—"Disadvantage had fallen from her and burden, leaving a calm delightful sense of power" (ch. 10, p. 267)—she must still learn how to make her access of insight and self-mastery into a way of life. Wilson/Wells advises three simple pro-cedures: "You want a *green solitude*. An infant. Then you'd be able to write a book" (ch. 9, p. 238). *Clear Horizon* (*CH*) (1935) tells of Miriam's steps along these lines, but they are not so easily taken. For the first, her determination to move away from Hypo's sphere of influence brings resis-tance from him, together with advice on writing "the first dental novel" (ch. 10, p. 396). As for his second expedient, details are omitted from *Pilgrimage*, but Richardson went only part way toward bearing Wells's child; she had a miscarriage in 1907. The equivalent in *Clear Horizon* is the breakdown that Miriam undergoes or verges on. Details are sketchy, both for Richardson's and for Miriam's medical histories,[13] but the significance of the period stands out more clearly when set against the corresponding ones in autobiographical tradition. This is the time of crisis when the horizon is clear but the way to it hidden or too difficult.

It is a period of leave-taking of the old life as Miriam divests herself not only of Hypo's sexual and personal domination but also of her job—"Ten years. One long moment of attention, more or less strained, day and night . . ." (*CH*, ch. 8, p. 386)—and of her closest friends, Shatov and the impulsive feminist Amabel, by the happy expedient of marrying them off to each other. Putting away the past is to leave oneself empty, though open to the future. There is at least the hope of finding the right place to rest: "Driving through her . . . came the realization that the 'green solitude' recommended by Hypo and spurned because every imagined leaf and grass-blade had looked so dreary when thought of in the presence of his outlook on life, might yet be hers perforce" (ch. 1, p. 300).

Miriam, like Dorothy Richardson, finds the right spot with a Quaker farm family in Sussex. It is a return to origins: the trees "looked into the depths of her, the unchanged depths awaiting them since childhood" (*Dimple Hill* [*DH*], ch. 2, p. 413). The recovery is not only of the past but of its values: "She saw upon the jocund, sympathetically listening grass-blades at her feet a vestige of the vanished radiance and looked thence into her mind and found there, bathed in its full light, the far-off forgotten world from which she had fled and, with a last glance at the sunlit trees, turned to run and seek it there" (ch. 2, pp. 420–21). Although she does

13. See Fromm, *Dorothy Richardson*, pp. 290–99, for what evidence exists on Richardson's condition and her evasive—yet dogged—references to it in her fiction.

not make her equation of the Quaker family and her own explicit, there is clearly a renewal of her earliest ties; when she receives news of the Roscorlas, her fingertips "remained steady, clasped about the letter that was to open the way to the richest depth of shared life imaginable upon earth, and thrilled with joy as they lifted and let it fall" (ch. 3, p. 430). With this "perfect human association," she arrives in "heaven" (ch. 4, p. 433).

The topography of her spiritual space has room for subdivisions as she finds herself "launched on the journey from her own world established in the room she had just left, to breakfast downstairs at the centre of the universe" (*DH*, ch. 5, p. 437). This figurative terminology becomes linked to terrestrial locations when she inspects the farm and its surrounding hills:

> "I never saw anything quite like your view," she said, "the way it spreads all round the horizon, and the huge distance across it to that green rim against the sky."
> "It's quite a way off," [Alfred Roscorla] said meditatively. . . . "It's quite a bit higher than we are. We're three hundred feet up. . . . From sea-level, not from the centre of the earth."   (ch. 5, pp. 446–47)

This precision about earthly measurements hardly serves to deflate Miriam's enthusiasm—the reverse when he goes on to connect the hills with the medieval peasant rebellion of Jack Cade. Beyond its historical associations, the enclosed prospect serves as a welcome limit of her horizons:[14] "No longer stretching out across the world and carrying her gently down towards an unpeopled sleep whence she would awake to renewed, impersonal adoration of her surroundings, [the farm's] radius was reduced to visible limits, ceasing

14. Miriam's awareness of her propensity for the horizon view and the composed limitations it entails is suggested in a previous passage: "All the while the party itself stood in my mind, left there, in exactly the same place on the horizon as when I had first contemplated it. I put things on the horizon and leave them there" (*DLH*, ch. 10, p. 253).

northwards where Jack Cade, life in hand to fight injustice, forever marched along the road. . . . she felt time cease. Her stretch of freedom . . . expanded now to infinity" (ch. 5, p. 449). Yet she does find it possible to extend her associative and literal view to the sea: "This discovery of the sea's nearness, the certainty of being able sometimes to see it from afar, seemed now to make perfect the circle of which this gentle hill-top was the centre . . ." (ch. 5, p. 466).

In such a setting and under these terms of figuration, the simple dignity of the Quaker family becomes elevated to a sacramental stature. Although their ritual piety is downplayed—in keeping with the tenets of their faith—at a climactic moment Miriam's view of them attains some afflatus. As the family prepares to end the day, Richard Roscorla reads from the Scriptures:

> The deep, vibrant monotone, simple, childlike, free from unfelt, tiresomely elucidatory expressiveness, leaving the words to speak for themselves, was the very sound of the Old Testament, the wistful sound of Hebrew piety. . . . leaving only the breathing spirit of their inspiration, sending the hearers down and down into depths within themselves, kindred to the depths whence it came, till the emotion creating this scripture became current and the forms seated in the golden lamplight fellows of those who had brought it forth, sharers of its majesty; a heritage bringing both humility and pride.
> "The valleys also are covered over with corn; they shout for joy, they also sing."
> (DH, ch. 5, p. 474; quoting Psalm 65)

This encounter marks Miriam's redirection in spirit although it makes no decisive shift in the outward forms of her life. It is a conversion to where one already is, and even the journey by which she arrives at this point is renewed at the moment of arrival. Gazing into a flower, the protagonist "had the feeling of being on a journey that was both pathway and destination" (DH, ch. 6, p. 485). Her journey is

not at an end, then, but becomes meaningful and justified
by the ends which it gathers along the way. Nor is the journey to continue only in the external world while the inner
world remains at rest, for even here there is continued exploration: "Be still and *know*. . . . Bidding her mind be still,
she felt herself once more at work, in company, upon an all-
important enterprise. This time her breathing was steady
and regular and the labour of journeying, down through the
layers of her surface being, a familiar process" (ch. 7, p. 498).

Although the volume closes inconclusively, with Rachel
Mary Roscorla taking pleasure in the prospect of a match
between Miriam and her brother Richard and with continued understandings and misunderstandings to be gone
through with her London friends, the protagonist has
reached a point of restoration from her past ills, if not complete recovery from (or of) her past, and a more steady
absorption in the ongoing life around her—later called "current existence, the ultimate astonisher" (*March Moonlight*,
ch. 4, p. 611). At this point, Miriam is highly skeptical of
literary efforts to express her achievement; when she is advised to "write the confessions of a modern woman," she
thinks: "Everything would be left out that is always there,
preceding and accompanying and surviving the drama of
human relationships; the reality from which people move
away as soon as they closely approach and expect each other
to be all in all" (*DH*, ch. 8, p. 525).

At this point, it would seem, *Pilgrimage* is indeed complete in the form announced by its title; a great autobiographical novel stands achieved. There are even gestures of
closure in the text that can be ascribed to no editorial hand
but must reflect Richardson's own sense of her enterprise:
"Farewell, farewell to youth. Recklessly she was plunging
ahead, parting life's clumped and screening leafage, breaking
through" (*DH*, ch. 13, p. 546). And although the last page
of *Dimple Hill* suggests that Miriam is to go off on another

Alpine journey, this would be consistent with the facts of Richardson's life—she made another mountain trip, to Vaud, not Oberland—between her first brief stay at Windmill Hill and her later extended ones between 1908 and 1911. Both continued journeying and extended meditational retirement are made compatible in the frame of mind established here.

But if the novel is figuratively completed, life goes on. Richardson was always at the mercy of the twin magnets of autobiographical writing, the pull to chronicle the past and the pull to compose it as a work of art. Her art-work achieved, her occupation threatening to be gone, she continued to write—performing another of the functions of self-writing, that of keeping oneself alive. As long as she was writing the continuation of her life, she was alive as a writer, and if this reciprocity had no theoretical limits, she could arbitrarily set one at 1915, at the publication of *Pointed Roofs*. There are no signs in the text that this novel is in the works but signs enough that Miriam is busy thinking through the challenges of becoming a writer.

Alas for novelistic—or autobiographical—form, she is also busy with the thousand other loose ends of her life, and *March Moonlight*, Richardson's uncompleted, posthumously published thirteenth volume is the most scattered, ill conceived, and bathetic of finales. Miriam develops an intense crush on a woman met in Switzerland, and for the first time we sense the homosexual urgencies that have all along been latent but have never been allowed to supervene in prior volumes. She continues to mediate the affairs of her paired-off friends, but they show themselves not only poorly linked in their marriage but also dwindling into suburbanization, for example, in sloughing off their shared passion for Emerson and sloughing off Miriam in the bargain. Her relations with the Roscorlas come to grief as sex and inhibition rear their heads; Richard Roscorla is not the marrying kind, it would seem, and Rachel Mary's friendship for Miriam disintegrates under the obscure stresses of possessiveness and disappointment. But the greatest disappointments of *March*

Moonlight are not in the events but in the prose; in place of the arts of representing consciousness that Richardson had explored as far as any modern master, we find large blocks of authorial summary in the detached, past tense as though the author were rushing to reach her stated goals without much attention to the minute particulars of moment-to-moment awareness. But if the latter is missing, where is *Pilgrimage*?

In 1912, as Dorothy Richardson was about to embark on her lifelong enterprise of writing her life, she found it necessary to seek new scenes and went to stay with friends at St. Ives, Cornwall.[15] Eventually she would spend most of her remaining years at various spots in Cornwall, with her lifelong companion, her husband Allan Odle. There is, perhaps, nothing to wonder at in this as the remote country provided many an artist with cheap accommodations during this period—the Lawrences and Murrys, etc., were close at hand in these years. Yet without ascertainable direct contact either with the literary society around her or with the vestiges of the milieu in which her closest avatar, Virginia Woolf, had been shaped, Richardson pursued her course, turning her life into a work of art, although sometimes subordinating art in the effort to tell that story whole.

15. See Fromm, *Dorothy Richardson*, pp. 63–65, for the details of her residence and a hint of the uncanny parallel with Woolf—and with Woolf's similar withdrawal into childhood images of seaside happiness.

20

"To Return to St. Ives"*

WOOLF'S AUTOBIOGRAPHICAL WRITINGS

———

Virginia Woolf completed no autobiography that can stand alone beside her name, and even the novel that approaches closest to her personal experience only debatably qualifies as autobiographical fiction. Of late, the publication of her letters and journals has brought home how much of her art turns on a few central facts subtly varied in a series of imaginative transformations. Throughout her life these facts remain connected not only with the governing figures of Woolf's imagination but also with the main lines of autobiographical tradition.

In 1926, Virginia Woolf and her husband made a Christmas holiday trip to Cornwall. She wrote a number of brief letters about the trip, one of them to her assistant at the Hogarth Press, Angus Davidson:

> It is bitterly cold; we are motoring over the moors to
> Lands End and other remote places. We look down

* Quoted from Virginia Woolf, "A Sketch of the Past," in *Moments of Being: Unpublished Autobiographical Writings*, ed. Jeanne Schulkind (Sussex, 1976), p. 115; hereafter cited as "Sketch."

into the heart of the Atlantic from our bedroom. All
my facts about Lighthouses are wrong. . . . This is
divine country—perhaps a little austere.[1]

There is nothing to mark the letter as significant, merely a
passing reference to the work she was then completing, *To
the Lighthouse*, where such a building is a central element of
the landscape and of the formal design. It is well known that
Woolf drew much of the detail for this novel from her
childhood vacations in Cornwall,[2] and we might have expected this trip to bring forth greater enthusiasm or more
complex associations. But these brief remarks to an employee
are barely expanded in letters of the same week to her sister,
Vanessa Bell, and to her then-intimate friend, Vita Sackville-
West. In one of these we learn that she is "putting the last
touches to my novel" (*Letters*, Vol. III, pp. 311–12; Dec. 29,
1926); she alternates between a writer's twin views of his
latest book—"inconceivably bad" and "best thing I ever
wrote." How then are we to explain Woolf's later diary
statement that "after *Lighthouse* I was, I remember, nearer
suicide, seriously, than since 1913"?[3]

There are a number of ways around this mystery. One
does not, perhaps, write about one's drift toward suicide to
one's beloved or to one's sister, whether to avoid causing
them grief or to prevent them from interfering with one's
plans. And there might be no mystery at all if we knew more
about the timing of Woolf's suicidal impulse. Her "after
Lighthouse" may refer to the preceding autumn when she
finished a first draft of the novel. There is a long diary entry

1. *The Letters of Virginia Woolf*, ed. Nigel Nicolson and Joanne
Trautmann (London and New York, 1975–), III, 310; Dec. 25, 1926;
hereafter cited as *Letters*.

2. For a downgrading of the autobiographical elements of the novel,
see Ian Gregor, "Spaces: *To the Lighthouse*," in *The Author in His
Work: Essays on a Problem in Criticism*, ed. L. L. Martz and Aubrey
Williams (New Haven and London, 1978), pp. 375–89.

3. *A Writer's Diary: Being Extracts from the Diary of Virginia
Woolf*, ed. Leonard Woolf (London, 1953), p. 229; Oct. 16, 1934; hereafter cited as *WD*.

called "A State of Mind," dated September 15, 1926, in which her depression is recorded, but by the time Woolf finished revising her novel in January, her spirits seem restored. Indeed, even by the end of that depressed September, despair had turned to something calmer, and she was able to go on with the rewriting. In her diary, she wrote of looking out over the ocean to envision her subject in the novel:

> I wished to add some remarks to this, on the mystical side of this solitude; how it is not oneself but something in the universe that one's left with. It is this that is frightening & exciting in the midst of my profound gloom, depression, boredom, whatever it is: One sees a fin passing far out. What image can I reach to convey what I mean? Really there is none I think. The interesting thing is that in all my feeling & thinking I have never come up against this before. Life is, soberly & accurately, the oddest affair; has in it the essence of reality.[4]

To shift the date of Woolf's suicidal depression to the previous fall, as she completed the first draft of *To the Lighthouse*, serves only to deepen the mystery of her bland recording of the Christmas trip to the scene of that work. She had anesthetized her response to the place of her most powerful childhood memories; she had transformed the lasting wound of her life into art, achieving an aesthetic distance measured, in her diary entry, by the vision of a "fin passing far out"—an object out at sea observed from a secure and elevated place on land. "We look down into the heart of the Atlantic from our bedroom," she had written in that Christmas letter.

Woolf was not always so lofty in her return trips to Cornwall. On an earlier revisitation with her sister, ten years

---

4. *The Diary of Virginia Woolf*, ed. Anne O. Bell and Andrew McNeillie (London, 1977–), Vol. III, p. 113; Sept. 30, 1926; hereafter cited as *Diary*.

after their mother's death, she wrote: "It is a strange dream to come back here again. The first night we groped our way up to Talland House [their summer home] in the dark, and just peeped at it from behind the Escalonia hedge. It was a ghostly thing to do: it all looked quite unchanged. Old people meet us and stop and talk to us, and remember us playing on the beach" (*Letters*, Vol. I, pp. 203–04; Aug. 13[?], 1905). Like ghosts, the sisters return to the place where they once lived, but the uncanny sensations such revenants evoke is felt by the sisters themselves not by the old people who remember them.

An even more energetic effort to return to the past and recover its life is found in three letters Woolf wrote from Cornwall after striking out on the spur of the moment to spend Christmas there in 1909. It is a country of the mind: "I have no pocket handkerchief, watch key, notepaper, spectacles, cheque book, looking glass, or coat. However, it is a hot spring day. . . . As for the beauty of this place, it surpasses every other season. . . . it is very warm, bright blue sky and sea, and no wind and smells heavenly" (*Letters*, Vol. I, pp. 414–15; Dec. 25, 1909); "Then there is the [Godrevy] Lighthouse, seen as through steamy glass, and a grey flat where the sea is. There is no moon, or stars, but the air is soft as down, and one can see trees on the ridge of the road, and the shapes of everything without any detail. . . . Thinking it over is the pleasant thing. . . . One gradually sees shapes and thinks oneself in the middle of a world" (*Letters*, Vol. I, p. 416; Dec. 26, 1909); "I start early tomorrow, and leave all this. It is very melancholy to be shut up in London again. Only the delights of human intercourse reconcile me to it" (*Letters*, Vol. I, p. 418; Dec. 27, 1909). We may join her in regretting the necessity to return to London, social life, and adult existence, but she had already achieved the mode of vision that was to be the form in which she rendered experience in her fiction: "One gradually sees shapes and thinks oneself in the middle of a world."

Not only are the aesthetic distance and the formal ordering of *To the Lighthouse* attributable to Woolf's manner of
responding to the scene of her childhood but also innumerable details of the setting and characterization in the novel.
The "ghostly" point of view of the revisiting sisters becomes
the disembodied perspective of the "little airs" in the fiction,
who make their deliberate way over the discrete objects of
the sleeping house. The *donnée* of the plot—a boy's frustrated
desire to make a trip to the lighthouse in the bay below the
family's summer house—is a remembered event. As reported
in the domestic newspaper the Stephen children produced
during these years, "Master Adrian Stephen was much disappointed at not being allowed to go."[5] Other details of the
standard biography identify the habitual visitors who were
eventually called upon to sit for their portraits. Even the
grand total of the eight children of the Ramsay family can
be numerically equaled, if not individually matched, with the
combined offspring of Leslie Stephen's and his wife's prior
and current marriages.

But this autobiographical novel is not written from the
author's reminiscental perspective; the point of view is not
the child's but the parents'—how it must have been for them.
Above all, the fiction represents the author's parents in a deliberate and consummate act of detailed mimesis. There is the
father's irascible temperament, his emotional dependence on
his wife, his progress through "R" in an intellectual project
(a philosophical argument in the novel; a dictionary of national biography in Leslie Stephen's case), his homely preference for simple fisherfolk and for the author who understood
them (Scott), his heroic stature as he dramatizes his agnosticism in a gesture when leaping from a boat at the goal of the
family voyage to the lighthouse—as if he were saying: "There
is no God." As for the mother, not only descriptive touches
but internal monologues render her beauty, her awareness of
it, her omnipresent care, her bounty and constraint in assuag-

5. See Quentin Bell, *Virginia Woolf: A Biography*, 2 vols. (London,
1972), I, 32; hereafter cited as Bell.

ing her husband's crying need for reassurance, her powers of creating social harmony, and her large recesses of unrecoverable inner life.

Like every autobiographical novelist, Woolf makes a number of careful displacements in the time and setting of the action so that it does not directly implicate her as a participant. For Cornwall in the west of England we have the Isle of Skye in the west of Scotland, though experienced commentators have emphasized that the landscape is Cornish not Scottish. Despite or because of her ignorance about lighthouses, Woolf is free to make the Godrevy light of her childhood summers into a dramatic focus of desire and fulfillment and into a shadowy emblem of reality and its appearances. Such minor distortions of factual detail are less the mark of fantasizing or evasion of the past than they are choices made in the interest of arriving closer to the truth of personal experience.

Of greater significance than the shifting of place is the alteration of the historical time of the novel from the pre-World War I era to a decade that encompasses the war. The period in Woolf's life covered by Part I may be said to have ended in 1895. (As Julia Stephen died in May 1895, the summer of 1894 was the last spent by the Stephen family at St. Ives.) Her father died in February 1904, some ten years after that last summer, and this may have suggested the ten-year lapse from the first part to the last, in which he is seen as pathetically alone but at the height of paternal stature. Besides the mother's, two children's deaths mark the novel. Prue's death was suggested by that of Woolf's stepsister, Stella Duckworth Hills, who died in 1897 as a young woman just blossoming when struck down early in marriage. The model for Andrew's death was the loss of Woolf's younger brother, Thoby, who died of typhoid fever in 1906. But Andrew is killed in World War I, a datum provided, like Prue's death, in a baldly bracketed, flat statement inserted into the flowing prose of ongoing life. The displacement from the end of the nineteenth century to a ten-year span reaching from shortly before to shortly after the first great war of modern annihilation gives Woolf the opportunity of generalizing from her personal loss to the cataclysmic losses of Western civilization.

Despite these historical and geographical shifts, *To the Lighthouse* remains an intensely personal novel, on intimate terms with the inner reaches of its characters and thus profoundly revealing of their originals, the members of Woolf's family. Soon after reading *To the Lighthouse*, her sister Vanessa Bell wrote Woolf:

> Anyhow it seemed to me in the first part of the book you have given a portrait of mother which is more like her to me than anything I could ever have conceived of as possible. It is almost painful to have her so raised from the dead. You have made one feel the extraordinary beauty of her character, which must be the most difficult thing in the world to do. It was like meeting her again with oneself grown up & on equal terms. . . .   (Bell, Vol. II, p. 128)

Woolf described her achievement in the same vein, but for her the presences of her parents were not merely "raised from the dead," as Vanessa put it, but "laid"—in the sense of spectres laid to rest. On completing the novel, she wrote: "I used to think of [father] & mother daily; but writing The Lighthouse laid them in my mind" (*Diary*, Vol. III, p. 208; Nov. 28, 1928). It was only much later that she explained what this involved:

> Until I was in the forties . . . the presence of my mother obsessed me. I could hear her voice, see her, imagine what she would do or say as I went about my day's doings. She was one of the invisible presences who after all play so important a part in every life. This influence . . . has never been analysed in any of those Lives which I so much enjoy reading, or very superficially.
>   . . . Then one day walking round Tavistock Square I made up, as I sometimes make up my books, *To the*

Lighthouse; in a great, apparently involuntary, rush.
One thing burst into another. . . . Why then? I have no
notion. But I wrote the book very quickly; and when
it was written, I ceased to be obsessed by my mother.
I no longer hear her voice; I do not see her.

("Sketch," pp. 80–81)

Some part of her success in laying the ghost of her mother
may be accountable to the enactment in the novel itself of
the ritual process of raising the dead. In the person of a
character with whom she closely identifies, the painter Lily
Briscoe, Woolf records a sequence of artistic activities which
issue in a vision of the departed, present again in the place of
one's most vivid memory of her. The climactic scene is an
enactment of the power of art, through its controlled use of
visual perceptions, to give calm and permanence to one's
memory of the lost world.

The artist character spends the final part of the novel
painting while trying to focus her memories of the woman
who has made the family cohere in the first part, ten years
earlier. As Lily paints:

Suddenly the window at which she was looking was
whitened by some light stuff behind it. . . . so as to
throw an odd-shaped triangular shadow over the step.
It altered the composition of the picture a little. It
was interesting. It might be useful. . . . One must keep
on looking without for a second relaxing the intensity
of emotion, the determination not to be put off, not to
be bamboozled. One must hold the scene—so—in a
vice and let nothing come in and spoil it. . . . Ah, but
what had happened? Some wave of white went over
the window pane. . . . Mrs. Ramsay—it was part of her
perfect goodness to Lily—sat there quite simply, in
the chair, flicked her needles to and fro, knitted her
reddish-brown stocking, cast her shadow on the step.
There she sat.[6]

6. *To the Lighthouse* (London, Hogarth Press collected edition
[1927]), pp. 309–10.

461

When the painter observes the space the dead mother once occupied, a movement of the air (one of the "little airs"?) causes a "wave of white" to move across the window, producing a useful and interesting "shadow." In this new visual development Mrs. Ramsay appears, less as a mystical presence than as an aesthetic object, a chiaroscuro relationship of light and dark. It was by a method similar to the one the painter employs that Woolf achieved an allaying of her personal ghosts, transforming them into aesthetic objects in *To the Lighthouse*.

Woolf's following return to St. Ives was indirect as her next major novel maintains a highly abstract rendering of human life and loss. *The Waves* (1931) is less an autobiographical novel than a mythic drama of the stages of human existence, though it contains unmistakable personal references not only to her family but to such friends as Lytton Strachey, Leonard Woolf, and perhaps T. S. Eliot. Yet the Cornish coast is there from the first pages' panorama of imminent dawn over the sea and the ensuing close notations of the changing light in a child's bedroom. These sensations are markedly similar to those she set down in a subsequent attempt to write her autobiography, which I shall consider shortly. For the moment we need to estimate the degree of authorial presence in the scenes from Woolf's own life with which *The Waves* is filled.

While preparing to write this experimental fiction (tentatively titled *The Moths*), Woolf worked out her ideas in her diary:

> Now about this book, The Moths. How am I to begin it? . . . I am not trying to tell a story. Yet perhaps it might be done in that way. A mind thinking. . . . But there must be more unity between each scene than I can find at present. Autobiography it might be called. . . . But who is she [the "mind thinking"]? I am very anxious that she should have no name. I don't want a

Lavinia or a Penelope: I want "She." But that becomes arty. . . .

However, I now begin to see the Moths rather too clearly, or at least strenuously, for my comfort. I think it will begin like this: dawn; the shells on a beach; I don't know—voices of cock & nightingale; & then all the children at a long table—lessons. The beginning. . . . this shall be Childhood; but it must not be MY childhood. . . .

(*Diary*, Vol. III, pp. 229–30, 236; May 28 and June 23, 1929)

The dual impulse toward personal memories and toward impersonal generalization shows up at once: "Autobiography it might be called. . . . I am very anxious that she should have no name. . . . I now begin to see the Moths rather too clearly . . . for my comfort . . . this shall be Childhood; but it must not be MY childhood."

When she had completed the last of the long internal monologues of her six characters—monologues of which *The Waves* is almost exclusively composed—Woolf wrote a diary passage of high exultation:

Here in the few minutes that remain, I must record, heaven be praised, the end of *The Waves*. I wrote the words O Death fifteen minutes ago, having reeled across the last ten pages with some moments of such intensity and intoxication that I seemed only to stumble after my own voice, or almost, after some sort of speaker (as when I was mad) I was almost afraid, remembering the voices that used to fly ahead. Anyhow, it is done; and I have been sitting these 15 minutes in a state of glory, and calm, and some tears, thinking of Thoby and if I could write Julian Thoby Stephen 1881–1906 on the first page. I suppose not.

(*WD*, p. 169; Feb. 7, 1931)

Critics have usually connected one of the novel's main themes—the passage of time and the losses of death—with Woolf's brother Thoby, who died many years before at an early age; the nonspeaking but central figure of *The Waves* is Percival, who dies a heroically promising but unfulfilled young man. The larger implication of Woolf's memorializing of her brother is that her total recall of their childhood and youth is his fitting monument—at the head of which the funerary inscription "Julian Thoby Stephen 1881–1906" might stand. Yet the fact that these memories were produced and their expression dictated by what Woolf calls "the voices that used to fly ahead"—now leading her so that she "seemed only to stumble after my own voice"—sounds ominous for her state of mind. Woolf makes the connection ("as when I was mad") and recognizes the danger ("I was almost afraid"). Still, the outcome of this return to the past is cathartic and exalting: "I have been sitting these 15 minutes in a state of glory, and calm, and some tears." For the closing pages of *The Waves* return to the setting on the Cornish coast and transform it into a universal symbol of the rhythm of life and death: "*The waves broke on the shore.*"

The book Virginia Woolf was writing when she died in March 1941 was her autobiography though she called it only a sketch. She had the month before substantially completed her last novel, *Between the Acts*, and had begun a "history of literature" tentatively titled "Anon" (of which numerous drafts remain in the Berg Collection of the New York Public Library). But since April 1939 she had been writing intermittently a work that, though incomplete, reaches to seventy-three printed pages and constitutes an extended narrative of the past—unlike the briefer memoirs and public lectures that are collected with it in the recent volume *Moments of Being*. "A Sketch of the Past," as the piece is titled in this collection, is also an extended meditation on the autobiographer's art, one of the most illuminating statements of the grandeur and misery of self-writing of which we are possessed. Beyond its integrity as a work of art in its own right, it is a series of footnotes to her fiction, its parallel passages incessantly jolting the reader's memory of the finest moments of her artistry, now rendered uncanny by our awareness that they are often translated from memory.

One such parallel occurs on the first page of the "Sketch" as we are brought back to the opening music of the human life cycle in *The Waves.* She sets down her "first memory," of "red and purple flowers on a black ground—my mother's dress"—sensory experience that immediately becomes fused with what "also seems to be my first memory. . . . It is of lying half asleep, half awake, in bed in the nursery at St. Ives. It is of hearing the waves breaking, one, two, one, two, and sending a splash of water over the beach; and then breaking, one, two, one, two, behind a yellow blind" ("Sketch," p. 64). From this fusion of visual data, auditory and other rhythms, and maternal associations (with the red and purple flowers, with the nursery bed), an overflow from sensation into self-consciousness is recorded: "It is of lying and hearing this splash and seeing this light, and feeling, it is almost impossible that I should be here; of feeling the purest ecstasy I can conceive" ("Sketch," p. 65).

Woolf begins her sketch at a point earlier than most autobiographers—earlier than most remembering adults—can reach, but it is not simply as a tour de force of memory that the passage is significant. It is an indication of the state of mind in which Woolf began her conscious life—a world suffused not only by heightened visual and auditory experience but also by the presence of the mother. "Certainly there she was," Woolf writes (using words in which she had enforced the presence of her character, Mrs. Dalloway): "There she was from the very first" ("Sketch," p. 81). The phrase, in both the novel and the autobiography, is more a gesture than a statement. It has the force of a performative, by which a speaker brings his subject into being.

From these evocations of her primary life rhythms and ways of seeing, Woolf passes swiftly to the family's life at St. Ives, to an affirmation of their continued existence in her mind, and to a favorite metaphysical speculation:

At times I can go back to St. Ives more completely
than I can this morning. I can reach a state where I
seem to be watching things happen as if I were there.
That is, I suppose, that my memory supplies what I
had forgotten, so that it seems as if it were happening
independently, though I am really making it happen.
In certain favourable moods, memories—what one has
forgotten—come to the top. Now if this is so, is it not
possible—I often wonder—that things we have felt
with great intensity have an existence independent of
our minds; are in fact still in existence?

("Sketch," p. 67)

Given this speculative possibility, Woolf is moved to generalize about her mother's ability to keep "the panoply of life
... in being," as she puts it ("Sketch," p. 83). She records the
mother "generalised; dispersed, omnipresent, ... the creator
of that crowded merry world which spun so gaily in the
centre of my childhood" ("Sketch," p. 84). Yet she must
record the mother's death as the point at which "St. Ives vanished for ever" ("Sketch," p. 117).

It did, of course, no such thing. Woolf is certain of that
abiding presence and of her mother's central place there:
"She was one of the invisible presences who after all play so
important a part in every life" ("Sketch," p. 80). Moreover,
a continuing relation to this presence is not only potent to
shape and direct the survivor but frustrating in its indescrib-
ability even for one immersed in it: "Yet it is by such invisible presences that the 'subject of this memoir' is tugged this
way and that every day of his life. . . . I see myself as a fish in
a stream; deflected; held in place; but cannot describe the
stream" ("Sketch," p. 80).

Woolf's habitual image for the medium in which the past
abides is flowing water—a traditional figure of memory,
turned in modern times into the metaphoric stream of consciousness:

The past only comes back when the present runs so
smoothly that it is like the sliding surface of a deep

466

river. Then one sees through the surface to the depths.
In those moments I find one of my greatest satisfactions, not that I am thinking of the past; but that it is
then that I am living most fully in the present. For the
present when backed by the past is a thousand times
deeper than the present when it presses so close that
you can feel nothing else. . . . Let me then, like a
child advancing with bare feet into a cold river, descend again into that stream.

("Sketch," p. 98)

Here is Woolf's declared motive and healthy justification for
autobiographical writing: it makes *present* life more vivid.
The placid surface of ongoing life is "backed" by the deeper
current of the past, and this awareness creates not an estrangement from the present but a heightened sense of its
reality. Yet the entry into the deeper current is cold; it is a
shock and requires some bravery, like that of a child on entering a cold stream.

Much of "A Sketch of the Past" was written under skies
crossed by screaming, bombing, and occasionally falling air-
planes, in the period known to history as the Battle of Britain.
Anticipating the consequences of that drama in German invasion—especially threatening near the Channel coast, where
the Woolfs lived—she and her Jewish husband drew up suicide plans. Though their daily life became less troubled as
pressure from the war was relieved, the possibility of death
became particularly vivid to her imagination; there is a closely imagined visualization of being killed by a bomb in her
diary of these months. She can usually withdraw from immediate pressures by turning to the presences of her departed
ones and writing them in her autobiography: "Scraps of
memoirs come so coolingly to my mind. Wound up by those
three little articles [of journalism which she had just written]
I unwound a page about Thoby" (*WD*, p. 355; Oct. 12,
1940).

The most impressive mark of the war upon Woolf's life
space was the transformation (by bomb damage to its banks)

of the river Ouse, which flowed near her country home, from
a stream into a lake—or more:

> Yesterday the river burst its banks. The marsh is now
> a sea with gulls on it. . . .
>   When I look up I see all the marsh water. In the
> sun deep blue, gulls caraway seeds: snowstorms: At-
> lantic floor: yellow islands: leafless trees: red cottage
> roofs. Oh may the flood last for ever. A virgin lip: no
> bungalows; as it was in the beginning.
>   (*WD*, pp. 358–59; Nov. 3 and 5, 1940)

"In the beginning" may refer simply to the undeveloped
countryside at Rodmell when the Woolfs first bought a
house there, before the bungalows and other developments.
Yet there is an unmistakable echo of the Creation, too, and a
preference for the original state of watery nature, which
holds in undifferentiated suspension random items from the
normally structured contexts of civilized life. In particular,
there is a return to the kind of imagination indulged in by
the child at Cornwall, looking into the Atlantic: "In the sun
deep blue, gulls caraway seeds: snowstorms: Atlantic floor:
yellow islands. . . ." The river Ouse has become the water of
memory where Woolf's lost presences abide.

As Christmas approaches, Woolf departs from memoir
writing and in her diary indulges herself in a "child's vision"
of the past:

> How beautiful they were, those old people—I mean
> father and mother—how simple, how clear, how un-
> troubled. I have been dipping into old letters and
> father's memoirs. He loved her: oh and was so candid
> and reasonable and transparent. . . . How serene and
> gay even, their life reads to me: no mud; no whirlpools.
> And so human—with the children and the little hum
> and song of the nursery. But if I read as a contem-
> porary I shall lose my child's vision and so must stop.
>   (*WD*, p. 360; Dec. 22, 1940)

Woolf seems unaware of the distortion—the notion of the
domestic Leslie Stephen as "reasonable" marks the distance

of this portrait from her usually bitter depictions of his unstable temper—but she is aware of her self-indulgence in
protecting this idyll of the nursery from her "contemporary"
adult view.

She persists in writing the memoir, even as with impend-
ing invasion "book writing becomes doubtful"—either an act
of dubious value or of unlikely completion. But: "I wish to
go on, not to settle down in that dismal puddle" ("Sketch,"
p. 100)—a metaphor of her mental state that severely reduces
her oceanic vision of plenitude and her flowing and multi-
layered stream of consciousness. Eventually, under attack by
her final illness, she can use the autobiography to fight off its
destructive influence: "A battle against depression . . . by
breaking into [the writing of *Between the Acts* for] two
days, I think, of memoir writing" (*WD*, p. 364; Jan. 26,
1941)—that is, by forcibly making place for the autobiography despite the push to complete her novel.

In the midst of this struggle, with the fiction more or less
complete but her memoir unfinished, Woolf walked into the
river Ouse with a heavy stone in her pocket.[7] Whether she
found there the images she sought, whether the waters carried her round to the coast of her childhood, whether the
current was that of heightened consciousness or merged unconsciousness, we cannot say. Yet the inference seems compelling that writing this most beautiful of autobiographies
was a dangerous act, a triumph in raising her ghosts to walk
again, and thus an invitation to join them in their mode of
being.

Still, the costs of autobiographical writing must be

7. A number of recent studies of Woolf's life have offered interpretations of her illness and suicide based on psychiatric or psychoanalytic teachings. These include Jean O. Love, *Virginia Woolf:
Sources of Madness and Art* (Berkeley and Los Angeles, 1977); Roger
Poole, *The Unknown Virginia Woolf* (Cambridge, 1978); and Phyllis
Rose, *Woman of Letters: A Life of Virginia Woolf* (New York,
1978). I have avoided dependence on psychological theories in interpreting Woolf's autobiographical writings, preferring the dubieties of
her own language to those of an alien jargon.

weighed against the benefits. The act of confronting oneself as aesthetic object, in order to write oneself down on paper, singles the autobiographer out for a struggle of self-transformation that might be called heroic. Virginia Woolf, in the next-to-last entry of her diary, wrote: "No: I intend no introspection. I mark Henry James's sentence: Observe perpetually. Observe the oncome[?] of age. Observe greed. Observe my own despondency. But that means it becomes serviceable. Or so I hope. I insist upon spending this time to the best advantage. I will go down with my colours flying."[8]

8. Ms., Berg Collection, March 8, 1941; quoted with permission.

Envoi
LIFE AS
NARRATIVE
▬

ONE DOES NOT SIT DOWN to write an autobiography without a narrative language in which to compose the sentences of one's life story. Where do the expressions of that language, the supplement of one's "natural" language, come from? A number of possible sources come to mind: from human nature, as archetypal figures corresponding to universal forms of thought or grammar; from cultural history, or more particularly, as a unique feature of Western culture; from a particular cultural institution, religion, which foregrounds concern for the meaning and end of individual life; from a less specialized institution, literature, where certain canonical texts establish the norms and often the working materials for later writers. There are other potential sources; I shall consider only these formidable alternatives.

A Natural Language of Autobiography? The cycle of growth from garden innocence through bitter adversity to eventual reconciliation is so widely experienced or perceived as to make claims for archetypal standing as a native disposition of the human mind. Such a view may be founded on a Jungian universal symbolism with its urge toward integration of personality or on a Freudian view of inevitably separative forces like the Oedipus complex or on the death wish as impulse of return. The position may be more flexibly phrased in accordance with purported phases of biological development and social acculturation, as in Erik Erikson's "life history" of "identity crisis" and other "developmental stages."[1] From this viewpoint, the writing of autobiography comes to be seen if not as a universal trait at least as connected with a distinct time of life; Erikson describes Freud writing his autobiographical sketch at sixty-eight, "about the age, it seems, for reminiscing." These latter generalizations may strike us as a *reductio ad absurdum* of the more orthodox formulations of universal drives and mental contents. Not only have men written autobiographies at widely different ages, but they have divided their life stages in many ways—by no means uniformly favoring the pattern of separation and return to which this study has devoted itself.

Autobiography as a Distinctive Phenomenon of Western Culture? Like most culture-centered viewpoints, no matter how anthropologically sophisticated, this one rests on a tacit definition of the object of inquiry in terms derived from the theoretician's culture. It is standard procedure in this argument to exclude the copious instances of non-Western self-writing, like those of Avicenna and al-Ghazali, as not *truly* autobiographies—usually because they are not confessional, that is, not Augustinian, conversional, guilt-ridden. (Sometimes the latter criterion is phrased in terms of Western guilt-culture versus non-Western shame-culture as a way of upholding a preference for works that satisfy the requirements of modern angst.) It has recently become possible, however, to scout these arbitrary limiting conditions, for a number of Chinese neo-Confucian self-writings have been shown to be thoroughly guilt-ridden and confessional.[2] This evidence

1. Erik H. Erikson, in *Life History and the Historical Moment* (New York, 1975), applies these terms, employed in his previous studies of historical individuals like Luther, to the nature of autobiography itself—exemplified not only in Gandhi's but in the psychoanalyst's own remarkable story, sketched in the opening essay. The quotation in the text below is from p. 32.

2. "The preoccupation with self is not exclusively the prerogative

does not promote the conclusion that even non-Western autobiography is confessional as much as it does the idea that self-writing takes place the world over, free of Western assumptions about its possibilities and limits. If even the narrow definition of autobiography as confession fails to render Western autobiography distinctive, what remains of this comfortable possession of a Western heritage?

Autobiography as Originating in Religion, Particularly the Christianity of Augustine?   There is an imperial, if not tautological, element in this view, which sees religion as a pervasive if not determinant force in culture generally and in Western culture particularly. If religion is so placed with regard to cultural expressions at large, its role in motivating or shaping autobiography as one of those forms of expression becomes less distinctive, less interesting. A more dynamic generalization about the historical bearing of religion on cultural forms may be more in point. I call it the Hadas three-step in honor of one of its exponents and in preference to the current term "displacement." In his work on the Hellenistic period, Moses Hadas speaks of an "alteration of motivation," which characterizes ancient art forms, plastic as well

---

of Western culture, nor for that matter is the occurrence of autobiographical writing. Sixteenth- and seventeenth-century China provides sufficient evidence of similar concerns"—Rodney L. Taylor, "The Centered Self: Religious Autobiography in the Neo-Confucian Tradition," *History of Religions*, 17 (1978): 267; "What I hope to show is that the hundred years from 1570 to 1670 witnessed a deep awareness of the human proclivity to evil, an urgent need to counter this proclivity, a readiness for self-disclosure, and a deep anguish over one's own wrongdoings, all to an extent and with an intensity never known before in Chinese history"—Pei-yi Wu, "Self-Examination and Confession of Sins in Traditional China," *Harvard Journal of Asiatic Studies*, 39 (1979): 6. To this evidence should be added the more general reflection that the greatest Chinese novel, *Dream of the Red Chamber*, is shot through with personal references and structured by the author's known motivations, though whether this makes it an autobiographical novel it is not in my province to say; see the introduction by Chi-chen Wang to his translation of the novel (Garden City, N.Y., 1958).

as literary: "The origin is in the service of religion; then when the religious motivation has faded the form is retained frequently without realization that it ever carried a religious burden, for the aesthetic satisfaction it provides; and finally it is endowed with a new meaningfulness."[3] Our brief review of changes in the use of typological motifs suggests the application of this three-step to the history of autobiography. The spiritual autobiographies of the seventeenth and eighteenth centuries were directed toward religious goals, primarily self-evaluation in behalf of prospective salvation. In the latter century, however, the practice of self-estimation became widespread and acquired some of the taints of habitual or mechanical practices; Benjamin Franklin's punctilious system of moral bookkeeping is a seriocomic illustration of the spiritual dryness which religious enthusiasts were fully aware of—and which they called the threat of "formalism." Finally, the burgeoning of literary autobiography in the nineteenth and twentieth centuries marks the emergence of new meanings to fill old forms, with the inevitable reworking of those forms and their language of expression. This is religious influence, indeed, but religion *manqué* or in the process of becoming something else.

Autobiography as a Genre, Subject to the Laws of Literary Influence? To test this hypothesis, we may draw upon the evidence of the preceding critical readings. Even without arguing the existence of a sharp break in the continuity of spiritual autobiography from the eighteenth to the nineteenth centuries, one can find little close influence of the great seventeenth-century self-writers on the Victorians. To be sure, Carlyle places George Fox at a commanding position in *Sartor Resartus*, as the symbolic hero of the chapter which begins his summative third book, the remarkable "Incident in Modern History," in which Fox made himself a suit of leather. Whatever the sly imputations that Carlyle or his per-

3. Moses Hadas, *Hellenistic Culture: Fusion and Diffusion* (New York, 1972 [1959]), pp. 212–13.

sona Teufelsdröckh may make on this theme, it hardly amounts to an autobiographical self-image resembling Fox's in his journal. Much the same can be said of the many references to *The Pilgrim's Progress*, which we have observed in autobiographical novels from Brontë to Richardson; there is scarcely any reference to *Grace Abounding* to be found in these texts though the pilgrimage pattern may inform their narrative designs.[4] This lacuna does not dispel the continued use of autobiographical figures from the seventeenth through the twentieth centuries. But it does belie more specific claims of direct imitation by one autobiographer of another—even Augustine or Wordsworth[5]—and with it the suggestion that autobiography is a literary genre, obeying the laws of convention and influence (however these are defined).

How, then, are we to account for the persistence of certain schemas of personal existence in a large number of self-writings, without relying on assumptions that are either sweepingly universal, culture-specific, or literary-generic? To avoid these theoretical bogs, can we approach an answer by drawing both from the experience of persons living in the world and from the conditions faced by the man who would sit down to write his life?

An initial sketch of an answer to such questions is provided in a recent essay by Paul Ricoeur, "Narrative Time."[6]

4. Even a work structured by Bunyanesque figures, like e. e. cummings's *The Enormous Room*—with chapter titles including "A Pilgrim's Progress," "Apollyon," "I Begin a Pilgrimage," and "An Approach to the Delectable Mountains"—does not narratively imitate Bunyan's autobiography.

5. The only extended English verse autobiographies I know of after Wordsworth are the West Indian Derek Walcott's *Another Life*—a splendid achievement in its own right—and John Betjeman's less impressive *Summoned by Bells*.

6. Paul Ricoeur, "Narrative Time," *Critical Inquiry* (Autumn 1980), pp. 169–90; the quotations following are from pp. 170, 180, 186. The essay and others in this issue that have keen bearing on the present discussion are reprinted in W. J. T. Mitchell, ed., *On Narrative* (Chicago and London, 1981). For a useful review of the presupposi-

It is Ricoeur's larger intention to return a diachronic dimension to the study of narrative, which has been reduced to purely synchronic analysis by structuralist narratology. To do this, he is led to pursue a parallel between the generation of narrative in history and literature and the temporal structure of human existence: "For each feature of narrative brought out by reflection on either history or fictional narrative, I shall attempt to find a corresponding feature of temporality brought out by an existential analysis of time."

Although Ricoeur's analysis entails a Heideggerian view of temporal experience in general, it does not posit any special conceptual content of human existence, that is, no universal symbols or developmental stages. Instead, it makes a plausible account of some standard operations in reading stories, comparable with the movements of temporal orientation which individuals make in thinking about their own past and future. Reading by means of the well-known hermeneutic circle becomes all but indistinguishable from fixing one's living past in memory and orienting one's coming life toward goals and outcomes:

> By reading the end in the beginning and the beginning in the end, we learn also to read time itself backward, as the recapitulating of the initial conditions of a course of action in its terminal consequences. In this way, a plot establishes human action not only within time, . . . but within memory. Memory, accordingly, *repeats* the course of events according to an order that is the counterpart of time as "stretching-along" between a beginning and an end.

tions of Ricoeur's position, see Daniel T. O'Hara, *Tragic Knowledge: Yeats's Autobiography and Hermeneutics* (New York, 1981), pp. 33–46. O'Hara goes on to apply some of its implications to autobiography, including "the central symbol or mythic image of the creative self" (p. 45) and the "pattern of literary history based on the idea of a Fall or of an eternal return" (p. 47)—which he finds inadequate. I regret that this book appeared too late to help me with my own formulations.

This description of the activity of readers in their shaping and interpretation of stories applies *pari passu* to the activities of writers as well, in their creation of binding memory links by plotting retrograde and forward narrative movements. These linkages are built up into configurations or sequential patterns that override the linear and otherwise evanescent succession of narrative units in story telling. To make a plainer claim: by writing (or by reading) a story, one affirms or locks in its internal sequences, generating not only a conviction about the appropriate ordering of events but also a sense of their fullness—a continuity reaching from what now recommends itself as the point of beginning to another, equally momentous point called the end.

Ricoeur goes on to apply these widely acknowledged activities in story telling and reading to the specific case of autobiography, considered as a narrative mode comparable with the epic of quest:

> In these stories, [narrative] repetition is constitutive of the temporal form itself. The paradigmatic case of such stories is Augustine's *Confessions*. Here the form of the travel is interiorized to such a degree that there is no longer any privileged place in space to which to return. . . . The [epic] quest has been absorbed into the movement by which the hero—if we may still call him by that name—becomes *who he is*. Memory, therefore, is no longer the narrative of external adventures stretching along episodic time. It is itself the spiral movement that, through anecdotes and episodes, brings us back to the almost motionless constellation of potentialities that the narrative retrieves. The end of the story is what equates the present with the past, the actual with the potential. The hero *is* who he *was*.

Although Ricoeur's language may verge too closely on the meaning-oriented approach to autobiography to satisfy all tastes, it has the virtue of keeping our attention on movements of narrative that are simpler and more essential. The forward directionality of narrative replaces the notion of a quest for self-discovery, the spiral movement of recapitulating earlier *données* replaces the idea of the goal as necessarily a homecoming, and the concept of ending as reaching a point of potentialities fulfilled replaces the narrower target of self-fulfillment.

"The hero *is* who he *was*" is a formula for the protagonist of an autobiography as the same kind of emergent being whom we know ourselves and others to be in life. Thus, the mimesis performed in self-writing—though it cannot be said to make direct copies of reality—acts by following the same patterns of gradual coming into existence as those which characterize individual lives. Writing and reading autobiography are temporally extended activities, which very much resemble the longer time formations that emerge in the course of living.

How far does living itself, then, provide self-writings with their forms? From the close correlation between temporal experience in general and self-writing in particular, we might suspect that autobiographies resemble lives not in the sense that they are a close representation of them but because they are stories of that which is itself a story. This suspicion is bolstered by the prevalence of words in our languages that refer both to incidents or sequences in life and to books or parts of books about them. We have not only names for portions of life or of text (passage, episode) but also words for special phases of living and for writings about them (romance, adventure). It comes as no surprise, then, that familiar synonyms for autobiography (life, confession) are themselves words of this kind. They are names for books that relate the course of a life, but that life—indeed, the idea of *a life*—is already structured as a narrative.

How do these considerations help to answer our opening conundrums? An immediate resolution of the nature-culture antithesis is offered by the reflection that every age and place has its stories, yet they are all happily distinctive in their historical or tribal context. For all the uniformities of plot, character function, or deeper structure that have been discovered by folklorists, anthropologists, and "narratologists," no one (let us hope) would wish to dissolve the stylistic distinctiveness of a community's stock of stories or the personal uniqueness of an individual's life tale within that community. Western autobiography shares in these stories' generation by universal social processes, but perhaps its most distinctive generic feature is its assertion of "individualism," although this ranges between extremes represented by Cellini (or Céline) and the spiritual autobiographers. It expresses this tendency by narrative elements which obscure the degree to which it participates in reciprocities of individual and group, which make its stories representative for the society if not the species.

Where does the language of self-writing come from? From the community's narrative discourse, to be sure, especially from those authoritative texts which embody the prevailing schemas of a life—whether simply human, heroic, or divine. We may take the further implication that life stories within the community are not likely to be regarded as a highly literary genre—enacted as they are by many nonliterary (and sometimes barely literate) men and women. Life stories, like lives, are modeled after idols of the tribe and constitute a subgroup sometimes difficult to distinguish from its other narratives of history and fiction. What distinction these lives attain is traceable to their variation of the community's sense of the sequence and shape of individual life itself, a communal sense, which they by turns enforce and help to modify.

Index

Index

Index

Designer: Wolfgang Lederer
Compositor: Heritage Printers, Inc.
Printer: Heritage Printers, Inc.
Binder: The Delmar Company
Text: Linotype Janson
Display: Foundry Bulmer